KU-022-822

CONTENTS

The Quaker Lloyds
in the
Industrial Revolution

Arms of Lloyd of Dolobran impaled with Stanley of Knockin;
oak panel from Dolobran Hall, about 1650.

The Quaker Lloyds
in the
Industrial Revolution

HUMPHREY LLOYD

HUTCHINSON OF LONDON

HUTCHINSON & CO (Publishers) LTD
3 Fitzroy Square, London W1

London Melbourne Sydney Auckland
Wellington Johannesburg Cape Town
and agencies throughout the world

First published 1975
© Humphrey Lloyd 1975

Set in Monotype Fournier

Printed in Great Britain by
The Anchor Press Ltd, and bound by
Wm Brendon & Son Ltd
both of Tiptree, Essex

ISBN 0 09 120880 7

ILLUSTRATIONS

Frontispiece: Arms of Lloyd and Stanley

The Publishers gratefully acknowledge permission for
reproduction from: Mrs R. E. Barclay, Mr A. S. Clay,
Mrs J. P. Fox, Revd C. D. S. Lloyd, Mr D. L. Lloyd,
Lord Lloyd, Mr P. G. Lloyd, Mr H. Pittaway, Mr J.
Taylor; and also from: the City of Birmingham Central
Libraries, the City of Birmingham Museum and Art Gallery,
the City of Bristol Museum and Art Gallery, the County of
Hereford and Worcester Record Office, Friends House
Library, London, Friends Reading Society, Birmingham,
Guildhall Library, London, the *Illustrated London News*,
Lloyds Bank Ltd and the National Library of Wales.

Stat fortuna domus, et avi numerantur avorum.

Virgil, Georgics IV, 209

PREFACE

This book is about the Quaker Lloyds in the time of the industrial revolution. Inspired at first by several finds of unpublished letters, it was foreseen as the biography of a family, but progressive researches while work on the material was being carried out have made it a family and business history combined.

First in Wales and then in the growing town of Birmingham, making their way in early iron and banking, the Lloyds for more than six generations were Quakers. Their Quaker period, from the 1660s to about the 1860s, is the period of this book, an era ending before the full onset of the modern time and before the present large-scale development of the Bank or of the manufacturing firms which carry on the name of the family today.

Since the end of the nineteenth century two works have stood as authority for Lloyd history, one published ninety years ago and more domestic in character, the other twenty years later and more general. These are: *Farm and its Inhabitants* by Rachel Jane Lowe, 1883, and *The Lloyds of Birmingham* by Samuel Lloyd, 1905. Both of them have long been out of print; but the real stimulus for a new study has been the coming to light, over a number of years, of four separate collections of family letters and papers, more than a thousand in number, not previously brought together. These comprise three collections of Lloyd manuscripts, all now deposited at Friends House, London, and a section of the Braithwaite family manuscripts which are held in private possession.* All had come down in different ramifications of the family. Interlocking to a remarkable degree, they apply in succession to the later seventeenth century, both halves of the eighteenth and the opening quarter of the nineteenth.

Starting from these, research was rewarded by new information and material in areas such as the iron trade in the time of the water-wheel, the growth of Birmingham, country banking, the position

* For a note of these and other manuscript sources see Bibliography.

of the Quakers, and the history of the family itself. The history of the early Lloyd iron enterprises, ignored in the past, was pieced together with the help of leases and business documents, from libraries and record offices, that were unknown to the present generation or previous writers. New light was found in unpublished Ph.D. theses relating to particular episodes or people and again through the locating of the lost deeds of a family inheritance in mines and minerals covering a century and a half. The partnership ledgers of the Lloyd bank at Birmingham, which was for a hundred years the predecessor of the present-day bank, were a happy discovery, and wills from Somerset House proved a source of unexpected particulars. The search for the illustrations themselves, together with the study of many plans, prints and portraits which cannot be reproduced, resulted in a supply of information and ideas; and the attempt has also been made to visit personally every place and site of relevance for the story, for even brickwork and ruins, like ground, are evidence in the excavating of history and nothing brings places to life like walking over them and talking to the people around.

In all these areas of enquiry the author acknowledges the interest which he has met with and the help received from very many people and establishments of whom but a few can be named. At the head must be placed the matchless local studies department of the City of Birmingham Reference Library under Dorothy Norris and her successor Dorothy McCulla, without whose guidance no writer concerned with the social history of Birmingham could proceed very far. To them I join Elizabeth Ralph, until lately the head of the City of Bristol archives office, A. J. Crowe, formerly librarian to the borough of Wednesbury, and Antony Gunstone of the Birmingham Museum and Art Gallery. With these rank the archivists of fourteen or fifteen county record offices, especially those of Worcestershire, Staffordshire and Shropshire, and the unfailing services of the Gloucestershire County Library.

On the background to the Welsh chapters I am in the debt of Ronald Morris, Llanfyllin, for much local information on the Dolobran district, Dr J. D. K. Lloyd, Garthmyl, who read and criticised these chapters in draft, Dr Michael Siddons, Croesyceiliog, for his researches into the Lloyd descent from early Welsh forbears, and G. Milwyn Griffiths of the National Library of Wales which includes among its functions that of record office for several of the Welsh counties. In the area of the early English iron industry I have had the advice and support, in particular, of Professor Michael Flinn of Edinburgh, Dr R. A. Pelham of Southampton and Dr Colin Owen of Burton-upon-Trent, and I am grateful to Mrs Joan Day for an introduction to aspects of the industrial archaeology of Bristol. As to the rise of the Lloyd banks, I have been indulgently treated by the Chairman and Secretary of Lloyds Bank who allowed me the run of the Bank's archives; and for the banking scene in the eighteenth century I acknowledge in particular the ready advice of John Leighton-Boyce, the author of *Smiths the Bankers 1658–1958*. To my kinsman Arthur Braithwaite I record my special thanks for lending me the indispensable Lloyd letters from the Braithwaite collection of family manuscripts; I acknowledge the cordial assistance of Dr Ruth I. Aldrich of the University of Wisconsin who has made a study of Charles Lloyd junior called 'the poet'; and I have had frequent agreeable advice and instruction from Edward Milligan, the librarian to the Society of Friends.

My wife, with her Birmingham family background, has actively abetted the research and much besides. More than sixty of my relatives have given me ready help, much of it substantial, including Wilsons, Braithwaites, Crewdsons, Howards, Foxes and many Lloyds, too many to list. But three must be singled out. These are Sampson Lloyd, the head of the family, for making me free of the Dolobran estate of which he has for many years been the owner; Helen Lloyd who read the whole manuscript from the family viewpoint; and Henry L. Lloyd, my principal consultant and collaborator, who has played an active part in the research and during several years has constantly contributed ideas and information.

During the two hundred years of the story, conventions in spelling moved on from the quaint and olden almost to those of the present. With a few exceptions all spelling in extracts and quotations, and occasionally the punctuation, have been adjusted to those of today. Seventeenth and eighteenth century dating down to 1752, particularly in those months most affected by the reform of the calendar, has been similarly treated. The information on sources given in the notes may make up for the want of it in former Lloyd biographies which Dr Arthur Raistrick regrets in *Quakers in Science and Industry*.

In 1820 Robert Southey, writing of his contemplated history of the Society of Friends, assures his correspondent, a Quaker Lloyd, that the history will be full and faithful but there will be no intention to offend.[1] In treating of Quakers while not a Quaker himself, the author trusts that he has not been led to do so, in Southey's words, 'erroneously or unadvisedly and thereby give offence'. He is indebted to many Quakers for much help.

PART I
Dolobran

I

CALLED IN SCORN QUAKERS

On the day when her husband was sent to prison Elizabeth Lloyd had been married less than a year and her infant son was four weeks old. The daughter of a considerable family, she had been brought up in Pembrokeshire in the turbulent days of the Civil Wars and the Commonwealth and she had come to Dolobran in Mont-gomeryshire in 1662 as the bride of the young Charles Lloyd. She did not know on that winter's night that ten years would pass before her husband was discharged from prison, that she herself would join him there or that most of her children would be born under the surveillance of a Welshpool gaoler. All she knew was that her husband had been summoned, with a handful of others, to be interviewed by the authorities, that he would be expected to swear loyal allegiance to the newly restored monarchy, which he could not do, and that he had not returned. She was alone, she had only servants to rely on and her people were two hundred miles away.

It was for no political reason nor from any disloyalty to the Crown that her husband would refuse to take this oath of allegiance and supremacy; it was because he could not swear. He had openly joined himself not many days before to 'the people in scorn called Quakers' whose teaching enjoined compliance with the gospel injunction to *swear not at all*; and to be a Quaker, and to show it by this refusal, was quite enough under the new Acts to place a man in gaol. All this Elizabeth knew. She could have no vision of the generations of her descendants who would preserve this conscience and this peculiar allegiance for the next two hundred years, and some for three hundred to the present day; what interested her was when he would get out. But Elizabeth Lloyd was a person of courage and common sense. Not yet herself a Quaker, she took the

3

strain at Dolobran at this distressing time and carried on, coping with the home and waiting on events for the sake of her husband and her child.

The setting of these scenes lies in the story of the two families, Charles Lloyd's and his wife's, the Lloyds of Dolobran and the Lorts of Stackpole. The town of Welshpool, where the prison stood, is about eight miles from Dolobran. It lies in the county of Montgomery but is quite near the Shropshire border and about twenty miles from Shrewsbury. It was conscious of being on the Severn, which was navigable up to only a few miles away, and it was proud to be reckoned a centre of the ancient district of Powysland. With the great Powis Castle on its doorstep, the seat at that time of the Herbert family, later Earls of Powis, Welshpool felt it could hold its own whether with the adherents of Chirk Castle to the north or of Montgomery or Bishop's Castle to the south. Welshpool was not a large place, and its living standards, outside the highest levels of society, were unworthy of particular comment. Its gaol, Elizabeth knew, was primitive and unpleasant in the extreme.

Dolobran is a house and estate in the nearby valley of the river Vyrnwy a sizeable tributary of the Severn passing a few miles to the north of Welshpool. The house (Plate 1) stands in the parish of Meifod, withdrawn from roads, overlooking a valley that can have changed but little in the past three hundred years. The estate was a landed gentry property, of about a thousand acres, which at that time consisted of the principal house and farm with its two corn mills and fulling-mill, together with a second house, and a number of subsidiary farms and smaller holdings occupied by Charles Lloyd's tenants. This property he had inherited at the age of nineteen when 'his father had dyed soe that he was left to his own disposall'. Enlarged in various ways by Charles Lloyd, by his father, and by his son, the house was spoken of as Dolobran Hall, as it is today, to distinguish it from other residences on the estate such as Lower Dolobran and Little Dolobran. At the present time it is a substantial farmhouse with all the alterations of later days, but one thing has been handed down in good order that Elizabeth Lloyd would have known from the day she came to live there. Over the fireplace in the main hall was a notable heraldic achievement, done in colour on a panel of oak, displaying the arms of

Lloyd and of Stanley for Charles Lloyd's father and mother (Frontis-piece). The emblazonment stands upon the authority of Charles Lloyd's father, who ranked, we are told, among 'the celebrated genealogists and antiquaries' of his day.[1] In the glowing colours of its many quarterings the shield recalls the long ancestry of the family reaching back to early Welsh kings, princes and patriarchs. It reflects a line carried back in authentic form to the time of the Norman Conquest, to Aleth, by tradition king of Dyfed, a region of south-west Wales, born about 1030, whose coat occupies the principal position in the shield.* By some, the ancestry has been taken back still further, to the misty times of Arthur and his knights, but those are 'high lines deduced from far above all memory' and the question of where record and legend merge must be left to the specialist in Welsh antiquity. The shield, however, remains, proclaiming to posterity that the line went back at least for four or five hundred years.†

About two centuries before the time when this chapter begins Dolobran had formed part of the domain of Llwydiarth, farther up the Vyrnwy, with its fortified manor house, held in Charles Lloyd's time by his kinsmen the Vaughans.‡ Llwydiarth is associated, for the Lloyds, with their ancestor Celynin ap Rhiryd, who came to Montgomeryshire in the fourteenth century and acquired the estate through marriage. Ancient tradition has it that he fled there having slain the Mayor of Carmarthen, an exploit which is outside the research of the present account but reminds us that peaceable Quakers may descend from violent men. About 1425, not long after Agincourt, the grandson of Celynin divided the lands of Llwydiarth among his three sons. One of these received Dolobran as his share, and it was this man's great-grandson, Ievan ap Owen of Dolobran, who adopted the surname of Lloyd at a period when permanent

---

* *Azure* a chevron between three cocks *argent* armed crested and wattled *or*.

† See Appendix I.

‡ An established farmhouse today occupies the site. In *The Beaufort Progress through Wales* by Thomas Dineley we read: 'Wednesday, July 30 1684, His Grace the Duke of Beaufort, Lord President of Wales, came to Lloydyarth [sic], the seat of Edward Vaughan, Esquire, in the county of Montgomery, attended with the Lord of Worcester, Sir John Talbott and several gentlemen of the Country, where a noble entertainment was provided, with good standing and provision for above 90 horse. Here his Grace made a stay all night with all Knights, Gentlemen, etc, of his Company and retinues.'

surnames were just beginning to be used.* Lloyd comes from the Welsh word meaning 'grey-haired', and the cherished nineteenth-century belief that the family name had derived from Llwydiarth cannot unfortunately be sustained.

But it is not until the time of Charles Lloyd's grandfather and father that anything like personal records begin to appear, and here we can glance at a fragment of family tree. This is convenient not only for reference on crossing the threshold from chronicles to history, but because from this time onwards the names in the family, particularly the Charleses, begin to repeat themselves a good deal. Charles Lloyd himself, for instance, is properly known as 'Charles Lloyd II'; his father was a Charles, and so were his son, his son's son and one beyond that again. But his grandfather was a John: These three Lloyds in the seventeenth century, John and the two Charleses, and the two next before them in the time of Queen Elizabeth all held the appointment of Justice in the county of Montgomery. Not long before the time of his imprisonment Charles

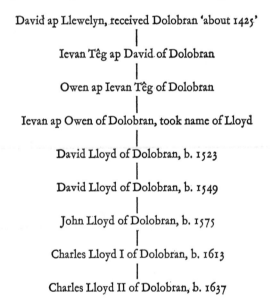

David ap Llewelyn, received Dolobran 'about 1425'
|
Ievan Têg ap David of Dolobran
|
Owen ap Ievan Têg of Dolobran
|
Ievan ap Owen of Dolobran, took name of Lloyd
|
David Lloyd of Dolobran, b. 1523
|
David Lloyd of Dolobran, b. 1549
|
John Lloyd of Dolobran, b. 1575
|
Charles Lloyd I of Dolobran, b. 1613
|
Charles Lloyd II of Dolobran, b. 1637

* But for this change, Ievan Lloyd would have been properly known, under the traditional Welsh nine-generation system, as Ievan ap Owen ap Ievan Têg ap David ap Llewelyn ap Einion ap Celynin ap Rhiryd ap Cynddelw ap Iorwerth of Dolobran (See Ellis, *Wales Past and Present*, 1870, p. 286.) There is no evidence for the view that the surname was first used by Ievan Lloyd's father.

Lloyd himself, still in his early twenties, had been nominated to be High Sheriff but did not take the office. Their selection for these services over successive generations is a pointer to the standing of the family in the district. They were respected members of the landowning class, they were baptized in Meifod church, and their politics, during the civil wars, were of a Parliamentarian flavour. Under the Commonwealth this would favour their selection as Justices. But it would count the other way in the mind of a Royalist magistrate committing Charles Lloyd to prison.

Charles Lloyd's grandfather, John Lloyd, had 'kept his abode' not at Dolobran but at Coedcowrid, the second house on the estate, the dower-house.* John Lloyd spent money on it, 'wainscotted the parlour thereof' and lived there in some state, 'having 24 men with halberts to attend him to church, where he placed them in his great pew under the pulpit'. But his successor, Charles Lloyd's father, the antiquarian, had lived in the principal house, Dolobran Hall. Born in 1613, this Charles turned to Shropshire for a wife. She was Elizabeth Stanley, daughter of Thomas Stanley of Knockin near Oswestry. She came of a line descending from ancient families in Cheshire and Lancashire, and linked, as the coat of arms shows, with that of the Earls of Derby. An episode in Elizabeth Stanley's pedigree seems to foreshadow that independence of spirit which comes out in her son Charles, the subject of this chapter. Elizabeth Stanley's mother had been a grandchild of Edward Burton of Longner near Shrewsbury, who had stood out for the Protestants in the time of Queen Mary, and whose story evidently appealed to Charles Lloyd. 'He was buried in his garden,' he records, 'being denied burial at Chad's in Salop because deemed anti-popish. He died of an extasie of joy after hearing of Queen Mary's death, he being much persecuted for religion in her reign.' To this day may be seen in the garden at Longner Hall a sarcophagus inscribed with the following lines, which Charles Lloyd writes out in his memorandum:

> Was't for denying Christ or some notorious fact
> That this man's body Christian burial lack't?

* 'The one was the mansion-house and the other the jointer-house that belonged to my friend Charles Lloyd and his ancestors.' Richard Davies, *The Convincement*, p. 143.

O no, it was his faithful true profession
Was the chief cause, which then was held transgression.
When Popery here did reign the See of Rome
Would not admit to any such a tomb
Within their idol temple walls; but he,
Truly professing Christianity,
Was like Christ Jesus in a garden laid
Where he shall rest in peace till it be said
'Come faithful servant, come, receive with me
A just reward for thine integrity.'*

Such was the background into which Elizabeth Lloyd had married and from which, as everybody in the district knew, the young Charles Lloyd was sprung. What of the young man himself? It is from the time when the family turned Quaker that the information begins to be so much richer and the days of scraps and guesswork end. For Quakers are consistent recorders. They keep letters. They write dates and notes in memorandum books. They do splendid obituaries about each other, which they call testimonies. They keep accounts. They make minutes of their Quaker proceedings. They record their births, marriages and burials. And, essentially, they hand these things down. It is something to do with the psychology of a minority. Thus, whatever the destruction, a respectable supply of Lloyd letters and manuscripts has come down, starting in Charles Lloyd's lifetime, and including even a dozen or two from his own pen.

Charles Lloyd's father had three sons, Charles, born 1637, John, 1639, and Thomas, 1640. Charles and his brothers were sent away to school. His father was a cultivated man. His mother had died in the 1640s 'when he was but young', so that, if this happened upon the birth of her youngest child, Charles may have been only eight or nine years old at the time of her death. The record tells us that 'his father took great care to have him educated at some of the best schools in the county where he was born and at some noted schools in the neighbouring county of Salop, in order to qualify for the university'.[2] This would be between about 1649 and 1654 when he

* These lines are written out in the notebook of Sampson Lloyd II, one of Charles Lloyd's grandsons; Lloyd MSS, no number.

was growing into his teens, and while at school he 'improved himself in learning, being of an acute lively nature'. John, the middle brother, on the other hand, was not sent to the university. His way seems to have been independent alike in education, religion and career. John Lloyd became what would now be called a Chancery master. 'He was brought up to the law in the Six Clerks Office in Chancery Lane, where he had a seat in the said office after he had served his time with his said master, and continued there many years,' and one of his sons followed him. John Lloyd prospered in this profession, and he married Jane, the daughter of a latter-day Sir Thomas Gresham, a name well known in the City. He must have gone to be articled or apprenticed to his said master by about 1655, when not much above fifteen or sixteen. John Lloyd's lot was thrown in with the Establishment, and his own particular form of loyalty to his native place was to present to the parish church, at Meifod *ubi natus et baptizatus est,* a silver-gilt flagon and paten, duly inscribed, which are still preserved and may be seen by the visitor.[3] For the brother of a leading local Dissenter this might seem to have been a rather pointed benefaction, but we read of John Lloyd being consulted in London in the 1670s to help Friends out of legal disabilities so he was evidently willing to be of service to them. John Lloyd was present at Leominster in 1686 at the second marriage of his brother Charles, on which occasion his signature appears among the witnesses. The date of his death is not known, but it must have been in the 1690s, probably 1695, since it is on record that it took place not long after the death of his eldest son, another John, who died in 1694.

Charles Lloyd went to Oxford in 1655. It has been declared by some writers that he went to Jesus College, but this has probably been assumed because of the Welsh connection of that college. The record tells us that he was at New Inn Hall, a former college commemorated today in the name of New Inn Hall Street. Charles Lloyd 'improved himself in his learning while he continued there above many of his fellow students' and gained the reputation of 'a man of very general knowledge in natural things and more especially in physick'. His brother Thomas in his turn, after attending Ruthin School, became a medical student at the same college. What length of course medicine required in those days is not known, but it is possible that Thomas, who later 'practised physick

for several years', was in residence longer than Charles, whose
time was cut short by the death of his father in 1657. It was upon
this event, when he was approaching twenty and had only been
two years at the university, that Charles went down without a
degree to take over Dolobran, 'and was left to his own disposall'.

His marriage to Elizabeth Lort took place about four years later.
During these years, in his early twenties, he was taking the property
under his own control and figuring as his father's successor in the
normal to-and-fro of the district. The only note we have of him in
this interval is that 'he was invited to court several persons of noted
families'. From the standing of the Lloyds this can be understood,
for he was an eligible young man. Some of the girls whose well-
intentioned mothers no doubt engineered these invitations would
have had their homes in the Welshpool region[4] but the family's
connection was a wider one than that, and in fact he found his wife
as far away as Pembrokeshire. And far away indeed it was. From
Dolobran to Pembroke meant 180 miles of travel by horseback,
most of it over Welsh roads, worse than in England, through
Leominster to Hay, over by Brecon to Carmarthen, and so away
to South Pembrokeshire, to the Little England beyond Wales.
There was no other route from North Wales to south-west Wales
having any pretensions as a carriage road,* and visits to the Lorts
would be limited, we may be sure, to summer-time only.

Reputedly of Staffordshire descent, the Lorts had held Stackpole
for four generations, their properties extending from Tenby in the
east to Castlemartin, south of Milford Haven, in the west. During
the Civil Wars and the Commonwealth they had showed themselves
adaptable to events. South Prembrokeshire, unlike most of Wales,
was not a Royalist stronghold, and Elizabeth's father and uncles
had acted to the best of their judgement in those violent, pendulum
days. But, in authority or out of it, defending Stackpole against
the Roundheads or serving as High Sheriffs under the Commonwealth, they were men of ability and leading figures in the district;
and her father, 'that thrice ambidexter' to his enemies, a graduate of
Wadham College, had been elected to Parliament not long before

* In a letter of 1688 from a Pembrokeshire relation to Sampson Lloyd at Leominster we read: 'After our return we go suddenly to North Wales. Somewhere on
the road I hope to see you, for we must go Ludlow way and to Shrewsbury, which is
the only coach way, as I hear, from S. Wales to N. Wales.' Lloyd MSS, 1/31.

Elizabeth's marriage. Links with a family so far from Dolobran are hard to explain unless perhaps through the Stanleys, for an earlier Lort, when High Steward at Stackpole, had acquired the estate from a Stanley.

Elizabeth's father was Sampson Lort of East Moor near Manorbier, his elder brother occupying the family seat at Stackpole. Her mother had been a Pembrokeshire Philipps, 'her heart manful and obedient, her wit sharp and her understanding quick'. Sampson Lort in his will names forty pieces of property, of which East Moor was the chief. A moated house 'of seven hearths', which was a considerable rating, it stood near the cliffs about two miles west of Manorbier. Here the young Lloyds would stay, riding no doubt with Elizabeth and her brother to visit Manorbier Castle, already four hundred years old. And a few miles away, at Stackpole Elidor church, on 2 January 1662, which was Elizabeth's birthday, she and Charles Lloyd were married.[5]

But in making this choice of wife there were some other influences at work in the heart of the young master of Dolobran. A description of him that comes down in the handwriting of his son is an attractive one: 'Charles Lloyd was in his person handsome, comely and portly, rather tall than of middle stature, personable every way, of a fresh lively countenance and generally cheerful and pleasant.' The account goes on: 'he loved to converse with sober, religious and ingenious people of all persuasions from his youth' and it adds, notwithstanding the ambitious mothers, that he was inclined to marry one of a religious family and a person who was religious also herself. This was the young man who within a year was to plunge body and soul into the new Quakerism with its harsh and continuing sanctions for himself, his wife and the future of his home and family. What was the spirit behind that handsome, cheerful exterior and what was the temper of the times in which that spirit had been incubating?

The young boy, it seems, was of an enquiring mind and a quick imagination. The contemporary records are predisposed, of course, in his favour, in his honour almost. They are written by Quaker pens, not without hindsight, by sons as of a revered parent, by clerks to Monthly and Quarterly Meetings in the name of his fellows and followers 'in the blessed truth', and they need to be assessed with open eyes. 'Religious inclined from his infancy:

strange dreams when he was but very young: concerned that he
might have an assurance of salvation for his soul: inquisitive with
his schoolmasters and tutors more than they were able to satisfy
him.' He certainly sounds like a seeker.

It was a turbulent time not in politics only but in religion too.
In his childhood there had been a domestic war; in his teens regicide
and the experimental institutions of a Protector; since he was grown
up, the death of 'Oliver' and the recall of a king. The years had
seen a turmoil of religious currents: an insecure Anglican Church;
a new Prayer Book; a resentful, Calvinist Scotland: many fierce
Puritan tides; the Presbyterian confronted by the Independent and
the Baptist: free congregations multiplying on all sides; men and
women in England thinking for themselves. Charles Lloyd had
lived with this; with his enquiring mind he had observed it. In the
Meifod area the Church was in conflict with the Independents: at
Anglican Oxford he had seen Quakers violently treated in the
colleges. 'He went,' we are told, 'for some time among the Independents.' 'He was for some time a hearer of Vavasor Powell, a
noted preacher at that time among the Independents, and when he
was at London he went also to hear the most famous preachers
that he could hear of, but he was not joined in Church membership,
so called, with any.'* 'The aim of the Independents was for free
and self-governing congregations, not under the scrutiny of some
central organisation bound to enforce orthodox opinion or practice.'[6]
A Quaker testimony of fifty years later, doubtless well distilled,
tells us that Charles Lloyd 'sought among such as were men of
great pretence and high notions in that time, called Independents,
among whom he resorted for some time though only as a seeker;
but he saw that they grew high and formal and selfish, and they
were but miserable comforters unto him, Priest and Levite-like, so
that he enjoyed no true satisfaction nor peace unto his soul while
he remained among them'. As regards the Lorts in distant Pembrokeshire there is an echoing note, that Elizabeth's family were
'zealously joined to the Independents, which religion was at that
time embraced by many sober and religious persons as the best
religion then esteemed', and which thus formed also part of the
religious outlook of Charles Lloyd's future wife.

* Charles Lloyd's early experience of London may have been gained while he was
a student at Oxford. It is not otherwise mentioned in the record.

The Quakers were one of the Puritan break-away sects. Under the compelling personality and preaching of George Fox the movement and its ministry had at the time of Charles Lloyd's marriage been spreading for about ten years. George Fox had been born in Leicestershire in 1624. He had grown up a tough but impressive young man, apprenticed to the shoe-making trade. He had early had an unquestionable religious call. He went about during his twenties – in the time of the civil wars – as an itinerant preacher, gaining experience and associating with several of those sects of the day which are best summed up by the contemporary term 'seekers'. It was through the support and encouragement of Judge Fell and his wife Margaret Fell in Westmorland in 1652 that Fox began to emerge as the leader of a movement, and it is from that year that the beginnings of the Society of Friends are usually reckoned. During all this period, and on to the end of the Commonwealth and beyond, the Quakers* were arousing the violent resentment of the established Anglican world and of the authorities behind it, and Fox and his followers steadfastly endured the harshest forms of repression, persecution and imprisonment that a largely unregulated age knew how to bestow. This severity they suffered both in England and in the new American colonies where the Quaker gospel soon penetrated. George Fox's message was a forthright one. It was a message of reliance, for salvation, upon God-given truth and light in the individual heart, of a personal and total submission to gospel guiding, and therefore, as he saw it, of a shaking off of formalised religious organisation and of any system of paid ministry. And in a forthright time this message was forthrightly given, in the way that pioneers do; and because it was exuberant and uncompromising it was as forthrightly resented, and it was put down by every abuse and exaggeration of the law and the legal processes of the day; yet all this served but to attract and to convince fresh adherents.

Two in particular of the movement's outward or visible singularities doubtless earned them more irritation and resistance than other sects. These were the refusal to remove the hat as a mark of official or social respect and the use of the singular or 'plain' language, 'thou' and 'thee'.* George Fox held that for one man to take

* *Quaker* was a nickname which is said to have caught on after Fox had bidden a bench of magistrates to 'quake and tremble at the word of the Lord'.

off his hat to another was an idle and worldly ceremonial, as idle as to bow the body, and he felt himself called to abstain from it and would bare his head before God alone. This both he and his followers consistently did and it proved a cause of affront to many a magistrate on the Bench. The effect of using 'thou' and 'thee', in the middle of the seventeenth century, is somewhat more difficult to appreciate. It seems that within recent generations, the ancient singular forms had been giving way to the plural 'you', particularly when addressing persons of quality. In informal speech and also in country places, as we know from Shakespeare, and of course all through the North today, 'thou' and 'thy' had remained in use, but the plural 'you' and 'your' had come to be used – and expected – by the fashionable and official worlds and by those who saw themselves as persons of more breeding or consequence than their neighbours. Fox would find in the use of 'thou' the echo of his printed Bible, where 'you' and 'ye' are only used in addressing two people or more; and the fact that he was not beyond a little conscious provocation can be sensed when he writes that 'the use of "thou" was a sore cut to proud flesh and those who sought self-honour'.

Charles Lloyd then, from his early days, had been of an enquiring and observing mind. He and his brother Thomas are on record as telling their friend Richard Davies that 'the great sufferings of Friends in that city of Oxford by the magistrates and by the wild and ungodly scholars did work much upon them; and they had some secret love for Friends then'. At New Inn Hall Charles Lloyd and his brother had been at one of the least Anglican of the colleges. This and one other were known at the time as 'two nests of Precisians and Puritans'[7] and may have received visiting Quakers in a less wild and ungodly manner than the rest. But whatever the inclinations, whatever the influences, Charles Lloyd's 'convincement', when it came, came suddenly.

The story of Charles Lloyd's convincement and arrest can be pieced together from Richard Davies and some other contemporary

---

* A distinctive code of practices and speech came early into use among the Quakers, most of which continued to be used throughout the period of this book and almost to the present century.

writings. Charles and Elizabeth had been married in January 1662 and their son Charles was born on 18 October. On a day 'early in the nineth month', i.e.November,* two visiting Quakers were holding a meeting for worship at the house of one Cadwaladr Edwards, 'that had been convinced in the prison of Montgomery' and who lived near Dolobran. This was the first meeting of its kind to take place in the Vyrnwy valley. Edwards, we read, had given notice of the day and time to his neighbours thereabouts, and on the day 'in came Charles Lloyd of Dolobran and several of his well-meaning neighbours'. The account goes on to declare that the Lord was not wanting, and the next morning the two preachers held another meeting. This took place at Charles Lloyd's own house, and from this point onwards, whatever his obligations, Charles Lloyd was openly a Quaker.

It caused something of a sensation in the district, for the Quakers were wildly misunderstood and one of the charges popularly favoured against them was even that of witchcraft. The report of the meetings went through the country, some saying that 'most of that side of the country were turned Quakers', and it did not take long for the Establishment to react. Within a fortnight Charles Lloyd and half a dozen others were in Welshpool gaol.† Their names are recorded. Two of them were women. Elizabeth Lloyd at this time was not one of them. She was making the best of things at Dolobran as we saw.

In the time of the Commonwealth the old device had been to require a Quaker to take the Oath of Abjuration, abjuring the authority of the Pope. This was done on the grounds that travelling Friends were often suspected as Jesuits in disguise, but also well knowing that a Quaker would not swear at all, 'envious magistrates making use of that oath', as George Fox wrote, 'as a snare to catch Friends in'. The King, however, had been restored, and the oath now tendered was that of Allegiance and Supremacy. It served as a snare just the same. The magistrate before whom Charles Lloyd and his friends were summoned was Edward, third Lord Herbert of Cherbury, a near neighbour, who however had his political line to follow, and 'after some discourse' tendered them the oath which

---

* Until the reform of the Calendar in 1752 the year began in March, not January.

† Not later than 20 November; see *Hannah Rose's Narrative*, at Friends House Library. She was the grandchild of one of Charles Lloyd's fellow prisoners.

all declined; and so to Welshpool prison they went 'where they were continued very close prisoners'.

The local Newgate was a rough, barnlike affair, of which photographs still exist taken before its demolition in the 1890s (Plate 2). It was about the size of a small warehouse and stood in the back lanes of Welshpool not far from the road that leads to Powis Castle. The reception awaiting its inmates was as unsavoury and as severe as in scores of other towns, particularly where Quakers were concerned. George Fox's Journal abounds in unspeakable close-ups of the prisons into which he himself was thrown, and, remote though it was, conditions at Welshpool were no better. A contemporary record tells the unvarnished tale: 'these prisoners', it reads,

were kept very close, some of them were substantial freeholders who were put in a dirty, nasty place near the stable and house of office, being a low room; the felons and other malefactors in a chamber overhead, their chamber-pots and excrements, etc, often falling upon them. Charles Lloyd, who was a little before in Commission of the Peace, was put in a little smoky room, and did lie upon a little straw himself for a considerable time.

In fact the Welshpool treatment seems to have been even below the standards of the surrounding centres, so that these six or seven, with some others in the same case, petitioned the County Magistrates about six weeks later for more reasonable treatment. On 8 January 1663 they presented a paper in which they declared that they were worse treated than the 'drunkards, liars, thieves and robbers' on the floor above, in being, unlike them, denied the visits of any friends. The paper went on to claim the benefits of the King's Declaration of Indulgence. This had been published only a month after their imprisonment* and it must at first have sounded like good news to them. Yet, 'notwithstanding all these former words and promises of the King, the supreme magistrate', the paper goes on, 'we have been persecuted more by you his inferior magistrates in this county than in many other counties.' The paper was signed by six men and four women, Charles Lloyd among them. But palace pronouncements were not always literally taken and there was no liberty for tender consciences in Welshpool. The most that the petitioners could gain was some improvement in their conditions,

---

* On 26 December 1662. This was the King's *first* declaration of indulgence.

and while not discharged they now began to be allowed visitors. What must have been the emotions of Elizabeth Lloyd who at last could visit her husband in that stinking place, and how must the future have looked to the young paterfamilias and his long-suffering wife?

This relaxation, so far as it went, took place about the end of January or the beginning of February, 1663. The next few months had further changes in store. It was about this time that Thomas Lloyd, now aged twenty-two, came home from Oxford knowing of his brother's imprisonment and doubtless having heard that visitors were now allowed. Thomas did not return to Oxford, he stayed on to do what he could and to bear a hand at Dolobran. This must have helped Elizabeth in the decision she now took to share her husband's existence at the gaol; 'she came to him', we read, 'in that nasty prison in her fine clothes, choosing at that time rather to live there with her husband in that filthy prison than to dwell in her own house without him'. Leaving her infant now four months old in the care of his nurse, she was 'made willing to lie on straw with her dear and tender husband', doubtless in that little smoky room, with little enough certainty of the future but at least now able to do something for her husband.

The next event concerns Thomas Lloyd himself. He, we are told, now became a Quaker, obedient, it must seem, to the promptings he had experienced at Oxford and 'being some time with Friends in prison and elsewhere' since his return. This does not mean that he himself was in gaol. For some reason at this stage he was not, as Richard Davies explicitly states, and this made it all the more possible for him to be serviceable to Friends, 'he staying pretty much at home and being with his eldest brother Charles Lloyd and in these parts'. In this situation Thomas had quickly got acquainted with Richard Davies who had probably been one of the instruments in his convincement. It was Davies who had organised the meeting in November near Dolobran. Davies was a Welshpool man, and one of the earliest leaders of the Quakers in that region. Within two years of Charles Lloyd in age, he had been apprenticed as a felt-maker and hatter, a quaint coincidence for one who became a Quaker. He was, like the Lloyds, known in the district and was related to some of the gentry. Besides his ministry and his travels far and wide, he used his connections and his wits, often in high places, for the service and the relief of Friends at centres as far apart as London and Bangor. Richard Davies died in 1708. He left behind him an engaging account of his times and work, on which parts of this chapter are based, and which was published after his death through the initiative of the Dolobran Quarterly Meeting, under the title of *An Account of the Convincement, Exercises, Services and Travels of that Ancient Servant of the Lord, Richard Davies: with Some Relation of Ancient Friends and the Spreading of Truth in North Wales.* It is usually known as *The Convincement.*

The Quakers were quite ready to do what they could to get fair play, as the incident of the petition shows, and Richard Davies and Thomas Lloyd who were both men of parts, 'not being prisoners', were now moved to undertake some propaganda among the local Justices which gave them an opportunity to lobby Lord Herbert on Charles Lloyd's behalf. It was about the beginning of April. Cann Office, the scene of the incident, is the name of a hamlet on the A458, not many miles from Dolobran, where the ancient inn is still in use and the site of the bowling-green, between the road and the river, can be easily conjectured. The story, as related by Davies, is worth giving in the contemporary speech:

My friend Thomas Lloyd and I were moved to go and visit most of the justices that had a hand in committing Friends to prison: we began at the farthest justice towards Machynlleth, and came down to Edward, Lord Herbert, Baron of Cherbury, at Llyssin aforesaid, who had committed Charles Lloyd and several other Friends; we understood on the way that he was at a bowling-green and several with him, near a place called the Cann Office, near the highway-side and not far from Llyssin, where we beheld them bowling. We considered with each other, which way to take, there being a peevish priest, the said Lord's chaplain, with them, so I asked Thomas Lloyd whether he would engage the priest in discourse or go to the said Lord, which he chose, and got into the green leisurely towards him, where most of them knew Thomas; but he went not in their complimenting posture. He stayed there a little while and they broke up their game, and while he discoursed with the Lord Herbert, I discoursed a little with the priest. Lord Herbert coming towards the priest and me, he said to the priest, Mr Jones, what have you got there? He answered, a Quaker and haberdasher of hats that lives in Welshpool. Oh, said Lord Herbert, I thought he was such an one, he keeps his hat so fast upon the block. Then, he intending and preparing to come down a great steep ditch, I stepped down to lend him my hand to help him and another priest would have stepped between me and him, but Lord Herbert refused the priest's help; and stopping a little said to the priest, here is a brother that stands by will say 'the blind leads the blind, and both will fall into the ditch'. The priest was so drunk that he could not stand by himself. This lord, being a very big fat man, took my help to come down, so we went along with him towards his own house at Llyssin, laying the suffering of our friends before him and that their sufferings were for their consciences-sake towards God. He gave us no grant then for their enlargement, but we heard that he sent private instructions, and they had more liberty.[8]

The sequel was an acceptable one for Charles and Elizabeth Lloyd. 'The gaoler,' as we learn from another source,

let Charles Lloyd have a chamber for himself and his wife and gave him leave to have his own bed to be brought there also, being more civil to him on some complaints of his cruelty made to the said Lord Herbert, though he continued his cruelty to the rest of Friends for some time afterwards.

Charles Lloyd and his little group had now been in prison five months, and with the spring there came one of those surprising changes that we cannot readily match in present-day experience. About May that year they were placed on parole and allowed the use of a house. Davies rather implies that it was a consequence of the démarche with Lord Herbert. Charles Lloyd's son in his memorandum book suggests that it was because of the persistence of the Quakers' refusal to play the gaoler's game. Probably some quite other reasons came into it that we cannot now know: but

after some space of time, when he found that he could not prevail on Friends to yield to his will and designs by his cruelty, to eat his meat and to drink his drink and to make use of his beds, he was more loving unto them and gave them more liberty and he let them have a house at the end of the town, to themselves, and they had quietness at that house to meet to worship God as often as they pleased without any disturbance.

This was the beginning of a state of affairs under which their imprisonment was to be continued in some cases for years ahead, certainly for nine years in Charles Lloyd's case, until 1672. Impositions of all sorts continued to be enacted and carried out, fines, distraint, confiscation of cattle, with many forms of severity and injustice, all through the period; but this degree of concession had been achieved, the first six months had been the most agonising, and the parole situation – 'he took their word for their safe keeping one another' – was now to continue throughout the piece. To record or to read that this man was ten years in prison for his faith is thus a statement that needs to be understood. The outcome of the new situation was that Charles Lloyd now 'took a house in town for him and his family to live in' and we may conclude that Elizabeth was able at last to send to Dolobran for the little Charles and perhaps his nurse as well and to get something of a second wind after the shocks and humiliations of the winter.

This seesaw of events was characteristic of the times. A kind of seesaw situation runs through the whole of the next twenty years of Charles Lloyd's history which is precisely the history of the persecutions of the Puritans in Charles II's reign. For there was a struggle going on at the centre over the right to dissent, a struggle between the King and the Parliament that swung first one way then the other, now bedevilling, now relieving the lot of the Puritan sects and not least that of the Quakers. This showed itself, in the 1660s, in a succession of new and repressive acts from the Parliament and intermittent indulgences from the Crown. The Parliament throughout this time, known as the Cavalier Parliament, was dominated by disgruntled Royalists who, under the resettlement of the kingdom, had not recovered as much of what they had lost under the Commonwealth, specially of land, as they considered they should. They were now determined to consolidate the new times in their own way and, predominantly Anglican, they concentrated their fire mainly on two targets, the Roman Catholics and the Puritans. In this way they were in opposition to King and Quaker alike. As the King's Roman Catholic sympathies grew, he more than once declared a general indulgence for non-Anglicans. Each time that he did so the Parliament was not slow in undoing it and in the passing of fresh acts, and these often outrageous shifts of fortune were sharply felt at the receiving end.

To list only the to-and-fro of Charles Lloyd's period of detention, from 1662 to 1672, is to show up something of what this meant. The King, on his return in 1660 had promised liberty of conscience to his subjects. The new Parliament was elected in the following year. By their Corporation Act, in simplified terms, they excluded non-Anglicans from the municipal bodies which regulated the sources of membership for the House of Commons. By their Act of Uniformity in 1662 every schoolmaster as well as every clergyman had to assent to the Book of Common Prayer. Their Quaker Act, in May of the same year, made it an offence either to decline an oath or for more than five persons to assemble for non-Anglican worship. This was the act invoked by Lord Herbert in November. These three acts set the pace. At Christmas, as we saw, the first of the King's indulgences was declared and he ordered imprisoned Friends to be released. It looked as though the seesaw had tilted, but they were not released; Parliament suppressed the order. The Conventicle Act of 1664 stiffened up the Quaker Act on meetings for worship and on oaths, prescribed new and startling penalties, even to transportation, and dispensed with the need for a jury to impose them. The Five-Mile Act in 1665 disqualified all ministers of religion who would not abjure resistance to government, Church or State from teaching or living within five miles of a borough. In 1671 there was a second Conventicle Act more savage than the first. During all this time Charles Lloyd was technically a prisoner. His release in 1672 was due to yet another tilt of the seesaw when the King, a Roman Catholic now, if only in private, made his second declaration of indulgence, suspending the penal laws against both the Roman Catholics and the Dissenters. On this occasion 491 Quakers were released from the prisons. They were set at liberty indeed but none too soon. Within a few months the seesaw had tilted again and Parliament had caused the King's Indulgence to be withdrawn.

But that was nearly ten years ahead. Thomas Lloyd now was still at Dolobran and Charles and Elizabeth Lloyd had the use of a house. Richard Davies, though in and out of prison, was actively helping and visiting Friends in Wales, contending with magistrates and clergy and often speaking up in churches himself. This was not at that time discouraged if the preacher was not interrupted, but matter that was not to the taste of the hearers could lead to arrest for causing a disturbance. However, though allowed to live out, Charles Lloyd was still a prisoner, he was 'not suffered to see his house for several years', and as act followed act the prospect for Quakers was a blank. They were accustomed to say afterwards that the period of their persecution lasted for forty years, meaning from the time when George Fox was first beginning to make his mark until, by the Toleration Act under the new reign of William and Mary, the more repressive of the recent enactments were abolished. In the Conclusion to his *Sufferings of the Quakers*[9] Joseph Besse writes:

> The foregoing collection contains a multitude of instances of the trials, afflictions and sufferings, cruel mockings and scourgings, bonds imprisonments and deaths, which this religious people underwent for the exercise of a good conscience during a violent storm of persecution of nearly forty years continuance.

Charles Lloyd's imprisonment corresponded with the height of this storm, which indeed abated little for the next fifteen years after his discharge, and it was only in the final years of his life, from 1689 to 1698, that he passed into calmer waters; but in 1663 he was still only twenty-five years old. Besse does not exaggerate in including deaths in his recital. Not less than two of Charles Lloyd's original fellow prisoners died in Welshpool gaol, Edward Evans after eighteen months and Humphrey Wilson after three years, 'of a distemper occasioned by the coldness and unwholesomeness of the place', and their widows survived them in the prison. Hundreds of other Friends died in prisons all over the country.

   We know of several personal events which marked the slow years of this Welshpool period. One of the first was the convincement of Elizabeth. This must have taken place at some point after she had joined her husband at the prison – 'she afterwards came to be convinced of the blessed truth' – and we may conclude that it would be in that same year of 1663 after they had occupied the hired house together. However, it can hardly have been before 9 April, on which date the following entry appears in the Meifod parish register: *Carolus filius legitimus Caroli Lloyd de Dolobran et Elizabethae uxoris eius baptizatus est*. To Elizabeth, not yet a Quaker, the baptism of her boy would be the natural course to take. One wonders if the Quaker father knew. Another event was the birth, the year after, of their second child, Sampson, and this was followed by four more children before they were released, all born at Welshpool and all boys. It seems that the mother went here and there to the houses of neighbours in the town, or perhaps of midwives, on these occasions; the infant Sampson was born 'at Ann Eccleston's at Welshpool', the infant George, the next child, 'at Humphrey Jones's house in Welshpool'. The event of the next year, 1665, was the marriage of Thomas Lloyd. His bride was Mary Jones, of a family who were hereditary burgesses of Welshpool, and shortly after his marriage he was himself imprisoned for refusing to swear. What concessions were allowed to Thomas by 'the cruel jaylor' are not recorded but we must make some assumptions. Probably he was placed on parole like his brother. Ten children were born to Thomas and Mary Lloyd during the following years, during which he was a prisoner for eight. It was during this period likewise, in 1667, that a passing visitor came to a meeting 'at Charles Lloyd's', i.e. at Dolobran, whose name would stir the Quakers round about. This was George Fox, on one of his journeys. He records in his journal that 'some opposers came in but the Lord's power brought them down'. Charles Lloyd was of course not present. He later himself visited George Fox in prison, at Worcester, in 1674.

An episode of these years brings Lord Herbert into the story again. Under the Second Conventicle Act the onslaught on non-conformists had been so stepped up as to become a very travesty of justice when the principles of Magna Carta are considered. The first Conventicle Act had dispensed with juries, requiring but two justices to apply it. The second reduced this to a single justice, prescribed new fines for preaching and even for permitting a meeting on any premises, gave sanction to the practice of informing by granting the informer one third of the fines, and authorised distraint for their recovery. In Montgomeryshire as in other places informers were not slow to appear, men who were often the lowest of the low and in league with the local gaolers. At Welshpool, one such, set on by the gaoler as Richard Davies tells, had worked it out that if he could surprise a meeting taking place at Dolobran he 'must needs have either Dolobran or Coedcowrid for his pains'. The informer in fact found a meeting of Quakers taking place at Dolobran and went to Lord Herbert for a warrant against them, who, however, seems to have had other ideas for, after being pressed if not badgered by the man for a warrant, he rounded on him exclaiming, 'is it not sufficient to put my peaceable neighbours in prison? Must I give a warrant to make such a rogue as this is rich, by ruining them and their families?' This incident occurred already nine years after

Lord Herbert had personally committed his neighbours to prison, and it would seem that he did not now feel proud of it even if the law had obliged him as a Justice to take official action at the time. Davies recounts that the informer, thus sent about his business, later came to think better of it and actually prayed the Quakers to forgive him; 'so he never informed against us afterwards.'

One particular activity coloured the later years of Charles Lloyd's imprisonment when 'liberty was given to them to go several miles from their prison provided that they appeared again at certain times that the gaoler did order them to appear again'. Charles Lloyd now made the first of his journeys to visit imprisoned Friends in other centres, a practice which we hear of again as he matured and as his ministry developed. On this occasion he went, as often, with another Friend; his companion was Richard Evans of Salop who was 'one of his first school-masters and knew him well' and who had likewise become a Quaker. This must have meant special leave for Charles Lloyd, for they went to visit Friends at Stafford, Warwick, Oxford and Bristol, in one journey. What income Charles Lloyd had at this time, how they found horses, or how long they were away we cannot know, but for an imprisoned man this was a considerable round. In these ways and by these events was the slow tramp of the years occasionally relieved.

There they lived, a growing family now, in a state of evacuation from their proper place, a condition of suspended reality. It must have been not unlike the wartime atmosphere that many experienced in our own times. One wonders how the children were brought up. By 1672 the three eldest, Charles, Sampson and George were reaching ten, eight and seven. Was there any school for Elizabeth to send them to so as to get any freedom for the younger ones as they came along? Elizabeth had an unemployed husband in the home. Perhaps it was he who taught them their letters. They appear as educated men in later life. Who were Elizabeth's friends? There was, we know, a little group of Quaker women sharing the imprisonment, living perhaps in the gaoler's house already mentioned, and she would also know the wives of some of the imprisoned husbands such as Tace,* the wife of Richard Davies. But what would have been the relations between the little Quaker set and their neighbours in the town? The women who had been committed to prison with

* Tace; pronounced to rhyme with Stacey.

Charles Lloyd in 1662 and just after were Anne Lawrence, Sarah Wilson, Margaret Lewis and Catherine Evans, and four other names are recorded later. Sarah Wilson, whose husband had died in the prison, was from the Dolobran neighbourhood. Anne Lawrence was from Herefordshire. It is not clear how she came to be arrested with the Montgomeryshire group; however, she became a close friend of Elizabeth's and, later, Charles Lloyd's second wife. Of the women officially discharged in 1672 three had suffered the whole ten years' detention, as Charles Lloyd had himself.[10]

We come now to a milestone, the Declaration of Indulgence by Charles II in 1672, which was marked by the release of Quakers and some other Dissenters all over the country. Suddenly, in September, Charles and Elizabeth Lloyd and twelve other Welshpool prisoners found themselves pardoned. That they were freed in time, before the Indulgence was reversed, was due to the initiative of some London Friends in getting the Pardon out to the counties for action. The instrument had been signed by the King and had received the Great Seal; but how, without other communication than the horse, was it possible to distribute urgently to several dozen sheriffs and gaolers all over the country a single document, in a leathern case and tin box, upon ten skins of vellum 'with the names of above four hundred persons repeated eleven times over in it'? The business could not wait. Winter was near, when everything would slow down. The seesaw might tip at any time. The story of the staff-work to solve this problem, carried through by a handful of their fellow Quakers, makes breathless reading; how copies were first made for the counties nearer to London, but 'we were yet more concerned for our suffering friends in the more remote counties and prisons in the northern and western parts of England and in Wales'; how an extract from the patent, called a *Liberate*, with the relevant names, was drawn up for each remaining county 'as those in Montgomery Prison in a distinct warrant for the sheriff of that county'; and how advantage was taken of under-sheriffs coming to London for the Michaelmas term; 'so that at last, through much labour, care and diligence, the difficulty we had been under came to be removed'.[11] Among the prisoners named in the Pardon were Charles Lloyd, Thomas Lloyd and Richard Davies.

Charles and Elizabeth Lloyd had just passed their tenth wedding-anniversary. Aged about thirty-five, they now had five children from ten years old down to twelve months. For close on a decade they had been living in Welshpool, in a house which, with such a family, must long since have become a home and which was now to be given up. What condition Dolobran was in on their return we cannot precisely tell. Cattle and possessions had been taken, we know, and the house had been used for holding meetings, but who had lodged there and who had worked the fields is not clear. It has been stated that the house had been partly demolished as part of Charles Lloyd's penalties, but without evidence as to how this would have benefited the authorities. There must have been everything for them to do and it must have looked an uphill crusade.

Another thirteen years of Charles II's reign were still to pass, before the accession of his brother James brought more substantial reliefs. During these years the family settled back into the house, a precious daughter was born, their seventh child, the boys began to grow up, and the parents must have hoped for a time of more tranquillity. But it was quite the contrary; for although the King

by his patent or pardon under the Great Seal did open the prison doors to the discharging of near five hundred of the said People at once, pursuant to his Declaration published for a suspension of the penal laws, yet the Declaration being thought an undue extent of the royal prerogative was soon revoked and their persons and estates again exposed to the returning storm and to the exhorbitant plunder and rapine of avaricious and merciless informers.[12]

Thus the harsh and dreary persecutions continued and were indeed from time to time officially spurred on as forgotten statutes with which to catch Quakers were invoked by the ingenuity of the persecutors. In spite of this, the ministry of visits for the encouragement of fellow sufferers, and sometimes for the confounding of the authorities, increased; and in 1681 a Yearly Meeting for Wales was instituted in parallel with the now established London Yearly Meeting which regulated the concerns of Friends centrally. During most of this time Charles Lloyd at Dolobran, Thomas Lloyd who was living and practising at Trefnant just outside Welshpool, and Richard Davies at Cloddiau* Cochion near by, were repeatedly fined and

* Pronounced somewhat like 'clothier'.

distrained upon and suffered short sentences of imprisonment under the now routine charges of *not paying tithes, meeting together to worship God* and *absence from the national worship.*

An example of fines for worship appears in the episode of the raid in 1674 on a meeting at Cloddiau Cochion by an informer, 'with 14 or 15 persons, most of them armed'. The assembly which they raided consisted of 'a small number of our Friends waiting in silence upon the Lord'. The informer – such is justice – was one David Maurice, a Justice for the County of Montgomery. The bill for worshipping God that morning was

T. Lloyd: for preaching	£20. 0. 0
The house: for allowing a conventicle	£20. 0. 0
The hearers: for attending it, 5. 0 apiece	

About the same time 'Charles Lloyd of Dolobran had ten young beasts taken from him upon a warrant from the said David Maurice, for preaching, on a day and at a place where the said Charles Lloyd was not that day nor many days before or after'. Ten young beasts would represent a substantial fine, particularly galling when an offence had not been committed. There are many other cases given by Richard Davies. An example of an old act resuscitated to make Quaker victims was one from the time of Mary, *De Haeretico Comburendo*, Of the Burning of Heretics. This a newly appointed judge in North Wales, Walcott by name, revived in 1667 and was determined that under it he would 'burn the men and hang the women'. And so he would have done but for the action of Thomas Lloyd and another Friend, who travelled to London, lobbied 'several Parliament-men' and were successful in procuring the repeal of the Act 'that sessions'. This was in truth a case of being 'serviceable to Friends'. Another example was the Act *De Excommunicato Capiendo*, Of the Apprehending of Excommunicated Persons, under which it seemed simple for a Quaker to be tidily arrested, with imprisonment to follow, for being an excommunicated person. Richard Davies narrates an occasion when, with the personal help of William Penn and the Chancellor, Lord Hyde, he obtained a directive for the restraint of this stratagem in the North Wales area, to the relief of many Friends who were under the threat of it.

Richard Davies and the two Lloyds had now become leaders among Friends in this region. Davies himself spoke Welsh as well as English. In reading *The Convincement* one imagines him as a brisk, talkative personality, preaching with the fluency and rich detail that comes out in his writing, argumentative, persuasive and shrewd, and at the same time having a way with him; probably a small man; black hair when young; grey at forty; a characteristic Welshman. There is no evidence that the Lloyds spoke Welsh or used it for preaching, though they may have understood it. It would be of interest to know at what period in the past their family had been bi-lingual, which down to some stage it must have been. Together, the three men upheld Friends in whatever ways were open to them. In their degree, all of them were personally known or related to many of the more prominent people round about, and as a result of this some of those who were in positions of authority 'were moderated towards Friends'. Lord Powis and his lady, for example, helped them several times. All of them, singly and sometimes two together, would visit, Paul-like, in these years, the centres of current persecution; or they would go out of their way to use influence to defeat the tactics of the opposition. Charles Lloyd and Richard Davies had gone together in 1675 to Bala, in the next county, to succour Friends at a time of onslaught there. Davies in 1677 obtained relief for a Friend in a tithe case at Ludlow by urgent recourse to a legal expert in London: 'I sent to London,' he writes, 'to John Lloyd, brother to Charles Lloyd of Dolobran, who belonged to the Chancery Office, and he sent me down a *Prohibition*; and I went to serve the priest and his attorney with it.' In 1682 Richard Davies and Charles Lloyd made a tour to visit Friends in Herefordshire and Worcestershire, organizing their journey so as to bring them at the right time to the Yearly Meeting in London. During this visit they made two of a deputation of six to petition the King on behalf of Friends in Bristol, when they waited on 'Lord Hide' at Whitehall to present their case by word of mouth. That year Charles Lloyd remained for longer than usual in the capital, partly because of illness, which was evidently a form of malaria; 'in the year 1682 and 1683 he continued at and near London near a year and while he was there he had the quartain ague which did continue on him a long time'. His son records that Charles Lloyd was 'several times at Bristol, and also several times at London at the yearly meetings there and at other times, and several times at the yearly meetings in Wales'.

Their three names had been likewise linked, in 1681, over the episode of the public disputation at Llanfyllin, a market town about five miles from Dolobran. The account by Richard Davies, as usual, is a vivid one:

About the year 1680 or 1681, came Dr William Lloyd, late of Martins in London, to be Bishop of this Diocese, called St Asaph. Persecution was very sharp and severe in several places about this time, upon account of Excommunication and the statute of £20 a month. But this new Bishop thought to take a more mild way to work, by summoning all sorts of Dissenters to discourse with him, and to seek to persuade them to turn to the Church of England. Among the rest, when he came to Welshpool in his visitation, he sent for us. Charles Lloyd, Thomas Lloyd and myself sought to speak with him, but I was that day bound for London so could not, but my friends stayed till they had an opportunity with him; and my friend Charles Lloyd gave me an account afterwards of what passed between them, which was to this effect: That the Bishop was much displeased that I was absent, and when he was told of my urgent occasion to go, and my stay on purpose for some time to see him, he said his business was greater, whatever my business was. That day they discoursed with him, his Chaplains and other clergy, so called, from about two in the afternoon till two in the morning. Afterwards they discoursed with him two days at Llanfyllin. The first day from about two in the afternoon till night, and the next day from about ten in the morning till an hour in the night, publicly in the Town Hall. The first day, at Pool, our friends Charles Lloyd and Thomas Lloyd gave their reasons of separation. In none of the three days would the Bishop and his clergy defend their own principles, or refute ours; but only held the three days on the general principles of Christendom and the Apostles' examples of water-baptism, and once a small touch at the bread and wine. Thomas Lloyd held the last day our reasons why we separated from the Church of England; which were,

1. because their worship was not a gospel worship,
2. because their ministry was no gospel ministry,
3. because their ordinances were no gospel ordinances.

But they would not join with him to prove any of them, though often solicited thereunto; Friends being sufferers must submit to all disadvantages; for they had not any notice beforehand of what matters they should argue till they came to the place of dispute, and the last day they forced Thomas Lloyd to about twenty-eight syllogisms, all written down as they disputed, to be answered *extempore*; and the Bishop said, he did not expect so much could be said by any on that subject on so little warning; and he said that they expected not to find so much civility from the Quakers; he highly commended Thomas Lloyd and our friends came off with them very well.[13]

What is of interest in this account is that it should have been these same three who were summoned to this theological marathon. Bishop Lloyd was a moderate adversary, not altogether ill-disposed, and he had other, more friendly encounters both with the Lloyds and with Davies later on. Eventually he became himself an objector against tyranny in high places for he was one of the seven Bishops who in 1688 were tried – and acquitted – for protesting against the claims of James II to dictate to the Church. For the Lloyds, now men in their forties and known to all, it must have been a satisfactory opportunity to demonstrate something of what they were and what they stood for.

By this time the elder boys were in their teens and daughter Elizabeth was approaching ten herself. Where Charles, the eldest, was apprenticed we do not know, but, reaching now the earliest known written item by any of the family, we find that the second boy, Sampson, was sent away in 1679, at the age of fifteen, to be apprenticed to Constantine Overton in Shrewsbury. One wonders how Charles Lloyd was able to arrange this. Perhaps it was through his old schoolmaster there. It is certain to have been through Friends. The item is a note in a pocket almanack of Sampson's for the year 1683, written opposite the calendar for October: 'A Memorandum that on the sixth day of this month 1683 at 11 of the Clock in the Afternoon there hapned a Earthquake in Sallop wch did shake me with my felow Aprentises in bed and made the house Crack. It lasted not one Minutt.' But much though this piece of reporting tells us we do not know to what trade either son was bound.

The year 1683 was an eventful one for the family. On 17 November George, the third son, died at Dolobran, aged eighteen. Allowing for the other deaths, this left as the final survivors, Charles, Sampson and the much younger Elizabeth. In the same year their uncle, Thomas Lloyd, emigrated to North America. He took ship with his wife and numerous family, endured a crossing of eight weeks, reached the infant colony of Pennsylvania, and within a month – as they eventually learned at Dolobran – Mary Lloyd died. At her burial we are told that William Penn personally 'appeared in testimony'; Thomas Lloyd was soon to be his right-hand man in the colony – indeed Deputy Governor. But there were further events in store. The year 1685 saw the deaths, within a month, both of the King, Charles II, and of Elizabeth Lloyd herself, his in March, hers in April. This was a poignant turn of events for Charles Lloyd – his wife departed aged only fifty-one, Dolobran without a mistress, his brother abroad, all this on the eve of the Indulgences by the new King James who, to serve the Catholics, ordained fresh reliefs to the Dissenters. Charles Lloyd would be grieving though perhaps hopeful as he rode to her burying at Cloddiau Cochion, five miles away, 'where there had been buried before her four of her children'.* She had been a staunch wife, she had endured much, 'she was a religious and virtuous woman of good life and conversation and of great self-denial, which was taken notice of by many who knew how she was brought up and educated'.

Quite soon Charles Lloyd married again. His second wife was that Anne Lawrence who had gone through the same term of imprisonment that he had and had been released under the same Indulgence fourteen years before. Anne Lawrence now lived at Almeley in Herefordshire where she acted as treasurer to the Monthly Meeting. As old friends and fellow sufferers she and the Lloyds had exchanged visits in the intervening years and it seems certain that the sons had stayed in Herefordshire, for at the same place and on the same day that their father, aged forty-eight, married Anne Lawrence, the young Sampson, aged twenty-two, was likewise married to a Herefordshire bride. This was Elizabeth Good, the child of a widow near Leominster,† and on 8 April 1686 the double wedding of father and son took place at Yarpole, about five miles from that place. The Quaker certificates of the two events present the signatures of more than fifty witnesses, among them those of brother John Lloyd and his son of the same name, who had made the journey from London. The form of words recorded to have been used by Charles Lloyd in taking Anne Lawrence as his wife is longer than in most Quaker certificates. As they are written in his own hand and rather crammed

---

* The outline of the little enclosure can still be seen in this remote place, in the meadow below Richard Davies's farm.

† For this connection see Chapter 3.

into the space, they are probably his actual words and as the declaration of a leader among Friends are not without interest: 'Friends, in the fear, love, light, life, power and presence of Almighty God and you here all assembled do I own and take this my near, dear and worthy friend Anne Lawrence to be my wife, according to the example of the men of God in former ages, and do further promise and intend by the assistance of his grace to be a loving, tender and faithful husband so long as it shall please God that either of us both shall live.'

Dolobran thus acquired a mistress again and for the next ten years, until 1697, was to enjoy a relatively more settled time. These were the years of James II and of William and Mary. Almost at once, under James, there was issued a new declaration of immunity, followed, in 1689, by the Toleration Act of the second of these reigns. Exactions for tithe still went on, but the time of the worst persecutions was behind and the story at length takes on a more domestic note. Charles, the eldest son, his marriage still seven years in the future, was living at home and working about the property. Sampson and his young wife were busy farming and raising a family of daughters at Kimbolton near Leominster. It is of Elizabeth that we begin to hear more.

Soon after her father's marriage Elizabeth, aged fourteen, was sent away to get on with her education, to distant London. In August 1687 her father is writing to her, newly arrived at the house of her mistress, Mary Pardoe, in Aldersgate, his first letter after the great departure. One can recognise it all. 'Glad we shall all be to hear from thyself by an epistle how thou hast thy health, how thou likest the city and thy coming thither', and again, 'how far thou hast improved thyself in writing, reading, spelling, sewing and in the service of God, and in anything else that is good and useful'; and lower down, 'my wife desires to be remembered to them all very kindly as well as thy little self, she longs for thee home'; and he ends, in effect, 'write quick, then Charles can bring your letter with him'. Though doubtless returning home in the summers, Elizabeth was still in London in 1690. She was now seventeen and taking her place in Quaker circles there as the niece of her lawyer uncle, John Lloyd, and the child of a senior Friend in the provinces. 'Many eyes will be upon thee unawares to thyself,' her father writes, 'some for good and some for evil.' And in the same letter, suddenly, one of those blinding phrases: 'let not thy earnestness to learn make thee neglect meetings and to see good friends, and especially *blessed and good George Fox, God's friend*, and mind me kindly to him.' Let us hope she found means to deliver her father's message. George Fox, in London now, was nearing the end of his days. Six months later he was dead.

Then, as now, marriages and deaths made news. It was in 1692 that the young Sampson lost his wife. He was only twenty-eight and for the next three years he was a widower. Who looked after the four little girls we do not know. In the following year both son Charles and daughter Elizabeth were married. By this step young Charles forged the first link in the long chain that was to tie the Lloyds into so many of the Quaker families in the iron trade of the West Midlands. His bride was a Crowley from the busy town of Stourbridge, about ten miles west of Birmingham. Why, when the bridegroom came from a country home so far away as Montgomeryshire, should the two families have been acquainted? One can only fall back on the Quaker connection – the bride's father, the senior Ambrose Crowley, was a leading Quaker. The young Charles was married to Sarah Crowley at Stourbridge on 6 July 1693. After the bridegroom and bride, the names of Charles and Anne Lloyd head the signatures to the certificate (Plate 5). Sampson the widower follows, together with the faithful Amos Davies, the friend of the family and clerk to the meeting at Dolobran. Sarah's father, Ambrose Crowley, who never learnt to write, makes his mark, 'A C'. Next come seven of the Crowley brothers and sisters. There is also one other signature of special interest for this history, traced in clear and rather ornamental characters, that of the Welshpool gospeller, Richard Davies. The marriage of John Pemberton, a young and well-to-do Quaker ironmonger (i.e. iron merchant) from Birmingham, to the slender Elizabeth, now home from London and living at Dolobran, both of whom had been present at the Stourbridge wedding, took place at the Dolobran meeting on 21 September.

During most of this time not much is heard of Charles Lloyd himself, and less of his wife. But now, from this date until his death in 1698, a sudden light is thrown upon his life and thoughts by about twenty letters, all written to son and daughter Pemberton at Birmingham. They bring us a picture of life at Dolobran when the old Lloyds are in their upper fifties. Charles Lloyd is growing infirm and is anxious about the future of the meeting. Anne is invisible as ever. On the premises there is a second *ménage* now for the younger Charles with his wife and infant children also live in the house. But it was Anne who was running the home. To Sarah, Anne was a mother-in-law, in fact a stepmother-in-law, and for all the old man's goodwill and benevolence the situation was not without its strains. In the family circle life takes its course. For Sarah in 1694 there is an infant, for Elizabeth at Birmingham a miscarriage ('those foul and dangerous stairs', writes her father with more than his usual force of utterance), and the next year a child for each. In December 1695 there is Sampson's new marriage to Sarah's sister Mary, a second Crowley alliance with its future iron-trade implications. On the Quaker front there is the provision of a new burying-ground near Dolobran, more convenient for them than at Cloddiau Cochion, while the event of the year 1694 is the holding at Dolobran of the Yearly Meeting for Wales.

From that year on, Charles Lloyd is often ill, 'I want a calash or litter or some conveniency beyond many that use them', and in writing to the dear daughter in Birmingham his concerns and anxieties come out. One of his most frequent topics is health. In letter after letter either John (of whom he thinks the world) or Elizabeth receives prescriptions and advice on the treatment for this or that disorder. It is clear that Charles Lloyd had 'practised physick' – like his brother, even if in a small way – he tells us of 'troublesome patients' – and his mind now often goes back to his studies as a student. His fund of knowledge, like his memory, is remarkable. He writes pages on the remedies of the day, and is lavish in specifics, for backache, for catarrh, for the smallpox, for infection of the gums. In a letter to Elizabeth, pregnant in Birmingham in 1697, we read:

I do not approve of all their oft bleeding thee, though it's the court fashion and mode of late, but it should be used in strong lively bodies of a strong habit. Thou art spare, thin and lean, and wants rather blood and spirits than to be so drained.

and a few days later:

Keep up thy heart and trust in the Lord and be hearty for many in thy case have such symptoms and do well enough... And as to their talk

1. Dolobran Hall near Welshpool, ancestral home of the Birmingham Lloyds.

2. The old gaol at Welshpool in which Charles Lloyd was imprisoned.
(Demolished 1896.)

3. Eighteenth-century iron forge near Dolgellau; aquatint by Paul Sandby.

4. Ambrose Crowley senior, of Stourbridge, 1635–1720.

And the said *Charles Lloyd* ✠ ✠ _ and *Sarah Crowley* ✠ ✠ as a further Confirmation thereof did then and there to thefe Prefents fet their Hands. And we whofe Names are hereunto fubfcribed, being prefent among others, at the Solemnizing of their said Marriage and Subfcriptions in manner aforefaid, as Witneffes thereunto, have alfo to thefe Prefents fubfcribed our Names, the Day and Year above-written.

			Charles Lloyd Junior
			Sarah Crowley

(signatures)

5. Signatures at the marriage of Charles Lloyd junior and Sarah Crowley, 1693.

6. Birmingham, 'The Square', favoured by Quaker families; from W. Westley's *North Prospect of St Philip's Church*, 1730.

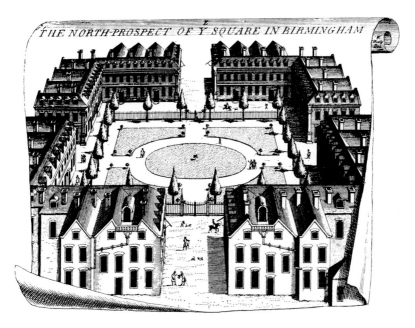

THE NORTH PROSPECT OF Ye SQUARE IN BIRMINGHAM

7. Thomas Pemberton I, 1697–1757,
cousin and brother-in-law of
Sampson Lloyd II.

8. Jane Pemberton, 1704–50,
wife of Thomas Pemberton I and
a daughter of Richard Parkes.

9. Pemberton's house and warehouse at Bennetts Hill; from a painting by Samuel Lines.

about wine, they mistake, tent wine is no wine of grapes but is made of the juice of Spanish mulberries and is binding like the syrup of mulberries, and is not heavy, feverish and inflaming at all, and is commonly taken by the Bristol women in their lying-in and weakness without danger. And vinegar also is of another nature than wine, used inwardly or outwardly, mixed or unmixed with water, and on cloths dipped therein applied to the back and lower parts. So is Jesuit's bark, sapling bark, pomegranate flowers and bark, acacia sloes, Japan earth, cole dragon's blood, and most opiates, especially made up with quince juice, as is that of Helemont's liquid laudanum cydoneated or prepared with quinces... Eat and drink anything prepared from almonds, as the milk almond comfits or macaroons, walnuts, good filberts, and fine bread or cakes, marmalade of quinces or quiddons or the syrup or mead of quinces, or what pleases thy palate and appetite best. I mention divers for variety's sake and to please thy fancy and desire better, lest they glut thee or not suit so well.[14]

But his advice is not offered on health matters alone. As a dedicated Friend, some of the letters turn into an unconscious sermon and others, whether to son-in-law or daughter, into a lecture, sometimes of the most personal kind; but it is never resented for they too thought the world of him. After Elizabeth and her husband had been staying at Dolobran in 1696, he writes:

Do not imitate proud dames and giglers who know little or less than thyself of truth, but be like a matron and thy father and mother's daughter... I question not thy love to us far beyond any of my children – and so I reckon thy husband as well as thee above them also – yet there is a little carelessness in thy carriage or strangeness at first. Thou goest not to them suddenly or takes them by the hands or clothes earnestly to invite them or ask them how they do and what meat and drink they will have oft, as thy husband uses to do which makes his carriage so pleasing and acceptable unto most, as I desire to be to my friends and guests, though perhaps thou thought of no hurt and leaves thy husband to entertain thy countrymen.

The greatest perplexity of the old man is over continuity where 'Dolobran and meetings' are concerned. This was partly from the scattering of the family, partly from his obligations to a meeting that was so much a child of his own, 'my own plantation and delightsome vineyard', and partly from uncertainty as to how son Charles was turning out. For Charles and Sarah were restless.

'Thy sister Lloyd is not yet resolved to stay here'; 'my son and daughter be uneasy and talk of going away. We bear much and be as quiet as we can be.' 'I fear it will hasten my hoary head to the grave more than all my prisons, debts and travelling.' (This is the one reference to prison in any of his letters.) But his mind runs constantly on the future of the Meeting. 'We be not yet clear of this place. It lays hard upon us that the meeting be better settled, lest it be scattered.' This is in 1695 when the Pembertons were already proposing that he and Anne should hand it all over and come to Birmingham. The next year the project was still being pressed, but this time they saw the way clearer, for at last there is a letter to Elizabeth, 'we do kindly accept of thy invitation'. Infirmity and the logic of events had prevailed. In October 1697, after troublesome delays on the journey, the old people arrived in Birmingham, the letters cease, and there a year later, in his sixty-first year, on 26 November 1698, Charles Lloyd died. At Dolobran Charles Lloyd had more than once mentioned his desire to be buried locally, but circumstances had set that aside and 'in his last sickness he showed no concern about it for he said it was a thing that had to be'. Thus, after a lifetime lived in Wales, he became the first Lloyd to be buried at Birmingham, bridging in his own person the Dolobran and the Birmingham branches of the family which the two sons were now to carry on.

His daughter Pemberton has left us a sensitive memorial of his last days, 'my brothers being all come with their wives'. There are also two testimonies, a personal one by his son Charles and a formal one in the name of the Dolobran Quarterly Meeting. These were drawn up in 1708, presumably to mark the tenth anniversary of Charles Lloyd's death. By this time he had become a hero to his son, now a conscientious Quaker himself, whose tribute begins, 'Shall Time blot out thy Memory or Multitude of Dayes cause thy Name to be buried, oh Noe'. To the Meeting, he was 'one of the Lord's worthies in his day' who 'hated none but Satan, sin and self' and 'whose memory will be had in Esteem when the memory of the Wicked will rott'.

2

FORGES IN WALES

Already since the end of 1697 an air of change had come over Dolobran where the house and estate were now in the hands of the younger Charles. He and Sarah lost no time in making their own plans and the next few years present us with a busy programme of innovation, including alterations to the house, a building for the Meeting and the launching of a Quaker school. But before any of these, and within six months of his father's departure to Birmingham, the new Charles had made a still more far-reaching move. He had taken the lease of a local iron forge.

To most of us a forge is another name for a smithy such as in the days of the horse was to be found in every village. On another plane, such terms as 'forgings' and 'forgemaster' are in present use in industry where the manufacture of certain kinds of large-scale fabricated metal products is concerned. But at that period, before the industrial revolution had advanced, a forge meant something different. It was the name used for one of the essential stages in the manufacture of iron itself. And as it may also seem surprising that there should have existed a unit of the iron industry in distant Montgomeryshire at all, a glance at the background may not be out of place.

The form which the product of such a forge normally took was that of bar iron. Bar iron was produced by the operations of refining and forming metal under heat, and would then be sold for working by smiths into iron articles of general use and necessity – from agricultural implements or chains and anchors for the country's ships to horseshoes and the humble necessary nail. But that was only the second stage of iron production. The raw material required for the forge was pig iron. This was produced at an installation known as the furnace (often far removed from the forge) where iron ore was converted into raw metal by a process of smelting with charcoal. Another, more primitive method of iron-making was still carried on in the country, it is true, as it had been for hundreds of years past, but production of workable bar iron was now mainly dependent upon the more economic, two-tier technique of the furnace and the forge.

In Charles Lloyd's day the number of ironworks in operation in England and Wales amounted to something over fifty furnaces and a hundred forges.[1] Originally iron production had been carried on chiefly in the Weald of Sussex, within reach of London and the Thames, but, in the interests of cannon for the Army and Navy, it had been subject to increasing regulation, and especially of wood-cutting for charcoal, which limited the iron available for the general market. The improved two-part process had therefore been spreading in response to demand, to other areas, and it is in the light of this trend that the presence of forges in Welsh counties (Plate 3) is to be understood. By the time of William and Mary furnaces for the making of pig were established in the Forest of Dean and South Wales, in the West Midlands and in the West Riding of Yorkshire, and also in some other centres such as the North Wales borders around Chester and Wrexham and in North Lancashire. So far as supplies of pig iron were concerned, therefore, a forge located near Welshpool was within reasonable distance, either by river or road, of both West Midlands and Wrexham sources.

But if such great expanses of the rest of the country, with their population, towns and trade, remained innocent of ironworks, how was it that the new iron-making had gravitated in this way to the western and north-western parts? The explanation is partly technical, partly commercial, partly due to the location of raw materials and partly to chance, and it is compounded of the following aspects: woodlands, water, ore, transportation, capital and enterprise. The industry depended, first of all, upon wood, because the fuel used in both furnace and forge was charcoal, and secondly it required streams or small rivers with sufficient fall to work the wheels for its bellows and hammers. Such facilities of wood and water might be thought to occur pretty generally throughout the land, but a furnace (though not a forge) needed also iron ore and limestone, and a furnace therefore required to be within reach of appropriate mineral supplies. This requirement the particular western distribution of the new iron districts satisfied; they were within range of suitable raw materials. For although the condition of the roads was much worse than anything we know today, especially in winter, the movement of loads by packhorse was practicable within limited radius. Movement over short distances would be effected by land where necessary, but where water was available goods would travel over long distances, both river and coastwise traffic being used; and these water facilities the new iron districts possessed, for they were most of them within reasonable reach either of a port or of that great old channel of commerce, the river Severn. The main iron-making districts thus enjoyed four of the facilities required: woodlands, streams, minerals and transportation. But on whose land and at whose risk were the new ironworks installed? A furnace or a forge was not set up by some group of experienced industrialists as might happen today, it was more likely to be started by a family, or by a landowner, whose property was already blessed with woods and water and who was willing to enjoy a revenue from exploiting them. The initiative for many of the new installations was thus often due to the enterprise of country landlords or property-owners having the capital and the wish to engage in new undertakings themselves or to grant leases to those prepared to do so.

In lower Montgomeryshire, in the Welshpool area, there were two iron forges at the time of this narrative. Both were on land belonging to the Powis Castle estate. One of them, built in the 1670s, was situated on the Severn at Pool Quay a mile or two below Welshpool, where there was a good weir to give a fall of water just at the point where navigation by barges began. The other, set up in the time of the Commonwealth by a local resident who had become a rich London merchant,* was located on the fast-flowing Vyrnwy at Mathrafal, by a corn mill where water and a dam already existed.[2] This was the forge, just across the river from the Lloyd property, in full view from the windows of Dolobran and less than half a mile away, that Charles Lloyd now took. The date on which he began to be not the neighbour only but also the tenant of Powis Castle was 25 March 1698 and his rent was £40 a year payable at

* At the risk of confusion it must be stated that he was Sir Charles Lloyd, baronet of Moel-y-Garth, near Welshpool, but he has no connection with anyone in this book.

Michaelmas and Lady Day.[3] He continued in occupation of this
forge for the next twenty years, and although we have no accounts
and no chronicler it is possible to piece together a certain amount of
information about it.

The view from Dolobran was closed in by a high rounded hill
largely covered with trees and known as Ffridd Mathrafal, much
the most conspicuous feature in the landscape, running up to 700
feet.* This area, below which the forge buildings stood, was included
in the rental, 'for fforge and Ffridd'. At the time when the forge had
first been set up in 1651 the Ffridd must have afforded the operator
some of his coppice-wood for charcoal, of which he would require
considerable quantities, for it is recorded that he had 'made a great
destruction of timber'. Indeed, a petition was made in the name of
Lord Powis to the House of Lords 'that a stop may be made (by the
tenant) of destroying any more of the timber and of carrying away
what is already cut, in order that there may not be a total destruction
of the estate';[4] but by Charles Lloyd's time charcoal supplies were
being obtained from several of the other large estates in the neighbourhood. The forge itself would be equipped with the simple
requirements of the day. These were a hearth, with water-powered
bellows, for refining the iron and expelling its impurities and a
second hearth with power-hammer for drawing out the metal into
bars, processes which had been in operation there for forty years
past. And it must have been an object of everyday interest and
familiarity to those at Dolobran, not only because it was on their
doorstep but because the only means of crossing to the Mathrafal
bank for a long distance in either direction was by a ford just below
the forge, which horse traffic from Dolobran would regularly use
whenever the river allowed.

There was a further association between the family and the forge
in the person of Amos Davies, who has already appeared in this
history as a friend and neighbour of the older Charles and as
his confrère in the lore of physick and of herbs. For a number of
years he had been clerk to the Dolobran meeting, and his beautifully
formed and educated handwriting graces the pages of their minute-
book.[5] He was likewise clerk of the Mathrafal forge. The clerk of
the forge was the manager, the man who was responsible to his
master for all that went on in the day-to-day operation and trading

* Ffridd is pronounced to rhyme with 'seethe'.

of an enterprise of this scale, and would occupy a certain position in the district. Amos Davies was in these roles a reliable and respected citizen, and until his removal to Salop in 1710, his influence was to make for continuity between present and past at Dolobran.*

The pool for the iron forge, though largely filled in with mud and reeds, is still to be seen, and so are the channel of the millrace connecting it with the river upstream and the tailrace to rejoin it below; and even the ruined masonry which carried the wheel survives, in vivid support of an eighteenth-century survey plan preserved at Powis Castle.[6]

As to why a newly fledged farmer and landowner should enlarge his activities by taking on an iron forge we may remember first that already, for twenty-five years, Charles Lloyd had lived under the sound of the hammer. Only those who have had that experience can know how the note of a tilt-hammer can pervade the vicinity, now faster, now slower, swelling louder on this wind or carried away on that, giving out all around an unconscious and rhythmic reminder of something going on. Charles Lloyd was conditioned to this, it was part of living at Dolobran. But we should also reflect on the iron trade connection on both sides of the family. Charles's sister Elizabeth had married a Pemberton, a well-to-do ironmerchant in Birmingham. His brother Sampson had just gone to that place to take up a similar occupation, forsaking farming in order to do so. The two brothers were married to two daughters of the Stourbridge ironmonger Ambrose Crowley, a man who had made his life in iron-dealing and iron-processing.† The two girls, moreover, were not only Ambrose Crowley's daughters, they were the half-sisters of his well-known son of the same name, later Sir Ambrose Crowley, whose methods and success were a portent in the iron industry. Sarah herself, Charles's wife, was the sister nearest in age to this elder brother and it may not be immaterial to guess at the pride she took in his reputation. When to this is added

* See Certificate issued by Dolobran Monthly Meeting when Amos Davies removed to Shrewsbury; minute-book, 27 December 1709; the normal name for Shrewsbury at that time was Salop.

† In the seventeenth and eighteenth centuries the term 'ironmonger' did not mean what we mean by it today. It was the word in common use for an iron *merchant*, of which John Pemberton and Sampson Lloyd are examples. But it was also more broadly used to include merchants who operated forges or slitting mills as well such as the Crowleys.

the probability (for which there are grounds) that Sarah Lloyd possessed some of the ambition of her conspicuous brother, we begin to perceive that Charles Lloyd might not look unfavourably upon the possibilities of an enterprise in iron.

When they took over Dolobran Charles and Sarah Lloyd had had only two children. They had one girl three years old, they had lost one, and the eldest son, who was immediately named Charles, was to be born in 1698, a month or two before the tenancy of the forge. But almost at the same time as these events, they must have been planning the substantial improvements at the house which were carried out during 1699. We have a clue to what was in their minds in embarking on it. Apart from convenience and amenity, they thought to keep up with the Pembertons at Birmingham. Eyebrows were raised in the family. 'Perhaps some may reflect hard on us for building,' Charles writes to his sister,

but I hope thou art not one of them. You have things so handsome and convenient with you that it may make some expect some things here like you. For my own part I think that most of you are satisfied that we have great reason to consider what we do, and I believe thou art not one of the most uneasy in our building. I hope it is near a period for this time.

A candid passage with a good deal between the lines. His father's widow, Anne Lloyd, now in her sixties, spending part of that year at Dolobran, writes in November to Charles Lloyd's brother Sampson, who was evidently her confidant: 'I have expected thee long but I suppose something hath hindered thy coming, which will cause my stay here this winter for anything I know, but *truly it is a place of change.*' Charles Lloyd's nature was not insensitive to family opinion. Perhaps his partner was the more thick-skinned of the two.

But their burst of building activity was only begun. When Charles Lloyd hoped it was 'near a period for this time' he knew that there was more to come, although it would now be not a private project but a collective one. The Dolobran monthly meeting was to have a meeting-house. Charles Lloyd, as the son of his father, and Sarah, who is recorded, in a paper written by her husband, to have 'feared the Lord and loved the blessed Truth and faithful Friends', were naturally placed as second-generation Friends to take a lead in the local affairs of the Society. In his father's time meetings had been held in Friends' houses, for several miles around, but Dolobran was the centre, already a burying-place was in use there,* and the time had come to create a meeting house beside it. The site, which was on Dolobran land and not many hundred yards from the house, was acquired for £40 by a local group of trustees for the Society.[7] On 20 April 1701 the first meeting in the new premises took place. This building, which incorporated a meeting-room and a small cottage, now became the regular venue both for business and for worship. The building still stands in its secluded position on the Dolobran estate, but the Quakers have almost died out in this part of Wales and the meeting-room, despoiled at different periods and without its panelling and fittings, is now un-used except for an occasional meeting held there by some Friends from a distance who manage the little property and keep up the cottage for occupation.

To round off their plans the Dolobran meeting set in motion a further development. They initiated a school, which was for the children of the meeting and others, in the new meeting house. A minute of 28 May 1701 approved the raising of an annual sum of £15 'for a yearly sallary for a school master', suitable enquiries were put about, and by the end of June their first schoolmaster had been installed. The man appointed was a young Quaker of eighteen named John Kelsall, whose importance for this narrative is con-siderable, for he kept a dairy.† This dairy is in many ways as revealing for the story of Charles Lloyd and his experiences in iron as *The Convincement* of Richard Davies is for the hardships of his father a generation before. Kelsall's diary, so far as the Lloyds are concerned, covers most of the years from 1701 to 1729, during twenty-two of which he lived and worked in the Dolobran valley. The period from 1701 to 1714 he spent in building up and running the school, where he had at times as many as forty or fifty pupils. For the first nine years he lodged at Amos Davies's at the forge, whence he would walk up to the school, over the river and across the Dolobran fields. In 1710 he married Amos Davies's daughter and went to live in the cottage at the meeting house. As a Quaker, he regularly attended the Dolobran meeting, became useful in its

* At least since 1695; Dolobran minute-book.
† John Kelsall's diary is preserved at Friends House, London.

affairs, and when Davies moved to Shrewsbury succeeded him as
clerk. Resident at Mathrafal, he had lived in the bosom of the forge
business. He was not at that stage recording ironworking details in
the diary because he was working as a schoolmaster, but he writes
of the local scene and of Lloyd matters at first hand. His familiarity
with life at the forge must have been no bad qualification when in
1714, to improve his income, he left teaching and took up the position of clerk at an ironworks in the next county.* But in 1720 he is
back at Dolobran, this time as clerk to a fresh iron enterprise of
Charles Lloyd's, which the diary illuminates with its inside information.

The situation of the Quakers as Dissenters had been relieved by
the Act of Toleration and some other acts following the accession
of William and Mary in 1688, but it was still being made uncomfortable on account of tithes. The Anglican majority in Parliament
had seen to it that the claims of the clergy for the payment of tithes
were secured whatever other concessions were allowed, and goods
might be seized by law in case of refusal. All through these years
Charles Lloyd was persistently dunned by the local clergy or their
agents and persistently refused to pay.[8] Exactions are recorded year
after year in his memorandum book. They show us that Charles
Lloyd ran a mixed farm as well as a forge.

As has already appeared, Charles Lloyd left behind him a memorandum book of family information which is very clear in the handwriting and in excellent condition, and as he lived a long life, dying
in 1748, and had several lucid years as a widower in which to bring
his book up to date, it repays study. One of the things it throws
light on is the personality of his wife. Sarah Lloyd was thirteen
years younger than her husband. After the first rather difficult years
of marriage it began to be clear that she had her own part to play in
the Quaker world. 'After we had been married seven or eight years,'
we read, 'she had a gift in the ministry...and she appeared for
several years with a living testimony and she was well received and
much esteemed by sensible Friends.' In 1707 she found herself
with 'a weighty concern on her mind' to visit Friends in the North,
and that same summer, at the age of thirty-one, she carried out one
of those preaching journeys, characteristic of the Quaker ministry,

* At Dolgyn near Dolgellau; an iron furnace then belonging to the Darbys, the
Quaker ironfounders of Coalbrookdale in Shropshire.

speaking at meetings in fifteen or twenty places in the Cumberland region, including Lancaster, Kendal, Penrith and Carlisle. Her husband accompanied her, 'though I had not any public testimony to bear in meetings', and but for a summons to Dolobran to receive some Quaker cousins from Pennsylvania the journey would have been extended into Yorkshire. But her ministry was well received and she applied herself in this service 'for several years afterwards and was often at the Yearly Meeting for Wales and in Worcestershire, Warwickshire and Herefordshire; and in Shropshire also she was oftentimes'.

In 1713 this work suffered a check. While at the Yearly Meeting in London 'there happened to be a great difference between her and a Friend belonging to the same Meeting of Dolobran, which difference proved very hurtful unto her'. Her husband's account continues: 'my wife was greatly wounded in her spirit by it and I doubt, by letting in reasonings, came to a great loss in her inward condition by giving way to thoughts that brought a cloud over her mind, so that *she seldom appeared afterwards in a public testimony in words in Meetings.*' Indeed, right down to the time of her death thirty years later, she seems to have detached herself and to have transferred her energies to other activities. Charles Lloyd was sorry about it but felt she had been unwise; he must have known her nature, they had been married for twenty years.

Another of the Lloyd wives appears in glimpses during these years. Anne Lloyd, the former Anne Lawrence, had a widow's path to tread from 1698 until her death in 1708. She lived during that time partly in Birmingham at 'son Pemberton's' and partly, despite the past, at Dolobran; and by her evident dependence on Sampson, the other stepson, now in Birmingham, her story reminds us of the Birmingham end of the axis. How she was left on her husband's death we do not know, for Charles Lloyd had died intestate.* She was not the mother of his family but she had shared his imprisonment and she had been his wife. But a notebook which she kept shows that she had a little income coming through her hands. She paid rent to the family at Dolobran and probably paid for her keep as well; in 1704, at Birmingham, she pays £3 10s. od. to son Pemberton 'for my diet'. She also writes down some lists of house-

---

* Letters of administration were granted to the second son, Sampson, who kept an eye on her affairs.

hold linen that belonged to her and two short inventories of her personal wardrobe, which take one back to the housekeeping of the day: '3 dosen of best napkins and 2 of corse ones', '7 tabel close' and six pairs of 'pillabiers' (which means pillow-cases), 'shifts', 'binds', 'piners', 'littel neck hanks'. And she puts down two or three recipes for useful preparations or remedies; 'to make lip-salve', 'for the itch or any breaking out'. Anne Lloyd died at Birmingham in June 1708, aged seventy, and was buried in the Friends' burying-ground there. She was the last member of the Welshpool Gaol generation. She had in her time been eleven years the mistress of Dolobran. 'She had a living testimony to bear for Truth in meetings, and when she was young she often travelled on that account in visiting meetings.'

For the next few years there is less information about the Charles Lloyds. It was not long before Queen Anne was dead and it was the period of George I and the 1715 Rebellion; but Dolobran was not much touched by such events nor influenced by the manners of the time. In 1708 the Lloyds had lost another child, 'pretty Tommy', aged about seven, who was buried in the new burying-ground at Dolobran. In 1712, when Charles Lloyd was fifty and the older children, Sarah and Charles, in their teens, a new daughter, Mary, the youngest of the family, was born. Meanwhile, in addition to Anne Lloyd's departure and her death, other gaps appeared in the circle. In 1708 Richard Davies had died. In 1710 Amos Davies left Mathrafal and went away to live at Shrewsbury. In 1711, Elizabeth Pemberton, who had several times revisited 'sweet Dolobran', died at Birmingham, aged only thirty-seven, and two or three years afterwards her husband married again. In 1714 John Kelsall and his wife removed to Dolgellau, giving up the school, which seems to have been shrinking in numbers, he was not replaced and it closed. The accumulated effect of these events, together with Sarah Lloyd's personal crisis in the Society in 1713 and withdrawal from her active role in the meeting, must have reduced old links and contributed to a certain decline in the local Quaker world.

In iron, during these years, the forge at Mathrafal had carried on from year to year, the rent-roll recording the regular payments of Charles Lloyd's rent, and a new clerk, though his name is not recorded, must have been found in Amos Davies's place. But Charles Lloyd's mind had for some time been reaching out towards fresh expansion. Suddenly, as it seems to us at this distance, there comes another of his bursts of activity, and within the space of three years, between 1717 and 1719, he gives up Mathrafal, builds his own forge on the Dolobran estate, and engages in an iron furnace at Bersham near Wrexham, thirty-five miles away, a venture which ten years later was to prove his undoing.

From April 1720 there is a good deal of light thrown upon these undertakings by Kelsall's diary, especially upon the new Dolobran forge. This was the date at which the former schoolmaster, lately clerk of a furnace near Dolgellau, and now thirty-seven years of age, returned to the Vyrnwy to be clerk to the new Dolobran forge. What is less luminous is the thinking that had led Charles Lloyd on, in his middle fifties, to embark simultaneously upon these two new enterprises at this particular time. Part of the background was of course his twenty years' experience of the Mathrafal forge, and from this and from his West Midlands connection he must have had an all-round familiarity with the state of the iron industry. He was in touch with the merchants, the 'ironmongers', to whom he sent bar iron, down river at Bewdley and beyond, and he had working relations with pig iron sources in Shropshire and in the Ruabon district to the north. Some years before his present programme, in 1710, he had contemplated taking on a second forge, at Pont-y-blew on the river Ceiriog near Chirk,* and he must already therefore have had ideas for expansion at this earlier date. But there was a contemporary reason. The country's production of bar iron did not match the growth of demand and was being supplemented by large quantities from Sweden. But in 1717, owing to reports of a Swedish plot for a landing in Scotland in support of the Jacobites, trade with Sweden had been prohibited and the embargo was in force for the next two years. A shortage of iron rapidly developing, the price of English bar advanced from £16 to £24 per ton, and the industry made substantial profits. This was

* Chirk Castle MSS, 6914 F, National Library of Wales, Aberystwyth. Charles Lloyd had negotiated for Pont-y-blew forge, which belonged to Sir Richard Myddelton of Chirk Castle, to the extent of heads of an agreement being drawn up under which he was to put the forge into repair and hold it for twenty-one years at a rent of £40, but there the matter had ended. The agreement was never executed.

the year in which Charles Lloyd began his moves not only for a
second forge but for a furnace as well. He must have satisfied himself that he had the capital for the double investment and that the
moment justified the plunge.

Let us look first at the forge project, the problems of which
Charles Lloyd thoroughly understood, and which, once started,
would be in many ways a continuation of the previous operation
across the river. He was relying on a new manager, it is true, but
he would continue to use the same river for power, the same
sources for charcoal and for pig and the same markets and methods
of distribution. The difference for us is that, through Kelsall, we
have information about these things that we did not have for
Mathrafal.

The Dolobran forge was located a few hundred yards down the
Vyrnwy from Mathrafal on the Lloyd side of the river. The site
was again at a spot where a millstream was already in existence.
Here, close to the small farm of Lower Dolobran, known even today
by the name of Forge Farm, was a water corn mill which had been
a feature of the property for generations past. Beside this mill the
Lloyds built not only a forge and all that it required by way of
outhouses, stores and stables but also a cottage for the clerk of the
forge with the date '1719' over the door. Here, too, to control the
supply of power, since the water would have more work to do than
in the corn mill days, they dug out a millpool. Though it has long
since reverted to meadow-ground, we know a little about this pool.
The spot was in full view from Dolobran, 'greatly to the embellishment of the capital house's prospect and from whence the Hall
itself makes a pretty figure'.[9] It also offered a new diversion, when
netted, yielding on one recorded occasion 'ten fine pikes' and on
another 'one very large and fine salmon and two small ones',[10] as
well as an economic value for the estate, being assessed a few years
later, in the opinion of a competent business man, as worth 'say,
£40 a year'.

For charcoal supplies the Vyrnwy district was a satisfactory one,
offering fewer difficulties and shorter hauls than either Dolgyn or
Bersham. Within ten to fifteen miles were landowners willing to
sell coppice timber for 'charking', there were 'colliers', i.e. charcoal-
burners, to chark it, and carriers to transport it to the forge. Pig
iron came from a number of sources. 'This morning,' as Kelsall

records, 'Mr Charles went for England, designing to go to several Furnaces about buying some Piggs.' His suppliers included furnaces at Oulton in Cheshire, Plas Madog at Ruabon in Denbighshire, and Boulden, Coalbrookdale and Leighton in Shropshire.[11] It even paid to bring it on occasion from as far away as Bristol, probably the good-quality Forest of Dean pig from which top-grade bar iron was made.

Outlets for the sale of Charles Lloyd's bar iron were of various kinds. First, the local market was important, among the smiths and landowners of the district. Kelsall, as clerk, was also the sales manager. He lost no opportunity of attending the fairs at centres such as Welshpool, Llanfyllin or Newtown, which at that time were as much market-places as places of social assembly. An itinerant salesman or 'chapman' was also employed, who would meet customers and collect payments at places as far afield as Chester or Birmingham and was often at Bersham furnace which he probably served as well. The more distant customers, the ironmongers of the Midlands, were reached at the busy port of Bewdley and the iron fairs at Stourbridge. Kelsall himself often went there. 'Being monthly day was busy amongst the ironmasters', he records; and he would go also to Birmingham, where he would call upon individual ironmongers, some of them related to his master, having names such as Pemberton, Fidoe and Crowley, and upon Charles Lloyd's brother Sampson. As to distribution, the Lloyds employed local carriers for their land traffic, both to the Ruabon area and to Pool Quay about ten miles off, where, except when the river was low, the goods began their journey down the Severn.

The bar was mainly of two qualities, merchant iron and mill iron. Merchant iron was the superior, tough grade, for the better kind of ironworking, made from the best pig. Mill iron was the standard product, used by the ordinary smiths and nailers, and did not need to be made from a particular type of pig iron nor forged to a standard beyond the average. But even mill bars had to be refined and drawn to a standard that would be workable at the slitting mills where they would be slit by machine into the thin rods required by the nailmakers. A note has come down to us showing how much this quality mattered. In a letter written to his son staying at Dolobran in the summer of 1721, Sampson Lloyd, then a senior Birmingham merchant, reports a customer's complaint:

I did not hear until yesterday that the last parcel of brother Lloyd's mill iron was come to Bewdley, where I saw Henry Wheelwright who told me. He desired me to write to Brother that if more care be not taken in drawing the mill iron they will not be willing to slit it. He says he is sure that you have changed the hammerman, for the iron is quite drawn different from what has been sent before. Pray desire Brother or cousin Charles* to take care about it so that we may not have such complaints. All the former parcel is not come from Bewdley. I cannot sell this last parcel at above £15 ready money. I do believe I may sell it at £15.10.0 at three months.

Sampson did not like letting a customer down. Nevertheless Charles Lloyd must have sent out hundreds of tons of satisfactory bar in all those years. A contemporary estimate suggests that the capacity of the Mathrafal Forge had been 180 tons a year and that that of Dolobran was 190.[12] But Sampson Lloyd's letter brings to mind two other aspects of the management of a forge, the plant and the employees. Kelsall makes a number of references to equipment and also to the men; the bellows must be repaired; a new hammer is sent for; the river is in flood and stops the forge. The essential men, the finer at the finery to refine the impurities in the iron, and the hammerman at the chafery† to draw it under the hammer into bars, are frequently mentioned; they are taken on, they are ill, they are given notice, they leave. There seems to have been a fairly high rate of turnover, if the diary is any guide, though whether this was due to something on the management side or whether there was a tradition of mobility among this type of craftsman we do not know. Kelsall's work on Charles Lloyd's behalf was thus of every variety, production, personnel, sales, distribution and accounts, besides including the role of trusted friend to his master and fellow Quaker.

The Lloyds had many other services from Kelsall during his ten years as clerk of the forge, treating him as their confidant in a number of family matters; and before turning to Bersham we may take a glance into his diary. During the winter of 1721 to 1722 Charles junior, then about twenty-three, was occupied over intentions of marriage with the daughter of an Uxbridge Quaker who

* This was Charles Lloyd's son who was assisting his father. He was really Sampson Lloyd's nephew, but 'cousin' was a favourite word rather loosely used by Quakers. Lloyd MSS, 1/50.

† 'Chafery' is an anglicised version of the French *chaufferie*. The furnace and forge processes had been introduced from the French-speaking parts of the Low Countries.

had interests at Llanrwst in North Wales. But when the negotiations
were in an advanced stage doubts began to appear, not as to the
excellence of the lady but as to the substance of the lady's father.
'Old Master, Mr Charles and self,' Kelsall notes in February 1722,
'were jointly busied to write and give him a plain account of our
thoughts and apprehensions in the said affair, having good grounds
to suspect he could not perform what he had promised'; and we
read that a few months later the lady's letters were sent back and
the matter was closed. The next year there were negotiations in
another quarter, this time for the hand of Jane Wilkins, from a
Quaker family at Thornbury, Gloucestershire,* who, however,
was residing with her uncle and aunt Exton at Burghill near Hereford. Between February and June 1723, Kelsall was employed as
go-between both in Gloucestershire and Burghill and it was only
after some uncomfortable, even acrimonious differences at the
parents' level that on 18 June, at the meeting-house at Ross, the
marriage took place. The couple started married life at the Extons',
who had a fruit-farming and cider business. However, before a year
was out there was more trouble. James Exton was disappointed in
young Charles, having expected him 'to take more delight in their
business and to carry himself more respectful and chaste towards
them than he did', and Kelsall was sent to Burghill as mediator,

for Master requested that they would secure to him their stock and £1,000
after their decease and then he would be contented to stay with him and
do his endeavour to please them; otherwise it would be hard for him to
continue pretty much at his own expense and have no certainty for
anything now or hereafter.

Relations remained strained until the next year, when James Exton
died. The young Charles seems to have lived partly at Dolobran
after this† and was certainly concerned as a partner with his father
in the ironworks.

The Charles Lloyds at this period were not without other pre-
occupations. They had lived through an exacting seven years since

* Jane Wilkins was under sixteen, ten years younger than the bridegroom,
according to Charles Lloyd's memorandum book; born 19 August 1707, married
14 June 1723.

† On 13 November 1725, Kelsall notes: 'Mr Charles abroad this day with the
workmen coursing.'

1717, during which his sixtieth birthday had come and gone. The elder daughter had been married in January 1719,* an additional commitment for Dolobran at the height of the building programme for the new forge. In 1720 Sarah's father Ambrose Crowley had died at Stourbridge. There had also been their son's matrimonial affairs to concern them, with little respite, for several years in succession. In 1725 Sampson Lloyd died at Birmingham; and through all this time Charles Lloyd had not one but two ironworks to control, both of them new undertakings.

Turning now to consider Bersham, we have to recall that the iron-works we have met with so far were forges, but Bersham was a furnace and this was a new departure for Charles Lloyd. A furnace produced iron from ore by smelting with charcoal. The iron made was usually in the form of pig, but at some furnaces the molten metal would from time to time be run off to form simple cast-iron products such as fire-backs, rollers, cooking pots or baker's slabs, or again heavy hammer-heads and anvils. These articles would not normally be the main product of the furnace but a secondary output appropriate to demand. But it was a curiosity of the times that so large was the sale of the cooking pot in proportion to other products, whether in this country or abroad, that it had given its name to the casting side of the industry which was often referred to as 'potting'. An important difference between a forge and a furnace was that, whereas in a forge the work of the hearths was a day-to-day affair, smelting at the furnace was continuous. For a period, a furnace would be out of action while stocks of charcoal were accumulated, but once in blast it would continue so for months on end, fresh materials and fuel being frequently fed in at the top and the molten metal intermittently run off at the bottom.

Charles Lloyd did not go into the new project alone but in partnership. His colleagues, R. Bratt, T. Lilly and Richard Wood, who were Wolverhampton men, were already, among their other interests, partners in a group of iron forges along the river Tern, a few miles to the east of Shrewsbury, and had hitherto, presumably,

---

* She married John England, a Bridgnorth Quaker. This marriage resulted in a half-way house on future journeys between Dolobran and Birmingham both for the Lloyds and for Kelsall.

been his competitors. The new enterprise was undertaken as to 50 per cent for Lloyd and 50 per cent the other three combined. Charles Lloyd's half may have been shared with his son, who worked with him for several years before his marriage and is known to have been financially committed in 1727. The other people in the story are the clerk of the furnace, Edward Davies, and John Kelsall who, based at Dolobran at his master's side, supervised the Bersham books and went there when necessary.

Bersham is a village lying a mile or two to the west of Wrexham in Denbighshire, where water-power from the small river Clywedog was in use for a corn mill. Alongside the mill an iron furnace had already been established for about twenty years but it had fallen into disrepair and the project involved rebuilding. The attractions of the site for a furnace were several. Near at hand were ironstone workings of suitable quality, so located that ore could be transported to the spot mainly downhill. Less water horse-power was required for the bellows of a furnace than for those of a forge, and none for any hammer, and quite a small stream was therefore adequate. Were the furnace turning out pig iron there were two forges in the neighbourhood to take advantage of it, while for cast products there were the markets of Wrexham and Chester within reasonable hauling distance.

It was upon the basis of technical and commercial attractions that the syndicate pledged their capital and planned the new undertaking, but it was Charles Lloyd with his 50 per cent share who carried out the negotiations. To the landowner their plans would assure both rent and a sale for his coppice timber; indeed Charles Lloyd declared that they would 'raise a large pile for their charcoal as big as Pentre Clawdd barn'.* During 1718 the reconstruction work was carried out, in 1719 John Kelsall records going there to see it while he was still working at Dolgyn, and about the same time Edward Davies was appointed to be in charge. In 1720 Kelsall himself became clerk at Dolobran. Kelsall, however, was not the Bersham clerk and the diary offers nothing like the picture of Bersham that it does of Dolobran. What it does give is an intermittent reflection of what went on, not a record but nevertheless

---

* Letter dated 28 December 1717, in the Erddig papers, to 'Esquire Mellor', the landowner, from his steward. Erddig is a property near Wrexham. The map reference for the site of Bersham furnace is: OS 1 in., Sheet 109, SJ 307493.

suggestive, and on occasion – when Kelsall had to spend more time there than usual – informative.*

For us it is unfortunate that Kelsall only returned to Dolobran in 1720. How much more should we know of Bersham, and especially of its beginnings, had he come there three years sooner. Charles Lloyd did the pioneering, as we have seen, and it seems probable that he was the partner who mainly ran it, for Kelsall frequently speaks of his going there. But no partner lived nearer than about forty miles away.

As for what was produced at Bersham, one presumes that a furnace made pig and might produce cast products as a make-weight. But in none of the records does it appear that pig was made at Bersham, not even for the Dolobran forge nor for that of the Tern partners. Charles Lloyd, in fact, was still buying pig from English furnaces in 1722. Yet, curious though all this now seems: we can hardly imagine a furnace that did not make any.†

On the other hand, though there are no details, Bersham was certainly making cast products. This is clear because Kelsall speaks of attempts to do so by new methods. Bersham, like other furnaces, was experimenting with substitutes for charcoal, and it is tantalising that we only know it from isolated allusions. On 3 February 1721, Kelsall notes, 'the furnace ceased blowing with charcoal and went on blowing with cokes for potting'. And Bersham was in a position to know what was going on. William Wood, Richard Wood's father, was well known among the pioneers in this research and the partners must have been *au fait* with the work that he was doing. The Lloyds, as Quakers, would know the Darbys at Coalbrookdale who had found out a method of smelting with coke a few years before. Kelsall himself, who had been attached for a few months to Coalbrookdale before going to work at Dolgyn, was on friendly terms with the Darbys' manager, Richard Ford, and would spend

---

* There is no edition of Kelsall's diary, but several writers have made studies based upon it; see especially H. Gwynn Jones, unpublished thesis, 'John Kelsall, a Study in Religious and Economic History', 1938; copies at National Library of Wales, Aberystwyth and University College of Bangor. This work has been drawn upon for several parts of Chapter 2.

† 'The principal product of the charcoal blast furnace,' says H. R. Schubert in *History of the British Iron and Steel Industry to 1775*, Routledge & Kegan Paul 1957, p. 246, 'was pig iron for the forge. Castings usually constituted only a fairly small proportion of the total output.'

the evening with him when on business visits to Stourbridge. It has even been conjectured that, by arrangement with the Darbys, a partition of the cast products market was intended, and that Bersham production was to relieve Coalbrookdale by catering for the Denbighshire and Cheshire district.* But smelting with coke was in its infancy, it was not at all generally understood and would not be so for another two generations, and the Darbys themselves may well have been fortunate in the properties of the coal from which their coke was made or the nature of the ore and other materials which they had used; so that Bersham, even with technical advice from Coalbrookdale, would still be trying to work out its own salvation.

Among the partners there must have been one or more forward-looking commercial minds. Perhaps one of the Tern men took the lead.† A pointer to their persevering with fuel experiments may be seen in the fact that in 1723 a coal supply was purchased at 'the Rhose', that is to say a surface working at the nearby village of Rhosllanerchrugog, which would assure them the raw material for their coke. Five years after the first, there is a second hint in the diary when we read that in September 1726 the furnace 'ceased blowing with charcoal on the 13th inst and began with *coals*'. This entry seems to repeat that of 1721 except that instead of 'cokes' Kelsall now writes 'coals'. If it means that they were now trying to produce pig iron with coal they were moving into a delicate area, for coal pig did not result in a very saleable type of bar, in fact was disliked, and it sold in only a limited market. But coal pig would do for casting. In this complex of speculation one is left with two impressions, of persistence in experiment and of management by remote control.

It seems that in the next spring, that is in 1727, the Lloyds were beginning to be short of working capital, especially at Bersham. In March, Kelsall was being pressed for payments at Wrexham fair. In April he had a fatiguing day sorting out 'some distracted matters' at Chester, and a few days later he was at Tern consulting the

* Ivor Edwards argues this in an article in *Transactions of Denbighshire Historical Society*, vol. x, 1961, p. 71.

† That they did visit Bersham appears from a note of Kelsall's when on 12 January 1724 Charles Lloyd suffered a fall from his horse between the furnace and Wrexham and was 'carried to town as if dead'. This Kelsall explains by observing that 'they had had too much brandy at the furnace'.

partners about 'the affairs of the furnace'. In July he makes a journey to London for a conference with William Wood and has 'much discourse about affairs but could not conclude anything'. Simultaneously there seems to have been a contraction of activity at Dolobran. If Kelsall's entries are any guide, there were no purchases or collection of charcoal going on that year from February onwards and none of pig since some time in the previous autumn. On 12 August 1727 an ominous step is taken. Kelsall is at Shrewsbury seeing an attorney on behalf of his master, where he 'delivered him the Dolobran Settlement in order to draw a mortgage of £900 now put to Master's use'.* On the 27th he is in Herefordshire, where young Charles is now living, and had 'pretty much talk about Master's affairs'. On the 30th came the moment of truth as Kelsall records in his journal:

A very sorrowful, troublesome and afflicting concern and exercise comes in course of time to be mentioned. It was not long after we returned from London that on great suspicion old Master Charles Lloyd found he was in more debt than he was able to pay. He himself by much solicitation discovered the same on 30th of 6 mo. 1727 (30 August); which debt was at last found out to be little less than £16,000, more by one half than what he was worth.†

Charles Lloyd now knew that he was broke.

Then there was no end to the alarm, the subterfuges and the disgrace, the harsh post mortems and the long tale of embarrassments that followed. Within a week, on 4 September, Kelsall was at Erddig, on behalf of his master, trying to sell the furnace and the mine, but without success. There must have been some hard riding between Tern and Dolobran first. The week after, on the 11th, he is at the Yearly Meeting at Marlborough where he discusses the emergency with several leading Quakers 'but could not conclude to raise any money'. A day or two later both Lloyds appear to have

* By a settlement on the marriage of Charles junior in 1723 a sum of £900 had been pledged for portions for the younger children of the marriage.

† John Kelsall's diary exists in two forms, the diary itself, and a digest which he made, known as the journal, from which this extract is taken. At the time of the disaster Kelsall is so appalled that he resorts to making entries in Latin.

decamped. Kelsall notes that on the 15th he 'returned home and found that old Master was gone from home that morning'. Charles Lloyd is then heard of in Birmingham. Perhaps it is best to suppose he went there to look for help. On the same day Kelsall received a letter from the younger Charles 'with directions how to write to him in London'. The next month Kelsall, summoned to Chester to attend upon the commissioners of bankruptcy in the place of his master, writes that 'they examined me of what I knew of Master's going off' and on 17 October Charles Lloyd was declared bankrupt. On the 24th Sarah Lloyd, aged fifty-four, who in her turn was upon the road 'desiring to get the best advice she could obtain in order to compose our unhappy affairs' was thrown from her horse between Shrewsbury and Bridgnorth, broke her leg and did not walk again for a year.

Although the financial collapse appears to have come from the Bersham end of the axis the failure was a total one. In November 'the prizers' descended upon the home ground and 'began to seize and prize the goods at Dolobran' and 'came this afternoon to the forge and weighed up the warehouse'. In December the local creditors met at Llanfyllin to prove their debts. The new year, 1728, opened in the same dreary way. On 2 January Kelsall records, 'I went to Tern. Found that Richard Wood did abscond, and J. Bratt being at London I could not do anything about the accounts.' Finally it was the turn of Charles Lloyd junior. Charles junior is not heard of much at Bersham in the diary but he was 'bound for about £6,000 for his father' and now became equally with him an object of the creditors' attention. Insecure in London, he had removed himself to France, his young wife remaining in Herefordshire, but he was now summoned for examination. 'At Pool,' says Kelsall, 'on 13th December I saw a letter from Mr Charles, dated at Boulogne in France and directed to W. Powel, being wrote in style much unlike a Friend.' It may even have been in abusive terms, for young Charles's line was to make out that he was not a partner and to dissociate himself from the affair. At the hearing at Chester in January he was 'very stiff and obstinate till several letters were produced of his handwriting owning himself a partner'; and so, in short, he too was declared a bankrupt.

At Birmingham Charles Lloyd appealed for aid to Friends, including his brother Sampson and his brother-in-law Pemberton, both in the iron trade, but there is nothing to say what reception he met with. He did not return to Dolobran. Kelsall says that he now lived in Birmingham, at New Hall.* He would be occupied with the care of his disabled wife and their daughter Mary, now in her teens. During 1728 and part of 1729 John Kelsall continued working to reach some degree of settlement with all and sundry. The creditors eventually received only five shillings in the pound. But Charles junior, who had meanwhile recovered his nerve, now prevailed on his aunt, the widow Exton, to finance him to the tune of £1,700 and in October re-opened the forge. 'Young Master,' says Kelsall, 'having purchased all the effects from the assignees, set the forge to work again, and I was clerk and manager again till the fifth month (July) 1729, when I removed to Dolgyn, soon after which he gave up the forge.' Kelsall had accepted a return to his old employment at the Dolgyn furnace† at a larger salary than under the Darbys, and he eventually did so before and not after young Charles gave up the forge. He and his wife may have become somewhat disenchanted with the service of the Lloyds. Kelsall himself, who was now in his fifties, suffered considerable ups and downs but remained a faithful, serviceable Friend, and died at Chester in 1743. The furnace at Bersham was acquired by John Hawkins, a son-in-law of Abraham Darby. At Dolobran the forge stood unused, the hammer was silent.‡

If the family's iron interests were thus in eclipse, so was their position in the Dolobran meeting. Charles junior, who was not a very admirable character, seems to have paid little more than lip-service to 'the blessed truth' of his father and grandfather. In a family record he accounts for his grandfather's not taking up the office of Justice by saying that 'he quitted it for the sake of the religion which was then taught and held by the Quakers, in which

* New Hall, Birmingham, the residence of the Colmore family, is recalled today in the name of Newhall Street. Charles Lloyd presumably found lodgings near by, not at the mansion itself.

† Dolgyn was now in the hands of the Payton family, Quaker ironmongers at Dudley, who appear again in another chapter.

‡ As the eighteenth century advanced, Bersham Furnace came into the hands of the Wilkinsons, father and son, who became known for improved methods of boring gun-barrels, and later as makers of cylinders for many of Watt's steam engines. Dolobran Forge, no longer in Lloyd hands, was converted in the 1780s for flannel-making, then a rising industry in North Wales.

profession he educated his family', an observation not expressed much like a Friend. It was the senior Charles who suffered the greater odium from the whole affair, for he was disowned by the Society 'on account of his late unwarrantable proceedings' and remained ashamed. The Society was insistent in its advice to members that business dealings must be honest and that no man should suffer from any dealings with a Quaker; 'that none trade beyond their ability nor stretch beyond their compass...and that they keep their word in all things.' Charles Lloyd's failure went against these principles and was the more resounding both from his own standing and from his father's reputation in the movement, and for these reasons eyebrows were raised very high indeed. In the quarterly meeting for Montgomeryshire and Shropshire, Friends from the first county would have excused him as a respected associate,* but those from the second would not. The issue was referred to the Yearly Meeting for Wales, the body which in 1730 formally disowned him; 'and we earnestly hope that so far as in him lies he will endeavour to make such restitution to the many sufferers that he has injured as may convince the world of his being in some degree on that foundation which alone can reconcile him to God and with his people.'

The situation of the family continued to decline. A fresh anxiety appeared when it was found that, in the documents drawn up in 1730 for the sale of such Dolobran properties as would satisfy the creditors, there was a technical mistake. By this mistake two things were made impossible at law, to realise the sum still required for the creditors and to safeguard a trust fund for portions for Charles Lloyd's daughters. His dismay at this blunder can only be imagined. To overcome it the Lloyds were obliged to go to the expense of petitioning Parliament to set aside the mistake, the House of Lords took the opinion of exalted lawyers, and a Private Act was obtained. Kelsall records on 3 March 1732 that he 'saw in the Votes today that my old masters, Lloyds senior and junior and wives, had got an Act of Parliament for selling lands in Montgomeryshire and raising out of the same three thousands and six hundred

---

* The Montgomeryshire Friends could not agree 'to join in a condemnation or denial of him the said Charles Lloyd'. Quarterly Meeting Minute Book, ref. 320, County Record Office, Glamorgan.

pounds'.* The conclusion was that Dolobran, Coedcowrid and certain adjacent farms survived in their possession, but other parts of the estate which cannot now be identified were sold.

The débâcle had not gone unnoticed in the district. Charles Lloyd had probably started his tenure of Dolobran with some sympathy on the part of his neighbours if only on his father's account and, though as a Quaker he would be separated in many ways, they had been accustomed to his operating ironworks for a quarter of a century past. After the smash young Charles took over. Whether the estate had been formally made over to him is not clear, but his father was far away at Birmingham and it was the younger man who was now their neighbour. It does not seem that local opinion regarded him very kindly. In 1732 he decided to put the whole Dolobran estate in the market, and the advertisement of the sale shows the points which he and his auctioneer thought would best sell it† but he ran into a closed ring of local opposition. No one would either bid or treat with him to buy it. 'It was surprising to us,' he wrote afterwards to his cousin Sampson Lloyd in Birmingham, 'that of several likely chaps but one deputed person came, but some time after we came to understand that Lord Powis and those concerned had so ordered it that none out of Montgomeryshire should purchase but themselves, and now they live behind the curtain expecting a great bargain.'[13] Dolobran did not find a buyer and there were successive mortgages on the property. At one

---

* *5 Geo. II, c.* xxx. 'An Act for supplying a Defect in a Conveyance lately made by Charles Lloyd senior and Sarah his wife and Charles Lloyd junior and Jane his wife; and for the sale of certain Lands in the County of Montgomery for raising Three thousand Pounds and Six hundred Pounds, and for other purposes therein mentioned.'

† The advertisement, from *The Weekly Worcester Journal* for 11 August 1732, reads as follows: 'On Saturday the 2nd day of September next will be sold, entire or separate, at the Fox Inn near the Market-house in Shrewsbury, under a Parliamentary Title, *Dolobran Estate*, with several other Tenements besides, all compact, about the yearly value of 220 Pounds, together with an Iron Forge with all conveniences newly erected, and about 100 acres of Coppice Grounds, situate and lying in the parrish of Meifod in the county of Montgomery, and within a few miles of two market-towns, viz three from Llanfyllin, and five from Welch-Pool. The Estate is well watered, and above 500 Pounds worth of fine young growing Timber upon it, the Mansion House, Gardens and Buildings belonging thereto are in good repair; the Buildings belonging to the other Tenements and Forge will be in compleat order before the day of sale; the Estate has all sorts of Game upon it, particularly Fish in abundance, and a right of large convenient Common.'

moment Charles hoped that his cousin Sampson might take over
the mortgages at a reduced rate of interest, 'understanding thy good
intentions some time past towards me'; and later in the same letter,
'dear cousin, if thee would be so kind as to help me in this condition
thee should have Dolobran made an absolute sale of to thee for thy
security'. Charles tried hard to sell the estate to Sampson but without
success.*

The younger Charles had two sons and seven daughters. He lived
until 1767. Little more is heard about him other than fresh mortgages, in 1755 and 1758 for example, and again in 1766,[14] and the
fact that in 1760 he in turn was disowned by the Society of Friends.
The occasion was his non-payment of a legacy due from the estate
of his uncle Exton who had died more than thirty years before.
His elder son, another Charles, did not marry. This son survived
his father by six years, dying in France in 1773, and the property
passed to his brother James 'of Coventry, wine merchant'. By this
brother the encumbered estate was at length sold, in 1780, to a local
lawyer, Joseph Jones of Welshpool, and so, after eleven generations
of direct succession, Dolobran passed out of Lloyd hands.†

Sarah Lloyd lived until 1743 when she died in Birmingham aged
seventy. The consequences of the fall from her horse in 1727 were
severe both at the time and afterwards. It was 'above a year before
she could walk'. She tried to be philosophical but felt frustrated,
as her energetic spirit would lead us to expect. 'Happy are they,'
she wrote to her husband in 1728, 'that can truly say Thy will be
done and not mine, *but it is close work.*' In his memorandum book
Charles Lloyd several times refers to the painful inconvenience
which she had to suffer year by year, 'notwithstanding that she had
the advice of them that were esteemed the best surgeons in Birmingham', and the fortitude that she displayed. With all this she managed
to get about and to visit her son at Burghill and her daughter, now
widowed and married again, at Coventry; also her sister Mary,
the wife of Sampson Lloyd. It seems that Mary Lloyd must have
come to her rescue at the time of the accident: 'my love to sister
Lloyd to whom as an instrument in great measure my life is owing'.
Indeed it was in hastening to her bedside, again on horseback, when

* For Sampson Lloyd's survey and valuation of the estate, see Chapter 5.
† For the return of Dolobran to the Lloyds in the nineteenth century, see
p. 274.

Mary was ill in 1743, that Sarah received the wetting which led to her pneumonia and decease.

Charles Lloyd himself lived on, a widower, to eighty-five, and died on 21 January 1748. During the twenty years between the bankruptcy and his death he had lived mainly in Birmingham and, after the death of his wife, with his daughter at Coventry. In 1742, after twelve years of exclusion, he applied to be re-admitted as a member of the Society of Friends. His application was considered at the Bridgnorth Monthly Meeting and was then passed to the Quarterly Meeting at Shrewsbury. This group, with the record of his injured creditors still in mind, having obtained from him 'a proper acknowledgment of his sincere repentance for his misconduct therein', and having formally checked what opinion was held of him among Friends in Birmingham, now re-admitted him to the Society.* This could never have happened to the son, whose quality must have been a source of disappointment to his father. But Charles Lloyd, notwithstanding his business calamities, had been a faithful Quaker and the son of his father, whose memory he venerated, and he had not been embittered on finding himself disowned. The verdict on Charles Lloyd must be that he was a better Quaker than he was business man. But he was not a leader. He filled a position at Dolobran, but he was open to be influenced by others. One can see this in the reasons he gave for enlarging his house, in his being 'made willing' to accompany his wife on her preaching journey and perhaps again in his embarking upon Bersham at all. Perhaps he was too much influenced by Sarah, perhaps she was more house-proud than he, perhaps there was a private attitude that a Crowley's husband ought to be a bigger ironmaster than other men.

Why did he fail? Over twenty years, as far as we can tell, he had made a success of Mathrafal. Without Bersham, he could have done the same with Dolobran. Perhaps his defect was of judgement, allowing him to take risks both in capital enterprise and in technical

---

* The Certificate, signed among others by the Abraham Darby of the time, ends with this characteristic passage: 'we do certify to you that we have received him into unity again, of which entry is made in our Quarterly and Monthly Meeting books, and we recommend him with his wife in sincere love and fellowship desiring the Lord Almighty may crown the evening of their days here with peace and hereafter receive them into the arms of his eternal and unspeakable mercy.' Bevan-Naish Quaker Library, Woodbrooke, Birmingham.

innovation that would have been better declined. To read his private memorandum book is to discover the man himself. It is the reflection of a rather humble, devout personality, ready to record, to pay tribute to others and to efface himself. His father, his wife and several minor characters stand out in its pages. But when one reaches the part that ought to display his own career it turns out to be mainly about Sarah. There is no reference in the whole book to iron, either to Mathrafal, to Dolobran or to Bersham, or to anyone associated with him in it, until one reaches a single passage, written probably in old age after his re-admission to the Society and sounding perhaps the proper note upon which to end an account of Charles Lloyd III:

Our great trouble was occasioned by my being very unadvisedly and inconsiderately concerned with some other persons in partnership and in more business than I had a stock* of my own and effects to manage with, which when it was completed and finished instead of being profitable proved a continual loss not only to ourselves but unto many others, which was a cause of great sorrow grief and trouble unto us; and more especially because thereby just occasion was given by me for people to reflect and reproach Truth and Friends by my acting so rashly against the good advices and orders often given by Friends against such disorderly practices in engaging in my business beyond my ability.

* 'Stock' at that time was the ordinary word for capital.

PART II
Charcoal Iron

3

THE IRONMONGER

Charles Lloyd's brother Sampson went to live in Birmingham much earlier in life than his old father or his elder brother were to do, but before entering the iron trade there he had already been farming for twelve years in Herefordshire. By the time he moved to the town in 1698, at the age of thirty-four, he had been married, had had four daughters, become a widower, married again and had two sons.

As the younger brother, Sampson Lloyd had got off the mark early, leaving Dolobran to be married at the age of twenty-two. His marriage took place in 1686, at a time of change in the family. He had returned to Dolobran from his apprenticeship at Shrewsbury in the previous year only a few weeks before his mother's death, his father's second courtship had marked the intervening time, and against this background his own courtship and the preparations for the double wedding at Yarpole near Leominster were carried through.

His bride, Elizabeth Good, belonged to a Quaker circle in North Herefordshire which had some of the characteristics of the Dolobran group and had suffered in similar ways during the recent reign. The Toleration Act was still three years ahead, the meeting house at Leominster had not yet been built, and meetings had been taking place in Friends' houses in the locality, at Almeley, at Wicton, at Yarpole, and at Kimbolton, in the occupation of Quaker families such as Pritchard and Clarke, Young and Eckley. Elizabeth's home was at one of these, at the Lea, a farm in the Kimbolton parish. Her mother Sibbell Good, a former Eckley widow, was a respected local Friend and the mistress of the Lea.

For Dolobran, the Leominster district was one of the nearer

Quaker centres, lying forty or fifty miles to the south. It was at Almeley that Charles Lloyd's fellow prisoner, Anne Lawrence, had settled after the 1672 Indulgence and her release from Welshpool. Leominster moreover was on the road to Pembrokeshire, the home of the Lort relations, with whom a family traffic was kept up. For these reasons the Lloyds were naturally in touch with the Herefordshire circle and it was easy for Sampson to have met Elizabeth there. What is more unexpected is that she was six years his senior, being at the time of their marriage twenty-eight years of age. The arrangement was that she and Sampson would live at the Lea and he would farm it.

Sampson Lloyd was a man who got on well with people in life, but he wrote little unless for reasons of business or duty or to gain some personal end. But a notebook has survived[1] which he kept during six or seven years at the beginning of his married life in Herefordshire. This notebook covers the period from his leaving 'Sallop' in 1685 to about the time of Elizabeth's death in 1692. Like many another its use tails off, but it gives some local colour, particularly over his last year at Dolobran and his first at the Lea. From this source we know of the 'feavour and ague', the tertian ague, to which he was subject, as his father was to the quartan ague. These were forms of malarial fever which were not overcome until a time when the country was better drained. Of one attack Sampson Lloyd records that 'I had a great fermentation in my blood which would hold me sore for about twelve hours every other day, but I had not above six bad fits because I had had agues afore and I abstained and took suitable things in time'; and he adds, 'spirit of Sal Ammoniack did me good'. But he and Elizabeth seem to have settled down satisfactorily to domestic life, and after about the time of the birth of their first child in 1687 the entries in the notebook become fewer and are more confined to the affairs of the farm.

The Lea Farm still stands on the rising ground to the east of Kimbolton village and it is still a farm.[2] It is nearly 300 years since Sampson Lloyd had it; it was already 300 years old then. It is a sturdy, spacious building, standing on a ledge of the hillside with the farmyard below, built of local stone with, today, a roof of slate. There is Elizabethan work in some of the chimneys. The cellars, filled in within living memory, were according to local tradition 'such as you could have turned a wagon and two horses in them'.

The house and scene must be still very much as they were in the 1680s.

The notebook shows the young Sampson Lloyd as a diligent, systematic farmer. The earliest record, curiously, is that of the Dolobran hay crop in 1686. This would be only two or three months after the wedding, and why the young husband should have been haymaking at Dolobran instead of at Kimbolton does not appear. That he was there in person seems certain enough, for if the entry does nothing else it offers us a contemporary schedule of the meadow crop at Dolobran, by fields and by dragloads, ending with the summary: 'in all, put in the barn to fill it up 160 and in the lesser rick 25 drags.' At the Lea, he notes most of the first year's harvests, as may seem not unreasonable in the beginner, detailing his own field-names now, one or two of them, such as Lea Dingle, still being in use today. Similar harvest items recur over the next four years in a cumulative record: loads of hay got in; dung spread; barley carried; 'memorandum that there was in the year '87 of corn and muncorn as followeth'; and another, 'that the quantity of wheat in the year '87 was 52 thraves'.* But perhaps the most engaging of these entries is by Sampson the stock-farmer, as follows: 'Comely went to bull the 28th of April 1687. Coal went to bull about the 10 May. Damsel about the 20th of May. Stately took bull the 21st day of May 1687. Jewel the 28th day of May.'

On the farm there was plenty to do. In the winter evenings Sampson Lloyd records some of the farming data that interests him. In the winter of 1687–8 one finds 'A Catalogue of what books I have', 123 entries serially numbered, including *The Pilgrim's Progress*, and, as a Quaker, William Penn's *No Cross, No Crown* and Robert Barclay's *Apology*. In another place he discloses an interest in trees and fruit. Such, at this time, was the father of the four young daughters who were born at the Lea in the first five years of his marriage, an Elizabeth, a Sarah, an Ann and a Mary, and such the husband who on 10 June 1692 saw his wife a victim of the smallpox, the little girls motherless, and himself, at the age of twenty-eight, a widower.

---

*Muncorn was mixed corn, usually a mixture of wheat and rye sown together. 'Thrave' is still used as a crop measure in country places: 'A thrave or threave of wheat, barley, etc. contains 24 sheaves, and in some districts 28 sheaves.' *Oxford English Dictionary*.

This was a time of sorrow and dismay for both Leominster and Dolobran, but particularly for Sampson and for Sibbell Good at the Lea. 'The sad news of my dear sister's death did very much surprise us,' wrote sister Elizabeth from Dolobran, 'for we heard not a word of her being sick till thy letter came.' Fifteen years younger than her namesake, Elizabeth goes on, 'the loss of such a mother is great as thee knows by experience and not only thee and thine but all our family shall find a great miss of her.' Charles and Anne Lloyd hastened to Herefordshire, but it was 'Aunt Good' as Elizabeth calls her who took on the care of the children while their father did what he could. This state of affairs was to last for the next three years.

It was in the summer after his wife's death that Sampson's brother Charles and Sarah Crowley were married at Stourbridge and during the time of their engagement one notices the first thoughts of a replacement in the mind of the widowed father. He had evidently been visiting Stourbridge and he writes in a letter to young Sarah, his future sister-in-law, in February 1693: 'the thoughts of the pleasant times we have had both here and elsewhere makes me very melancholy by reason I am alone (if compared to the time I was with you) but I hope ere long to see you. But in the meantime think not that I have forgot M—. I desire that thou may give me thy judgement which I greatly esteem.' This letter is endorsed 'Sister Mary being then at Bristol but came home soon after to Stourbridge'. Sarah, whose judgement he thus solicits, had just had her seventeenth birthday. Mary was fifteen and a half.

In December 1695 Sampson Lloyd did marry Mary Crowley, then eighteen to his thirty-one, but the intervening time had not been without its difficulties. Writing to Sampson at the Lea in August 1696, when Mary was expecting her first infant, his father, Charles Lloyd, refers to this: 'be kind to thy second self who married thee against many objections, let her be easy and her fruit, which I desire God may bless.'

Three and a half years passed before the new marriage took place, years which are a blank so far as any record of Sampson Lloyd is concerned. Except for the recording of births, marriages and deaths, which, happily for posterity, Sampson Lloyd kept up for many years to come, the entries in the notebook dried up before Elizabeth's death and the widower did not resume them. There are no letters.

Sampson would seem to have withdrawn himself and no doubt sought satisfaction in his work. The next evidence is the marriage certificate, dated 10 December 1695. It was winter, and the company was smaller than at brother Charles's wedding two years before. Sampson's father was ill and regretted that he could not get to Stourbridge, but on the certificate Mary's father makes 'his marke'. From Leominster, the bridegroom is supported by sister Young and her husband Constantine Young of Lustonbury near Yarpole. John and Elizabeth Pemberton are there from Birmingham, but sister Lloyd is having a baby at Dolobran. The rest of the names are friends from Stourbridge and district. Sampson Lloyd brought his new bride back to the Lea. Over the following years she had many children, outlived them all except two, and died at ninety-three, but she did not live long at Leominster. Within three years, in 1698, the great move to Birmingham had taken place. She and Sampson by then had two sons, Charles and Ambrose, but it is a time of which little is known except for two events. The first was the death of the eldest of the girls, Elizabeth, aged ten. The second is not so quickly told.

In the winter of 1696–7 Sampson Lloyd had been pricked High Sheriff for the County. This was a distinction which for a Quaker was an embarrassment, for a Quaker could not accommodate himself to the forms and oaths required in the official world, neither were the authorities favourable to the appointment of Quakers to such posts, and had it been realised in London that he was of their number his name would have been passed over. Sampson Lloyd may also by this date have foreseen his removal to another county and was perhaps already concerned in some of the preliminaries towards it. The problem was how to be excused. He now turned to his new brother-in-law, Ambrose Crowley junior, who was the eldest of the family, a man twenty years older than Mary and the child of another mother. This Ambrose had left Stourbridge and was at the height of his fortunes in the iron trade in London. It happened that just at this time Crowley had become a member of the Court of Common Council of the City of London. This was a road which would lead him, in his own career, to the appointment of Sheriff, and though he had ceased to be a Quaker he approved of Sampson as a brother-in-law and was in sympathy with his case and prepared to exert himself. The extent of Crowley's influence and the effect of the action that he took can be seen in the letter he wrote to Sampson Lloyd on 6 January 1697.

I received your two letters and have taken all the care imaginable for getting of you off, which had been done this night but that the Council did not sit. Lord Chancellor has promised that you shall be discharged on Sunday night when the Council sits, and he has promised Edward Harley Esquire the like, upon the affidavit Richard Dancer made that you were a Quaker before a Master in Chancery the day after you were mentioned in the Gazette. Accordingly we have fee'd the Clerk of the Rolls to attend on Sunday night at Kensington with the Welsh Rolls and I intend to be there myself to see it accomplished. Peter Bowen has been very diligent in it. On Tuesday night you may expect to have an account sent who is chose in your room.

Crowley adds a postscript which has some interest historically: 'Whitehall was burnt on Tuesday and Wednesday, else the Council had sat this night and you had been discharged.' On Sunday the 13th, however, nothing hindered the Privy Council from meeting, the essential people attended, and late that night the promised account was penned by the worthy Dancer, who was one of Crowley's confidential clerks:

I am just now come in from Kensington it being past 11 of the clock and these may certify you you are discharged of being high sheriff and another pricked in your room, which the King did with his own hand; and the Roll being put up in the Privy Purse the Serjeant at Arms could not give an account of the person's name that is now chose but he will give me an account tomorrow and by the next post you may expect to hear who is pricked in your stead.

To this letter there is a still more laconic postscript: 'It hath been a hard push to get you off.'

Sampson and Mary were to become the ancestors of all the Birmingham Lloyds. Their removal to Birmingham is, therefore, not without significance for the history of the family and, to an extent, for Birmingham, and we can now consider certain questions such as why they left the Lea, what prospect Sampson Lloyd could expect at Birmingham and what kind of place he found it when he did so.

The first of these – why they left the Lea – seems the most problematical. Sampson Lloyd had been farming for twelve years and he had been brought up to farming before that. Did young Mary fret for the West Midlands? Was Sibbell Good difficult over the daughter-in-law situation? Did farming fall on bad times? Did Sibbell die – and who would the farm belong to if she did? No useful clue is discerned. But what then inclined them to Birmingham? Let us consider a little further how Sampson Lloyd would stand and what the prospects might be in Birmingham if he went there. He had, first, his reputation in Herefordshire as a respected citizen and the undeniable fact that he had been nominated as High Sheriff. But Leominster was not near Birmingham. Forty miles was a long way away. Sampson Lloyd was the younger son. There is nothing to suggest that his father was well off, unless in land, and Charles Lloyd had been preyed upon too long as a Quaker to have built up much worldly substance. By 1698, Sampson Lloyd's first wife and also probably his mother-in-law being dead, the Lea may possibly have become his to dispose of; but where his second marriage is concerned we know more, for part of the Lort inheritance had come his way. The uncle at East Moor had been childless, male successors among the Lort relations had failed, and Thomas Lort's mind had turned to his sister Elizabeth in Montgomeryshire. There had been a personal affection between them – although only half brother and sister they had been brought up in the same home at Manorbier – and Thomas Lort may also have had sentiments both of indignation and compassion over her experiences at the prison. Evidently he had a liking for her Quaker husband. At his death in 1686, making separate arrangements for his own widow, he left East Moor and some other property, not to his sister, who had recently died, but to 'my beloved brother-in-law Charles Lloyd of Dolobran and his heirs male for ever'.[3] The value was £1600. Charles Lloyd had two heirs male, his sons Charles and Sampson, and this property, as they married, he had settled upon them, half to each, to pass in turn to their widows and heirs after them. Sampson and Mary Lloyd had later agreed to realise their share and it seems likely that they did so in connection with the Birmingham project.[4]

Sampson Lloyd had also a family connection in Birmingham, and he had the Quaker connection. That he had taken his place among the Quakers in North Herefordshire is not in doubt. He lived in the bosom of the circle there. Within a year of his marriage he had subscribed £5 to the building of the meeting house at Leominster. His child Elizabeth had been buried in the Quaker burying-place at Almeley. He was a Dolobran Lloyd and the son of an acknowledged figure in the Society. At Birmingham his sister had married into a Quaker family, and his Crowley wife and Crowley sister-in-law were from a family of the same persuasion not many miles from that place. At Birmingham, if they went there, Mary would be near her people, there would be the families on either side and the Quaker network extending both. There would be the unhindered worship. In spite of tithes and the other disabilities of a minority these things could be some insurance for a newcomer. It happened also that both the Pembertons and the Crowleys were in iron, the heads of both families ironmongers, the one at Birmingham, the other at Stourbridge. Whatever occupation Sampson Lloyd might consider he would therefore find himself, socially, within the atmosphere and the idiom of the iron trade. And were he to turn in that direction himself he would be in a fair way at least to hear about the iron market and its ways and perhaps to make contacts within its fringe.

Sampson Lloyd had, finally, his personal qualities. He was good at getting on with people and he was of an independent spirit. He had left home at twenty-two and had managed his affairs for himself over a good many years. He had wits, and we know that he was to do well at Birmingham during the next twenty-five years. Beyond these it must be allowed that he had enterprise, for he must have had, if nothing else, the urge to get out and take a chance.

They would find Birmingham an untrammelled place, free and liberal in its attitude, accommodating to newcomers and to Dissent. These characteristics were due mainly to two things, its civic status and the Five-Mile Act. Birmingham had no civic status, it was neither city nor borough and did not become either until 140 years later. It had therefore, unlike Coventry a few miles away, acquired neither the traditions nor the restrictions of a borough. It had no Member of Parliament, it had no guilds or apprenticeship regulations. It had no bishop. It was a busy, undistinguished, expanding market town. But because of these things it was unaffected by one of the key restrictions of the Clarendon Code by which no minister of religion who would not swear support for government,

Church and State might live or teach within five miles of a corporate borough. Already therefore for a quarter of a century Birmingham had been at liberty, which the corporate boroughs were not, to receive such nonconformists as cared to go there, and Birmingham had attracted some able and independent-minded families as a result. Yet though an expanding town it was not large. According to Hutton[5] its population was about 15,000 but was already beginning to grow. But to have any fair picture of the extent of the place at the time when Sampson Lloyd went there it is necessary to dismiss from the mind almost every notion of the Birmingham of today other than a handful of street-names, the parish church, and the contours of the area immediately about them.

Taking the third of these, Birmingham occupies a part of that exposed watershed which here separates Trent from Severn and stretches roughly from Dudley to the Lickey Hills. Its own particular stream, the Rea,* flows north-east towards the Trent, while others, rising only a few miles away, flow south-west towards the Severn. The town had originally come into existence at a point where travellers might ford the local river. This was followed by a bridge and soon by a market, parish and parish church. The road that made the crossing ran from Warwick in the east to Dudley in the west, boroughs of far more ancient importance than Birmingham. You came in from the country on the Warwickshire side, down through the hamlet of Bordesley and so over the water into Digbeth. Climbing the hill by St Martin's Church and the Bull Ring to High Street (then known as High Town) and the upper part of Bull Street you emerged into the country again, and the Birmingham of Sampson Lloyd would then already lie behind, partly on the escarpment but largely in the lower parts about the bridge.

The streets and ways of the place would be little more than lanes between the houses, either unpaved or cobbled, undrained, unlighted and very unclean. The truth of this may be judged from an account of them as they still were more than fifty years later:

The streets were with few exceptions devoid of pavement, the carriage-ways being of sand and mud and the footpaths flagged only in front of the principal shops. Huge ruts and puddles of water were found in every

* Pronounced 'Ray'.

street, both in the carriage-ways and the footpaths, and the latter were almost as much used by the horse traffic as the former. Heaps of manufacturing refuse, broken glass and crockery, coal-slack, brick-ends and other refuse obstructed the ways; and while the streets were innocent of drains they were effluent of evil smells of every kind, and pigs and other animals were quite as often to be found among the mud heaps in the carriageways as in their styes and sheds.[6]

The same account tells us that

the most unpeopled streets of a former period were now busy with life and bustling activity. From morning to night continually swept along them a busy tide; and trains of heavy carts, extending for more than a mile, loaded with coal and lime and bars of iron from the district round, stretched from one street to another and far beyond them.

This state of affairs, extending ahead as it does over the next two generations, is worth keeping in mind not only during the Birmingham career of Sampson Lloyd but during the greater part of the life of his son, Sampson II.

The reference to manufacturing refuse in this account is of interest. It reminds us that Birmingham, which had been a leather-working centre in the early times, was now a place of smiths and metal-workers. Its people had sources of iron and also of coal for hearths in the neighbouring districts of Staffordshire, and they were known as well for their sword-blades when there were wars as for more peaceable implements when there were not. Already, more than a hundred years before, a traveller could note that 'I came next...to Birmingham, swarming with inhabitants and echoing with the noise of anvils, for here are a great many smiths'.[7] Apart from one or two water mills used as blade mills, most of the output was produced in the lower parts of the houses or in small smithies at the back, so that the refuse at the doors is not difficult to account for. There is another illuminating reference from the previous century which says that 'there be many smiths in the town that use to make knives and all manner of cutting tools, and many loriners that make bits, and a great many nailers'.[8]

Other small towns and villages distributed about the coal belt to the west and north-west of Birmingham, in the district later to be

known as the Black Country, were likewise peopled by metal-
workers and particularly by nailers. This district turned out the
hand-forged nail in its cottages and sheds, village by village and
street by street, and it continued to do so during at least two
hundred years until the advent of the machine-made wire nail of the
nineteenth century. During the eighteenth century the demand for
the hand-made nail was insatiable, as building, industry and the
requirements of the armed forces, of the shipbuilders both naval
and civil, and of the trade with the colonies constantly increased.
Thousands of local men, women and children came to be occupied
in this elementary form of manufacture, for while different places
specialised in different types of nail* no new mode of manufacturing
nails was invented during this long period and only by the labours
of more and more nailers could the market be satisfied. There was
also a second influence tending to stimulate and expand the nail
business. Earlier in the seventeenth century the water-powered
slitting mill had been introduced into this country. This device
was a mechanical method of cutting bar iron into rods suitable for
the use of the nailer. By superseding older and clumsier methods,
the new process had reduced the price of rod and therefore of nails,
and this, as well as the pressure of demand, was a spur to the
industry.

Both these influences were having their effect when Sampson
Lloyd came to Birmingham and, since the raw material of nail-
making was iron, the result was an increase in business for the
ironmongers. Thus the requirements of the smiths in Birmingham,
of the nailers round about and of an expanding day-to-day economy
combined to draw upon the iron industry for more and more supplies. This meant more rod, more bar and more pig, whether from
sources at home or from abroad, and there was a brisk business in
iron of all sorts. Even a Charles Lloyd in distant Montgomeryshire,
taking on the Mathrafal forge in this year of 1698, could not but
feel the benefit of it. But it was in the Birmingham region that the
iron trade had its centre, principally at three places, at Birmingham

---

* Rowley Regis, for example, made rivets, hobnails and small nails; Bromsgrove,
all small work, chiefly hobs, brush nails and flemish tacks; Sedgley, larger nails and
spikes; Halesowen, large work such as spikes and pipe-nails, and Dudley, horse
and mule shoe-nails, which claimed to require greater skill than any other. See
E. I. Davies, thesis, 1933, 'The Hand-made Nail Trade of Birmingham and District',
University of Birmingham Library.

itself, at Stourbridge twelve miles to the west and at Bewdley another ten beyond.

None of these places were at all close to iron supplies of the first quality, either iron-ore deposits or iron furnaces. The traffic had its centre here because of two factors, transport and a market. It was more economic for the ironmasters to refine or to slit iron in the Birmingham district, near the customer, than to install their forges and slitting mills alongside far-away iron furnaces, so long as they could command charcoal for the first of these processes and water-power for both. Provided they could have these facilities, and given adequate transportation they could afford to bring pig from furnaces at considerable distances.

The ironworking industry could satisfy these requirements to a large extent in the Stour valley. The river Stour rises at Halesowen near Birmingham and flows into the Severn a few miles south of the river-crossing at Bewdley. Owing to the contours of the district its descent is such that damming to provide the coveted fall of water for power was practicable at comparatively short intervals. Here, therefore, on this small river, were mills of all sorts and it was here, either by converting or by new construction, that forges and slitting mills multiplied. It was said that, at one time, in its course of twenty miles the Stour was turning the wheels of thirty ironworks, more than on any other English river of similar length. Charcoal for the forges, though much in demand in ironworking districts, was still to be had within cartable distance, even if some of it came from as far as the west bank of the Severn. For the slitting mills, coal was easy to get and it was cheap. The well-known 'thick seam' slanting across the watershed was partly a surface seam and was at this period easily worked. In these ways power and fuel are accounted for, and customers were at hand as we have seen, but how did Birmingham, the Stour valley, or Bewdley manage for transport?

For the managers of industries with heavy products such as coal or iron or salt, transportation at this time meant a perpetual struggle. Where there was no water you had the appalling roads to contend with. The reference to carriage-ways of sand and mud in Birmingham reminds us of these conditions, for the observation could be well applied to the roadways round about. Where the going was friable or soft, as in a sandstone district, roads were worn down to an extraordinary degree so that Hutton could write of 'the wagon, that great destroyer of the road'. Where an area was hilly such conditions were made worse by the scouring of the surface water. The Birmingham area had both these characteristics. Some of its approaches were so worn down that it was said that a wagon-load of hay could be driven unseen along their hollows and that some of them were, in places, as much as twenty feet deep. The name of a Birmingham street, Holloway Head, commemorates this aspect to this day. Outside the towns many of the ways were unsuitable for carts for miles at a stretch. In the time of Queen Anne very few turnpikes had been constructed. Where there was a road a little better than the rest wagon trains crowded along it, so much so that travellers by horse or chaise would set out while it was still dark to be ahead of them. But on most of the roads the packhorse was the contemporary carrier, as for centuries before, its load disposed in two panniers, a hundredweight on either side. A road worn down by trains of packhorses became more and more v-shaped, which puts us in mind of many a country bridle-path of today: both in form and in name recalling the roads of Sampson Lloyd's day. Indeed they were as commonly known as ways, unworthy of a better name. It was only three years before, in 1695, that Charles Lloyd at Dolobran, Sampson's father, had written to John Pemberton, of a traveller to Birmingham in December, 'I wish he may come safe to you, by reason of bad weather and floods which have been great, and the continuing rains are like to make them *and the ways* more dangerous and worse.'

But if trade was not to stand still these were the roads that industry and merchants must use. And here the economics of distance come into account. After about the first ten to fifteen miles it became more expensive to move goods by road than by water, the price of water carriage, so comparatively effortless, remaining low over great distances. But the distances between Bewdley and the Stour valley, or again from Stourbridge to Birmingham, the busy consumer's town, were not above a dozen miles and hence manageable where carriage was concerned. Except for a couple of miles near its mouth the river Stour could not be navigated, but from Bewdley in two directions opened out the gentle waterway of the Severn, a free river unattended by either locks or tolls. Northward to Ketley and to Shrewsbury and, at some seasons, to Welshpool it stretched. Southwards it stretched to infinity, or so the iron men must have felt. Past Worcester and Tewkesbury and Gloucester it led on to the port of Bristol with its limitless trade. This trade was as busy on the coastwise track, to the Falmouths, the Exmouths and the south coast places, or to London, to Newcastle and other North Sea ports, as it was to the new colonies across the Atlantic, to the coasts of Europe, to the Africas and beyond. By way of this artery pig iron could reach Bewdley from the north or from the south. From northwards, it came downstream from the furnaces of Shropshire or, allowing for some road-carriage, from Cheshire and North Wales and so by the Severn from Pool Quay; or again, using coastwise passage via Chester, from the important furnaces of distant Cumberland. It was still economic from there. Downstream, to the south, the river passed under the flank of the great smelting district of the Forest of Dean, from which, as from Cumberland, some of the best-quality pig iron was drawn,* and Bristol was the gateway to the world. By way of Bristol arrived, from London, the imports of that mercantile place, from Sweden, the desirable bar iron of which England consumed so much, and, as time went on, the pig received from North America; and beyond Bristol lay the distant, wide-open markets for cauldrons and for nails.

Up and down the waterway flowed the trade. It was carried for the most part either in 'frigates' or in 'trows'. These terms, in the context, meant sailing craft of about 30 to 60 tons burden, suited some to the upper parts of the river, some to the lower, and some to the tideway for Bristol and South Wales. Severn trows were square-rigged craft at this period, with masts as high as tall trees (Plate 10).† So many might be seen at the moorings of towns on the waterway that these towns took on the appearance of inland ports. But not the whole of the river's course was physically suited for sailing, and there might be no wind. The other means of progression used by these vessels was that of two-legged traction. Gangs of men,

---

* 'This Forest iron,' as Yarranton explains, 'is of a most gentle, pliable soft nature, easily and quickly to be wrought into manufacture. It is sent up Severn to the forges', wrought and manufactured 'at Stourbridge, Dudley, Wolverhampton, Sedgley, Walsall and Birmingham' and 'a great trade made of it'. Andrew Yarranton, *England's Improvement by Sea and Land*, 1677, vol. I, pp. 56–9.

† 'The trows, or larger vessels, have a main and top mast about 80 feet high with square sails, and some of them have mizzen-masts. They are generally from 16 to 20 feet wide and 60 feet in length.' J. Phillips, *A General History of Inland Navigation*, 4th ed, 1803. 'Trows' is pronounced to rhyme with 'snows'.

'bow hauliers', harnessed like the sledge-dogs of Hudson's Bay, dragged them up or down the river, both with and against the stream. They were rough crews, waterside halting places became notorious on their account, and we are told that those sturdy philanthropists the Darbys, iron-men themselves, did their utmost to promote towpaths over riverside property that the horse might take the place of the man. By means of these craft, lowering their masts to pass under the bridges, a slow but regular service was operated up and down the stream to the advantage of trade of all sorts.

Small wonder that Bewdley figured as a key point in this traffic. It was the great exchange station for land and water and it was a river-crossing as well (Plate 11). Through Bewdley the Stour valley received the greater part of its raw material. To Bewdley was carried a good part of what the Stour valley turned out. At Bewdley were maintained the stock-houses of the great ironmasters, and iron prices were quoted 'ex-Bewdley' as we should say. At Bewdley, at busy seasons, as many as four hundred visiting horses could be watered and fed.[9] It was a handsome, prosperous place. And in the middle, between Bewdley the port and Birmingham the outlet, lay Stourbridge, among the works and the mills and the warehouses, Stourbridge the manufacturing place, with its busy inns and monthly mart which John Kelsall was later to frequent, the crossroads of the Stour valley trade. And Stourbridge was the home of the Crowleys. It was Mary Lloyd's home town.

Sampson and Mary Lloyd moved to Birmingham with their five children in 1698, the year in which his father was ending his days at the Pembertons. They resided at first in Worcester Street, where the new business was started and an iron warehouse opened. But the house which became their permanent home was a commodious, new-built terrace property in Edgbaston Street, to which they moved in 1710.[10] Occupying a frontage which the developer had intended for two houses, it was a double house and is recorded to have contained 'two staircases of a superior kind, panelled rooms, and decorated doorframes on the upper floor'. It stood on the lower side of the street at a spot where the ground fell agreeably to the meadows and the river below. It had ample stables and outbuildings, plenty of garden ground, and evidently, from an old plan, a way out into the fields. It had room for a warehouse, and seems to have been just the property that a rising ironmonger would be glad to secure. These premises, which as his will declares Sampson Lloyd later purchased for £400, were used by the family for residence and business during the greater part of the eighteenth century, and so suitable were they that the house next door, with several similar attractions, later became a second Lloyd establishment. The houses of Edgbaston Street were not at the bottom of the town and not in the new residential part at the top; they were between the two, respectable, substantial and conveniently placed.*

Sampson Lloyd's brother-in-law, John Pemberton, was well established in the town. His family had been goldsmiths and they had been ironmongers, and the latter was the description that this Pemberton applied to himself. But he was a forward-looking man and he was more than an irongmonger; he had become a property developer as well. For Pemberton was one of the leaders in the extension and embellishment that was proceeding in the upper parts of the place. He was himself the possessor of a handsome residence built by his father on the high ground known as Bennetts Hill, a locality then still entirely rural. It was situated opposite the beginning of the present-day Newhall Street and was one of the best houses in the town; it had splendid views in every direction and it must have caught all the winds which that windy situation enjoys. But Pemberton could afford comfort within, and it was here that Charles Lloyd had taken shelter, when old and infirm, under the care of his daughter Elizabeth. Among the new roads and streets that were being created it is to Pemberton that is attributed the concept and undertaking of 'The Square' (Plate 6). This was an ambitious innovation of sixteen excellent houses, only a stone's throw from the Quaker meeting house, and was to be occupied by persons of quality, including some in this history, during the next 160 years until swept away by an innovator of another century.†

---

* Edgbaston itself, known today as a district of Birmingham, was then a neighbouring village, towards which Edgbaston Street, in earlier days, had conveniently led. The house, known as No. 46 when numbering was first introduced but altered at a later date to No. 56, was blitzed in 1941, after having been used for many years as shop premises.

† The Square, later known as the Old Square, was demolished in the 1870s under Joseph Chamberlain's 'Improvement Scheme' to allow the construction of Corporation Street.

As in Wales, so in Birmingham it was the time of the second-generation Quakers when the movement had started to put down roots. Quakerism had come early to the place, and the first meeting house had been established there in 1681.* This was a cottage with garden in Bull Lane, converted, to quote the official license received under the Toleration Act in 1689, to the purposes of 'a meeting place for dissenters from the Church of England who scruple the taking of any oath'. The garden became a burying-ground and continued in use for more than a century; but the cottage was superseded by the building, in 1703, of the better-known meeting house in Bull Street upon a piece of land purchased from John Pemberton, still in use for the same purpose. Sampson Lloyd, now nearer forty than thirty, had soon been accepted as a useful addition to the Quaker community. He served, in his first year, as a representative to the Quarterly Meeting at Warwick, he is named among those who were active, during 1702, over the fund-raising and other business which the project for a new meeting house required, and when the property was conveyed to trustees he figures among their number. This was the second new meeting house to the building of which Sampson Lloyd had subscribed since he was first married and was under construction just at the same time as the sister project at Dolobran. The Bull Street meeting house is described in Hutton's *History* as 'a convenient place and, notwithstanding the plainness of the profession, rather elegant'.

It has to be understood that, during the period covered by this history, Birmingham Quakers thus had, one after the other, two meeting houses, one in Bull Lane and the other in Bull Street, each of them furnished with a burying-ground, which are referred to as the 'old burying-ground' in Bull Lane and the 'new burying-ground' in Bull Street. Bull Lane was the short stretch of road from Bull Street to the present-day churchyard and was known at various dates by several different names. Forming today a part of Colmore Row, it had been named in turn Colmore's Lane, Newhall Lane, Bull Lane, and Monmouth Street, appearing in the 1681 conveyance as 'Colmore's lane turning towards Edgbaston out of the common

* The principal source for this account is information in the Quaker records at Bull Street, parts of which are brought together in a manuscript book of C. D Sturge in the Bevan–Naish Quaker Library at Woodbrooke College, Birmingham (ref. JK9/4041).

T.Q.L.—D

way', that is to say out of Bull Street. The site of the Bull Lane burying-ground, as mentioned in another chapter, was just at the exit of the Great Western Arcade of living memory. But neither Bull Street nor Bull Lane, which owed their names to a popular tavern of times past, must be confused with the Bull Ring, at the centre of the town, so named from a popular public sport.

At Stourbridge Mary Lloyd's father, Ambrose Crowley, was an established citizen in his sixties (Plate 4). Crowley's house was at the bottom of the hill where the road to Wolverhampton crosses over the Stour. Here he had his business premises, an iron forge and a warehouse, and close adjoining stood the new meeting house, the land for which he had leased to the Society in 1688 and of which he was a trustee. Throughout the last quarter of the century Ambrose Crowley had been building up his position. Born at Rowley Regis, he had started in domestic nailing, he then became an ironmonger and he finished as a Stour valley forgemaster. He was in addition a supplier of anvils and hammerheads for forges, as appears from a letter of his son's, and he also had his own steel furnace and was a dealer in steel. He was a partner with the ironmaster John Hanbury of Pontypool in a works near Treforest in South Wales[11] for the rolling of the new 'black plate', the basic material used in the future tinplate industry; and he had interests in the installation and operation of water supplies by means of 'water engines' at Exeter* and at Barnstaple.† He was a pillar of the Quaker world at Stourbridge, at Chadwich near Bromsgrove, and in the mid-Severn counties at large. It was at his house that Richard Davies was to lodge in 1706 on the last of his ministering journeys. To lose sight of Ambrose Crowley under the refulgence of his son's achievements would be as unjust as it might seem easy. He was a successful man in his own right and he was a patriarch among Friends. He had lost his wife soon after the birth of the first child, the younger Ambrose, in the 1650s, but he had married again, and among the dozen or so further children who made up his family were Sarah and Mary, the Lloyd wives whom we have already met. Ambrose

---

* G. Oliver, *History of the City of Exeter*, 1861. In 1711 Sampson Lloyd is consulted by the Crowleys on the appointment of a new manager for 'Exon Waterworks'; Lloyd MSS, 1/59.

† Income was still being received from Barnstaple by Ambrose Crowley's executors several years after his death. Lloyd MSS, 2/18b.

Crowley, like others in this story, was to be the ancestor of countless Lloyds of future generations.

But Sampson Lloyd was not a man of sixty, he was a young man in his thirties, and it is Crowley's son Ambrose who figures, all through the time of Queen Anne, not only as his brother-in-law but as his associate, friend and business *vis-à-vis*. For Sampson Lloyd, the newcomer, had had the good fortune to hit it off with the forceful and ambitious Ambrose and to find the means of being of service to him, especially in the West Midlands part of Crowley's iron empire; and there can be no doubt that to Sampson Lloyd's business association with that conscpicuous man, as much as anything, may be traced his successful launching into his new occupation. For this Crowley was the exceptional personality, and the word 'empire' is not too strong a description of the position that he was creating for himself in the history of the early English iron industry.*

Crowley was a ball of fire. Brought up among the nailers, it was he who in 1684 not long after he was out of his indentures and had set up as an ironmonger in London, had addressed to 'none but the considerable ironmasters that principally trade in or near Birmingham' a demand that they should buy him off for £10,000 if he was to stop his intended new nailing enterprise in the North East and not to undercut them, as he sets forth, by 'at least 40s. a ton'.[12] Already at that early age he had an iron warehouse in Thames Street, he was building up his connection as a supplier of iron wares to the Navy, and he had had the bold idea of setting up manufacturing installations of his own at Sunderland and was later to do the same near Newcastle. For the Stour valley boy had determination, and he also had business vision. He saw that the dockyards, few in number, were a splendid potential market for nails and for many other needful iron manufactures. He saw that they were concentrated in the Thames and on the south coast. And he saw that water transport from the north-east coast was cheap, to London and to Portsmouth as well. Crowley was right. The story of how he built his fortune, of the growth of his operations, and of his administration by remote control of these distant industrial establishments, in which he was far ahead of his day, are not the proper

* The biographer of the Ambrose Crowleys is Professor M. W. Flinn. See especially his *Men of Iron*, Edinburgh University Press, 1962.

subject of this chapter. But as a man he was important for Sampson Lloyd, for, among so many larger operations, he retained and developed his Stour valley connection, using his brother-in-law, the ironmonger, to a large extent as a fulcrum for getting things done. This was the man who, the son of 'a Quaker, no gent nor any pretence to arms', had pulled the strings at Kensington in 1697, had left Friends, was to build himself a mansion and a wharf on the river front at Greenwich, to become a Sheriff of the City of London and, in 1707, to be knighted. Crowley was a powerful ally.

To the regret of the biographer, no letter of Ambrose Crowley senior has come down. Ambrose Crowley senior could not write. From Sampson Lloyd there are hardly more than can be counted on the fingers of one hand. But the younger Ambrose was a copious correspondent, and by good fortune about thirty of his letters have survived among the Lloyd papers. All except one are from Sampson Lloyd's Birmingham period, and all are addressed by Crowley either to his own family or to Sampson Lloyd himself. These latter are mainly upon iron matters and, although we have little light upon Sampson Lloyd's start in the iron trade, we do gain some glimpses of his business between 1702 and 1704. These letters show him already, after four years, holding a position of stability and respect, carrying on as an ironmonger on his own account both in iron and in steel, supplying bar iron for his brother-in-law's slitting operations, advising him on candidates for employment, reporting on available mill sites and standing as arbitrator in disputes which Crowley might enter into from a distance.

The correspondence has its entertaining side. Crowley at forty-five was a self-made man, a captain of industry and a dominant personality. His energy and his intolerance of opposition burst out through his letters at every turn. 'A mill of my own I will have, for the greatest plague that can attend mankind is to be obliged to deal with cheats.' This was an opening shot in the saga of Richard Wheeler, a prominent slitter of bar for rods, whom Crowley in 1703 accused of substituting common iron for best, causing customers to complain of the quality of Crowley's best nails.* 'I no more dreamed of your being in the fault,' he writes to Wheeler, 'than I did of your being picking pockets under Newgate'; or again, 'I am

---

* Most nails were made from common or 'coldshort' iron, but in this case Crowley was requiring a supply made from best or 'tough' iron.

sure he that robbeth upon the highway is not guilty of half the evil
that you are'; and to Sampson Lloyd, of Wheeler and another,
'they have continued so long in their *roaguery* that you may as well
make the blackamoor white as make them honest'. And 'as for the
notorious cheat of taking my iron that was tough and good, that I
bought of Mr Sampson Lloyd, and delivering this base sort in lieu
of it', Crowley claims a difference of £1 17s. 6d. per ton on eighty
tons of rod received over four months from Wheeler's mill, making
£110, 'and the consequential damage may be five times more'.
This is a respectable quantity of material and would result in
thousands of nails, but it is the indignation in the phrase 'that I
bought of Mr Sampson Lloyd' that is of interest. Already Crowley's
supplier was a reliable figure in the district and known to be so.

Sampson Lloyd was also a confidant of Crowley's over the
problems of the Stourbridge *ménage*. Mary Lloyd's mother had died
in 1701, and by the time that the younger Crowleys were growing
up their father, in his seventies, was beginning to feel his age; not all
his daughters were 'disposed of', not all the sons were yet launched,
and the old man was becoming uncertain in the management of his
affairs. Letter after letter from London now reaches Sampson
Lloyd, on how to prevent the father-in-law from lending money,
or how to divide the business among the younger sons, who did not
have the abilities of their exalted half-brother. In 1707 John,
aged seventeen, is dissuaded by Crowley from going to sea, as one of
the older boys had wished to do, a form of break-out which appears
in some other Quaker families in this history. In 1710 the father is
rebuked for fresh lending when such matters were thought to have
been regulated; 'Honoured Father,' writes Crowley, Sir Ambrose
now, 'I am mightily surprised that you should run into these unnecessary hazards'; and again, 'I find you have not resolution enough
to withstand the temptation of rogues and villains who comes to
involve you in your old and helpless age.' In this situation, with
John and James bickering over the forge and the steel-merchant
interests, the household in the hands of the unmarried Judith, the
father's loss of grip, and the daughters taking sides, and all this
under broadsides from London, Sampson Lloyd is desired to intervene. But he steers a wary course. He sees the facts of the situation
and discounts Crowley's fulminations. A letter that we have is
revealing. Having been urged by Crowley to go to Stourbridge

and sort things out, 'I went not yesterday to Stourbridge', he writes, 'I was a little more backward in going because I understand there is such heats and animosities amongst some there that I despair of being of any service in that place at present'; and, 'in a short time thou mayest have further satisfaction from some of us, but I do not love to make mischief or make complaints if I can avoid it.'

One of Sampson Lloyd's first responsibilities in Birmingham had been the welfare of Anne Lloyd, his stepmother, whose trustee he seems to have been, if that is the proper term. His father, Charles Lloyd, had made no will and it was to Sampson that letters of administration had been granted.[13] Relations with the Pemberton family at Bennetts Hill, where John and Elizabeth had a girl and a boy, were close. Mary Lloyd on her part had been increasing her family. She had arrived in Birmingham with five children, three of her predecessor's and two of her own. By 1710, when they moved to Edgbaston Street, the total was thirteen, aged from twenty-two down to one, and had not two others died as infants there would have been fifteen children in the house. It was a good thing that it was a capacious one. Her husband had achieved his design of breaking into the metal business and was coming to be regarded as an established person. He was during these years, as we have seen, a regular supporter of the Bull Street meeting and a participant in its practical concerns. He kept in touch both with the family at Dolobran and with cousins from Pennsylvania who visited England from time to time. Isaac Norris was one of these, on whose account in 1708 Sarah Lloyd had been recalled from her ministering journey in the North. Another was James Logan, Penn's Secretary in the colony, who, returning in 1709 for two or three years and visiting Birmingham and Stourbridge, aspired to the hand of Judith Crowley. This design, which proceeded so far as to produce some intimate correspondence, lasted for several years and can hardly have been all on one side.[14]

But in 1711 this situation took an unexpected turn when the circle was shaken by the sudden death of Elizabeth Pemberton at the age of thirty-seven, 'my very dear sister' as Sampson Lloyd writes in his notebook. 'Her relations have lost the joy and glory of their family, her husband a treasure that was constantly too near him to leave him capable almost of judging of her value'; so wrote Logan to Judith Crowley after Elizabeth's death. Elizabeth had been the youngest of the brothers and sisters, born the year after the release from imprisonment at Welshpool and the only daughter to grow up. That she had something of the gentleness of disposition of her father may be felt from letters such as she wrote to her sisters-in-law as they came into the family, to Sampson on his becoming a widower, and again in her account of her father's last days.

Rather soon after Elizabeth's death it was John Pemberton's turn to think of Judith. Judith was still in touch with Logan, across the sea now, though she had not felt free to accept him. This the family at Birmingham knew, and they now took Pemberton's side. But Judith was not to be pushed, and before another year Pemberton is paying his attentions to a lady in Bristol, whom in fact he presently married. At this stage Judith makes an end of it and seems to have put brother Sampson in his place as well. Perhaps he deserved it. 'Dear Brother,' she writes in August 1713,

I am favoured with thine. As to Cousin Pemberton's request I think 'tis altogether needless to give myself the trouble of writing another, for you may assure yourselves, had Cousin been the most excellent of your sex, my thoughts are too exalted to lay a claim after he has addressed elsewhere. Cousin may depend upon it he'll meet with no interruption from me for I cant yet believe myself to be at my last prayers. I hear that he sets out for Bristol on fifth day, I wish him a very good journey.

She finally dismissed Logan also. Judith Crowley was not at her last prayers; she remained unmarried for ten years longer, saw the death of her brother at Greenwich in 1713 and of her father at Stourbridge in 1720, and was married in 1724 when forty-three to Cornelius Ford, a clergyman of the Church of England. Brought up a Quaker, she was buried, as Ford's widow, in the parish church at Birmingham. Her epitaph, in the notebook of Sampson Lloyd II,* reads: '1756, 29, 4 mo. Aunt Judith Ford died and was buried at Birmingham near the pulpit, in the middle aisle in the old church. About 76.'†

Sampson Lloyd's trade with the Crowleys did not come to an end with the death of his brother-in-law in 1713. It was continued with Crowley's son and successor, John Crowley (not to be con-

* Now in the possession of Sampson Lloyd of Bagpath, Gloucestershire.

† Such arrangements could be made at that time on payment of one guinea extra.
J. Hill and R. K. Dent, *Memorials of the Old Square*, Achilles Taylor, Birmingham, 1897.

fused with the brother John at Stourbridge), at least up to the time of Sampson Lloyd's death in 1725. While Sampson Lloyd had many other customers in the Birmingham district the Crowley connection colours the whole history of his career in iron, that is to say his Birmingham period, the last twenty-five years of his life.

The Crowley correspondence is illuminating because it shows how, once established, Sampson Lloyd found himself right at the heart of the iron trade of the day. We get glimpses of the market at Stourbridge for iron and for steel, the slitting mills of the district, the warehouses of Bewdley, the price of bar and of rod, the carriage rates from London on goods of smaller weight and of the Severn traffic if they were heavier. We get glimpses of leading men in the trade. The Foleys, already mentioned, of a local family, developed partnerships in Crowley's time which spread widely into the iron-producing regions of the Severn basin, and became great men, leaving many a Foley Arms to remind us of their name. Another was John Wheeler of Wollaston, a Foley partner, better regarded by Crowley than his brother, Richard Wheeler, as we saw. The Knights of Wolverley, who at first were partners in the Foley network and then largely succeeded to the mid-Severn part of their empire, also appear from 1709 onwards. In 1711 Crowley writes, 'I thank you for the account you give me of Mr Richard Knight's best tough rods. I shall keep private what you mention of the price'; an example, no doubt, of what Yarranton calls 'the curious intreagues of trade'. In another memorandum Sampson Lloyd, as middleman, receives a hastener from Crowley: 'I hope you have taken care to hasten the 15 ton of mill bar now at Bewdley, to Stourton, being I am in want of it.' Stourton was the name of a mill on the river Stour where some of Crowley's bar iron was slit. In 1710, when the younger Crowleys are beginning to be useful, their eminent half-brother writes to James, 'desire brother John to keep his promise to advise us what iron is to be had at Bristol, the sort, quantity and price'. In 1712, James Crowley had begun to take on the steel merchant's side of his father's business, to whom one of the clerks at Greenwich writes, 'Sir Ambrose bid me write to you that he believes in February next he shall have at Bristol a good quantity of steel iron,' imported no doubt by Crowley from Sweden, 'and shall be able to furnish you cheaper than you can buy at present, therefore do caution you not to buy more than what will serve your occasions till that time, but do not talk of this'. And in the same year Sampson Lloyd is asked to give his own steel requirements for a year ahead: 'I am now providing steel for the next cheap land carriage and desire you to let me know what quantity of broad and narrow and rod steel, and the respective sizes of each, will be a sufficient sortment for a whole year.'

In 1717, in the flash of a single sentence, we see the extraordinary dominance of water transport over land transport. John Crowley, Sir Ambrose's successor, whose pig iron is made near Newcastle, has a consignment to send to Sampson Lloyd in Birmingham. Today, without looking at the map, we should all have a fair idea of the route between these two places. Crowley's route might not occur to us. '*My pigs have met with some delay*', he writes, '*at Bristol, occasioned by the master's not taking a regular cockett at Rye, but I now expect every post to hear of their being at Bewdley.*' (A 'cockett' was a document, obtained from the customs at a port, certifying that goods brought in which had already paid duty might be shipped out without paying any more.) In the light of this example of contemporary channels of distribution the purchase of pig in Bristol for Charles Lloyd at Dolobran may seem the less surprising. And as to prices, in 1717, when admittedly the market was rising owing to the prohibition of trade with Sweden, Sampson Lloyd is commissioned to buy for Crowley in the following terms: 'I shall take it very kind if you please to buy me as for yourself any quantity of mill bars or rods not exceeding 150 tons, provided you can do it on reasonable terms. I think £17.10.0 for bars at Bewdley or £19.10.0 for rods delivered at my warehouse at Stourbridge may do.' John Crowley and his friends did not like the embargo, for the removal of which he was organising a Petition to the King; 'and I doubt not but we shall have your assistance at home and at Birmingham', he writes to Sampson Lloyd. Four years later, as we saw, when the market had fallen again, Sampson Lloyd was fearing he would have to take £15 for a parcel of his brother's bar 'or £15 10s. at three months'. But business on the Crowley scale meant profit for the West Midlands ironmonger.

Pig iron was not the only product reaching Sampson Lloyd from Bristol in these years nor was his Severn traffic only a one-way

affair. His trade had led him to that western metropolis quite early
in his Birmingham period. He found there not only iron at the
Bristol Fairs, not only a thriving, independent, interlacing colony
of Quakers with a yearly meeting of its own, he found a change
from Birmingham and he found friends; and through the links that
he established, although he could not know it, he was opening the
way to an association of the Lloyds with Bristol that was to last
for a hundred years.

Bristol was no Birmingham at that time. It was a proud city with
ancient traditions and it was the second port in the Kingdom.
Despite the stench, twice a day, when its river became a muddy
ditch and the ships lay on their sides, it was still in part a walled
city and it was the capital of the south-west. Bristol had been the
scene of some of the harshest of the Quaker persecutions. We saw
how men such as Richard Davies and Charles Lloyd had visited
Friends there and had made the case in London for their relief.
But it was now the second generation, the Quakers whom Sampson
Lloyd found in Bristol were the sons and daughters of those who
had suffered the onslaughts in an earlier reign, and conditions were
settling down. The earliest letter showing Sampson Lloyd's connection is dated 2 January 1708. It gives us a sidelight on Sampson
Lloyd as a man whom they were all fond of but who was a hopeless
correspondent. The letter is from John Andrews, a wine merchant,
and at the same time a partner in the Quaker enterprise trading as
the Bristol Brass Wire Company, whose partners we shall meet
again. 'Honest Sampson,' Andrews writes,

perhaps thou expectest I should have wrote thee somewhat in relation to
what we talked of about J.C. but I had not quite adjusted the preliminaries with his master before he went off; but beg no excuse for my
silence because I only treat thee in thy own way; for in short if thou wast
not more sociable in conversation than free in writing thou wouldest not
have merited the value thy friends have for thee. But prithee once in thy
life write (without being spurred by business) to let thy old acquaintance
know that thou art in the land of the living and how thyself, spouse and
flock are.

On more than one score this letter must have made its reader grin.

Later the same year Elizabeth Pemberton is staying at nearby
Bath, for the waters, and is called on by several Bristol Quakers,

including Benjamin Cool, another Brassworks partner, 'and John Andrews often'. In October 1711 yet another of the partners, Edward Lloyd, is writing affectionately to Sampson Lloyd, this time on hearing of Elizabeth's death. This was a Bristol Quaker whose wife was the sister of John Andrews but whose connections with the Dolobran stock, if any, has eluded research. Some of Sampson Lloyd's family were sent down the river, in order to learn a trade. These were Sampson and John. Sampson, aged eighteen, whom we must now call Sampson II, was in 1717 to be apprenticed to Thomas Sharp of 'the Brasswarehouse in the Castle Street at Bristol', which was a local description of the brass-wire firm. Sharp does not seem to have been a partner but it is evident that he was a Quaker. In December 1716 John Andrews had written to Sampson Lloyd, 'I have at last received the Committee's answer in respect to thy son.' This sounds like a committee of the partners which would regulate the admission of apprentices, and in 1717 Sampson II duly arrived at his master's.

But Sampson, though he lived to be eighty and did important things later in life, was not in good health at Bristol. In February 1718 John Andrews writes to Birmingham, 'perceiving thy son Sampson to look ill', to tell the father quite a tale of afflictions, 'but thou knowest it must be got artfully from him in his own time and way'; and again the year after, ''tis hard to know his case for I guess he hath no confessor'. Sampson Lloyd II always did keep his cards close to his chest. But he had to admit that he was unwell; 'I think there is a few relics of the old distemper left,' he writes to Birmingham; 'I do not think it of much consequence yet I thought it was best to let you know of it'; and he describes what his symptoms are. This is in 1718, in a letter in which he also mentions the apprenticeship of his brother John, apparently to a soap-maker at Gloucester; 'Jacky is very well. His master and mistress are very kind to him.'

In January 1719 there is a clue to their father's travelling habits. Sampson Lloyd is planning one of his visits to Bristol. 'As soon as this comes to thy hand,' he writes to his son, 'I would have thee go to Cooke's coffee house and tell them if they have not disposed of the room I usually sleep in to keep it for me, and I would have some of them lie in the bed to air it before I come.' This is the man who thirty years before had been noting the effects of the ague.

Perhaps he still had it to fear. There were no centrally heated hotel bedrooms in Bristol. The year after, when the apprenticeship had lasted only three years, Sampson junior was obliged to go home. He had suffered too long and too severely from what seems to have been a septic blood condition, and perhaps too from the unavailing efforts of his medical men, and he was thoroughly ill. 'Sampson saith he is better though I think far from health. He is thin.' So wrote the obliging Andrews. Sampson reached Birmingham in April 1720 and continued unwell at home for another two years. Altogether he was five years ill and he was twenty-three before he threw off his complaint.

The year 1720 was an uncomfortable time for the Birmingham family. Besides Sampson's illness and the approaching death of old Ambrose Crowley they had the case of young John to cope with. John had run away from his master. He had made his way first to London but had been returned to Bristol, and after further rebellion he was sent up the Severn to his father. There he arrived penniless and hungry, having left the trow at Worcester, walked the next twenty-five miles and 'lain all night on the Lickey'. But this was not the end of it. In Sampson Lloyd's will, 1724, we read of John that he was 'gone abroad, as is supposed beyond Sea, and hath not been heard of for a long time past', his father directing John's share to his brothers and sisters should he not return within ten years, but to be refunded 'in case he shall at any time return and require the same'.

Sampson Lloyd died on 3 January 1725. His will follows some conventional principles. He duly leaves to his widow the value of the Lort inheritance which had been settled upon them at her marriage but which they had realised when he started in business. But the will has its revealing side and it has its highlights.[15] The case of John is one of them, another is that of daughter Elizabeth, the wife of Thomas Morris. To her, unlike her sisters, who each received an outright sum, Sampson Lloyd leaves £12 a year 'to and for her own sole and separate use without her husband's intermeddling or having anything to do therewith'. Sampson Lloyd did not think much of Thomas Morris. The testator was a plain-speaking man and the phrase about 'intermeddling' sounds just such as he would approve. It is of a piece with his forthright expressions to Judith on the subject of marrying away to the Colonies: 'I desire thee well to consider of matters and for my part I am of the same opinion that I have been'; and 'if matters should break between thee and Brother I am of opinion thou wilt repent it.' It is of a piece with his letter of 1721 on the Dolobran mill iron at Bewdley; 'pray desire Brother or cousin Charles to take care about it that we may not have such complaints.'

Sampson Lloyd leaves £10 a year to Charles and Sarah Lloyd, 'my dear brother'. He was always attached to Dolobran. He often stayed there and so did members of the family. He did not live long enough to know about the collapse at Bersham but he knew all about Mathrafal forge, and about Dolobran forge after that. He must have known Kelsall both as schoolmaster and as clerk. Sampson Lloyd was more successful than his brother. They both had the charm, from their father, but Sampson Lloyd had qualities which Charles did not. He adapted better, he had a shrewder brain and he had grip. His handwriting is positive and rapid, the writing of a man 'spurred by business', where his brother's is reflective and neat. At the time of his death, aged sixty, eleven of his sixteen children were still living, though some of these died rather early in life. He had portioned four daughters and his estate at his death was worth about £10,000. It was nearly forty years since Comely went to bull. Sampson Lloyd had left the country and gone to the town. Himself a second son, he had founded a line, he had pioneered a business and he had set the stage both at Birmingham and at Bristol for the marriages of the next generation and for that expansion from trade into manufacture which is the subject of the next chapter.

4

THE TOWN MILL

In this and the next chapter a single presence gradually dominates the scene, for these chapters are the story of Sampson Lloyd II. By his marriages, one of which led to a considerable fortune, he made connections for the family in different parts of the country. Through his sons and daughters, and through their marriages, he headed an ever-branching pedigree. Through his business life, as a merchant, in iron on Midland rivers, in the founding of one of the earliest banks, he pointed paths for his descendants to follow. In his Quakerly way he learned to succeed in the conditions of his circle and of his day. But Sampson Lloyd did not have these things at first; he did not have even a wife. He had only his own qualities and his position in the ironmerchant's business with his brother. The present chapter tells of these brothers and of their business and how they turned a corn mill to the purposes of iron.

The family business at Edgbaston Street was now, in 1725, in the hands of Charles and Sampson Lloyd, who were still in their twenties.* By this time each of them had had some experience at the iron trade. Charles, already married (Plate 14), may have been in it for ten years, having been brought up in it by his father. Sampson, a bachelor, had graduated in the business and built up his health

---

* It will not escape the reader that we have already met another pair of brothers named Charles and Sampson, Charles Lloyd, the young men's uncle, at Dolobran, and Sampson Lloyd, their father lately deceased. The Quakers were not alone in the repetition of names from one generation to another, and in family chronicles this can be confusing. Lloyd pedigrees have long adopted the device of adding I, II or III to repeating names. In some cases, where this might be ambiguous, a label has come to be used, e.g. 'Charles Lloyd the banker'. As regards the present pair, Charles, for reasons appearing on a later page, tends to be known in the Welsh fashion as 'Charles the mill', but Sampson is 'Sampson Lloyd II'.

since his withdrawal from Bristol in 1720 and was playing an active part. Both in business and socially they were the new generation in action, and they were doubtless busy also with their executorship. We can see some of these things reflected in the record of a business visit which John Kelsall made to Birmingham in August of this year of 1725, when Mary Lloyd was newly a widow and the young men newly in control. Kelsall arrives at Birmingham, with two of his children, on '2nd day', i.e. a Monday, and notes what he did that week:

Second day. Went that evening to see Sampson Lloyd and his mother.
Third day. Went to see some friends in town, as John Pemberton and Charles Lloyd...and to see the new steeple-house with the children (St Philip's church).
Fourth day. Settled some business with Sampson Lloyd.
Sixth day. To Stourbridge. Dined at the Talbot with the ironmasters. Then finished my business with Sampson Lloyd, received of him £100 in bills and money and sold him 4 tons of wrought iron.*
Seventh day. At Birmingham. Went to Sampson Lloyd (who obliged him by releasing a ton of the wrought iron for another customer).
First day. I dined, after meeting, at Sampson Lloyd's who was very civil and kind.

Where Charles Lloyd's house was located at this time, which Kelsall visited, is not recorded, but Charles was the eldest son and he was the senior partner and it was natural that Kelsall should call there as well as at Edgbaston Street, just as he also called on members of the senior generation such as John Pemberton in the Square.

Marriages were at this time in the air. Charles was already settled and had two or three small children. Charles's wife was Sarah, the daughter of Benjamin Carless, ironmonger, of a well-established Quaker family with property in Birmingham.† Of the Pemberton cousins, Rebecca was already married and her brother Thomas soon would be. It was now Sampson's turn, with his share of his father's estate, his youthful feelings and his new standing in the town, to

* On the same date Kelsall 'stayed up late at the Talbot' with Richard Knight, the ironmaster, and another companion. It would seem that business gatherings have not greatly changed.
† Particulars of the Carless family, over many generations, are given in J. Hill and R. K. Dent, *Memorials of the Old Square*, Achilles Taylor, Birmingham, 1897, p. 135. The name is printed in a well-known pedigree as 'Careless' and this has been repeated by some writers but is incorrect.

wish for a home of his own, and as his marriage in 1727 to Sarah
Parkes is of importance for this history for many years to come we
must pause to consider who the Parkes family were and take a look
at Wednesbury where they came from.

The closest acquaintances of a Quaker ironmonger at Birmingham
in the 1720s would be, first, Quakers and, second, ironmongers.
Sarah's father was both. Richard Parkes and his family had come
from Wednesbury to Birmingham in 1713 when Sampson was a
boy. The house which they had acquired was the one where the
Pembertons had lived until the time of Elizabeth's death, but on his
second marriage in 1712 John Pemberton had set up his new establishment at No. 1 the Square. The high house on Bennetts Hill*
where the old Charles Lloyd had died was thus still a well-to-do
Quaker home. The Parkeses had four daughters. The eldest had
found a husband about the time of the family's move, but it was
here that the others grew up and from here that each was married.
The family had as a matter of course taken its place in the meeting
and in the Birmingham Quaker circle and would know the other
families in this chronicle. Richard Parkes was not a Wednesbury
man. He had been born in 1665 of Quaker parents at Hook Norton
in the Banbury district, and was not connected with any of the other
Parkes families in Wednesbury.†

Wednesbury is an ancient parish in the district later known as the
Black Country. Like the district as a whole, its life has turned on
its minerals and was already doing so in Richard Parkes's day.
Located on the north side of the watershed, that is to say in the Tame
valley, Wednesbury was a place richly endowed by nature with
coal, ironstone, limestone and clay suitable for bricks, and for many
generations, subject only to the means of getting at these deposits
and to the natural supply, has lived by exploiting them. In the time
of Richard Parkes, when the means were primitive but the supply

---

* As mentioned in Chapter 3, Bennetts Hill was then simply a part of Birmingham; there was not yet any street of that name. The house shows up plainly in Buck's
South West Prospect of Birmingham, 1731, and a small plan of the property can be
seen in Bradford's *Plan of Birmingham*, 1750.

† Register of Births, Oxfordshire, Book 85, p. 9, Friends House Library; and
Parkes Papers, bundle 5. A source relied on for some of the opening parts of this
chapter is the collection of deeds and other papers accumulated over a number of
generations by the Heirs of Parkes. These are deposited at the Staffordshire County
Record Office.

abundant, Wednesbury was sending ironstone to the furnaces of the Stour valley, coal to the forges of the Tame, and was receiving from the slitting mills of each the rod iron which it sold to the smiths and nailmasters of the neighbourhood.[1] Richard Parkes had known how to set himself up among the ironmongers, marry the daughter of one of them and, employing his profits in local property, to interest himself financially in the mineral potential of the future. Intelligent and shrewd, he must have been very able in business and had made himself a man of substance and an established figure in the town.

His wife must have brought him a fair fortune quite apart from what he made himself, for she was of the Wednesbury family of Fidoe. Her father Henry Fidoe, an active Quaker, had run one of the largest rod iron accounts in South Staffordshire.[2] The Parkeses had seven children but all their three boys had died.[3] Perhaps the Quaker scene at Birmingham was a more ample one and opportunities of all kinds better than at Wednesbury. This could have weighed with them, as parents, in a Society where you had to 'marry in' or quit. At any rate thither they went, there they brought up the young daughters and there, one by one, the marriages took place.

This was the background against which Sampson Lloyd's marriage took place. By 1727 the two elder girls were gone, one to Wednesbury and the other to Bristol, but it is of interest that the other two were secured against all comers by the cousins Lloyd and Pemberton.* Alike in age, favoured as suitors, married in the same year, the two men were to be associated over Wednesbury matters for a generation to come and their descendants for a century after them.

The weddings took place in June and November 1727, Thomas Pemberton to Jane Parkes, twenty-three (Plates 7, 8), at Wiggins-

---

* The Parkes, Lloyd and Pemberton connection can be simplified as follows:

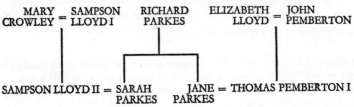

MARY CROWLEY = SAMPSON LLOYD I	RICHARD PARKES	ELIZABETH LLOYD = JOHN PEMBERTON
SAMPSON LLOYD II = SARAH PARKES	JANE = THOMAS PEMBERTON I	

hill,* and Sampson Lloyd to Sarah, twenty-eight, at Bull Street. This day completed the Parkes marriages. Sampson and Sarah settled in to matrimony and a year later was born the little boy who is known today as Sampson Lloyd III.

An absentee from the wedding was Pemberton's sister Rebecca, the 'little Beckie' who, with her brother, had been left motherless in 1711. Rebecca Pemberton had been married for some years to a nephew of Sarah Parkes, John Fidoe, another Wednesbury marriage link and another ironmonger. But John Fidoe, who was a man both of substance and initiative, like the Parkeses had quitted Wednesbury and upon his marriage had set up house in Birmingham, no doubt very comfortably, at No. 13 the Square. Here he was a neighbour of his father-in-law, whose part in that development is reflected in the wording of John Fidoe's purchase deed, 'lately built ... in a place in Birmingham aforesaid called the Square ... upon part of a close of land late of one John Pemberton and called or known by the name of The Priory'.† There was but one child of this Fidoe marriage, Elizabeth, after her grandmother Lloyd, born in 1721, whom we are to meet again for she became John Fidoe's heir. Fidoe was an active person and an example of the busy ironmongers of the day. Back in Wednesbury he was a buyer and seller of land. Some was coal-bearing land upon which he and his cousin Henry Fidoe carried on mining operations with considerable enterprise. In 1727 they were contracting, under licence from the patent-holders, for the supply of what would later have been known as a Savery–Newcomen atmospheric pumping installation but was called at that time a 'fire-engine', to distinguish it from pumping engines worked by horses.[4] The problem of water, even in the shallow workings of the period, bedevilled Wednesbury not only in Fidoe's time but for a hundred years to come. Another local mineowner, Lord Ward, had for some years had a similar steam-engine at Dudley, which Kelsall saw when travelling to Birmingham in 1725: 'here at Dudley Castle', he records, 'is an extraordinary fire engine that throws up 60 hogsheads of water in an hour's time. I saw it going at a distance.'

* Wigginshill, a few miles off, amounted to a second Birmingham meeting house at this period, Quaker marriages taking place there as well as at Bull Street.

† Parkes Papers, bundle 8. Today the spot is covered by the modern thoroughfare known as the Priory Ringway.

As an ironmonger, John Fidoe is taking steps in 1724 to find himself a London warehouse. He is also engaged in the nail traffic, and in 1732 we catch a glimpse of his commercial relations when a price-restriction agreement is recorded 'between John Fidoe and certain ironmongers of London respecting the sale of nails'.[5] On this side of his activities he was in partnership with his father-in-law, John Pemberton, as is shown by the following item of economic intelligence from a letter of Sampson Lloyd's to a brother iron-monger in 1737:

I had as I thought above twenty ton of iron in the Irish Channel during the rough weather, which made me uneasy, but I had a few days since the good news that the Captain, not liking the weather, kept in the port of Liverpool where I believe she now is. Cousin Fidoe and Uncle Pemberton have sent their nails the same way this twenty years and never had but one accident all that time, and that owing to a ship's falling foul on another, and there is seldom a week without a vessel being in her passage with some of their goods on board.[6]

The coastwise circuit round Wales was very likely being used by the Lloyds to bring Cumberland pig to the Severn; their cousins' nails were consigned to Liverpool in the opposite direction. Through all this we are frequently with Fidoe both on the road and in distant London; 'I designed to set forward for home on Second day next but am detained till the Fifth day following by reason I have sold my mare and this morning took a place in the coach'; or again, 'S. Robinson designs coming down with me for sister's wedding and if so must desire the favour of my father to send the chariott on Sixth day next to Warwick', or, as we might say, 'ask Father to meet us at Warwick on Saturday'.

The two Lloyd brothers meantime were launching out in a new direction when they acquired, in 1728, the corn mill in the centre of Birmingham known as the Town Mill. This event, which was their first move into productive industry as distinct from trade, was to enhance the fortunes of the family at least until the end of the century.

The thinking which preceded such a decision may have been connected with the approach of Sampson Lloyd's marriage. The

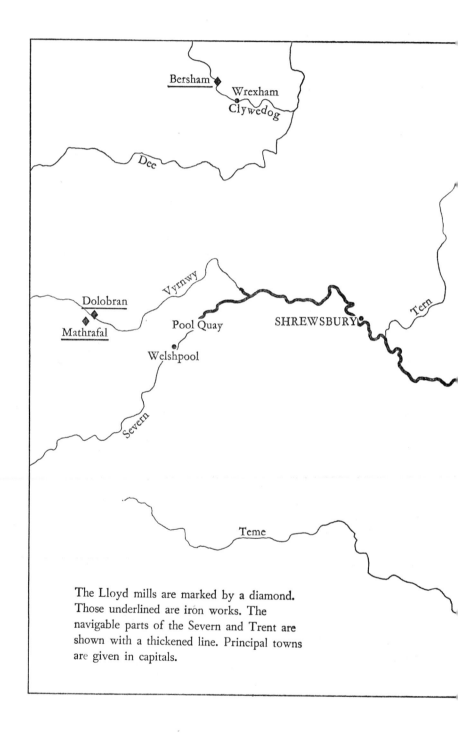

The Lloyd mills are marked by a diamond.
Those underlined are iron works. The
navigable parts of the Severn and Trent are
shown with a thickened line. Principal towns
are given in capitals.

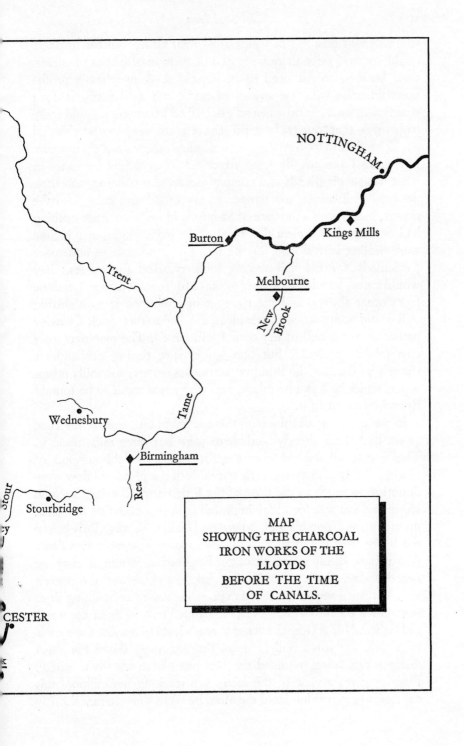

NOTTINGHAM

Kings Mills

Burton

Trent

Melbourne

New Brook

Tame

Wednesbury

Birmingham

Rea

Stour

Stourbridge

CESTER

MAP
SHOWING THE CHARCOAL
IRON WORKS OF THE
LLOYDS
BEFORE THE TIME
OF CANALS.

ironmerchant business had supported their father, but the brothers could see that, once there were two of them married with families, their business might need to be expanded. A merchant's profits must fluctuate with the swings of trade, and as recently as 1724 there had been a period when an established ironmonger could write to his wife that 'our trade at present is at the very lowest ebb and could I tell how to keep myself in employ otherways I do not care how soon I was wholly freed from it'.[7] They would be aware in what ways their friends and competitors were expanding, and their personal inclinations and temperaments would also enter into the matter, but down to the date of Sampson Lloyd's marriage nothing had developed. It is clear that most of the ironmongers at this time were dealing in rod iron for the making of horseshoes and more particularly for the nail-making industry. Rod for nailers, they would argue, should be cheaper to make for oneself than to purchase from other slitters, and the thought of having their own slitting mill would occur, among other ideas, as it had to their uncle Crowley before them ('a mill of my own I will have'). The manufacturing cost might be similar but one would save paying out another slitter's profit. But the limiting factor was power, for mills meant water, which was at a premium, and where was water to be found? Everybody wanted it.

In the parish of Birmingham there was but one stream, the Rea, as we have seen already, and there were but three mills upon it. These were all located near together in the neighbourhood of Digbeth bridge. They were the old mills of the place and they were doubtless as much as the flow of the little river, allowing for such scope as there was for obtaining a fall of water, could be prevailed upon to turn. Cooper's mill, otherwise Heath mill, was a little below the bridge and the other two were above it. The river Rea flows down into Birmingham through Edgbaston, where it may be found today. Soon after leaving Edgbaston, where the stream already turned several wheels, a man-made waterway had long since been taken off the natural river, 'a channell cutt to drain the water to Digbeth Mill'.[8] Here the water was at a level to operate the wheels of a mill, the town mill, and so, flowing away down the short distance remaining, rejoined the Rea just above the town bridge. Plate 15 gives a view of the scene. On reaching the millpool this cut received on the left hand the Moat brook, a short stream flowing out from the moated manor house of the De Bermingham family, which itself powered a small mill known as the blade mill, Grittlestone mill or Moat mill. Of these three mills the town mill was the most important. It had been the town mill since the time of Queen Mary, and Mill Lane is still there today. It appears to have served at different stages for the staple requisites both of corn milling and fulling, for part of the property is called in a deed 'the fuller's garden'. In the 1720s it was a corn mill. It was a superior mill with four wheels and no doubt many an eye in the town was cast upon the power which it afforded.

Whether the young Lloyds had foreseen any tangible prospect of getting such a prize into their hands may be doubted. It is more likely that the opportunity came suddenly. The mill had been for a number of years in the occupation of the Farmer family, Quakers, ironmongers, gun-makers (oddly), and later to intermarry with the Lloyds. This family had the mill as a flour business. James Farmer had had it through the 1720s, and in 1728 a new lease was prepared in favour of Joseph Farmer, intended to take effect at Lady Day. This lease was never executed. Instead, an identical document was prepared, effective the same date, the lessee's name simply being altered from Joseph Farmer to Charles Lloyd. Why it should have been Lloyd who secured the mill when Farmer dropped out would be fascinating to know. All we can say is that the miracle happened and it was to Charles Lloyd that a lease for ninety-nine years was conclusively granted.* All this action took place less than four months after Sampson Lloyd's marriage.

The mill was not leased to the brothers as partners. It is 'Ch. Lloyd's slitting mill' that Kelsall visits in 1729; 'went to see Ch. Lloyd's slitting mill at work, which seemed very strong and convenient.'⁹ How then did they regard the transaction, and how did they plan to divide and apply their energies? The programme before them would have two aspects. On the one hand the mill was a corn mill, and it was, in this sense, an activity that did not dovetail with their existing business in the slightest. That its power might be

---

* 206567 and Gooch 253, draft lease to Farmer and lease to Lloyd, Birmingham Reference Library. On this evidence, the statement that the slitting mill had been established in 1702 by Sampson Lloyd I (T. S. Ashton, *Iron and Steel in the Industrial Revolution*, Manchester University Press, 1924, pp. 215, 244), repeated by several other writers, has to be dismissed.

diverted to the slitting of iron for rods was a possibility that did fit their business and must have seemed a real windfall. And as to the management, it is Charles who takes on the running of the mill, while Sampson keeps the responsibility for the ironmonger's side. To manage the mill, at the outset, meant learning to be a miller, and this new skill had to be mastered. Besides the milling technique it meant acquiring a knowledge of the grain market and of the price of flour. These functions Charles undertook. But at the same time they quickly began their conversion for rolling and slitting iron. Within eleven months Kelsall sees their slitting mill *at work*. How they got the new machinery together is not recorded. For corn-grinding, the traditional timber, brass and millstones would be proper. For slitting, steel was required. The process, in simplified terms, was to take a piece of bar iron, draw it out under heat by means of rollers into a strip, and then pass the strip between cylin-drical steel cutter-plates so formed that they would slice it into rods. Their raw material, bar iron, as ironmongers they would know well how to obtain; for their fuel, coal, they were near the South Stafford-shire supply; the machinery was probably made up among the smiths and metal-workers in the town. They must have had plenty to do in that year of 1728, but they would congratulate themselves on the turn that their business had taken.

In the second half of February 1729, in the midst of the excitement and uncertainties of the new mill, when the infant Lloyd was less than four months old, Sarah lost her father. Richard Parkes had been failing, he had made his will in the previous May, and Sarah Lloyd now found herself one of his heirs. Richard Parkes had left the whole of his property to his daughters 'as tenants in common'. All of them were by this time married and, under the system of the day, their four husbands became interested in the revenues and in the satisfactory running of the estate. What a situation for Sarah and likewise for Sampson to experience, so early in their married life, to become quarter heirs of a wealthy ironmonger and property owner.

Richard Parkes had pursued at Wednesbury a long-sighted policy of property acquisition. He had begun to be active during the 1690s in making purchases of land there and had carried this process on at least to the time of his removal to Birmingham in 1713. From the deeds which have come down it is clear that his investment had included house property, some purchased and some built by himself, surface land and mining rights. A house which he had acquired in 1707 and for a time had resided in was Oakeswell Hall, which was one of the two principal mansions of the parish and is illustrated in Shaw's *Staffordshire*. His property purchases have an interesting history on account of the special character of the land in Wednesbury, that of lying over important coal, ironstone and other mineral deposits. Because of this, a piece of land could have two values, as surface ground in the ordinary sense and as land with minerals below it, and an owner if he chose could sell these two different assets separately; he could sell the same piece of ground to two purchasers, to one the surface and to the other the rights beneath. Such a possibility, while it might suit the seller, created two owners with potentially conflicting interests in the same piece of ground. In this way the stage was set for a long chain of disputes and litigation that would keep the lawyers busy for years to come. It was, of course, equally in order to sell a plot in the ordinary way, mines not excepted, in which case the purchaser would exploit them or not as he pleased. Richard Parkes had acquired some of his property by outright purchase and some as purchases of rights under other people's land, and a terrier has survived dated 1729, the year of his death, showing that he died possessed of surface and mineral rights in 202 acres and mineral rights only in 512 acres.

A further interest lies in the *proportion* of his holding in mineral rights only, which was more than 70 per cent of the whole. How had Richard Parkes come to own so large a share of the minerals under the parish? The explanation is that the principal local landowner, Shelton, was getting out. In 1708 Shelton conveyed to Parkes on lease for 500 years one half of his 'mines' for the sum of £400, at the same time entering into partnership with Parkes for the working of them. Two years later, in 1710, he dissolved the partnership and granted Parkes the other half of the rights, for a similar term, this time at the price of £500. In this way, for £900, Richard Parkes obtained a property which, passing to his daughters, was to continue in the hands of their descendants, collectively at first and in due course severally, for more than 150 years.* Richard Parkes was

* In his will (Parkes Papers 12/1), referring in due sequence to his freehold and leasehold properties, he bequeathes, first, all his 'lands and tenements whatsoever

a far-sighted man. He could sense the potential of the minerals in the district, but it was not the iron which interested him most, it was the coal. Parkes had acquired the leases in the time of Queen Anne, twenty-five years before his nephew, John Fidoe, was installing pumping equipment at Wednesbury, but already steam had been on the horizon. No one in Parkes's position would be unaware of Thomas Savery's pamphlet of 1702, *The Miner's Friend, or an Engine to raise Water by Fire*, or of the promise held out by the new motive force of 'rarefaction'. What Parkes did was to back vision by investment. What he could not know was that this inheritance, when able to be technically exploited, would one day be developed by his descendants into a business that would command a price approaching half a million pounds.

This was the inheritance that passed to the daughters in 1729, and because they received it in common we are concerned with the two elder girls as well as with Sarah Lloyd and Jane Pemberton. For these four and their descendants, styling themselves the Heirs of Parkes, were to hold together for generations to come as a kind of family club or syndicate, concerned alike in the income to be obtained and the administration that would produce it. Mary Parkes, the eldest, had married in 1715 Joseph Wilkinson of Wednesbury, described sometimes as ironmonger, sometimes as gentleman, who also held mining property in the town. There was a tradition among the Lloyds that her father gave Oakeswell Hall to Mary, but if so it must have been by an arrangement between the sisters, for he does not leave it to her in his will. Mary's fourth share in the inheritance passed down in the Wilkinson family. Elizabeth, the second sister, in 1720 had married John Scandrett of Bristol, of one of the established Quaker families there, a grocer by trade, and had one daughter, Sarah, through whose marriage Elizabeth's fourth share was to become the concern of the Harford family of that city. The first heirs of Richard Parkes can be summed up as follows:

---

with their appurtenances', and secondly 'all such mines of coal stone and other mines whatsoever whereof or wherein I am possessed or entitled to only for some term or number of years together with all such liberties and powers of searching digging for getting stacking rucking up and carrying away the same as I am entitled to and all my estate title and interest therein'. It is easy to see what a surface owner might be obliged to face. For the terrier see Parkes 11.

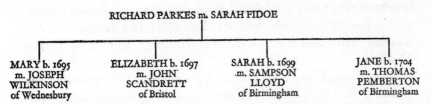

RICHARD PARKES m. SARAH FIDOE

MARY b. 1695	ELIZABETH b. 1697	SARAH b. 1699	JANE b. 1704
m. JOSEPH	m. JOHN	.m. SAMPSON	m. THOMAS
WILKINSON	SCANDRETT	LLOYD	PEMBERTON
of Wednesbury	of Bristol	of Birmingham	of Birmingham

Thus, at the time of their father's death the four girls were all young married women, two of them only recently wed, and Parkes had already lived to see a child of three out of the four marriages who might carry on the inheritance in the future. He died at the age of sixty-four and was buried at Birmingham in the Friends burying-ground at Bull Lane.

An extraordinary succession of deaths now took place in the Parkes family. Within the space of three years, first Sarah Lloyd, then Mary Wilkinson, then their mother, and then Elizabeth Scandrett all died, leaving only Jane Pemberton and an assortment of desolated husbands behind them. Sampson Lloyd had been married barely a year and a half, and was a widower at thirty. Though now his, the Parkes inheritance at first would taste a little sour. But like his father before him he had a business to attend to.

However, young fathers need wives and their children need homes, and in two years time Sampson Lloyd married again. This time it was at Bristol that he found a wife – Rachel, daughter of Nehemiah Champion IV of that city, merchant. Besides business interests, Bristol was full of Quakers, it was a real colony; and families such as Andrews, Champion, Goldney and his cousins the Scandretts and the Harfords, among many more, were well established, most of them prosperous and many rich. From describing themselves by the older names such as grocer or wine merchant many of them – Bristol fashion – were now *merchants*. Nehemiah Champion was a merchant in a big way of business, largely in iron and iron products, but likewise in cider, pitch, wine, timber, in fact almost anything of a profitable sort that he understood.[10] As a partner in the Bristol Brass Wireworks he was also in the processing of metals other than iron. Prudent, busy and successful, the Bristol Quakers formed an influential business network, carrying on at the same time a well-conducted Quaker community, with its meeting, charities and all the apparatus of a determined minority, and their intermarrying more complex than at Birmingham. Rachel Champion's mother had been Susanna Trueman, of a family that had married with Scandretts and with Harfords and other Bristol Quakers.

Rachel herself had been born in 1712 and was thus thirteen years younger than her suitor. Perhaps this had something to do with her refusing him on his first asking for her hand. The story is gravely recounted in a paper of the time of Sampson Lloyd's grandson who doubtless supplied the personal touches:

He has been heard to say that when he first went to pay his addresses to her he was repulsed and had arrived beyond Gloucester on his return home, as may be supposed in no joyous frame of mind, when he could not divest himself of the persuasion that she was the proper person for his wife, insomuch that notwithstanding his repulse he determined immediately to return and renew his solicitations. He was successful in his suit and the marriage proved a happy one.[11]

It was another of Sampson Lloyd's narrow shaves. To guess at the balance of his emotions during the forty miles to Gloucester and forty back to the house in Unity Street is perhaps a delicate matter. He was wounded in his affections, his pride had had a fall, but behind these it was his strategy, his design that was frustrated. He had already formed a valuable connection with the daughter of Parkes the ironmonger. This could be another, and it is not surprising that a daughter of Champion the merchant, should seem a 'proper person for his wife'. What singles him out is that he went back.

Rachel's emotions when he sent in his name the second time, could we know them, would also be an interesting study. However, they mended matters between them and, the formalities being dispatched, on 17 November 1731 at Bristol the marriage took place. Again we are fortunate to have the marriage parchment.[12] The Bristol witnesses include some of the names we have noticed, Harford, Scandrett, Stretch, and quite a gathering of Champions including no less than three Nehemiahs. The only Birmingham witness is Olive Lloyd aged twenty-three, Sampson's unmarried sister, who had also been present at his earlier marriage and who, in the fashion of the day, would accompany him and his lady to Birmingham as he brought her back to the strange town and to their new life with the little Sampson now just three years old.

For Sampson Lloyd the time from 1727 to 1731, from his first to his second marriage, had been five years of change and upheaval, some of it harsh, most of it unforeseeable. The next ten were to be a more settled time for both the brothers as they advanced from their thirties into their forties and built up their position in the business and in the town.

The great change had been the acquisition of the mill. This had altered the character of their business in two ways, by expansion and by diversification. Starting as a trading enterprise, it had expanded into the processing of iron and thus acquired a manufacturing character. But in order to do so it had first diversified, from iron, into the conversion of grain to flour, a new field altogether, although this, while requiring their best adaptability and wits, no doubt enlarged to a useful degree the business connections of the two men. Let us look again at the first of these developments, the expansion from ironmerchants to slitters, from trade into manufacture, and come to the corn-milling and flour-trading later.

The demand for nails was perpetual. It had provided a livelihood for the earlier Crowleys, who were makers of nails, and contributed to the fortunes of Sir Ambrose who exploited them; it had assured the prosperity of the great iron syndicates of the Foleys and the Knights, for a demand for nails meant a demand for bar from the forges; it had put money in the pockets of the ironmongers in this history, who traded in bar, such as Fidoe, Pemberton, Parkes and the elder Sampson Lloyd; it had provided an incentive, earlier, for the introduction of the mechanical slitting mill, cheapening and facilitating the reduction of bar for readier handling by the nail-makers, and it had showed profit to those who now operated such mills; it nourished a race of camp-followers, of ironmongers' agents, warehouse-keepers and clerks, nailmasters, nailfactors, petty middlemen and chapmen of all degrees; and it was always expanding. It grew with the expansion of the economy and the increase of the population, it responded to the requirements, war by war, of the forces of the Crown, it appeared with fresh vigour in the colonies of the day, in North America especially, where the ubiquity of timber construction made the nail an essential article of import. Thus, no new nail-making process appearing until well into the nineteenth century, this backward and primitive industry continued, generation by generation, to advantage the merchant and sustain the slitter. And the Lloyds were now both. The story of the Lloyds for several generations is in a sense the story of nailing, for all through the eighteenth century, whatever else they undertook, they were to continue in the role of rod-ironmongers, buttressed by slitting and by an increasing chain of other production activities. Through all this time it was their trade that mattered. The production was the servant of the sales.

But what of the other side of the picture? What of the nailer carrying home on his back the sixty-pound weight of rod, to be returned, in a week, as a like volume of nails that he and his family have made in their poor back shop? What of the long hours, the grinding middlemen, the miserable wage or the substitution of shoddy goods for part of it? What of an industry that did not change in its conditions during several centuries, in which already years before Sampson Lloyd sold bar or his sons became slitters, a prophet of reform could cry out upon the middlemen as 'cunning Egyptian task-masters' or upon the ironmongers as 'rich, covetous and uncharitable'?[13] The Lloyds were ironmongers for a hundred years. What were the ethics of this trade, and what was the posture of the Quaker ironmongers in it?

It is tempting to judge the actions and attitudes of the men of another day from the standpoint of the present. It would be easy to protest at the iniquities of a bygone system, or to condemn as humbugs the members of a Society, known for its humanitarian principles, who were happy to draw advantage from it. But the historian has to remember the conditions of the day in which his actors acted and the notions current at the time, and to recollect that at that moment such conditions and such ideas were modern, the most up-to-date that there were. We have to reflect on the slow stages by which the social conscience has moved forward, and to remember that we are treating of the days of George II. The Quakers were indeed kindly men, benevolent in their view of their neighbour and known for leanings towards reform. They moved with the times in these things, and sometimes faster, but they still had to live in their day. It has been estimated that in the eighteenth century, at the height of the demand, nail-making accounted for more than a third, possibly a half, of the entire output of the iron-

making industry in this country,[14] and the Quakers perceived no
shame in domestic nailing, though they already were beginning to
do so in slavery. Those who were ironmongers were quite prepared
to thrive on the making and supply of rod, and the Lloyds with them.

We can thus get some view of the operations of business at
Edgbaston Street. The Lloyd firm were iron and steel merchants
and dealers in metals. What goods did not pass direct from their
supplier to their customer they would lodge in their warehouse,
from which they would keep up a supply of mill-bar to the slitting
mill near by. It was from here that the output of the slitting plant
passed, very largely, to their customers the nailmasters, whose
business it was to put out rod to the nail-maker and to market the
resulting nails. There is no evidence that the Lloyds were nail
merchants or held stocks of nails themselves; this would be a retail-
ing function, but they themselves were suppliers of rod to the trade.
A reflection of this may be seen in the fact that their head clerk did
retail nails, in his own name, from the Edgbaston Street address,[15]
a proceeding that his principals evidently had no objection to and
which the firm's contacts with the nailmasters would facilitate. A
dispatch note to Thomas Kirton from the clerk, James Goddington,
for six hundredweight of nails details nine different sorts making
up the order and gives weight and price per thousand. 'Among
the nails,' Goddington writes, 'I have made bold to send you three
thousand of waggon clout nails; it's a sort I sell a pretty many of
with horsenails.' On the other hand some ironmongers, we know,
dealt regularly in nails. John Pemberton's firm did, and had done so
for years. 'I want some good screw hinges to be sent with some of
Mr Pemberton's nails'; so Crowley had written to his brother-in-law
while house-building at Greenwich in 1704;[16] and we have had a
glimpse of Pemberton's coastwise nail traffic in the 1730s and of an
agreement drafted by his partner, Fidoe, for sales through London
outlets. Small wonder to find a tavern in London still called The
Bag o' Nails. But, from the evidence, the Lloyd interest ended at
the rod stage.

The water-driven slitting mill was a continental invention which
had been developed in the Low Countries, in Germany, and in
Sweden, to replace more primitive methods of preparing iron for
the use of smiths. It had first been introduced into this country about
the end of the sixteenth century, and in the time of Charles and

Sampson Lloyd there were about twenty such mills at work.[17] Its introduction, so significant for the nail industry, had given rise to the legend that the design of the slitting mill was first brought back to this country by a young iron-maker disguised as a musician. This tale of industrial espionage is told by several writers in different forms. In one version it is a Stourbridge Foley who pipes his way to Sweden for the secret. In fact a Richard Foley, though not the introducer of the new device, did install a slitting mill at Kinver on the Stour about 1625, of the type used in Britain for the next hundred years or more. The design of this mill may have come from abroad, but to say that he got his know-how from Sweden – or in disguise as a musician – may sound improbable. Yet there could have been an echo of reality behind such stories. Years afterwards Crowley himself, in 1701, had sent one of his brothers to visit ironworks and forges in 'Sweedland', and his imperious but competent and detailed questionnaire and instructions for this mission still survive.[18]

A slitting mill was really a rolling and slitting mill, since the first of these two treatments was necessary before the second could be brought into play. A convenient way of understanding the operation is to look at the eighteenth-century illustration in Plate 13, in conjunction with the remarkable, non-technical description of the Lloyds' own mill by a London sightseer who visited it in 1755:

> Next morning we went to see Mr L—'s Slitting mill, which is too curious to pass by without notice: its use is to prepare iron for making nails; the process is as follows: they take a large iron bar, and with a huge pair of shears, worked by a water-wheel, cut it into lengths of about a foot each; these pieces are put into a furnace, and heated red-hot, then taken out and put between a couple of steel rollers, which draw them to the length of about four feet, and the breadth of about three inches; from thence they are immediately put between two other rollers which, having a number of sharp edges fitting each other like scissors, cut the bar as it passes through, into about eight square rods; after the rods are cold they are tied up in bundles for the nailers' use.[19]

The visitors saw the rolled iron, in its strip-like form, being passed immediately through the cutters and turned into rods (in section, about a quarter to three eighths of an inch square); but the strip need not be slit into rods, it could have other uses, some of it being formed into sheets either by further rolling or by hammering. The mill was thus a two-purpose establishment. This slitting mill in the heart of the town caught the attention of Birmingham people for many years to come, right on to the turn of the century by which time the next generation of Lloyds were men in their fifties. In 1731 there appeared the earliest of the Birmingham town maps and in this the millpool is represented, as a feature, the only such millpool in the town, duly marked as 'Lloyd's slitting and corn mills'.[20] Twenty years later, in 1750, in a new town map, the entry is 'C. Lloyd's slitting mill' with detail as to the layout of the premises, yard and gardens adjacent (Plate 12).[21] (Charles Lloyd had died but the lease had passed to his son of the same name.) In 1755, as we have just seen, the mill is singled out as something not to be missed by the visitors from London. In 1800, it enjoys the same reputation. In a poetical composition of the day, in the course of which two of the gods from Olympus are conducted round the town, we read

> Then LLOYD's fam'd mill for slitting IRON RODS
> Was honor'd by the presence of the GODS;

below which the guidebook-minded author prints the following flattering footnote: '*a very ingenious and curious process for slitting Iron Bars into Rods for Nailers.*'[22]

Towards the end of 1735 an event took place which had the effect of throwing a good deal of light upon the next years of this authentic history. This was the marriage of Olive Lloyd, the sister of Charles and Sampson, as a result of which posterity possesses about 120 letters between the two Birmingham brothers, her husband and herself. The letters are mainly of the later 1730s though they cover about twenty years altogether. They include more than sixty from Sampson Lloyd's pen and have both a domestic and a business interest.[23]

Born in 1707, Olive Lloyd was one of the younger children of her father's second marriage. She was about ten years younger than her brothers, and was now aged twenty-eight. Her bridegroom was Thomas Kirton, the son of London parents, a Quaker, who is described as 'of Brimpton in the county of Berks mealman'. The couple settled in fact in the Newbury district and lived for many years at Speenhamland and later at Crookham. Another Kirton, an uncle, occupied a corn mill at Newbury nearby. Thomas Kirton's business indeed was basically that of a flour merchant, and it may have been through the Lloyds' flour-dealing connection that he first met his wife. He dealt also at times in timber and iron and nails and doubtless in other lines as opportunity offered. His bride is recorded as 'daughter of Mary Lloyd of Birmingham in the county of Warwick widow'. They were married on 19 November 1735 at Wigginshill, about a dozen witnesses signing the certificate, including several Lloyds, John Fidoe and one of the Pemberton cousins.* Olive does not write much herself, which her husband complains of, but she did a service in preserving the letters after his death. For Kirton, whose letters to his wife are rather shallow stuff, but who was good company as well as being Olive's husband, Sampson Lloyd seems likewise to have had a soft spot. He writes to him with a good deal of candour, especially on iron-trading matters. Indeed he sometimes seems to be coaching Kirton, who may have been developing an ironmerchant's activity on the strength of his new Birmingham contacts. The letters certainly afford some good glimpses of the writers.

Sampson Lloyd, as we have said, was an iron and steel merchant and a dealer in metals such as brass and tin. He would also get odd jobs carried out among the Birmingham metal-workers to oblige his friends and writes Kirton a technical message about a brass pan ordered for Kirton's aunt at Newbury mill: 'please to tell Aunt Kirton the dripping pan is made and what they call bright, but it's no otherwise than from the hammer; the man says he never made one quite bright in his life but that this will soon come so by scouring.' Examples of such commissions include a malt mill (for £2 2s. 0d.), a quantity of rolled iron, doubtless from the Lloyd mill, and some cast-iron boxes; and sometimes he would send Kirton other things as well: 'I had everything ready to send the 25th,' he writes in June 1738; 'thy letter came just in time to have the cabbage seed put in the box. There goes therein two brass locks and a small box-iron and its holder. The small paper of seed is in one of the locks.'

Sampson Lloyd always steered to his advantage when he could

---

* The signatures also included an interesting Birmingham figure in the shape of Samuel Bradford of the 1750 *Plan of Birmingham*, whose family name is preserved in the present-day Bradford Street, passing close to the site of the town mill.

see it clearly enough, but in his trade he had to use his judgement and, like other men, he made his mistakes. Of an unfamiliar commodity which he was invited to take up, 'I shall by no ways deal in it,' he writes to Kirton, 'till I can see my way very clear both in buying and selling,' but he is frank enough to declare on another occasion how his judgement of a man had been at fault and what it had cost him: 'I have been engaged for some days past in looking after a chap which I cannot yet hear of but that he is gone off and owes me no less than £980. I relied on the man's honesty more than his ability but I find myself egregiously deceived.' And sometimes he was in doubt about his judgement of a market: 'I have been a little foolhardy in buying spelter, what the event will be time must discover.' 'Spelter' is the commercial word for zinc.

At an early point in the correspondence Sampson Lloyd answers some questions which Kirton had asked him on steel prices: 'as to the German steel at 40/– that's reasonable; the English at 27/– is very high unless it is drawn in bars as small as German which we here call faggot steel, but if it be blistered he gets full much by it'; and in his next he gives the Birmingham price as 25 shillings 'though it affords great profit at that'. 'Blister' was the name used for steel produced by the contemporary English case-hardening or 'cementation' process, uneven in composition, but in demand for ordinary purposes. These letters recall the 46 shillings per hundredweight at which Crowley had supplied German steel to Sampson Lloyd's father thirty or forty years before. When it comes to iron we find Sampson Lloyd giving Kirton some pointers in the ways of the trade. He introduces him, for instance, to one of his own suppliers, a well-known importer of Swedish and Russian bar at Hull, 'my friend Richard Sykes' ('thou mayest be assured he will not impose on thee'), of whom Kirton may expect to obtain if required 'Gottenbro iron', 'Stockholm', 'Peterburgh' or 'Government of Siberia iron'; or alternatively recommends him to a London merchant 'who will advise thee where thou mayest be supplied with the Spread Eagle' (the emblem of the Tsars being used as a brand name). 'The advantage in dealing in Hull is to have the prime sorts on the common terms.' He also explains to Kirton what his practice is about insuring iron in transit from Hull to London; 'its my method to insure when I have a value on a bottom, but if it doth not exceed £100 I generally take the chance of it.'

At the same time Sampson Lloyd is at work on his own account: 'I have met with upwards of 450 tons of Peterburgh this season.' he writes in 1736, 'but I bought it at several ports and none within thy reach,' adding, 'I am yet short of it.' And again on 1 January 1737, 'I have ordered what I think I shall want to mid-summer next.' 'I think there can be no hazard in providing till the middle of July, there's no prospect of its being cheaper.' In April he is warning Kirton of a rise: 'Some persons apprehend there will be a farther duty laid on all foreign iron this Session, thou wilt do well to be cautious in parting with much till their result be known.' The foreign iron, especially Russian, was acceptable to the smiths and nailers on the one hand, and therefore to the slitters and ironmongers. It was disliked by the furnace and forge-men and also by the coppice-owners, as iron from the colonies in North America was disliked, in one case on the simple grounds of unwelcome competition, and in the other because the sale for their woodlands depended upon the consumption of charcoal.[24] A letter of Sampson Lloyd's in February 1738 reflects the controversy:

> Our English ironmakers and wood gentlemen are very busy to form a strong interest this Session to get a further duty laid on foreign iron in order to advance their own, but that is so high already that I hope they will not carry their point. If they do, it will be a most destructive scheme to the iron manufacture of this Kingdom and quite disable us from exporting any goods made thereof.[25]

As a merchant, Sampson Lloyd preferred the trade to be free and did not much mind where he obtained his bar. He adds, rather testily, 'it is not for every man that hath a bad trade to apply to Parliament to made good the deficiency'. In the event, the conflict of opinion was such that no conclusion could be reached, and no new tariff was imposed for several years after this particular agitation.

That Sampson Lloyd kept a sharp eye on the wider horizon is also evident from a remark in a letter to Kirton in 1739 about the export outlook, on the eve of the War of Jenkins Ear. This is of interest not only as a merchant's reaction to a political situation but because there are so few references to national events in Quaker correspondence, least of all to wars. Quakers disapprove of wars, and it is as though there was a tacit understanding that if possible they were not mentioned. In the whole of the manuscript material for the time of Sampson Lloyd I and right down to the end of the 1730s the only reference to anything military is by his apprentice son at Bristol in 1718 when he declares in a letter home that, through a phenomenon of sound, the workers in the local coal-pits had heard gunfire at extreme distances 'in the late wars'. The Jacobite rebellion of 1715 is not mentioned, the name of Marlborough never occurs, not even in the correspondence of Crowley who had left Friends and joined himself to the established Church and who lived and moved at the centre of affairs in the metropolis. One therefore notices, in 1739, when France and Spain were ranging themselves together against this country, some observations of Sampson Lloyd on his return from a business trip to London. 'Iron is in an uncertain situation,' he writes.

As I met with offers on reasonable terms I have guarded against a sudden alteration and would advise thee to do the same. But I hope something or other will intervene to accommodate the present commotions. I fear the consequence of a war will be the loss of a very valuable branch of our trade, which the French are gaping open mouth for.[26]

Sampson Lloyd was thinking of the war risks affecting the excellent market for iron products in the American plantations.

All this time the town mill was not only rolling and slitting iron, it was grinding corn for flour, for its acquisition had taken the firm into what would now be called the food industry Here was another example of the kind of adaptation we saw in Wales where both the Mathrafal and Dolobran ironworks had taken advantage of water already harnessed for corn-grinding. Thus at Birmingham it was no brash new manufactory that the Lloyds had taken on, it was a traditional corn mill with all the appurtenances of such. The lease shows us this. Framed to convey the apparatus of an ancient craft, and drawn up in terms that lawyers must have used of mills all over the country, it offers a vivid picture to the imagination. The description of the parties themselves lends a slightly medieval flavour to the business, for while the lessee is Charles Lloyd of Birmingham in the County of Warwick ironmonger, the landlord, rather unexpectedly, is the Right Reverend the Lord Bishop of Bangor. The lease grants to the lessee 'all that water corn mill commonly called the town mill and also all that piece or parcel of meadow ground commonly known by the name of the near mill meadow'. For good measure and legal reasons it goes on to include 'all houses edifices structures buildings gardens foreyards backsides dams banks stanks* sluices floodgates watercourses advantages and appurtenances whatsoever to the said water corn mill and mill meadow or either of them belonging or appertaining'. If one brings together the layout of the property as shown in the old Birmingham maps with the view of it in the 1731 *Prospect* one can feel what an evocative recital this is. The mill buildings, the miller's house, the two gardens, the mill yard, the considerable dam pounding up the stream to form the pool and assure the fall of water for the wheels, the flood gates, and the sequence of banks and waterways, both above and below, for the want of which the water could neither reach the spot, do its work nor be channelled away as it ought, all are pictured by the ritual words. Four acres of elbow-room in the mill meadow was an advantage; it had probably served for the spreading out of cloth to dry when the mill had been used for fulling, and it was to pay off in another hundred years for building development. The rest of the provisions in the lease are all interesting but too many to list. They regulate, as they should, the management of the water, the rights of the neighbours, especially of the blade mill just above, the maintenance of the waterways and buildings, the use of the land and the rights of the parties should the use of the mill be changed. They also state the rent, which was £74 a year.

Appended to the lease is a schedule of the equipment to be handed back to the landlord on termination.† In this schedule are detailed some tools and spares, the mill's stock of grindstones and the wheels themselves. As to stones, the mill had six pairs, ranging from three to seven inches in thickness and from five to eight feet in diameter. Two of the stones were 'broke through the middle'. Four pairs were 'peakes', of the popular millstone grit quarried in the Peak District, one pair 'flints', a serviceable made-up stone imported from France, and the sixth pair is entered as 'collougns', signifying a desirable

* 'Stank'. First meaning, a pond; second meaning, the dam forming a millpond: *Oxford English Dictionary*. The reader may choose.

† Fifty years later Sampson Lloyd, to whom the mill had then passed, mentions this obligation in his will. But the lease, on its expiry in 1827, was renewed to the Lloyds for another hundred years and we need hardly suppose that this pledge was ever literally redeemed.

hard volcanic stone from Andernach near Cologne in Germany. The wheels are specified as 'four water wheels overshot', a point which may throw light on the probable dimension of the wheels and the height of the dam and which allows comparison with Cooper's mill below. A wheel is overshot or undershot according to whether the water to drive it passes over or under. It can be seen from the *East Prospect of Birmingham* that Cooper's mill had to make do with undershot wheels, but the Lloyds had enough head of water at their dam for the more efficient overshot type. Knowing the length of the millrace, the height of the dam can be estimated from the slope of the valley in relation to the contours, suggesting that the diameter of the wheels was about five feet and the dam a little higher. To get the most power, since five feet is not a large diameter, the wheels would be made wider in compensation. Two were retained for grinding corn, and two were adapted for the slitting process, in which the rollers must run 'contrary ways about'. The document itself, on a single parchment measuring a foot and a half by two feet, is the counterpart lease from the Gooch collection. It concludes with the signature 'Cha: Lloyd'.

By good fortune three of Charles Lloyd's letters to Kirton have survived, dated in 1737 and 1738, and these, taken with information in some of his brother's letters, give us a snapshot of the man as he was at this time after ten years' experience at the mill. They show us a man different from Sampson both at business and in temperament. Charles Lloyd managed the mill. On the flour side, he was in charge of the whole operation, raw material, employees, processing and selling; but where the rolling and slitting of iron was concerned, while Charles managed the production, his brother, the iron-merchant, carried on the sales.

Charles Lloyd, like his brother, was friendly with Kirton in Berkshire with whom he shared an interest in flour, and the letters touch upon technical matters in the mill as well as on the market for flour itself. In the second half of 1737, after a visit to Birmingham, Kirton had sent Charles Lloyd a millwright named Barlow, one of those travelling specialists skilled in the technicalities of mill operation. 'Brother Charles seems much pleased with the alterations of the old millwright,' writes Sampson Lloyd to Kirton in November, and a month later it is Charles himself who reports, throwing in a note as to a labour matter that was on his mind:

I deferred writing till now being willing to give thee an account of our proceedings in the corn mill. It has been set going four weeks or there-abouts. My friend Barlow has altered my slitting mill's wheels very much to my mind; he has saved me more water than will turn the corn mill. I am fearful my man I intend for the business will not be capable of learning. If thou couldst procure me one that was a thorough workman shall be very much obliged to thee. I can make the place worth 10/6 per week, he finding himself everything.[27]

A letter in the following April gives a glimpse of the demand for flour in the town and the hazards of drought where the Rea water was concerned. 'If thou thinkst it worth while to send any,' he writes, 'believe can dispose of it, for I cant supply my customers, not dressing above five or six loads per week and when the weather gets drier cant do so much.' Sampson Lloyd, on his side of the house, professes ignorance of the flour business, perhaps out of deference to his brother. When a carrier is going to Newbury he writes to Kirton, 'I gave him a note to thee to bring a sack of flour for me, yours being finer than what is to be met with here. I believe brother Charles would be glad of another. I am a stranger to that com-modity, but by brother Charles's talk it would be worth sending a whole load of.' But this pose does not constrain him from one of those pithy economic *dicta* which light up the commercial scene. 'I find wheat and meal,' he writes to Kirton, 'comes now to this town both up the Trent to Burton and up Severn to Bewdley and so by land here, so that I guess we have been above our neighbours, though I dont know the price.'

It seems likely that the brothers made a sufficiently good combina-tion. Sampson Lloyd was active and enterprising but prudent, his brother was busy and competent but rather casual. Charles Lloyd lived at the mill house, where he and Sarah were bringing up seven or eight children, and where Charles was something of a plantsman, exchanging garden favourites with his friends. But he was carefree in matters of routine, not always paying small debts, and unpunctual on occasion over the rent of the mill.[28] Yet, if casual, he was a human and likeable person. In a business letter to Kirton he pleads pre-occupation: 'I am a little hurried in my mind with the disagreeable news of cousin John Fidoe's death. He died this morning early after a short illness. Yesterday evening he was thought to be in a fair way of recovery but suddenly altered and went off.' This was the ironmonger of The Square, only in his forties, a contemporary and a neighbour. In another letter Charles writes, characteristically, 'Thy invitation to my wife she takes very kind, but as she is got into the old pickle it will not be safe for her to stir this spring.'

A few years later, in April 1741, Charles himself died, and it is from Sampson Lloyd that Kirton receives the bulletins at Newbury where Mary Lloyd is visiting her daughter. On the 4th he is told of a 'feverish disorder', of two doctors called in, and 'I cannot but apprehend he is in great danger'. On the 8th he is 'exceeding weak' and the constant Sarah 'will not leave him, though she is advised to it in regard to the condition she is now in'. On the 18th we read the following revealing lines:

My last carried thee the disagreeable news of brother Charles's removal from us. Have little more to say on that melancholy scene but it is what will not soon be effaced. I shall be glad to hear that Mother bears it with that patience that is requisite on such occasions to those whose ultimate happiness is not placed in the compass of this life, but in such a shock I know that affection takes the place of reason and it is some time before the latter can recover itself. Be so good in thy next to transmit me the subsisting account between Brother and thyself. I have not yet seen his accounts, but as I fear he did not keep them very exact shall be pleased with thine to set me right therein.[29]

There would certainly be a lot for Sampson to do; Charles Lloyd was not only inexact in his paper-work, he had died without leaving a will.

The later history of Charles Lloyd's mill and of Charles Lloyd's widow are not without interest. It seems that under Sampson Lloyd, who now controlled the business, the corn-milling was discontinued. Charles having died intestate, and none of his nine children being more than sixteen years of age, letters of administration were granted to his widow. Sarah Lloyd would thus become the owner of the lease as well as the occupier of the mill house. It cannot be doubted that she would be content for Sampson Lloyd to keep on the mill as a slitting mill, upon which the Lloyds paid the rate for another sixty years. The parish levy books afford a certain amount of information. These records, which are preserved from 1736 on-wards, recite the contributions raised from occupiers 'for the necessary relief of the poor' and thus amount to a partial directory of the town's inhabitants.[30] The levy on the mill property had been assessed on Charles Lloyd, the lessee, in 1736 at 6s. 1od. per month, making a yearly due of £4 2s. od. In 1744, under the name of Mrs Lloyd, the figure is only 4s. 5d. or £2 13s. od. From this period there is no hint of Sampson Lloyd's having carried on corn-milling nor any reference to prices either of grain or flour. It is likely that the spare power was employed to increase the slitting capacity, the poor rate being modified on the grounds of the contraction from two kinds of production to one.

In the 1750s either Sarah Lloyd or her son assigned the lease to Sampson Lloyd who, in due course, disposes of the property under his will as part of his own estate. At his death in 1779, after she had moved to nearby Dudley Street, he leaves 'unto my sister-in-law Sarah Lloyd relict and widow of my late brother Charles Lloyd deceased eight pounds eight shillings a year in order to pay her rent'. Sarah Lloyd survived him by only two months. She died in 1780 aged seventy-six and her name disappears from the levy-book entries that year. But Sarah Lloyd's death was far removed from that of her husband in 1741, to which time this story must now return.

5

IRON AND WATER

In his business Sampson Lloyd was now alone. His father had run
it single-handed, but the business had grown and Sampson himself
had had a partner. His brother's young sons were going into other
trades, and his own boy was not yet in his teens, but Sampson Lloyd
was not daunted by the situation and he was now to put forth so
much initiative and achievement that it is clear he welcomed it.
Within the next ten years he had advanced his manufacturing
operations to the Trent, acquired a property in the country, and
become a partner in a business at Bristol; but these were coming
events, and it is time to see what we can of his family and of the
local scene in this Birmingham of 1741.

At the time of Charles's death Sampson Lloyd was forty-one
and had been married to his second wife for a little under ten years.
Their family was not getting on very well for during this time
Rachel had had six children and buried five, the average length of
life being a little over one year. There is nothing to show any
tangible explanation apart from the death-rate of the day. Sampson
Lloyd records in his private notebook that in London at about this
time the mortality of children under two years old amounted to
34 per cent of all deaths, and of children under five years 44 per cent.
It must have been hard going for Rachel Lloyd, still under thirty,
and not for the mother alone. Sampson Lloyd writes to Kirton of
'these repeated losses and afflictions', allowing himself to add, 'they
are bitter crosses'.[1] The survivor was Mary, born in 1736. Thus,
after two marriages and thirteen years of matrimony, Sampson
Lloyd still had only two children, 'Sampy', from his first marriage,
aged twelve, and the little Mary, five. Mary, who was known as
Molly, had come often into her father's letters. 'Our daughter is

mistress here and doth just as she pleases, she can now walk very well and would be glad if her relations would come to see it'; and when Mary is three, 'our daughter is the rudest girl in town'. Mary grew up, the eldest daughter of the family, to become the wife of a banker in Lombard Street.

The letters report the loss of a number of the Birmingham relations. Through these obituary references we get a kind of directory to the circle and can also see the guesswork and ignorance which surrounded the causes of their deaths. First it is 'Uncle Pemberton' of the Square, in 1736. 'Uncle Pemberton is yet alive but his death is hourly expected. He hath been very severely handled by the distemper and applications, having had I think eighteen blisters.' John Pemberton, always a forceful man, had become more testy with his years, for Sampson Lloyd adds, 'as it happens, he hath not been perfectly sensible since he was taken ill so that it makes his case the easier, otherwise it would have been very hard for a person of his way of thinking'. The next is that of John Fidoe, also of the Square, in his early forties, whose departure in 1737 we saw in a letter of Charles Lloyd's, though without anything like a diagnosis; and he is followed in 1741 by Charles himself. Another was Sarah Lloyd, formerly of Dolobran, aged sixty-eight, 'Aunt Lloyd' to the new generation, whose death took place in 1743. Handicapped from her accident but still riding, she had been 'very much wet by several great showers of rain' on the road between Coventry and Birmingham, but she did not change her clothes, was 'taken ill with a shortness of breath and a great inflammation in her lungs', and the standard treatment of bleeding 'had no effect to ease her of her disorder'.[2] Within three years of Charles's death, Sampson Lloyd loses two more brothers. In 1742 he writes to Kirton, 'Yesterday we had the misfortune to lose brother Ambrose after a long and lingering indisposition. It is what we have daily expected for a considerable time past, there having been no prospect of his living.' Ambrose was forty-four. Next it is Thomas, aged only thirty-six, in 1744. 'Brother Tommy hath been ill for two or three months past; I wish his complaints dont end in an inward decay which indeed they strongly portend,' and three months later these fears were realised. Some years later Rachel Lloyd herself was 'visited with a long weakness which ended in a decay'.[3] One may guess at tuberculosis. Rebecca Fidoe on the other hand, John

Fidoe's widow, when aged about sixty, is reported 'very weak and poorly and if she dont mend cannot continue long. She is thought to have an ulcer in her lungs.' And of Thomas Pemberton, her brother, whose illness is severe but unspecified, we learn that he had 'met with a temporary relief by scarifying his legs, but his time here cannot be long'.* Sampson Lloyd always does his best to offer some version of the case. When it comes to his infant children we do not, however, meet with particulars except in one case in 1740, that of Champion Lloyd, aged ten months. This child was taken ill with 'a convulsion fit which held it several hours. It lay in a very bad way in violent agony for about a week and then died. We apprehend the teeth was the chief cause.' How glib and medical in their terms would modern parents be in accounting for such afflictions.

But the scourge of the times was the smallpox, which recurs like a refrain through the correspondence, as in the letters of earlier generations of this history. The development of vaccination was still more than twenty years away in the future. Every two or three years Birmingham was sure to be visited by this lethal scourge. In 1737, 'the smallpox is exceeding rife in town, having some weeks past had a great mortality thereby'; in 1741, 'the smallpox is exceeding rife here, never more so'; and we read of particular kinds and particular cases, 'the unkind sort', 'the favourable sort', or again 'the confluent kind'. Some kinds leave more of the unsightly pockmarks than others, some cause real alarm; but they overtake all and sundry.

In the middle of the 1740s the sailor brother, Jack, makes an appearance in the story. For twenty years we must suppose John Lloyd had been at sea, but he was evidently in touch with the family again. Arriving at Portsmouth in the *Princessa*† in 1746 he was desirous of obtaining his release, for which the family, when they heard of it, were willing to advance the sum required.[4] Though 'fearful of being turned over to another ship suddenly', John Lloyd obtained his discharge, upon payment, about a month later. He himself had entered the Navy in 1742, probably as a merchant

---

* Lloyd MSS, 2/90, 10 July 1757. Medical opinion suggests that 'Cousin Pemberton' was probably suffering from Bright's disease, a complaint not named for another seventy years.

† The *Princessa* was a 74-gun ship which had been taken from the Spanish in 1740 in the War of Jenkins Ear.

seaman pressed for the war. He was not an ordinary seaman but an experienced man, an A.B. at 24 shillings a month, the ship's muster-book showing deductions, upon his release, amounting to more than six months' pay: for clothes £3, for dead men's clothes 4 shillings, and for tobacco nearly £5.[5] After his discharge John Lloyd settled in the Birmingham district and was buried in 1751 at Bull Lane. It is interesting to see how, through situations such as this, even so landlocked a centre as Birmingham could be concerned, upon occasion, with sea-faring matters, and that in fact the colonies, the West Indies, the foreign markets or the Friends in America were not so out of range as might be thought. The seas and the rivers, and not only the roads, were the highways of trade and of affairs.

As the letters to Newbury show, travel by road was an everyday matter. Accepting their primitive standards, Sampson Lloyd's generation was daily concerned with mails and carriage, with routes and risks, and, basically, with the horse. Between Birmingham and Newbury the most regular route for mail was via London; but there was also the cross-country post which, though more direct, took longer. When it came to goods there was a similar dilemma. Did one wait for a cross-country carrier which meant delay, or send them through London at higher rates? If by London, the system was by a land and water combination, for the Thames, in part, as well as the Trent and the Severn, served as a commercial waterway. James Goddington in the Edgbaston Street counting-house writes to Kirton in 1738 about a consignment of his nails: 'most goods out of this country go by way of London at this time. Carriage is 4/– and upwards per cwt. If it should come down to 3/– shall take an opportunity to forward them to Mr Pocock who will ship them I presume, without any charge to you, on board the vessels that go for flour.'[6] John Pocock was a brother ironmerchant and factor near Blackfriars, who often acted for Sampson Lloyd as his agent.

The road traveller might use either vehicle or horseback, but in the 1740s the horse, to many, still appeared more personal and as safe. It might otherwise be surprising to find Sampson Lloyd urging his mother, at the age of sixty-three, to choose horseback for the ninety-mile journey to visit Olive at Newbury: 'Mother hath some thoughts of seeing you about or before Michaelmas. She intends to go by coach as far as Islip though I shall rather persuade her to go throughout on horseback.' When Mary Lloyd did this, either one of the family or the groom attended her. A young traveller would always make his journey on horseback. A few weeks after Olive's marriage Sampson Lloyd writes in a letter to her husband, 'I am pleased to hear thy self and horse are reconciled to carry double. It is a very comfortable and agreeable way of travelling.' But a journey on horseback had its hazards as road travel generally did. So felt the solicitous husband. When Thomas Kirton is away in London on business he writes to Olive, 'when goest to Mill pray take care at mounting the little horse to not curb him too tight nor suffer him to be held too hard, for it will make him prance and perhaps fright thee; but prithee let him go off gently and if he is a little pert at first he wont be vicious nor do thee any harm.'

A journey in those days was a risk and the phrase *through mercy*, used over so many years in reporting safe arrival,* was not just a formula of the people called Quakers, it was written from the heart and thankfully read at the other end. The roads, the sea, childbirth, infancy and illness, these five were still the anxieties of daily life at the time of our story, and the letters show us this. Kirton might write, when Olive was away, of his 'desires of hearing as often as the post comes or I shall have a crow to pull with thee', and he might tease her when she did, 'pray dont be so brief in thy next, for notwithstanding there's some beau spelling in it I value every line', but, though not a letter-writer herself, it was largely for her sake that the letters were written and afford us the picture that they do.

Quite soon after the death of his brother at the mill Sampson Lloyd took the step of investing in a country estate. This was the property that for a number of generations after his time was to be the principal headquarters of the family, known in Birmingham for so many years as 'Farm'. The purchase was negotiated between the autumn of 1741 and the spring of 1742. Evidently inclination, financial position and opportunity combined at this time to support such a decision. There is no doubt that after Charles's death Sampson Lloyd found himself comfortably off. The ironmonger side of the business was now his. The Spanish war was stimulating the trade. The mill was operating through a manager in Charles's place. In addition to these sources of income, he had been for twelve years a quarter heir of Richard Parkes. In a family sketch we read that,

* Lloyd MSS, 2/98, T. Kirton to his wife, 1736, offers an ordinary example: 'These are to acquaint thee, through mercy I got well home yesterday morning.'

from this marriage, 'he came into the enjoyment of a considerable property from which during the minority of his son Sampson he had a considerable income.'

The possibility of a country establishment was an idea that he had toyed with for some time. In 1739, *à propos* of a move which Kirton was contemplating, he writes, 'my own inclination often prompts me to a more retired situation but I am so linked in and encumbered that I see no room to creep out till Sampy is of age to relieve me'. Sampy was eleven years old. But the occasion upon which Sampson Lloyd had declined the purchase of the Dolobran estate itself deserves a fuller account.

Some time after the bankruptcy, as we saw, Charles Lloyd IV had made attempts to sell Dolobran and on failing locally had turned to his cousin in Birmingham. Sampson Lloyd, then thirty-six, was not untempted, but salesmanship mingled with sentiment on the one side was met by hard-headed appraisal and valuation on the other.[7] Sampson Lloyd does seem to have been at this bait for some time. His cousin, in August, 1734, urges him to take the decision so as to keep the property in the family. Until the next spring Sampson Lloyd did nothing. He then travelled to Mongtomeryshire, and in a letter dated Dolobran, 5 May 1735, after a detailed study of the estate giving a purchase value of £3,360, he sums up: 'As I have business at home to employ both my thoughts, time and stock, and that to pretty good advantage, I think it would be folly in me to buy an estate that would any way engross my time therefrom.'

But six years later he finally felt able to embark upon a country purchase. Owens Farm, of fifty-six acres, with its Tudor farmhouse, was about two miles out of Birmingham. It was situated at Sparkbrook on the borders of the old parishes of Aston and Moseley and, changed though the locality is today, was at that time right in the country as it still was a hundred years later. The price that Sampson Lloyd paid on 29 April 1742 was £1,290.[8] At first he kept the farm as it was, but his planting of the avenue in 1745 shows that he already foresaw the siting of the future house, which was not built for a further five years. When it was, it made an important departure in the history of the family, continuing in Lloyd occupation for 170 years.

On the business front Sampson Lloyd was equally ready to take

10. Severn trows moored near the bridge at Worcester. C. and N. Buck, *South West Prospect of Worcester*, 1730.

11. Bewdley, the port of Birmingham in the eighteenth century; lithograph from a drawing by S. Ireland.

12. The town mill area in 1750; from Samuel Bradford's *Plan of Birmingham*.

13. Slitting rod iron in the time of Sampson Lloyd II; from M. Diderot, *Encyclopédie des Sciences, des Arts et des Métiers*, 1773.

14. Charles Lloyd, 1697–1741 ('Charles Lloyd the mill').

15. The town mill at Birmingham in 1731 from C. and N. Buck, *South West Prospect of Birmingham.*

16. Powick iron works and Nehemiah Lloyd's house; by E. F. Burney, 1784.

17. Powick iron works about 1800; from a survey plan in the Hampton estate papers.

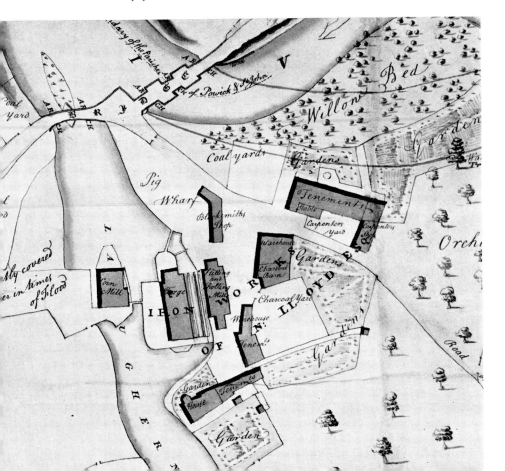

what he judged to be good opportunities. Two of these were concerned not with iron but with other metals that he dealt in, steel and brass. One had been taken during his brother's lifetime, but independently, in 1739. Once again it is to the merchant of Newbury that the information is given, for whom, as well as for the writer, advantage is held out in the letter. Sampson Lloyd announces the construction of a steel furnace near Tetbury, on the Gloucestershire–Wiltshire border, in partnership with John Willetts, possibly a Birmingham steel-maker. The information, however, is tantalising for we hear no more of the enterprise. How two Birmingham men came to engage themselves in a concern at such a distance is not explained. It is clear that Sampson Lloyd did not merely erect the furnace; he had an interest in finding custom for its output, which probably consisted of small iron bars converted partly or wholly into steel by the 'surface-cementation' method, that is to say, the imparting of extra carbon to the wrought-iron, under heat, so that it became 'steeled'. But the location of the works, its fortunes and its future history remain a mystery.

As Tetbury is not many miles from Bristol it may have seemed less remote than might appear. Certainly it was through the Bristol connection that he took an interest in another new enterprise, the Warmley Company. This was a partnership set up at Bristol in 1748 for the production and working of metals such as brass, copper and zinc, in which Sampson Lloyd's own firm dealt. His Bristol links had been strengthened both through his wife's connections and through the goodwill which he had built up himself during twenty years of business life, and the new partnership had something of a family flavour, comprising four names, William Champion who was Rachel Lloyd's brother, her step-uncle Thomas Goldney, her husband Sampson Lloyd and a Liverpool Quaker, Thomas Crosby, who had married into the Bristol Harford family. For Sampson Lloyd had at this time in Bristol not only a Champion father-in-law, three Champion brothers-in-law, and Harford cousins, but also a newly acquired Goldney relationship. His father-in-law at sixty-four had surprised his friends by announcing a second marriage to a woman twenty-seven years younger than himself. Champion's new bride, a widow of thirty-seven, was the sister of the Quaker merchants, Thomas and Gabriel Goldney, who had thus, although only his own age, become Sampson Lloyd's step-uncles.* William Champion was the active partner with the technical knowledge and ambition, an inventive and original figure. Sampson Lloyd and the others were not executive. William Champion is known for his pioneering work for the manufacture of spelter in this country. As early as 1732 Sampson Lloyd had supplied imported spelter to the original Champion firm, the Bristol Brass Wireworks, but the new company was a breakaway. Its works were set up at Warmley, to the east of Bristol, on a small tributary of the Avon. It is not our business to enlarge upon eighteenth-century non-ferrous metals manufacture, but it was recorded in 1761 that the proprietors, still the same four, 'never divided less than 5 p.c. yearly from the beginning of the works about thirteen years since'.[9] These works in fact became one of the largest industrial establishments to be found at this period.

The market for non-ferrous products was profiting at that time from the Seven Years' War, and William Champion was wishful to expand the business. A memorandum addressed by him to the partners, dated 7 July 1761, recommends a scheme for adding to the existing brass works a new copper works, to be financed by accepting additional partners and doubling the capital. The new partners were to include local colliery-owners who would undertake to supply the two works 'with good coal 20 p.c. cheaper than any other works of the like nature', and the capital was to be increased from £50,000 to £100,000.† With a quarter stake in an undertaking of this scale, in addition to his other Bristol interests, it is not surprising that Sampson Lloyd, a proprietor who was also a metal merchant,

---

* Thomas Goldney, like his father, another Thomas Goldney, is frequently met with in Bristol enterprises during the eighteenth century. Among his many interests, he was a proprietor of the Darby ironfounding business at Coalbrookdale in Shropshire and in 1752 was to form Goldney, Smith & Co., one of Bristol's earliest; banks. See booklet, *Goldney, a House and a Family*, by P. K. Stembridge, 1969; A. Raistrick, *Dynasty of Ironfounders*, Longmans, Green, 1953; and C. H. Cave, *A History of Banking in Bristol*, 1899.

† The interest of this paper is in the light that it throws upon the company's assets and upon its distribution arrangements. The assets are presented as: estates or land, £3,103; dead stock, otherwise buildings and plant, £21,807; and quick stock, i.e. stocks at works and distribution points, £30,885; total £55,795. The buildings and plant include twenty-five houses, a spelter works, twenty-two copper furnaces, fifteen brass furnaces, a wire mill, three rolling mills, five water battery mills, a 'fire engine' and a windmill. The value of stocks at distribution points is given as: £7,094 'in our warehouse at Liverpool kept by Mr John Par, our agent there'; £6,324 at London; £478 at Dublin; and £8,558 at Warmley.

should be a regular visitor to that city. But afterwards, as mentioned in another chapter, Champion overreached himself and the company declined into reconstructions and failure. Sampson Lloyd for many years participated in good profits. Eventually he was a victim of the collapse.

In 1746, two years before the formation of the Warmley partnership, Sampson Lloyd took on an important new commitment in the development of the iron business. This was the acquisition of a forge of his own for the making of bar iron, which he required both to sell as a merchant and to use in the Birmingham slitting mill. The forge was about twenty-five miles away, not on any Birmingham stream but upon the Trent at Burton. The idea of taking on a forge in addition to the mill would be naturally present in the mind of a forward-looking ironmonger, for the leading iron men had all the processes in their repertoires, forging, rolling, slitting and, many of them, the smelting of iron ore into pig before that. Probably Sampson and his brother Charles had discussed such a possibility. But to find a forge anywhere near Birmingham, let alone to acquire it, was almost like crying for the moon, while to discover a mill of some other description that might be converted was little easier.[10] Water-power was at a premium, one had to go a long way to look for it, and for a forge there must be charcoal as well. How did it come about that Sampson Lloyd should come by a forge at Burton-upon-Trent?

Birmingham business men knew all about Burton, just as they knew all about Bewdley, for each was the terminus of a great river artery within economic hauling distance of Birmingham. Sampson Lloyd had made the point himself when he remarked in a letter to Kirton that meal and flour found their way to Birmingham through these two centres of transportation. But he was familiar with Burton for another reason; for many years Swedish and Russian iron had been reaching Midland ironmongers from Hull by this route. Burton was likewise a distribution centre for many other goods besides iron, both those arriving upstream, destined for Birmingham and beyond, and those passing downstream, from the town's agricultural hinterland, for the coastwise traffic to London. And Burton was at no impossible distance from Edgbaston Street for a busy business man on horseback.

The Trent when it reaches Burton is already a considerable river, far different from the millstreams of the Birmingham plateau. The local weirs sustained several mills and one of these had been converted, twenty or thirty years before, into a forge 'for the hammering and plating of iron'. But the lessee had become bankrupt and the forge had gone down hill.* So it was that, fortunate once more, Sampson Lloyd acquired the lease, at the going rent of £9 a year, with sixteen years of its term still to run. The condition of the mill, and perhaps his own excitement, can be sensed from an allusion in a letter to Newbury dated 5 April 1746. Excusing himself from an engagement he writes, 'I am absolutely bound to stay at home for about a month to come, having engaged in a forge about twenty miles off which I must put into a going way before I can stir.'[11]

The forge building, which was only pulled down in the 1940s, stood on the left bank of the Trent at the head of the long slanting weir, about half a mile below the town bridge.[12] It was one of a trio of mills. These were, at the lower end of the weir, the corn mill (in a flourishing state to this day though no longer water-operated), 'the most valuable mill in the county', with a fulling mill alongside, and at the upper end the forge, flanked by a lock for the purposes of the river traffic, the stream thus serving four uses simultaneously. These installations were the property of the Paget family of Beaudesert in Staffordshire, the head of which, the Earl of Uxbridge, was the general landlord. Sampson Lloyd's wheels were dependent here not upon a head of water pounded up in a millpond as at Birmingham but upon the volume of the Trent as it approached the weir. This, we are told, was such that 'in the driest summer, water is never wanting to drive the several wheels about, and yet the whole is so contrived by the help of floodgates that the greatest swells of it seldom do much damage'.[13] Thus, in a drought, though the waterway downstream might be short of water for navigation, the water engineers had seen to it that the mills were not. This was a desirable mill to have secured. In this mill Sampson Lloyd would see many advantages: steady power,

---

* Other uses had included the production of thimbles and of gun-barrels. Letter of Wm Wyatt to the Earl of Uxbridge, 27 February 1762, with lease of forge dated 1721. Paget Deeds, D603, unlisted, E472, County Record Office, Staffordshire. For this and much other information on the industrial history of Burton and district the author is indebted to Dr C. C. Owen and to his thesis, 'The Development of Industry in Burton-upon-Trent prior to 1900', 1968, deposited at Sheffield University.

labour at hand, pig iron to be had from Staffordshire and Derbyshire, charcoal in the country around, and coal at nearby workings,
together with local markets, regular carriers and a location at the
crossroads of one of the country's principal trade routes. It was a
prize, as the town mill had been, and must have been considered
so in Birmingham.

Though not previously part of his personal experience, most
of the procedures in the forge would be familiar to a man in the
ironmerchant's business. The finery, the chafery, the bellows and
hammers, would be little different from the kind of equipment we
saw at Mathrafal and at Dolobran. In addition, this mill had rolling
equipment, not the narrow-gauge rolls of a slitting mill, but such
as were used for reducing iron to 'plate', which could then be
appropriate for further cutting and fabricating, some of it to make
hoops for Burton barrels; so that, writing to his master in 1762,
the steward of Lord Uxbridge could declare of this mill that 'the
only business which now is or has been carried on for the last
fifteen years is the making and plating of iron'. All this, once put
into working order, Sampson Lloyd would delegate to a manager,
going often enough to Burton himself to encourage and direct.
The forge was to prove a success. There are some particulars of it
in a later chapter, for it was still in the family down to the time of
Sampson Lloyd's grandson and was only given up when new
methods had made charcoal iron a back number and the Lloyds
were turning to other interests. Sampson Lloyd was to be more
successful on the Trent than his uncle Charles had been on the
Vyrnwy.

From this time on, Sampson Lloyd must have become really
busy. He was blessed with the ability to delegate, for he was a
merchant and would rely upon managers at the mill in Birmingham
as well as at the forge. Ten years earlier he had been able to find
some elbow-room in business life. In the summer of 1737 he had
recommended Kirton to take 'some weeks abstracted from business',
explaining that 'it is what I sometimes do myself, and often find
a recess no great hindrance before the year revolves, for a little
relaxation invigorates the faculties more than people of business
are aware of'.[14] He had also been a good correspondent in those
days, but now the letters dry up. It may be that what he wrote did
not survive, though Olive Kirton did preserve a few of his letters.

But during the ten years from 1746 to 1756, there are only four from Sampson Lloyd and those are mainly to give reasons why he cannot visit Newbury or abstract himself from business as before. There is, in fact, an unwelcome gap, and partly as a result of this some events cannot even be dated. Several more children were born during this time, completing the family, Nehemiah in 1746, Charles 1748, John 1751 and Ambrose 1754, but we have none of the engaging particulars of their childhood or their childish complaints that we had for the earlier children, nor of how their mother did. Of the wider family there is only the slenderest news, little of the Kirtons, and almost nothing upon the events or incidents of business or daily life. We have therefore to make our way, partly in blinkers, into a span of years which includes the building of 'Farm', the emergence of the younger Sampson, and the death of Rachel Lloyd.

To the general want of information there is one dazzling exception. For a few days in the summer of 1755 the curtain is lifted upon the Birmingham scene through the journal of two visitors from London who arrive in the town to stay with the Pembertons at Bennetts Hill.[15] During this visit the days are passed mainly in the company of Lloyds and Pembertons, Thomas Kirton also chances to be staying in Birmingham, and we get glimpses of the homes and properties of the two families as well as of local 'manufactories' and of the town iself. The programme of the visitors is divided between the sights of Birmingham and a day in the country 'accompanied by our friends', and concludes with an excursion to see Coventry and Warwick Castle. The factories visited, each one of interest for this history, are an iron furnace near the town 'where the iron ore is smelted and run into pigs', the Lloyds' slitting mill 'to prepare iron for making nails', and 'the manufactory of Mr Taylor, the most considerable maker of gilt-metal buttons and enamelled snuff boxes', the accounts of which are quoted on later pages. The description of the town, written down by no unintelligent observer, belongs to the first day after the arrival of the visitors on the Saturday evening:

The next morning we employed like good Christians; and after dining with our kind host, reconnoitred the town, which is another London in miniature. It stands on the side of a hill, forming nearly a half-moon; the lower part is filled with the workshops and warehouses of the manufacturers, and consists chiefly of old buildings; the upper part of the town, like St James's, contains a number of new, regular streets, and a handsome square, all well built and well inhabited, besides two chapels, and meeting houses for every denomination of protestant dissenters. There are two churches; one in the lower part of the town, an old building, which has a very tall spire; the other is a very grand modern built church, having a square stone tower with a cupola and a turret above it.

But some of the social and domestic touches are also worth reproducing. The note on the Pembertons' house, if taken with the layout of the property in the 1750 *Plan of Birmingham* and the views of the house with its commanding position in the *South-west Prospect* of 1731 and in Samuel Lines's oil painting (Plate 9) has a remarkable guide-book quality. The account is of particular interest in describing what had been, over the preceding sixty years, the home successively of John and Elizabeth Pemberton, Richard and Sarah Parkes and, more recently, of Thomas and Jane Pemberton, although this Pemberton, the visitors' host, was now a widower. Written at Warwick on the Thursday evening, 31 July 1755, the report discloses the elegance of the Pemberton way of life. The initials used are not difficult to interpret:

I ended my last with an account of our being got to Birmingham on Saturday last; where, after the usual salutations and enquiries, and a dish of tea, which set my companion's head quite to rights, we walked in Mr P—'s garden. This consists of two parts, a handsome flower-garden about half an acre, square and walled in; neatly laid out, and as neatly kept. On the left-hand stands a convenient summer-house, opposite to which is a gate opening to a long grass-walk, having a row of fan elms on each side, with borders of various kinds of plants and flowering shrubs; this walk parts the fruit and kitchen garden; at the end is another walk on the left-hand, with rows of tall fir-trees, etc. The house stands on the highest ground of the town, over which the garden commands a good view of the country on that side for some miles. Being destined to abide here, we spent the evening with Mr P. and his son, Mr S. L. jun, Mr T. K. of Newbury, and another gentleman, who was till then a stranger to us, but of that agreeable sort with whom one soon grows acquainted. Our supper was elegant, our wine good, and the evening was spent very cheerfully.

On the Monday it is the turn of the Lloyds to entertain the visitors, who dine and, after a promenade to another part of the town, spend the evening at their house. And on the Wednesday, their last day, they dine at Edgbaston Street (dinner is probably at 2 o'clock and they take their dish of tea about 6.00), walk to Sampson Lloyd's estate at Bordesley, and finish up with a party at the Castle Club.

We dined at Mr L—d's. In the afternoon we walked to his country seat, (about two miles from the town) which he calls his Farm; it consists of a large genteel house and gardens, stables and outhouses, which are mostly new buildings, very neat and convenient; before the front of the house is a long spacious lawn, planted on each side with rows of elms, leading to the road; the dairy and other branches relating to the farm lay at some distance from the house, which renders it more cleanly and agreeable. After drinking tea, we returned, and spent the evening at the Castle Club over a half-pint and cheat. The company was pretty large and very cheerful; my companion in particular became extremely joyous. But I am afraid we Londoners rather encroached too much on the good-nature of our Birmingham friends; for cheat after cheat so disordered their economy and destroyed their scheme of frugality that in the end neither the landlord or his drawers, or any of the company, could count the reckoning: so that we either cheated him or ourselves at last.

This is much the earliest eyewitness report of any visit to Farm. It shows that the house had been completed before 1755 (the elm avenue would be now ten years old) but the reference to a 'large genteel house *and gardens*' suggests a date already several years past, otherwise there would hardly be genteel gardens for the visitors to see but more probably the desolation of builders, or at any rate grounds bare and newly laid out. This points to the house having been completed quite early in the 1750s.*

It was during these earlier 1750s that Sampson Lloyd had taken the step of relinquishing the whole of his Parkes interests at Wednesbury in favour of his son, the sociable young man of the 'R.P.' visit. Sampson Lloyd was fifty-four at the time and his son was twenty-five. Let us see what had been happening among the Heirs of Richard Parkes during the time since young Sampson's mother had died, and then consider what thoughts may have led his father to such a decision.

The Heirs of Parkes at this stage, twenty-five years after the will, were either the sons, sons-in-law or widowers of the four sisters, three of whom had died quite soon after marriage while Jane, the

* A pamphlet of 1912 by Samuel Lloyd of Farm states that the house was completed in 1750. The date of 1758 given in R. J. Lowe, *Farm and its Inhabitants* (privately printed), 1883, p. 30, would not appear to be justified. For a view of Farm as it was a hundred years later see Plate 30.

wife of Thomas Pemberton at Bennetts Hill, had died in 1750. Thus the present successors were: for Mary Wilkinson's fourth share, her sons Joseph and Richard who were young men in London: for Elizabeth Scandrett's share, her son-in-law Edward Harford at Bristol who had married her daughter Sally Scandrett in 1747: and for Sarah Lloyd's and Jane Pemberton's, their widowed husbands, Sampson Lloyd and Thomas Pemberton. The members of the syndicate taking charge of day-to-day Wednesbury matters were the Birmingham cousins, Pemberton and Lloyd, whose two names often appear in the documents during the 1730s and 1740s, Pemberton being the more executive of the two. The partners had been progressive in installing more than one 'fire-engine', of contemporary type,* by means of which they would achieve a limited control of water in their coal workings, especially if not required to be pumped up many feet. The deeds and records show them, as proprietors, facing the responsibility to compensate when coal-getting interfered with a tenant's husbandry.

Among the more picturesque and unscrupulous of the local mining worthies we meet with two named Burslem Sparrow and Thomas Tomkys, whose relations with surface owners seem to have been chronically awkward, and whose reputation was that they would sign anything and do the least. In 1735 there had been a rumpus of this sort when a surface tenant had gone for Sparrow and Tomkys on the grounds that by their coal-getting operations, which in those days were more or less of a surface affair, they had made 'great waste, spoil and destruction', plucking up fences and laying waste a surface area of eleven acres. Sparrow and Tomkys, as mining tenants, were perfectly within their rights in getting the coal but they were neglecting their obligation to compensate, and a comprehensive operation of restitution was imposed. And because the Heirs of Parkes as superior landlords were party to the granting of the surface rights Pemberton and Lloyd are found as signatories to the deed requiring Sparrow and Tomkys to make good. Cases of this kind occur all through the piece, and it is hard to see, under the terms of the will, how it could have been otherwise. But Sparrow and Tomkys were a thorn in the flesh. They were known to be so

---

* Such engines would be not much advanced at this date upon John Fidoe's 'Savory-Newcomen' type of the 1720s. The innovations of James Watt were still in the future.

as far away as Harford circles in Bristol.[16] They had likewise neglected their obligations in a case affecting John Fidoe's representatives, the trustees of his daughter and heiress, Elizabeth Fidoe, one of whose tasks on reaching her majority in 1742 had been to exact new agreements from Sparrow and Tomkys for carrying out unfulfilled obligations. This is of interest to us because her Wednesbury property later passed largely to the Lloyds and was merged with the Parkes inheritance. From his share in this inheritance, as the old paper tells us, Sampson Lloyd had enjoyed 'during the minority of his son' a considerable income. It was at the price of complications such as these that he had enjoyed it.

The transfer to Sampson III, for so we must think of him, was by means of a formal assignment dated 20 September 1753. What is transferred amounts to one fourth part of the rights in the Parkes properties. Some of the plant or installations are examples of early engineering: 'the engine houses, reckoning house and smith's shop', and again 'the three fire engines' now used 'in and about the getting of the said mines'. The considerations which the lawyers set out as motivating the transaction are of interest. First there is the token sum of ten shillings, which the father duly acknowledges, but we also learn that the transfer is made 'in consideration of the natural love and affection which the said Sampson Lloyd the Elder hath for his said son Sampson Lloyd the Younger and for the advancement of his fortune and making some provision for his present subsistence'. There was no obligation upon Sampson Lloyd to hand over what was an ordinary life interest. The transfer was an act of his own choosing.

Sampson Lloyd himself was no longer a young man at the time of the transaction; he was well into his fifties, he was successful in his affairs and he could afford to forego the income. He was at the same time under pressure at business, he was without a partner, and there had been signs that his energies were not inexhaustible,* so that it may have suited him to be relieved of the Wednesbury commitments. Further, his relationships with the younger Sampson

* He had had occasion two years before to cancel a visit to the Kirtons on that account; he writes from London, 'I fully intended Berkshire in my way home but the extreme heat of the weather here for some days past affects me much and sends me out of this city sooner than intended, as it also disconcerts the measures I had taken, and obliges me to proceed homewards directly by slow and easy marches in the cool part of the day.' Lloyd MSS 2/85 (1751).

are different from those with the other children. This eldest son is half a Parkes, the only one in the family. It cannot be doubted that, in all the circumstances, the father would wish to see him graduate respectably as the eldest, take his place in the circle, and grow to the business. It would do no harm to place responsibility and an income in his hands and give him something to manage; he could understudy his uncle Pemberton and consult his father as well. He was being given what a later pen described as 'an independent and honourable position'.

It is also likely that Sampson Lloyd was looking in a special way to the effect of more responsibility upon the development of this son. Where the young man had been apprenticed is not known – to his father perhaps – nor how he was shaping at business or worked in with father. It is the tradition in the family that he was 'remarkably handsome with a fine tall figure' and, in these early years, gay and worldly beyond the Quaker mean; and we are told that, though a leader among Quakers in after years, he was at this time given to field sports, dressed in the mode, 'visited in high society and became at last a companion of Lords and Ladies', and that he was 'a correspondent on familiar terms with some of the most fashionable of the grandees of his day.[17] Another story told of him is that when a young man, staying out late at night, his father was accustomed to wait up for him. On one occasion, coming in later than usual, the son remarked 'I think, father, thou must be tired of waiting for me'; to which his father replied, 'I am glad thou art beginning to think.'

At some stage after the handover of 1753, and not before the visit of 'R.P.' and his companion in 1755, the younger Sampson changed his ways. The change was both abrupt and noticeable and there are several versions of how it came about. It is said, for instance, that the remark of his father's just related left an impression upon his mind; that he was struck by a text uttered by a poor Friend which inspired him to new resolutions; that an address at a Quaker meeting 'which he used occasionally to attend', touched him deeply: that he was moved by the religious experience of a beautiful woman. And the story goes, told by his son many years later, that his resolution, once taken, was so sudden and drastic in its effect that he 'determined all at once to give up the world'; that he invited all his gay companions to dinner (at the Bull's Head at Meriden, 'a central point of their hunting meets') and frankly told them of the change; that he 'at once ordered his tailor to make him a sober suit of Quaker apparel'; and, final touch, that 'when the tailor came and laid the clothes down on the chair he felt as if they had brought him his coffin'.[18]

The beautiful woman we cannot pass over. She is linked both with this Sampson and with the prosperity of his line, and she makes much the best story. She was his second cousin Elizabeth Fidoe, whom we first met as an infant in the 1720s, her mother a Pemberton, her grandmother a daughter of Dolobran, and she was the present owner of her father's Wednesbury estates. In a book of autobiography, founded upon recollections no doubt, if, to our taste, somewhat glamorised, written by a friend of the family a hundred years later,* a reconstruction of the affair may be read, the writer declaring that she had heard it in his venerable age from Sampson himself. In it the writer tells of Elizabeth's popularity and wit; of Sampson and his aspiring passion: of her prostrating illness, 'for a time an inmate of an asylum', and her gradual convalescence; and of how, 'though several years older than myself', he had at length gone in compassion and honour to offer her his hand. We then read that 'she cordially and gratefully thanked me', but 'she had passed as it were through a bitter death since I had seen her'; 'the elegant taste of her dress was exchanged for the delicacy of Christian simplicity'; she had found the peace of God all-sufficient and would not exchange it for anything this earth could give; 'I entered the room admiring a woman, I departed from it in deep communion with an angelic spirit'; and we learn that the impression of that hour was the turning-point of his life. Whatever credence is placed upon this moving report, it sustains the tradition that Sampson had diverged from parental ways and had been breaking out, and he now comes back into the fold.

---

* The writer was Mary Ann Schimmelpenninck, an authoress of the romantic period, 'vividly imaginative and impressionable', a daughter of the prominent Quaker family of Galton at Birmingham and the wife of a Dr Lambert Schimmelpenninck. Her recollections were dictated in the 1850s when she was rising eighty; see C. C. Hankin, *Life of Mary Ann Schimmelpenninck*, Longman, Brown, Green, Longmans & Roberts, London, 1858. The drama of Elizabeth Fidoe, if it can be dated at all, should probably be placed in about 1756. That the story should ever have been related of the father, Sampson Lloyd II, as in Lowe, op. cit., is evidently a mistake.

Already, in 1755, we find him involved in a Wednesbury compensation claim, nothing to do with Tomkys or Sparrow, but one directed against his own newly acquired interest, the syndicate itself. He is discovered in London, with lawyer's papers and his uncle's directions, calling upon Lord Ward on behalf of the Heirs of Parkes and reporting to Birmingham by post.[19] The syndicate had been mining coal, evidently for a number of years, under surface land owned by his lordship who now required a reckoning. The conduct of the affair is genteel, the damage considerable. One pictures the old lord and the young mine-owner. 'I went to Lord Ward's who received me in a very friendly manner'; 'he did not seem at all inclinable to cavil when I mentioned our opinion that between £400 and £500 would make him ample reparation.' At the next interview, ten days later, after some talk of 'reference', i.e. arbitration, the terms are stiffened up, but the other side still temporised. It is clear that they went on temporising, for the parties continued in difference for more than two years longer until Lord Ward died, at which stage arbitrators were appointed and the new peer gave the Heirs of Parkes his bond for £2,000 to abide by the award which, in the event, was pitched at £400.[20]

At Birmingham, apart from family and business, the elder Sampson Lloyd was now a responsible person among Friends. For ten years past his name had been appearing with regularity in their business records, as it was to do for another twenty to come. Acknowledged an Elder in 1752, he is recorded as representing the Birmingham meeting in the regional affairs of the Society, at the monthly meeting for North Warwickshire and at the quarterly meeting for Warwickshire, Leicestershire and Rutland, signing certificates, serving as a trustee for property and figuring in the raising of funds for current needs;[21] and no doubt he and his growing family – seven in number now – would fill up a bench or two at Bull Street on 'first day' mornings. He was also often away, as in the past, at Bristol, at London, and of course, more locally, at Burton. Visits to Newbury are rather the exception than the rule. But in 1756 Bristol was to claim his time in an unexpected way. The infant Ambrose, carrying on the Stourbridge name, had arrived in 1754, but now Rachel's health began to cause anxiety. As in the generation before, the waters of the little spa at Hotwells, or 'the Hotwells', in the Avon Gorge, 'where they have good apartments for entertaining diseased persons', were the great resource of these Birmingham families, and to a girl brought up in Bristol more than most, and there in the summer of 1756 Rachel Lloyd spent several months. The water, which averaged 78° Fahrenheit or about the temperature of milk – not very hot – was regarded for many years as a treatment for diabetes and later also for consumption. Through most of the eighteenth century, patients and other visitors were attracted there, a pumproom and lodging houses appeared, and a fashionable régime developed, spreading to Clifton on the higher ground above, so much so that some of its patrons attended as much for the company as for the cure, and Lloyds, Pembertons and Fidoes are heard of at the Hotwells right on to the turn of the century (Plate 23). Rachel's illness is hinted at in June when her husband travels urgently to Bristol from London. Olive visits the patient in July, Kirton in August. In September Sampson Lloyd writes to him from Hotwells that 'she continues in a very weak way, more so than when thou wast here; I shall rejoice to see her get better'. Rachel did not get better. In the notebook of Sampson Lloyd is the following entry:

My very dear wife Rachel died 16, 9 mo, 1756. She was visited with a long weakness which ended in a decay. She went down for the benefit of the Hotwells but received none. After an absence of seventeen weeks she returned to Birmingham, 13. 9 mo, 1756. She lived but three days after her return. She was buried in the old graveyard, Birmingham,

and he inserts her age, according to his private habit, '44.3.6'.

Sampson Lloyd was a widower for the second time. The business had grown out of recognition but there was an heir-apparent now, soon to be made a partner, and the story of the next fifteen years is that of father and son in combination. At home, three of the family were still under the age of eight, the youngest two years old. But a fresh upheaval in the family provided the solution, for in 1757 not only was Molly married, to a Hanbury, near London, but there followed the deaths of Thomas Pemberton and of Thomas Kirton also. Upon this event the childless Olive gave up the Berkshire house and, just as she had accompanied her brother home after his marriage, so now she came to keep house for him as a widower and look after the children.

So at Edgbaston Street he carries on. But, while contemporaries

might slip away, the figure to outlive so many of her breed is his
mother. Mary Lloyd is eighty. She is still there. 'Mother gets on in
years and frosty weather affects her asthmatic complaint,' he had
written in 1755. It was at about this time that she too joined the
Edgbaston Street household. Sampson Lloyd never moved to Farm,
though in his later years he spent 'much of his time at his house
and estate at the Farm which he took much pleasure in cultivating'.
But Edgbaston Street suited him as a widower, and Edgbaston
Street was commodious. Besides the elders there were still five
children in the family, Rachel fourteen, Nehemiah twelve, Charles
nine, John seven, and Ambrose two. For Olive it was a situation
demanding skills she had not required before, but she was not in
charge of all of them all the time. Sampson Lloyd sent the boys to
school at 'Friend Goodere's', at Worcester. The third one, John,
was young to be a boarder. Perhaps subconsciously it proved a
balancer to the upheavals at home.

This time of domestic change and readjustment coincided, in
national affairs, with events which offered new and compelling
opportunities for iron-businesses. Rachel Lloyd's death had taken
place just as the Seven Years' War began. The turmoils and rivalries
in India and North America could be settled only by arms, and that
involved European countries as well. As England went to war
under its new leader, William Pitt, the sources of Baltic bar iron
became closed, supplies from the American colonies were not
enough to replace them and the price of English iron moved up
substantially.[22] Thus, from about 1756 to 1763 the war brought
large profits to ironmongers and Sampson Lloyd and Son, as they
now began to style themselves,* were able to sell all they could
make. It is no doubt largely for these reasons that we find them, in
these years, adding pig to their other products through the acquisition of a furnace in Derbyshire, advancing their manufacture of bar
iron again, this time to the Severn, and taking part in a transport
monopoly on the Trent. Though he might not see it so, the bereaved
husband was now to release his powers in meeting this war-time
challenge and turning it to advantage. His wife was departed, the

* An early reference to the change of style is met with in the sales records of the
Knight Ironworks in 1757 (Kidderminster Public Library).

children young, Olive would see to the home, and he could turn his mind, with his son, to a fresh round of business expansion.

Iron prices had advanced almost as soon as the war began. Everybody in the industry was busy. The demand for rod at Birmingham and for bar and strip at Burton continued to rise, the merchant's side of the business was buoyant, and Sampson Lloyd's mind must have constantly dwelt upon how to achieve more manufacturing capacity and the profit that this would bring. A second forge would not be out of court on the present outlook, nor would another slitting mill, if he could find the water for either; and for that matter he was paying a rising profit to others on pig for conversion at Burton, which could be saved if only he had a furnace of his own. Before the war ended in 1763, somehow, against the wits and competitions of other determined men, all these things come the way of Sampson Lloyd. He must have enjoyed an exceptional private intelligence system to continue, as he did, both hearing of opportunities and being in the right place at the right time to seize them ahead of others.

The achievement of their own iron-furnace was a milestone in the firm's history. A slitting mill, forges, *'and an iron furnace at Melbourne near Derby'* were the installations attributed to Sampson Lloyd in the old paper. He would now have all three processes at his disposal. At Michaelmas 1758, a lease of the furnace was obtained from Francis Hastings, Earl of Huntingdon.[23] Probably Sampson Lloyd heard of this chance through his Burton connections, for the Melbourne estate, at that time Huntingdon property, is only about ten miles down the Trent Valley from that place. The furnace was one of several old Derbyshire furnaces, 'heated by charcoal of wood and blown by means of a water wheel', which were sited not far from the Trent and had long been used for smelting ores procured in the Ashby-de-la-Zouch coalfield.* It stood in the fields of Melbourne Common, upon quite a small stream, the New Brook, which nevertheless sustained an imposing millpool, as may be seen from the survey plan of an earlier earl, dated 1735,[24] and gave sufficient fall for a 17-foot wheel. Here the Lloyds had suitable resources on all sides: ironstone from Ashby, charcoal from Charnwood Forest, limestone on their doorstep at Breedon-on-the-Hill,

* Others were nearby at Foremark and at Hartshorn. John Farey, *General View of the Agriculture and Minerals of Derbyshire*, 1815, vol. I, pp. 395, 401.

a short haul for their pig to the waterway at Kings Mills and a convenient one to Burton, by land, whether for processing at the forges* or for the requirements of other consumers. To gain an impression of smelting procedure at such a furnace, which can have been little different from that carried on at Bersham in Kelsall's time, we have only to turn again to the description by 'R.P.', three years before, of a furnace visited near Birmingham on the fourth day of their stay:

Next day we went to see an iron furnace at a small distance from Birmingham, where the iron ore is smelted and run into pigs. The furnace is built like a lime-kiln, and kept continually burning. The ironstone or ore being mixed with a quantity of charcoal is put in at the top, when, falling on other parts of the same kind already burning, the charcoal catches the fire and as it burns sinks lower in the furnace with the ore; as it descends, the fire burns fiercer, being continually blown by two pair of monstrous bellows. These, moving alternately by means of a water-wheel, throw in a continued stream of air, which increasing the fire in the charcoal, and the ironstone being mixed with it, it melts away into a proper receiver, and the dross runs from it in streams of liquid fire. When a sufficient quantity is thus fluxed the metal is let out into a wide frame in the ground, filled with sand, which is hollowed into trenches of the shape of the pigs of iron, and many pigs are cast together joining to a long middle-piece called the sow.†

More than two hundred years later Melbourne furnace was excavated. Charcoal iron had long ceased to be made, the mill had been abandoned and the site re-adapted to cultivation; but its memory survived, as happens in the country, in the name of 'Furnace Farm' just along the stream. Photographs taken on the excavated site well illustrate 'R.P.'s' description, including the kiln-like furnace structure which was found substantially undamaged. The archaeologists of this dig are thus the only men of the present day to have set foot inside a charcoal ironworks operated by the Lloyds. The sites and, it may be, the foundations of most of the others can still be visited and identified but the furnace at Melbourne no one will see again. The Furnace Farm area was submerged

* Besides the Lloyds' forge at Burton, another had been started there in 1755 by the Thornewills, a leading firm in the town, who would likewise require suitable pig.
† See Note 19 to Chapter 4.

in 1963 upon the creation of the Staunton Harold Reservoir.*

The furnace at Melbourne was not the only prize that came into Sampson Lloyd's hands at about this time. When the chance came, he took on a second forge. This further works was as far to the south-west of Birmingham as Burton was to the north-east, a distance of about twenty-seven miles. Sampson Lloyd might have wished it nearer but a mill had to be taken where it offered. This one was located near Powick, about three miles to the south of Worcester. Here the Teme, flowing down from Ludlow and the Welsh hills to join the river Severn, is crossed by the Worcester–Powick road, and at this point, just above the medieval bridge, stood the forge.[25]

Just as Burton was placed upon one great river route, the Trent, so Powick was close to another, the Severn, connected to it by a short stretch of the Teme from the Severn to Powick bridge (map page 103). Road transport still being little improved, a forge on the middle Severn was not inconveniently placed. From the port of Bristol or the Forest of Dean, and alike from the furnaces of Shropshire and beyond, the pig iron would be 'brought to the forge door',† coal would come down from Staffordshire through Bewdley, and the river would carry the output, the bar iron, to the West Midland merchants and slitters, all at waterborne rates. Charcoal would be no problem, for at that distance from the Stour valley there would be no competition. Powick forge was thus not so far from Birmingham as it looked and should be an economic proposition. In fact it was carried on by the family until after the end of the century.

The regulation of the water must have taxed the Lloyds' experi-

* The furnace site was excavated about 1960 by Mr W. H. Bailey of the Sheffield Trades Historical Society, and was photographed by Mr John Shields of Breedon, to both of whom the author is indebted for their assistance. Mr Bailey gives the following particulars: 'The furnace is a blast furnace of the rectangular stone construction which was usual in its day, and the bellows were driven by a pitch-back water wheel. A portion of the rim of the wheel and the floats remains and from this, and the stone breast of the wheel pit, the diameter and width of the complete wheel are known to be 17′ 0″ and 22″ respectively. We have samples of the ore used and cast iron made. The furnace stack is 26′ 0″ square and was probably about 20′ 0″ high. It was demolished to the present height of about 8′ 0″ before the site was covered over with soil and restored to agriculture.' See Appendix II.

† Advertisement in the *Weekly Worcester Journal*, 27 February 1736, when this forge had been in the market to be let or sold.

ence of mill-management for the vagaries of the Teme are as
interesting as the history of the site. The Teme was a rapid and
variable river, the subject of unpredictable spates due to Welsh
rains in its upper catchment region and capable of rising many feet
in a few hours. It could easily rise from the level illustrated in
Plate 16 to the doorsteps of the houses above, and does so to the
present day. The site had been used for milling, originally corn-
milling, from time out of mind. But to appreciate the water situation
it has to be understood that two streams meet at Powick bridge, a
greater and a less, the Teme and its tributary the Laughern brook.
These streams, forming a kind of 'v', were in early times independent of each other, and it was upon the Laughern brook, not the
Teme, that a corn mill had been built. The Laughern brook,
flowing down from the west side of Worcester, was by nature a
gentle stream, immune from the caprices of the Teme, unalarming
in times of flood, short of water in the summer. But in the fifteenth
century a great landlord, the Prior of Great Malvern, who controlled the manors on both sides and wished to improve the pro-
ductivity of the corn mill, had joined these two waters.[26] From
that time on the mill enjoyed a power-supply more copious than
before but much more temperamental. This was the supply which
also served the Lloyds at the forge. For there were now two mills,
one on either side of the water: the corn mill on the north side,
ancient, the forge on the south, modern, unrelated commercially
but using the same water. They were thus allies in time of flood but
rivals in drought, for even the turbulent Teme could fall low in dry
seasons, and, right into the nineteenth century, the corn mill was
in covenant with the ironworks to employ only one wheel when the
water fell below an agreed level.[27]

It was to share in this power supply that the forge, with its
'new-built houses' for the workmen, had been put up, though of
comparatively late years as mills go. In the contemporary lists of
ironworks, which we have noticed before, Powick forge does not
figure under 1717 but it appears in the 1736 list.[28] It had presumably
therefore been erected in the 1720s or early 1730s and was still
being described as 'new erected' in the later part of the century.[29]
But there is no lease, and research has not yielded the name of the
builder or of the landlord, nor is it known, except by inference,
when Sampson Lloyd took it. This cannot have been until after

about 1758 or 1759, when documents show the forge to have been in other hands,* but the post-war slump in the iron trade which began in 1763 would probably deter a man of business from new ventures in that industry even if the opportunity offered. From 1764, moreover, Sampson Lloyd was occupied in setting up a banking enterprise; yet it is to Sampson Lloyd and not to his son that the forge is attributed in the records. From these considerations it seems reasonable, first, to place Powick during the Seven Years' War, and, for want of more evidence, to assign it to the early 1760s. The price of iron had risen again in 1759. There would at least have been an incentive for plunging.

The skill that Sampson Lloyd needed at Powick would above all be in the selection and managing of his managers. He was not a production man as brother Charles had been, he was a merchant. But he was also a boss, and he was now running four works through managers with success. At Powick he would require a man equal to both works and water problems, but one who was also capable of taking on more. For soon a new installation was added, alongside the forge, upon the same water. This was a rolling and slitting mill.[30] The Powick manager would now have two mills to answer for and three processes, while Sampson Lloyd's own total, leaving aside the steel furnace (if still working) and the Warmley brassworks, would be a furnace at Melbourne, a forge and rolling mill at Burton, a forge and a rolling and slitting mill at Powick, and a second rolling and slitting mill at Birmingham.

The year 1759, 'the year of victories', was not only the occasion of a further rise in prices and the middle point of the War; it was the year of Sampson Lloyd's sixtieth birthday. At Birmingham, in the monthly meeting of the Society he had become one of the most senior of the elders. Upon the certificates which the meeting would issue when a member was removing to another town or intending a religious visit to Friends in other parts, his signature was now placed first.[31] Among his services to the North Warwickshire quarterly meeting is an application to London for advice upon the

* 'Late in the tenure of . . . Thomas Maybury afterwards of Mary Croft widow afterwards of the said Sampson Lloyd . . .'; Conveyance, BA385/77. 'Mr Maybury of the forge' only died on 25 September 1758; Powick parish registers. Both references are at County Record Office, Worcestershire. Compare Abstract of Title to this mill at Central Electricity Generating Board, Moseley, Birmingham, which, however, does not afford the missing information.

uncomfortable situation of Friends not illuminating on rejoicing nights. Plassey was followed in 1759 by more successes than in any year in the history of British arms, and events such as those at Quebec, Minden and Quiberon Bay were marked by the wildest rejoicings. The war spirit was dominant. But Quakers did not bear arms, illuminate their houses or take part in fireworks and bell-ringing, and they suffered, as Sampson Lloyd's letter expressed it, 'from the insults and abuses of the populace on what is called a thanksgiving day'. In a riot at Birmingham, on a day appointed to celebrate the taking of Canada from the French, one Quaker residence had 115 squares of glass broken.[32] In reply to his request, London sent down 'an account of Friends' proceedings in this city on a like occasion'. But if Sampson Lloyd was sixty he still took some of his longer journeys on horseback as he had advised his mother to do twenty years before. A letter reporting arrival at his uncle Goldney's house at Clifton, where he was attending a Quaker funeral, shows the extent to which road conditions still made news, as well as recalling some of the stopping-places on the Bristol road:

I found the road to Upton very good; from that place to Gloucester tolerable except part of the Lawn which was extremely bad; hardly passable from Gloucester to Newport, worse than ever I knew it; and from Newport here the best I ever rode it.[33]

Sampson Lloyd's road was the present-day A38, except that in those days the route did not pass through Tewkesbury to Gloucester but through Upton-on-Severn and, from there, on the west side of the river. 'The Lawn' was a stretch on this section near the present village of Corse. The Newport mentioned is about half way between Gloucester and Bristol, less well known than some of its namesakes but at that time a regular stage on this journey.

On 11 November 1762 the younger Sampson Lloyd at length married. The ceremony took place at the Devonshire House meeting in Bishopsgate Without. Writing home to Birmingham that evening his father reports, 'we had a very comfortable and satisfactory meeting this morning at my dear son's marriage, which is a good omen'.[34] The bride was another Rachel, a daughter of Samuel Barnes 'of Clapton in the parish of Hackney, an eminent silk-dyer who held high standing among Friends as a member of the Society and frequented Gracechurch Street meeting'.[35] When

Samuel Barnes made his will twenty years later he had at least formed a good opinion of his daughter's new family, appointing three Lloyds as either executors or trustees and using the services of one of them as a banker. The house which the couple presently took, and in which they were to spend their first twelve years, until 1774,[36] was at No. 18 Park Street. We know little about the young wife personally except one fact: at the time of her marriage she was sixteen years old. The bridegroom was thirty-four.

In the same year as the marriage, two developments in the family's affairs at Burton were in progress. By the first, their tenure of the iron forge was consolidated, the lease having expired, through a new lease granted by Lord Uxbridge to the Lloyds direct. By the second, they found themselves partners in a new group, holding, as the Earl's lessees, the transport rights over a twenty-mile section of the Trent below the town. Both leases exist and so does some of the correspondence between the Earl and his confidential agent, the steward of the manor of Burton. This was William Wyatt, a local timber merchant, who figures as the Earl's eyes and ears, reporting what goes on, overseeing existing tenants and negotiating with new ones. Knowing that the lease of the forge would be falling in, the Lloyds had taken the initiative the year before, applying for a new lease and drawing attention to the money they had spent upon improvements. They had no wish to give it up. Trade was good, the forge had proved 'advantageous' and they now had the convenience of their own pig supplies from the furnace at Melbourne.

After due negotiations the new lease was secured at the old rent of £9 a year, plus a premium of £450, a slight improvement upon Wyatt's figure of £500, which Mr Lloyd had 'startled at'.[37] The lease, bearing date 23 May 1762, was for a term of ninety-nine years or three lives 'if any of them should so long happen to live'. The three persons named were Sampson himself, thirty-four, his sister Rachel, nineteen, and his brother Nehemiah, sixteen. This tenancy continued in force to the third death and beyond, which was his own in 1807, by which time new arrangements had been negotiated.

The special interest of the lease is in its references to the several water-users about the weir and their conflicting water requirements. Three of them were mills, as we saw, the corn mill, the fulling mill and the ironworks, and the fourth was the lock, 'standing and being in the said forge yard for the use and service of the Navigation'. Besides abstaining from fulling and corn-grinding and from converting their mill to these uses, the Lloyds were required to refrain from releasing water from their gates or sluices 'for helping or assisting any boat or boats over the scours shoals or shallows below the said lock'. These words focus vividly the physical hindrances which the lessees of the waterway had to live with, that is, shallows in time of drought, and likewise the techniques employed for countering them. The remedy, the releasing of 'flushes' or 'flashes' from a lock or mill-gate to float a grounded boat somewhere downstream, was a carefully regulated right. The navigation operators could do something to help themselves by releasing a flush from their lock, but they could improve upon this if they controlled one of the mills at the weir as well. In fact, in this case, they had control of the corn mill. Here they could release water for their boats but must respect the needs of their neighbours, a duty with which interest sometimes conflicted.

The various installations of the Lloyds present an interesting assortment of water-control situations. At Melbourne, although the stream served mills above and below, the high dam assured so good a head of water that, with care, no special problem need be expected. At Birmingham the mill was on an unimpeded leat with its own dam and millpool, and the regulation of the water was uncomplicated; here the principal obligation was to avoid unduly deranging the flow of the tailrace which affected the power for the mill below and the condition of a public ford between. At Powick there was a double problem, that of acting with the corn mill to combat the excesses of the Teme but of partitioning the water in time of drought. But the situation at Burton was the most intricate, for here the dilemma was to reconcile the interests of four competing users, where some required the level conserved 'to drive their wheels about' while others wished the water drawn off in order to float their boats. At Burton, however, these were not new problems for those at the forge, who for sixteen years had been accustomed to making it work. The Lloyds knew the other water-users as close neighbours, indeed the lock, which though derelict may still be seen, was practically in their own back yard. But the Lloyds did not know, when renewing the lease of the forge, that in less than a year they would be parties to a lease of that very lock and of the Navigation itself.

The river lease had lately expired and Wyatt's business was to make fresh arrangements for the Earl to approve. The monopoly was secured, not without competition, by a new group consisting of three local personalities, a Birmingham business man and Wyatt. Which of them took the lead must be a matter for conjecture. It is unlikely to have been the ironmonger at Birmingham. Based twenty-five miles away, Sampson Lloyd does not look like the leading spirit, and moreover, a Quaker may still have been an oddity to some of the Burton men. Wyatt, as a timber merchant, would have an interest in the good management of the waterway, but as steward of the manor he could hardly negotiate with himself. The two cheesefactors, Robert Palmer and Joseph Wilkes, would take a business interest in the facilities of the Boat Company, as it was called, for cheese from the upper Trent, by way of Hull for London, was one of the principal cargoes of that river. But perhaps it was Hawkins the lawyer who played senior partner. His name is recited first, and an invitation to the Lloyds as necessary allies on the weir would come well from a man in his position.

To these five men, Hawkins, Palmer, Wilkes, Sampson Lloyd the younger (it is he who is named in this lease), and Wyatt, the proprietorship of the Boat Company duly passed.[38] A letter of Wyatt's shows that it cost them £2,500 for the lease and £6,000 for the gear and goodwill, total £8,500. What they took on was expressed to be 'all that the said Navigation of the said river Trent with the appurtenances thereof, as the same is at this time perfected, in as large and ample a manner as the same has been held and enjoyed by the late Henry Hayne gentleman and by his son John Hayne'. The picture can be filled in by one or two of the other stipulations. They were to keep the waterway in repair, convenanting that they would 'well and sufficiently repair cleanse and keep in repair all the trenches cuts and passages for water and all the dams locks turnpikes pens for water watercourses cranes wharfs warehouses warp passages and all other things proper and convenient for the said Navigation'. And they were to play fair and preserve good water manners, for they were not to 'prevent or hinder the water of the said river from serving the mills thereupon other than in taking and using a necessary quantity of water for the use and service of the lock and for flashes to carry boats in low water over the shallows below the said mills'. Of the five, it was the Lloyds at this stage, whose interests faced two ways where water rights were concerned. It may have reminded them of the conflict between surface interests and mining rights at Wednesbury. But before long the 'new navigators', as Wyatt calls them, did better. Within three years, by remarkable commercial good fortune and, it may be, with a little help from one of them, they acquired in addition the leases of both the corn mill and the fulling mill.[39] Between them they thus totally disposed of the power at the weir, water administration became an internal matter within the group, and their hold was complete.

The importance of the new situation, for the Lloyds, arises not simply from their one-fifth share in the deal but from the way in which it led to their continued presence on the Trent long after the traffic on this stretch of river had given way to the new canals and also from the history of the Boat Company itself. The latter had been a short one, about fifty years. As recently as the time when Crowley had been consigning goods from the north-east coast to Sampson Lloyd's father at Birmingham, the Trent had been usable only as far up as Nottingham and Crowley's iron had gone round by London and Bristol. The Trent had only been made navigable to Burton in 1712. The years since then had been a time of pioneering, of monopoly, of feuds, and of determined men defending themselves against encroachment using all the stratagems of river warfare. The lower Trent had always been a first-class channel of trade, even better in some ways than the Severn though freight rates were higher. Coasting vessels could pass, via the Humber, right up to the inland port of Gainsborough, whence goods could go on by river craft to Nottingham. But in the time of William and Mary the Paget family had obtained by Act of Parliament the right to develop the river further inland. After a period of delays the new stretch had come into use, the trade of the hinterland had grown and there had even been visions of a connection through Staffordshire to the Severn.* The new section

---

* 'The river Severn is navigable to within twenty-five miles of Burton,' states a paper of 1698 in the Coke MSS of the Marquess of Lothian at Melbourne.

thus opened by the Pagets, which, for all its locks and shallows, added twenty miles to the river's usefulness, extended upstream from a point near Nottingham at that time named Wilden Ferry and known today as Cavendish Bridge. The navigation rights were held under Lord Paget (not yet Earl of Uxbridge) by two characters named Fosbrooke and Hayne, based one at Wilden Ferry and the other at Burton, who, in combination, exploited the traffic. Fosbrooke's boats worked largely downstream to Gainsborough, Hayne worked the part above, and each supported the other. The feud with the older riverside interests who resented both the stranglehold and the competition, the battles of boats at Wilden Ferry, the determination of the Mayor of Nottingham to chain off the passage of Nottingham Bridge, may not be re-told here, but the buccaneering episode of the block-ship cannot be passed over. The principal stage-point on the course of the new navigation was at the Kings Mills, a group of mills a few miles above Wilden Ferry, near Castle Donington, where the formidable weir was by-passed by one of the newly built locks. In 1749 Hayne and Fosbrooke, more exasperated than usual, sank a barge filled with stone in the lock itself, so forcing all goods to be trans-shipped over their premises and upon their terms. Here Hayne, declaring that the statutory toll was not enough, held commerce to ransom and denied passage to enemy vessels for eight years, until his death in 1757. It was the mills at this spot that the Lloyds were to operate during fifty years of the nineteenth century, and it was an enterprise of these antecedents in which they now participated at Burton. From the waters of the Trent, which they already employed for power, they thus drew fresh advantage in terms of transportation.

In his business Sampson Lloyd was alone no longer. Expressions in Wyatt's letters such as 'the Quakers' and 'Mr Lloyd and Son', reflect this clearly enough. It is his son who joins the Boat Company. Now, in 1763, they were two, and at sixty-four Sampson Lloyd was glad of it. At his father's death he had been one of five brothers, but he had long been the only one. The family history had been his history. In the future they would be numerous again, how numerous he could not know; but for twenty years, like the sand in the hour-glass, their fortunes had descended in him. Now he could look round on his achievements, he had a partner again, he could begin to ease off; but his course was not finished yet.

PART III

'This Trade of Bankering'

6

INTO BANKING

A fresh tide was now running in Birmingham as in the country at large and the next twenty-five years were a surging time. The Seven Years' War was over,* a spirit of expansion and improvement was in the air, and whether in trade and finance, in communications, in scientific enquiry and technology, or in matters of civic and human conscience, Birmingham kindled to it. The town had been growing steadily. Soon, with the new progress and prosperity, its population would quadruple. Previously its leading men may have been pushing and successful but they had been individualists. A new collective attitude, a readiness to band together, to canvass new projects, promote Acts of Parliament and raise subscriptions for large schemes was now the fashion, and changes of all kinds began to be made. It was not long before the Lloyds were drawn into this current and they played their own part in giving it momentum, for in addition to their iron interests they were now to engage in banking, a development as important for the town as for the family. In fact, whether in Birmingham or in London, no less than four of the five sons of Sampson Lloyd II became members of banking partnerships and both his daughters married bankers. As he had, however, two families, the girls coming in the middle, and as in 1764 when this chapter opens the younger sons were still in their teens, the story of Sampson, the eldest, can be followed first, leaving Nehemiah, Charles, John and Ambrose until later. Indeed the creation of the town's first bank and the rise of Sampson Lloyd III must be, against the background of the new Birmingham, the next matters for our attention.

* The Peace of Paris was signed in the same month as the Burton navigation lease, February 1763.

Before coming to the bank it is worth while to consider by what system of credit and exchange a town of 30,000 inhabitants with no formal banking service had, down to this time, conducted its daily business and what improvements a new banking enterprise might be able to offer, for some of the operations of the aspiring banker would correspond to those of the present day and some would not. Deposits had come to be entrusted, in London, to specialists such as the goldsmith, the security of whose strong-rooms was accepted and the respectability of their connections esteemed, and sometimes, in other towns, to an established merchant if he were sufficiently well thought of. For convenience in the transmission of payments, unexpired trade bills could be obtained from many traders and merchants in return for cash, as could cash in return for bills. For the financing of longer-term needs, lending was carried on, often on the security of mortgage or bond, both by tradesmen and by private persons having the fortune and the inclination to do so, and lending supported from sums on deposit could make for commercial advantage. These were informal banking processes, the 'trade of bankering' in action, so that some goldsmiths came to be known as goldsmith bankers and some merchants as merchant bankers; but all the time, behind these processes, there was the bill system, unfamiliar today but then an everyday matter. In the absence of the cheque for credit transactions or of any mechanism for the clearing of cheques,* let us see what this bill was, how credit worked, and what part a banker might expect to play within such a system.

Until well on in the eighteenth century, except in London, credit in England worked almost entirely without banks. The device which, sanctioned and protected by the law, to a great extent made this possible was the inland trade bill or bill of exchange, known simply as a bill. We have to put aside the idea of a bill as meaning an invoice or notice of a sum requiring to be paid and think rather of the bill of exchange as used in international commerce. For this is the bill as understood in the 1760s, not just the notice of a sum to be paid, but a two-way affair, comprising, on one piece of paper,

---

* A London clearing house was established by private bankers there about 1770, for their collective convenience, but until well into the nineteenth century little use was made of it outside London. W. F. Crick and J. E. Wadsworth, *A Hundred Years of Joint Stock Banking*, Hodder & Stoughton, 1936, p. 12.

both directions for the payment of a required sum and an undertaking to pay it, a device which, regulated by Parliament and respected by tradition, had been long in use, and, despite the eventual spread of the cheque, would continue so for a century to come.

A bill normally carried two names. It would be made out, 'for value received', for a given sum, by the person to be paid, and had then to be signed and returned by the person to pay it. The first was called the drawer and the second the acceptor.* When Richard Wheeler delivered rod iron to Crowley he drew a bill on Crowley for the price of the iron, and this Crowley signed and returned as his undertaking to pay. This was called 'Wheeler's bill on Crowley' and, as it happened to concern eighty tons of rod at £17 17s. 6d., it would be a piece of paper expressing Wheeler's right to receive £1,430 from Crowley. The same method would be used were it only for an ordinary amount such as £5 or less. A drawer might require the sum to be paid as soon as the acceptor received the document for signature and this was a bill payable 'at sight'. Or again the sum might be expressed to be payable on demand. But, where an agreed delay was allowed for settlement, the bill would stipulate payment at a deferred date such as sixty days from the day when it reached the acceptor. And as everyone knew that the sum had to be paid on the sixtieth day, such a bill could be used by the drawer, up to that time, in several alternative ways.

There were three principal ways in which the drawer could employ his bill after it came back to him accepted. First, he could keep it and claim the sum on the sixtieth day. Secondly, by endorsing the name of a new payee on the back, he could use it as cash for making a payment of his own, and the right to claim the value at the due date then passed to the new holder. At Stourbridge in 1725 John Kelsall says that he received from Sampson Lloyd a payment of '£100 in bills and money'. Thirdly, at the price of a discount, normally 5 per cent per annum, and entering the name of the purchaser on the back, the holder could negotiate it, i.e. obtain cash

---

* A drawer might, if he wished, direct the payment to be made to a third party instead of to himself, so creating a three-way transaction as in the case of a present-day cheque. The earliest known example of any bill bearing the name of Lloyd is a bill of this type, drawn on Sampson Lloyd I at Birmingham by a drawer in Bristol on 29 February, 1712, payable to a third party. For simplicity, the type discussed in the text is the two-way bill.

for it, and on the proper date the purchaser would collect the value in full, thus recovering the discount as a profit. The facility of negotiating or discounting a bill in return for cash could usually be had of the established retailers, manufacturers or merchants in a town or from officials such as the local receiver of excise or taxes. In remoter districts it was necessary to go to some town to achieve this business. Forty years before banking began in Birmingham John Kelsall would ride from Dolobran to Chester or to Shrewsbury for the purpose. At Shrewsbury he was supplied by the head of the Drapers' Guild with trade bills in return for cash which had accumulated from his local sales of bar iron. These would be bills drawn on London merchants by local members of the Guild requiring settlement for the sale of Welsh cloth, and Kelsall would use them to pay for Dolobran's pig iron supplies. The merchant, in return for the discount, was obliging Kelsall as a banker.[1] For those in large towns it was easier. At Birmingham, Hutton tells us, before there was any bank, 'about every tenth trader was a banker or a retailer of cash' and 'at the head of these were marshalled the whole train of drapers and grocers until the year 1765 when a regular bank was constituted by two opulent tradesmen, Messrs. Taylor & Lloyd'.[2]

When it came to the final stage, that of collection, and the holder of a bill required cash, the onus was upon him, be he drawer or indorsee, to present it for settlement. To get his money it must be claimed from the acceptor, who knew from his bill-book what amounts were to be met. The claim might be made, according to the case, either by sending to the acceptor's place of business or to an agreed intermediary; or, in many cases, by arranging for your correspondent or agent in a major centre (most commonly in London) to collect from the acceptor's correspondent in that place; or, since an endorsed bill could have originated from anywhere in the country, the holder might have to claim his settlement by post, calculating the time for the purpose. Alternatively the acceptor might simply credit the holder's account, if he already knew him, in the ordinary way. But everyone knew that, under the law, payment must be punctually made. Bills were thus constantly on the move and, compared with some other forms of currency such as coin or Bank of England notes, a bill, unless a total sham, was safer, each new holder having recourse to the name before should settlement not eventually be forthcoming.* The names on the paper were what mattered, not the acceptor's only but the others as well. A reputable trader did not care to make a payment with a bill that might cause doubt or difficulty. Therefore, especially if remitting to a correspondent at a distance, where the value of local names was unlikely to be known, he would only use bills with good names on them, waiting if necessary until he had such to send. 'Within the next month,' writes Sampson Lloyd to Kirton in 1741, 'please to expect £100 in good bills. Those that are to be depended on are now a little scarce.' A few weeks later three bills are dispatched, with names specified, making up the sum due, 'the first I received that I thought suitable'. One of them is 'Sir Henry Gough's bill on Hoare and partners for £50', an example of a Birmingham figure, the lord of the manor of Edgbaston, transacting business with one of the early London banks. It is unlikely that Gough had been paying for iron with the bill, and more probable that he had taken it to Sampson Lloyd to get it cashed. The system has been described as 'a ramshackle system'. The bill did not have the precision of the cheque. The amount of a remittance was limited by what the contents of the bill-box would make up. But it was the only system there was and everybody understood it, and the examples give glimpses of credit in action, dependent, as it must be, upon judgement and trust, and of the 'dirty bits of paper that eighteenth-century bills often were',[3] the legal, negotiable instruments of credit.

It was the flow and return of bills between the provinces and London that made credit transactions possible at a distance; and it was merchants accustomed to dealing at a distance and thus able to oblige others, as Sampson Lloyd was, who mainly made it so. London was the grand exchange-point for credit. In London there had developed enough financial machinery for bills to be accepted, transmitted or collected as a matter of routine, provided one had a brother merchant or correspondent to act as one's agent and kept him in funds for the purpose. For the conduct of business such London arrangements were not only convenient, they were indispensable. Sampson Lloyd's London correspondent was John Pocock, 'factor in Queenhithe', a merchant in corn and iron who

* In two letters to Kirton, Sampson Lloyd II gives an account of a forged bill which he investigated on behalf of a neighbour; Lloyd MSS 2/80 and 2/81, 7 January and 9 February 1745.

acted likewise for Kirton at Newbury. In 1736 Sampson Lloyd
introduced Kirton to Richard Sykes, the iron-importer at Hull, a
leader in the Swedish trade, with whom he places an initial order in
Kirton's name, the goods to be sent coastwise to London. Directing
Sykes how to obtain payment, Sampson Lloyd writes, 'When the
iron is on board and the bill of loading sent, mayst draw on John
Pocock for the money at 30 days date, where it will meet with due
honour.'[4] In this case a merchant in Birmingham, Lloyd, relying
on the confidence between them, was telling a merchant at Hull,
Sykes, to obtain payment from a merchant in London, Pocock,
of a sum incurred by one at Newbury, Kirton, and pledging Kirton
to assure a sufficient balance with Pocock after thirty days. There
were no banks at Newbury or Hull in the 1730s; a London merchant
was used as a credit intermediary to carry out a banking function.
It is not, however, our business to follow out all the applications of
the trade bill or its regulation under the law, but simply to get it
into focus. This we need to do because the bill was one of the
central devices in the merry-go-round of credit, and because we can
so get a better idea of the system in daily use before country banks
and of the central influence exercised in these matters by London.

This brings us to the question: if a banking house appeared in a
town for the first time, what would the new banker expect to do,
and why should the public make use of him? He would, according
to the bias of his town and the trade in the district, have scope for
some of the familiar banking activities of today, the accepting of
funds for safe keeping subject to their return upon demand, the
making of loans against security of one kind and another in accord
with the usages of the time, and the provision of cash in exchange
for bills at a customary discount and of bills, at a premium, in return
for cash. He would act as a merchant in bills, as a middleman prepared to remit (and receive) payments on behalf of his customers,
whether from the account of one man to another in the same town
or, by means of his London connection, to any place in the country,
and to develop for these purposes all that apparatus of recording,
timekeeping and collecting that his customers would expect. His
claims to enjoy such business would rely, first, upon their assessment
of his integrity, and then upon their view of his business capabilities,
their estimation of his substance and of course their impression
of him as a man to deal with in daily dealings, and not a little upon

an established London connection, for the want of which the more moneyed and sophisticated customers would go elsewhere. But in the society of the day, and under such organisation of affairs as we have considered, he need come before his neighbours with no more exalted or technical pretensions than these. There were no professional institutes or examining bodies, no letters to place after your name, a man's name and a man's business were known in a town, and what is clear enough is that since up to that time, where the elements of banking were concerned, it had been a do-it-yourself community, the momentum was there, and banking functions, if not under that name, were being carried on, in partial degree, on all sides. The opportunity for a banker was to gather up some of this activity into one set of hands, and so to channel and develop it as to proffer to his townsmen, a little more streamlined, a little more concentrated, a little more effectual and convenient, and at a profit to himself, the facilities that they were improvising for themselves. In a time of demand for credit, the services that he could offer in the discounting of bills would assist the flow of business, and his bank notes would facilitate the circulation of money. It was in such conditions that in 1765 Birmingham's first bank was set up, the banking enterprise of Taylors & Lloyds.

The new firm was a partnership of four business men, a father and son from each of two families. Both the seniors were respected in the town, both prosperous, both wealthy, Taylor very wealthy. Neither their integrity nor their substance were doubted. Both had certainly been carrying out the simpler functions of banking, in the course of their normal business; and if Sampson Lloyd would discount his neighbours' bills, as we have seen, and had working arrangements in London, in the interests of his own affairs at least, we need not doubt that John Taylor did the like and perhaps more so, for Taylor's business had its own branch in London. There does not appear to be any evidence to show how far either of the sons was experienced in such matters at the time when the bank opened, though the younger Sampson, in his thirties, must have thoroughly understood his business. But, if the seniors had the experience, were the seniors going to attend at the new premises daily, busy and responsible as they were, and not always, either of them, in the town?

Or how far would they depute their reputations and the cultivation of this new ground to the younger partners? Let us see who the Taylors were and what considerations may have moved either side, for the venture was soon established and the two families continued in partnership for nearly ninety years before one of the two names dropped out.

John Taylor (Plate 20) was at the height of an exceptional career as a manufacturer. Said by one writer to have started life as a cabinet-maker, by another as 'a mere artisan', his fortune at his death in 1775 is said to have been £200,000, and by some £250,000. Birmingham was always the town of a thousand metal-workers, constantly developing and producing as many different kinds of article. Prominent among them at this stage in the century was the celebrated race of toy-makers. 'Toy' was the word used for the many minor objects of use and fashion in demand by a gay and dressy age, at first in steel then in brass and other materials, buckles, buttons, snuff-boxes, seals and hundreds more; Taylor, in the toy industry himself, is described by a Birmingham contemporary as 'our great button-maker'. He is said to have been debonair and cheerful in manner, but he was practical, able and successful and he was much more than a button-maker. He was inventive in technical matters and advanced in the management of production, and his products had 'a decisive elegance and an obvious indication of good taste that ensured a good sale and large profits'.[5] An example of his ingenuity is recalled in the *Birmingham Post* for 24 October 1938:

He was a hard worker himself, and his wife assisted him both in the painting and the varnishing of snuff-boxes. Taylor, one finds, had discovered a method of transferring floral and landscape designs onto the boxes, which were then varnished. The origin of some of the patterns with which he decorated the boxes while the varnish was wet was a secret known only to himself and his wife. They were the impressions of his own thumb.[6]

This novelty, which is recited in every account, was doubtless soon dropped by Fashion but seems symptomatic of his enterprise and market sense. His house was in High Street, his manufactory in a lane at the back near the present-day Union Street. A visit to the latter establishment in 1755 by the travellers from London whom we met before is described as follows:

We returned from hence to the town and saw the manufactory of Mr Taylor, the most considerable maker of gilt metal buttons and enamelled snuff-boxes. We were assured that he employs 500 persons in those two branches, and when we had seen his workshop we had no scruple in believing it. The multitude of hands each button goes through before it is sent to the market is likewise surprising. You perhaps will think it incredible when I tell you they go through seventy different operations of seventy different work-folks, but so we were informed. Whether it be exactly true or not I cannot affirm, the number seemed to me uncountable; though from what dwelt on my memory afterwards, reflecting on what I had seen, I could not find so considerable a deficiency as to raise a doubt of the truth of it.

John Taylor saw himself as a great man. He enjoyed his success, he enjoyed being High Sheriff of Warwickshire and the mansions and properties that his money enabled him to acquire.* He would be proud of his part in the new bank; and the bank would owe much to his name, for he was regarded by his fellow townsmen as 'one whose name was a guarantee of success and without whose support no undertaking was likely to command public approval'. Of his son, John Taylor junior, on the other hand, little seems to be known at the time we speak of, and this brings us to the Lloyd side of the venture.

In what ways had John Taylor and Sampson Lloyd been associated, other than as fellow-townsmen, before a bank was planned? There is no support for the statement that Taylor was in partnership with the Lloyds' cousins, the Pembertons, for they were iron-mongers but he was a button-maker.[7] On the other hand there can be little doubt that Taylor, the manufacturer, obtained some of his materials from Lloyd, the metal merchant and that they respected each other as men of affairs. The Sampson Lloyds, however, except in a sense, with their cousin the Heirs of Parkes, had never been in partnership with others and it is of interest to try and see how the project was developed and which party took the initiative. Two papers throw some light on this. The first is the draft of a letter by the younger Sampson dated in November 1764, several months before the bank opened. It shows that, while premises had already been taken, the relative participation of the two sides had

* He was High Sheriff in 1756; he became, by purchase, lord of the manor of Yardley and the owner also of Bordesley Hall.

not yet been finally agreed, that Hanbury, the brother-in-law to whom it is written,* was being canvassed as a London partner, and that the Lloyds on their part felt there would be hard work and much to learn; but it discloses that the Lloyds had private as well as commercial motives for entertaining the scheme. The letter begins with a reference to what seems to have been an ill-guarded remark by somebody in their counsels:

I observe the strong light in which thou hast placed the case of our neighbour. We own ourselves also to be concerned though we cannot but say we believe it was entirely accidental, and faulty mostly through inconsideration—the outlines of the thing being then hardly sketched out nor the least determination come to whether at all or at which end to begin. Considering a partner in London necessary, no one thou mayst well think could be so agreeable to us as thyself. I confess my regard for thee prompted me greatly to covet thy being a party but I so fully expressed myself on this head in my last that I have but little room left to say further. It was a scheme I had very little thought on and of which the success cannot be presently determinable, but if found at all it must seemingly be the consequence of pretty great application, everybody here being strangers and the nature of it different to what it is in London if not in most places.

My father is actuated chiefly with a view to striking out somewhat that might afford employment and advantage to his young family (which he has been thoughtful about of late not a little), on which account I also confess my own diligence had of late been pretty much awakened, especially as the old channel of our trade has been considerably obstructed.

We think less than the share we proposed in our last to hold would scarce demand the necessary attention but the one-third we tendered thee still waits thy acceptance. We have gone so far as to take a house at the upper end of Dale End at £30 per annum. J.T. has been for some days in London. He seemed desirous of holding more than half but that would hardly be consistent or agreeable. When we intimated our concern on your behalf he said he thought you would hardly find it worth your notice nor could it be so to anybody if divided into many parts.[8]

The second paper is another letter, dated in December 1764, a fortnight later, when the scheme was evidently being talked about. It was written by Samuel Garbett, a leading business figure in Birmingham, who informs his correspondent that 'some of the capital

* Osgood Hanbury in 1757 had married Sampson Lloyd's elder daughter Mary.

people in this town are establishing a bank, viz., Abel Smith, Esq., banker of Nottingham, John Taylor, Esq., our great button-maker, and Sampson Lloyd an ironmonger in this town, he is a man of unquestionable substance, a most amiable character'.[9] In the light of these two letters it is possible to get a view of the birth of the new enterprise: the idea mooted evidently by Taylor, his name taking precedence in the style of the business, 'desirous of holding more than a half'; Taylor's approach, an eye to the main chance, 'hardly worth notice if divided into many parts'; the importance of London, 'at which end to begin'; Hanbury proposed as a partner, 'a partner in London necessary', but (Taylor's solution) Abel Smith's bank* as London agent, 'J.T. has been for some days in London'. One perceives also the caution of the Lloyds, 'success not presently determinable', 'pretty great application', 'everybody here strangers'; but motivation on two grounds: for the son, the recession in the iron trade since the War, 'the old channel of our trade obstructed': for the father, the prospect, in that glorious phrase, of 'employment and advantage for his young family'. '*Actuated chiefly*', this may have tipped the scale for the Lloyds, the two sides committed themselves and on 3 June 1765, with the details determined and premises secured, the new firm opened for business.

In the event, the capital, of £8000, was arranged between the two families on a fifty–fifty basis, the partners subscribing £2000 each. Dale End (Plate 19), a continuation of Birmingham's short High Street, was a busy thoroughfare, forming part of the main road to Coventry which passed in those days through Coleshill. The house, at No. 7, afforded a room for the clerks, another for the partners, and accommodation for a housekeeper, but neither house nor site would bear much resemblance to bank premises such as we think of today. Birmingham was an old-fashioned, congested place. The weekly cattle market, which by tradition took place in

* Smith and Payne were one of the very earliest country banks. The Smiths had been banking at Nottingham for many years and had latterly opened in London as well. Abel Smith was probably known to Taylor in London. Although concerned in the planning of the project he did not join the new partnership. He was content to know that they were the first bank in the Birmingham region and to have secured their London representation. Contrary to Sayers, op. cit., 8, it is clear that Taylor, not Lloyd, is to be recognised as the founder of Taylors & Lloyds and so, at longer range, of Lloyds Bank itself. (See J. A. S. L. Leighton-Boyce, *Smiths the Bankers, 1658–1958*, National Provincial Bank, London, 1958.)

the street, was carried on in Dale End, under their windows 'to the great danger and inconvenience of persons living and resorting there'. Both families had plenty to do in their other concerns. The merchant's business at Edgbaston Street and the control of the distant mills and forges had kept the two Lloyds busy enough up to this time. There is a tradition that the younger Lloyd, Sampson Lloyd III as we must call him, took the principal executive part in the new bank. If he did, the younger Taylor, John Taylor II, must likewise have shown a talent for it, for it was these two, the sons, not the fathers, who presently took part in establishing a sister bank in London.

To launch two banking ventures in five years at so early a stage in banking history suggests the unity and spirit of the partners. Country banking was in its infancy. In 1750 there had been, outside London, hardly a dozen banks in the whole country, and Taylors & Lloyds can claim a place in the van of a movement which in the later part of the century was to snowball on every side. But in setting up its own London house the Birmingham concern was again exceptional. Much the most usual relationship was that between country banker and London agent or, as London would have it, between London banker and country correspondent. Very few country banks formed their own London house, with the additional demands, but also the additional opportunities and advantage, which such a course involved. Smith & Payne had done so a few years before, and had at first acted as London agent to Taylors & Lloyds; but, in 1770, five years from the start, the Birmingham men opened a London bank on their own account. Once again Smith & Payne seem to have co-operated, even if they may have lost something thereby, for one of the new partners was William Bowman, hitherto a cashier or assistant to the Smiths, who now became resident partner and manager of the new concern. By taking this step the Birmingham partnership greatly strengthened its position. Not only did they enjoy in Lombard Street the services of what was, naturally, their London agent, information, consultation, cash at command, the handling of bills, and very many other facilities, but they had these things of their own people, they were proprietors.

The style of the new bank, which was set up at No. 14 Lombard Street, opposite where the head office of Lloyds Bank stands today, was Hanbury, Taylor, Lloyd & Bowman, the names of Taylor and

Lloyd reflecting the Birmingham connection, the capital £20,000. Osgood Hanbury, instead of becoming five years earlier a junior partner in the first bank, appears now as principal partner in the second. Hanbury had been married to Mary Lloyd for thirteen or fourteen years. To her father he had become a useful son-in-law and he was friendly with her brother Sampson. As a London tobacco-broker with a handsome property in Essex, it is not obvious how he had come to find a wife in Birmingham, but the to-and-fro of the Quaker fraternity accounts for unions more distantly separated than that. There had nevertheless been some common ground in a previous generation for, before Hanbury's father was in tobacco, his people had been in iron in South Wales where they were known to the Lloyds and also linked with the Crowleys, and they had come originally from Worcestershire. Osgood Hanbury, as a prosperous Quaker merchant, was qualified to carry conviction as a banker in much the same ways as the Lloyds. In addition he was established in London and hence his name was placed first. With Hanbury's standing, Bowman's know-how, and the thrust and connection of the two Birmingham men, this second bank was to be a strong combination and, manned by members of the several families, was to flourish in London for more than a century, until eventually taken over by its own Birmingham parent.

To obtain a view of these twin banks and of the new Birmingham–London axis we have run several years ahead and must turn to the other movement which was stirring Birmingham and which was to affect Lloyd interests in a number of ways. The two banks were beginning business at the outset of the fabulous canal era; and it was the new banking and the new canals, providing better organisation of credit and capital and better means of transportation, which together made possible the great expansion of the last quarter of the century. Today, when so many canals have passed out of use and the image of those remaining is of hump-backed bridges and an antique mode of progression, it is impossible to recapture the enthusiasm that attended their introduction, and difficult enough to realise the reasons for it. But this becomes easier if we can conjure up in the imagination a world of agriculture, trade and industry that was without the lorry, had never heard of a railway, and had only the road and the river for transport; a world, however, in which the badness of the roads still beggared description* and rivers did not run tidily from town to town.

It might be thought that a Birmingham firm would profit mainly from such canals as might start or end at Birmingham, but the benefits of the new waterways were felt by the Lloyds far beyond that, so much so that we must call to mind a little of what was going on. It had been before the end of the War, in 1758 and 1759, that the success of a pioneer canal had set the country talking. The new canal was short and it was simple, but it pointed the way; for it had everything, basins, tunnels, embankments and a lofty aqueduct that carried it over a navigable river. Its object, the conveyance of 'coals' from a local coalbed to a local town, the public could easily understand, and the fact that those coals could be sold at half their former price, yet still at a profit, appealed to business everywhere. This great and experimental engineering venture was known as the Bridgewater canal, but it was not in Somerset. It was in Lancashire, on the north side of the Mersey, the river that it crossed was the Irwell, the coal-owner the Duke of Bridgewater, and the town that it supplied was Manchester. The country was at once agog. Let town be joined to town, markets to their supplies, industry to its raw materials; let land carriage and coastwise communication be reduced to a minimum, let sea be joined to sea and inland navigation unite the leading ports of London, Bristol, Liverpool and Hull; let the Thames and Severn, Mersey and Trent, all be joined by water.

This programme was everywhere tackled with determination, Birmingham in the van. Within three years the town was joined to the best coal in the district, within five the Trent was linked to the Severn, Birmingham was connected to both, and in eleven to Liverpool and Hull. The connections from the Midlands to the Thames took a few years longer. And because of the nature and pattern of their business nearly all these innovations brought advantage to the Lloyds. The layout that Sampson Lloyd had been forming during forty years was matched by the new communications at every

---

* With the increase of trade, especially in heavy goods, many of the roads had become worse. The turnpike network had yet to enter upon its main expansion. The road to Dudley, Hutton wrote in 1781, 'is despicable beyond description'.

turn. Not only was the new water brought to their own town, not only did the town's canal lead directly to their coal-workings at Wednesbury, but their country ironworks, at Powick, at Burton, disposed as they were beside the new network or its extensions, were brought nearer at low cost and, eased of their heavy land freights, could streamline their connections in new ways both with markets and with suppliers. And it need not be added that the only bank in the town could not but gain from the new prosperity. The coming of the canals set a seal, as it were, upon Sampson Lloyd's business career.

For this was a Midland scheme. The junction of the three rivers can be thought of in the form of an inverted 'Y' having its base on the Mersey, one arm on the Trent, the other on the Severn, and forking at a point near Stafford. Birmingham lay somewhere in the crotch. Birmingham drove its own canal north-west from the town, designed to bring the best coal to its door and to link up with the new trunk system. Since the main trunk scheme, the Y, was conceived not as one but as two canals, the 'Trent and Mersey' and the 'Staffordshire and Worcestershire', several Acts of Parliament had to be promoted. The time-table was as follows, and let us recall that the bank had opened at Birmingham in 1765:

	Trent and Mersey	Staffordshire and Worcestershire	Birmingham Canal
Act obtained	1766	1766	1768
Canal in operation in part or in whole	1777	1771–2	1769–72

The first stretch to be opened, in 1769, was the Birmingham line as far as the delphs* at Wednesbury, whereupon the retail price of coal in Birmingham immediately fell from 15s. to 8s. 6d. a ton. The waterway was brought right into the town, ending in two basins, one for general goods near Newhall Street, the other near Suffolk Street for coal. Neither the Heirs of Parkes nor the business at Edgbaston Street and Mill Lane can have wished for better. The line to the Severn, with its advantages for Powick, terminated not at Bewdley but, for engineering reasons, some miles downstream at a hamlet called Titton Brook where the Stour falls into the

* A delph was the shallow surface mine of the period.

Severn, and here a new town sprang up like a seaport in the heart
of the kingdom which received the name of Stourport. But it was
the line to the Trent, the other arm of the Y, that aroused public
debate, a debate which the Lloyds, with their interests in those
parts, followed with considerable attention.

Ought the new canal to join the Trent at Wilden Ferry and so
avoid the uncertainties of the Burton navigation, or terminate at
Burton and save sixteen miles of capital expense? Controversy
raged. Pamphlets and publications appeared. If the first plan were
adopted, both the navigation and the Burton ironworks would be
by-passed and so would the furnace at Melbourne. A letter of
Josiah Wedgwood's, who was a leading figure in the movement
and was sparing no pains to see these great schemes through, reflects what was going on. Wedgwood had reason for his efforts.
The roads were bad, his goods were both heavy and breakable, and,
located in Staffordshire, his land-carriage charges were a bugbear.
His driving idea was access to London without land-carriage. He
had been holding a public meeting in Birmingham of 'landowners,
gentlemen, traders and manufacturers', talking to leading personalities such as the Garbetts and the Taylors, and expounding the
merits of canals both regional and local. 'We made it appear pretty
evident to the gentlemen of Birmingham,' he writes to his brother,
'that £10,000 per annum would be immediately saved to them in
the article of land carriage to and from the river Trent so soon as
the canal was brought to their town.' Written on 3 April 1765,
the letter suggests that a decision about the Trent terminal had just
been taken,* for Wedgwood mentions that 'Mr Taylor is just
entered into partnership with one Mr Lloyd in the banking business;
and Mr Lloyd, it seems, is one of the proprietors of the Burton
navigation, which will be injured by our intended canal as it is
proposed to carry it beyond Burton to Wilden in order to keep clear
of their locks and shallows'.[10] What was current intelligence for the
Wedgwoods would be a blow for the Lloyds. The line adopted
wound gently along the Trent valley, at some points less than a
mile from the river, but Burton was by-passed. Burton, in due course,
secured a lateral canal to connect the town to the Trent and Mersey,

---

* The Wilden Ferry plan was preferred in conformity with a memorandum in
the names of James Brindley, the Duke of Bridgewater's engineer who was also the
engineer to this project, and John Smeaton, who took over upon Brindley's death.

the benefit of which the ironworks enjoyed; but the Boat Company was hit. Their locks and shallows went against them, and Lord Uxbridge must have regretted that the river had not been more improved. The reasons for the Lloyd participation in this enterprise we saw in the last chapter; they had to be in it because of their gates on the weir, but after 1777 the river traffic became progressively less profitable, though the Boat Company continued to work the navigation for local needs. How the syndicate fought back over a number of years is related in a later chapter, but the navigation had to face a progressive decline. From the Lloyd point of view it was the forge that profited from the new transportation through having acess to the Trent and Mersey by the lateral canal.

It has been said that the Lloyds took the lead in promoting the Birmingham Canal and that they were the moving spirits in its construction.[11] In fact this was not the case, and it was only in 1771 that the name of the younger Sampson first appeared on the committee which managed the canal under the act.[12] But, as Taylors & Lloyds, they became its treasurers, as they did for other schemes of improvement that Birmingham was introducing at this time. One of these was the scheme for a general hospital, put forward in the same year that the bank was formed. Birmingham had only its workhouse infirmary for the needs of 35,000 people, and the idea of better facilities for 'the sick and lame' was one of the humanitarian projects that were beginning to exercise men's minds, if not unmixed with the expediency of medical assistance for their workers, 'too valuable to allow of any risk being incurred by neglect'.[13] Led by Dr John Ash and supported by 'the nobility and gentry of the neighbouring country and the principal inhabitants of the town', a subscription was raised, a site obtained and a building begun. The list of subscribers exhibits all the foremost local names; Garbett, Colmore, Galton, Matthew Boulton among others. Taylor and Taylor contributed twenty and ten guineas, Lloyd and Lloyd fifteen and seven. The two seniors served on the first committee and the bank was appointed as 'receivers of contributions'. We return to the family's part in these innovations on a later page.

Meanwhile there was the iron trade to be looked after, the bread and butter behind the new bank, but the limelight is on other matters at this time and there is little to record of the mills either at Birmingham or Powick and not much about Burton or Melbourne. At Birmingham, the slitting mill had been taken over formally by Sampson Lloyd senior in 1760 from his brother Charles's widow. At Powick a slitting mill had been added alongside the forge. This seems to have been fairly soon after its acquisition by the Lloyds, as a slitter's infant was baptised there in 1766. The younger Sampson, before his brothers were of an age to join him, was active on the merchants' side; indeed, he was still personally buying and selling iron as late as 1775. He was also supervising the outlying ironworks. There is a glimpse of him at Burton in 1771, as a buyer of cordwood for charcoal, when there had been a rumpus about the price and Wyatt is selling it to someone else: 'I am told Mr Lloyd says he has been ill used in respect of this wood,' Wyatt writes to a correspondent, 'but does not explain himself. You may remember that he had the first offer of it at 12/– per cord which he refused and, after trifling for two months, offered 11/6 per cord as the utmost price he could give.'[14] Only one side of this incident is recorded, to Sampson Lloyd's disadvantage. Perhaps he was a bargain-driver; or perhaps, that year, when the second bank had just been launched and he was also preparing to move house, he had too much to do, had let the matter lie and then felt aggrieved. A Birmingham neighbour records about this time that 'Cousin Sampson is under a great weight of care, so that I believe he scarcely remembers anybody long together'. Two other indications seem to support this view: the temporary return of Sampson Lloyd senior in 1771 to 'the old business' and the surrender of the Melbourne furnace in 1772. The first is in a letter from one of the sons-in-law: 'although I understand the old business may require again thy presence I trust it may not be of long continuance.'[15] This sounds as though the old man, now seventy-two, had been giving more time to the new bank than to the older business, but something had evidently happened to recall him. The discontinuance of the Melbourne iron furnace took place at Michaelmas 1772, one of the permitted breakpoints under the lease,[16] but the reasons remain a matter for conjecture. Whether its pig had been going mainly to the forge at Burton or mainly to the general market, no good commercial reason for a break appears unless it were the new competition from coke-fired furnaces which was beginning to cause the decline of charcoal pig. The Boat Company could still carry the output, canals or no. Perhaps there were difficulties over managers in that country place; or perhaps at a moment when the new banks must have been occupying so much of their attention the Lloyds were willing to discard what had been the little sister among their ironworks in the interests of the new diversification.

By the 1770s the younger Sampson was entering the most active period of his life. He had stood up to the spadework of establishing two banks and to the responsibilities which they were adding to his position. He had increasingly to combine the activities of a good townsman and a good Quaker with the requirements of the several businesses and of his own family. Among the interests that he looked after in these years, were those of the Heirs of Parkes at Wednesbury.* His uncle Pemberton, who had managed the properties in former years, had died in 1757 and the house at Bennetts Hill was occupied by Thomas Pemberton II, the son, but the younger Pemberton was not the man that his father had been and did not have business ability. The Wilkinson stream was likewise running thin as the present Wilkinson representatives, Joseph and Richard Wilkinson, were elderly, childless and located in London. At Bristol the representative of the Scandretts was still Edward Harford the younger, whose wife had been Sally Scandrett. Harford was a rich man with Bristol interests, and, like the Wilkinsons in London, was content to entrust his Parkes interests to Birmingham management. This meant, in effect, the younger Sampson Lloyd, who now, with the nominal help of his cousin Pemberton, managed the estate and accounted to his cousins for the revenues.

The nature of the inheritance caused plenty of demands upon Sampson Lloyd's time. Apart from houses and cottages, the freehold parts of the estate were mainly composed of numerous strip-like pieces of land disposed haphazard among the old manorial common fields, and this involved him in relations with tenants of all degrees. The leasehold part consisted of mining rights under other people's property, rights which were gradually being exploited for coal-getting and the working of which, to the detriment of the surface-owners, often led to difficulties. The negotiations about the compensation to Lord Ward, by that time Viscount Dudley, have

* The principal source for Heirs of Parkes matters is the Parkes Papers; see Preface and Bibliography.

been noted in a previous chapter, and the Tomkys and Sparrow partnership, the sons of the men we met before, were as much a thorn in the side of a landlord as ever their fathers had been. The lawyers for their part might well declare in a deed that 'the said freehold and leasehold lands mines and premises lie intermingled and undivided in common fields in such manner that it is very difficult if not impossible to ascertain with exactness what quantity of coals and other profits are gotten from the freehold and leasehold premises distinctly and separately'.

The nature of the inheritance was not Sampson Lloyd's only preoccupation. He had also to reckon with the incompetence of his cousin Pemberton for whom, in the year when the London bank was forming, a rescue operation had to be mounted on account of his debts. Pemberton was forty at the time of this affair, which came to a head in April 1770[17] when he was in debt both on his own account and as executor to his father. He was unequal to extricating himself and extreme remedies were required. To satisfy his creditors it was arranged that he should assign the whole of his personal estate and effects to trustees, who would realise what was necessary, pay the debts and re-convey any surplus. The trustees were Sampson Lloyd the younger and John Ash, then Birmingham's leading doctor, and among the assets assigned was Pemberton's quarter share in the Parkes inheritance. By September 1771 the task had been completed and the debts cleared up, partly by the sale of assets and partly by raising £1000 on mortgage from John Taylor; but the trustees still had to reckon with Pemberton's share in the obligations which these carried, one of which was his one-fourth liability under the impending settlement with Lord Dudley, 'some difficulties and disputes having arose over the getting and working of certain mines of coal which lay under an estate belonging to his Lordship'. The trustees therefore reconveyed the surplus not to Pemberton but to a new trustee for so long as the settlement should be pending and Pemberton's part of the compensation unpaid. To such lengths did the Parkes will and Pemberton's extravagance oblige Lloyd and Ash to go. In 1771, while all this was still going on, the discredited gentleman removed from Birmingham and withdrew to his wife's district, to Balby near Doncaster.* His disgrace,

---

* Pemberton had lost his first wife, Mary Harris, a Quaker from the Newbury district, and was married to a second wife, Sarah Broadbent, a Yorkshire Friend.

eventually, was remitted by the Birmingham monthly meeting, which certified to Friends in Yorkshire that he and his wife had honourably discharged their debts,* but it had been a thankless extra for the trustees.

The affairs of the inheritance were growing more complicated to manage. In addition to deaths, the intestacy of one, the insolvency of another, all added to the paper-work and lawyers' charges and brought nearer a desire for some simplification. In the case of the Wilkinson brothers, one of whom was a London linen-draper and the other a silk-mercer, their share in the leasehold rights was disposed of during the 1770s, one eighth to their cousins collectively, the other to one of them, and their share in the freeholds to a mortgagee, John Poole, a gentleman in London. Thus by 1776 part of the inheritance was in the hands of an outsider having no Parkes blood and the circle was no longer entirely among the cousins. It was as a result of such complexities, falling mainly upon a Birmingham cousin because he was on the spot, that in 1778, fifty years from Parkes's death, an important step was taken to ease the situation. This was to split up the freehold lands, the fully owned part of the estate, into separate and independent freeholds and abandon the tenants-in-common aspect. A surveyor worked out a division, and a Deed of Partition was executed, which extended to eleven skins of parchment, weighed nearly two pounds, and recited almost every plot in the parish, its area, occupier and the contiguous landholders, the parties being Harford, Lloyd, Pemberton and Poole.† Although the leasehold rights could not be unscrambled in the same way something had been gained. Sampson Lloyd as manager could begin to focus his attention upon a specific fraction of the freehold that was now his own, no longer held in common with his relations.

At Birmingham, as a banker and as a Quaker, Sampson Lloyd was being extended during these 1760s and 1770s, when he was in his thirties and forties. The year 1769 saw the inclusion of his father and himself in a new body which, feeling its way at first, was to

---

* Minute-book at Society of Friends, Birmingham, quoted in C. D. Sturge's MS book, 'Friends in Birmingham and Neighbourhood', at Bull Street meeting house.

† The share of Poole, who does not figure in the records of the inheritance after this date, was held under mortgage and would appear to have been surrendered, the estates being held thereafter between the other partitioners only.

continue as the town's principal regulating authority until after the conversion of Birmingham into a formal borough in the next century. This was the body known as the Streets Commissioners, the establishment of which was obtained, and its powers advanced, by several Acts of Parliament, secured, as for other towns, by petition on the part of the citizens. The Commissioners' first objects, simple enough but crying out for attention, included the elementary cleaning and lighting of the streets, the reduction of hazards and obstructions, and the regulation of the street markets. Any such functions had been beyond the thoughts of the antique manorial administration, 'the government of a village', which was still all that this large centre of population had. As the town grew further, a number of the Lloyds were to play a part in the proceedings of this body, over the eighty years of its history, some of them as its chairman, and they were the Commissioners' bankers from the outset.[18]

On the humanitarian side, both for the town and for the bank, the rate of progress was less satisfactory, for after a brisk start the construction of a general hospital had been halted for want of support. Public interest was diverted, it is said, on account of a canal investment and, later, in favour of building a new theatre. Launched in 1765, the hospital project languished for more than ten years, the bank being creditors for nearly £3000, and it was only in 1776 that it began to be revived. Public subscription was then slowly renewed, the bank accepted interest at 3 per cent 'for what they paid in advance', and in case of further delays 4 per cent, and at last in 1779 the hospital was opened.[19] Public participation had been so slow that the committee had the double task of satisfying the old creditors and paying for the new work as well. The embarrassment of Sampson Lloyd at the bank, on the town's account as well as his own, can be felt from a letter to Matthew Boulton, a member of the original committee. Boulton, inventive and enterprising, was an important man, but he was not always a good payer. On an occasion when it had become necessary for the bank to call in a debt from Boulton Sampson Lloyd adds in a postscript to his letter, 'There is also thy bond on the hospital accounts. We lie under a great and unnecessary burthen, as also the community in general suffers, for want of gentlemen's exerting some spirit in behalf of that charity.' This thrust was delivered in 1777 before the revival of momentum had been achieved.[20]

At Bull Street the increase in the traffic and general to-and-fro was disturbing the quiet of the Quaker meetings to such a degree that it was decided to brick up the elegant Queen Anne windows facing onto the street and improve those looking out at the back (Plate 31). Sampson Lloyd was one of the three members charged with carrying this alteration through.[21] He and his father were elders in the meeting, and were also serving as trustees, at this time, of buildings and land, and he is active again in 1778 and 1779 in further improvements and in organising subscriptions from members of the meeting to pay for them. His usefulness to the Society may be gauged from the fact that in 1777 he was chosen as clerk to the Yearly Meeting in London. This was a responsibility undertaken each year by a member from anywhere in the country and one which Sampson Lloyd was to carry again in 1782.

In 1772 he and Rachel had moved to No. 13 The Square, John Fidoe's old house. They had lived for ten years at No. 18 Park Street, but they had been growing short of space, seven of their seventeen children having already arrived. It was in this house on 22 March 1776 that the lunch party took place (called dinner in those days) at which two well-known London figures were entertained. These were Samuel Johnson and James Boswell, and the visit, as related in the *Life*,[22] sheds some light on Sampson Lloyd both as a host and as a Quaker.

The two travellers were spending the day in Birmingham *en route* from Oxford to Lichfield. Boswell had not seen Birmingham before but Johnson knew it well and had friends in the town, for he had lived there for some time as a young man and his first wife had been a Birmingham woman. Having lodged at Henley-in-Arden they arrived in Birmingham early and went to call on Johnson's old friend Edmund Hector, a prosperous surgeon whose house was in the Square at No. 1. But Hector being out, 'we next called on Mr Lloyd,' says Boswell, 'one of the people called Quakers. He too was not at home, but Mrs Lloyd was, and received us courteously and asked us to dinner,' an invitation which Johnson remarked 'came very well'.

That it was a Lloyd whom they visited does not necessarily mean that Johnson already knew Sampson Lloyd and his wife, but there could be more than one reason for the visit. Johnson, who was thirty years older than Boswell, had an old admiration for John Taylor from the 1730s, and it is likely that he had known the Lloyd family in those earlier days; but, Taylor having died the previous year, Johnson would be curious to make the acquaintance of his banking partner whom he would have heard of in letters from Hector. There was also another link, for Johnson in his youth had known the Crowleys and Lloyds at Stourbridge where he had been sent to school. He had even at that time had 'a kindness' for the youthful Olive Lloyd, afterwards Kirton, who was Sampson's aunt and who, like Taylor, had died the year before. There was no want of common ground. Johnson himself was just then at the height of his fame, 'a literary dictator'.[23] His name would be known to Rachel, who understood what to do with callers, unexpected though they might be.

We are not concerned to trace Johnson's day in Birmingham or to accompany Boswell on his visits, whether with Lloyd in the morning to see 'some of the manufactures' or after lunch with Hector, 'to the great works of Mr Boulton'. Our business is 'at dinner at Mr Lloyd's, where we were entertained with great hospitality'. This is another good mark for Rachel Lloyd, who was within a month of her eleventh confinement, a circumstance that may have been in Boswell's mind when recording that his host and hostess 'had been married the same year with their Majesties and, like them, had been blessed with a numerous family of fine children'.

But the hosts were Quakers, and the sociable occasion was to be marred on this account by a Johnsonian outburst. Boswell had been aware of a prejudice about the Society on Johnson's part which might make for awkwardness and he had played for safety. A chance, however, defeated his restraint. As men of letters, both he and Johnson would take an interest in fine books and would have an eye for any book produced by John Baskerville, the Birmingham typographer, who during the 1760s and 1770s had been putting out some of his best work. The Lloyds had in the house the Baskerville edition of Barclay's *Apology*[24] and it was a passage on baptism in this Quaker classic that led to the altercation. Here is the episode as Boswell relates it.

As Dr Johnson had said to me in the morning, while we walked together, that he liked individuals among the Quakers but not the sect, when we were at Mr Lloyd's I kept clear of introducing any questions concerning the peculiarities of their faith. But I having asked to look at Baskerville's edition of Barclay's *Apology*, Johnson laid hold of it; and the chapter on baptism happening to open, Johnson remarked, 'He says there is neither precept nor practice for baptism, in the scriptures; that is false.' Here he was the aggressor, by no means in a gentle manner; and the good Quakers had the advantage of him; for he had read negligently and had not observed that Barclay speaks of *infant* baptism, which they calmly made him perceive.

His host, as the argument continued, seems to have given away the advantage by misquoting John the Baptist (though not in heat or aggression) a point which, feeling that face had been saved, Boswell contentedly notes, concluding his account as follows:

Mr Lloyd, however, was in a great mistake; for, when insisting that the rite of baptism by water was to cease when the *spiritual* administration of Christ began, he maintained that John the Baptist said, '*My baptism* shall decrease, but *his* shall increase.' Whereas the words are, '*He* must increase, but *I* must decrease'.

A tradition of this incident was still in circulation among the Lloyds in the following century, of Johnson fiercely denouncing the book and throwing it on the floor to the alarm of the children but going round later to the bank and calling out to his host in loud tones, 'Sir, I am the best theologian, but you are the best Christian.'[25] But if Johnson did this, Boswell does not mention it; Boswell was not there, he was at Matthew Boulton's with Hector.

Sampson Lloyd at this stage in his career was approaching his fifties. He was as sociable and urbane as ever, but beneath it there was a kind of intensity in his dealings. Hard-headed he certainly was and he lived to exacting standards; he was conscious of who he was, how things should be done, and where the advantage ought to lie, and he was pained if they went otherwise, and sometimes outraged.

There are signs of these things in some of the episodes of his rise. 'The utmost' is an expression that he uses in negotiation, with Lord Ward on the compensation for the land-damage, and with Wyatt as a buyer of cordwood. He is rather ready to bridle. There is the figure for rent 'which Mr Lloyd startled at'; there is the raising of the eyebrows at the idea of less than half stake in the bank, 'hardly consistent or agreeable'; the postcript to Boulton about gentlemen's want of spirit, rather pointed and a little tart. There is also the desire to be sure, the caution, over the banking project itself, the success of which 'cannot be presently determinable'. And at the same time, though he and his partners had been willing to carry the hospital overdraft for some years without interest, he did not like doing it. 'Madam,' he is said to have replied to a customer who asked for something to be done without charge, 'we do nothing for nothing for nobody.'[26] He was a man who had plenty of money and expected to make more. But there was another side to his character. From the day when the tailor brought him the clothes and he 'felt as though he had brought him his coffin', he becomes increasingly the devoted Quaker and does all 'with integrity and honour', and not every member of the Society was summoned to be clerk to the Yearly Meeting. Sampson Lloyd was regarded as a cheerful Quaker, 'his religion cast no gloom over his countenance',[27] and he brought to it the engaging manners of his youth. It would seem, from this distance of time, that, in him, his religion and his other qualities went together and that, upon the whole, Samuel Johnson may have been right.

7

THE BANKERS

For the Lloyds, the later part of the eighteenth century was a time of increase in numbers, gathering esteem and change of emphasis in business. Their numbers had begun growing in the 1770s as marriage and partnerships opened up new horizons; members of the family were to lend their influence both to Quaker causes and to objects of public humanity, and as the century closes we shall see the balance of their affairs alter, the banking advance and the iron decline. Against such a background we now have to consider the banking sons of Sampson Lloyd II, and his banking sons-in-law, in Birmingham and in London.

During the 1760s and 1770s, while Sampson Lloyd III was making the running in Birmingham and in the two banks, his father's second family had been arriving on the stage. They were much younger than Sampson. Between him and Ambrose, the youngest, there was a quarter of a century.* Their father, without a wife now and approaching his seventies, had plenty to concern him on their account, the marriages of the girls, the apprenticeship of the boys, how each was to 'begin the world', and all within the confines of the Society; and the marriage connections of the sons no less than their sisters' would be important to his mind for more reasons than one. But Sampson Lloyd was to see all the family handsomely settled. The two girls' husbands, both London men, were to be of service to the younger members, and as two of the sons made London marriages themselves there grew up a considerable outpost of the family, all linking in with the Quaker fraternity there.

* Sampson had been born in 1728. The dates of birth of the second family were: Mary 1736, Rachel 1743, Nehemiah 1746, Charles 1748, John 1751 and Ambrose 1754.

Sampson Lloyd was favoured to end his days with seven grown-up children, six of them married, from whom, could he have known it, would spring forty-four Lloyds in their own generation and 120 in the next.

Older than the others, Mary Hanbury had already been married for ten years at the time of her sister Rachel's marriage in 1767 to another rich London merchant, David Barclay. And David Barclay so identified himself with the Birmingham family, that we must see what manner of match this was.

David Barclay II, as we have to call him, was an interesting man (Plate 25). A grandson of Robert Barclay of the *Apology*, he was a member of an important firm of American merchants with his father in Cheapside, and became a partner in Freame & Barclay, the Lombard Street banking house which in the next century became Barclays Bank, and was a proprietor of Barclay, Perkins & Co. at Southwark Bridge, the brewers. He was linked by marriage to the Gurneys, the Buxtons and the Hoares – and to the Hanburys – all with their copious Quaker ramifications, and was respected for his benefactions in useful and important causes.[1] His own house at the time of his marriage was at Clapton, about three miles from the City, and his father's at No. 108 Cheapside, opposite the Church of St Mary-le-Bow, where the ground floor included the warehouse and counting house of the merchants business. Barclay was thirty-six and Rachel twenty-four, and Rachel was his second wife. He had one daughter surviving from his former marriage and may well have wished for a son, but in twenty-five years he and Rachel had no child. They removed in their first year from Clapton to an exceptional house and estate at Youngsbury, a little to the north of Ware.

Rachel admits on becoming engaged that she is not in love, though she thinks that Barclay is, but she is flattered at 'so desirable a connection'. Staying at her sister's in Essex at the time of the engagement, she writes to her 'dear brother Nimmy' in Birmingham:

I want to hear from thee, and I desire to be informed whether my intended marriage hath been a circulating subject of conversation among my townsfolks. Do tell me what my acquaintance say. Who objects to his age? Who says I am not fit for a mother-in-law? Doth not many pity the poor girl who is likely to have so tart a Mamma? Do sum up and tell me for I want to know the sentiments of my friends and neighbours.*

The Osgood Hanbury family, for their part, lived at Holfield Grange near Coggeshall in Essex, then a dignified early Georgian mansion which was for many years one corner of a busy family triangle, Youngsbury–Coggeshall–London, all at manageable horse distance from each other.

That Barclay lost no time in being of service to his new in-laws, even before he was married, appears over the situation of John and Ambrose when they were out of reach of home and undergoing the smallpox by inoculation; how he sent a friend to visit them while they were ill, reported to their father ('John has had a large crop and Ambrose a very small one') and had them to stay at Clapton to convalesce. The boys had been placed under the Quaker doctor, Thomas Dimsdale, one of the pioneers of inoculation against this disease, which was still a terrible scourge. Dimsdale had set up at Hertford the contemporary equivalent of a nursing home, where patients could be looked after during the inoculated attack.[2] But it was a harrowing decision for parents, for the complaint had to take its course and a patient sometimes died, and it is of interest to reflect that it was Sampson Lloyd, aged seventy, not the parents of the younger generation, who in 1767 first committed his children to so advanced a treatment. Anxious entries in memorandum books and letters show that during the next five to ten years his lead was gradually followed, first one family and then another taking the step, but for very many years to come a mild result would be a matter for thankfulness. 'I suppose thou hast heard,' Rachel writes to her father, 'that my brother and sister at Coggeshall are come to a determination to inoculate their four eldest children. I shall wish to be with my sister during a part of their absence for the occasion must create anxiety.' 'Richard Gurney,' wrote her brother Charles some years later, 'has lost his latest child under inoculation. It is an affecting circumstance.'

For Ambrose, Barclay is active on the father's behalf both when the boy is being bound to a linen-draper and in his marriage negotiations. For John, who was older than Ambrose, Barclay proposes a plan for five years to be spent at a merchant's in Philadelphia,

* Lloyd MSS 2/179, 17 July 1769. For mother-in-law we should now say stepmother.

considering that 'John's firmness and stability renders him very fit
for such an undertaking', and he names the merchant house in view.
For Charles, who was destined for the Birmingham end of the axis,
David Barclay does more. He arranges for this brother to be taken
into his own family's merchant firm to gain experience in the
skills of the counting house. Add to this Charles's own marriage to
one of Barclay's near relations and one is not unprepared for the
friendship which grew up between the two. Years afterwards,
when the merchants business had been given up, Charles Lamb
writes of an occasion on which he and Charles Lloyd were the
guests of Barclay at the Cheapside house, and relates how he was
beckoned out of the room by Charles Lloyd 'to go and sit with
him in the old forsaken counting house' and to be told of 'the great
amount of business that used to be done there in former days'.[3]
The only one who did not receive direct help in his career from this
influential man was Nehemiah. Nehemiah did not go to the metropolis to seek his fortune. Iron was to be his trade, though he also
became a partner in the Birmingham bank after his father's death.
But to Nehemiah and Charles, the Birmingham brothers, we are to
return.

'Cheerful in his temper and conversation', Sampson Lloyd was a
person who was accustomed to making the best of things. At
Rachel's wedding in 1767 it was as a widower that he received his
guests, supported by Olive Kirton who shared his home. The
marriage was followed by a gathering at Farm, where the handsome
drawing-room which had just been added may still be seen. One
other person still living with them was his mother, Ambrose
Crowley's daughter, a name to carry the mind back nearly to the
beginning of this book. Mary Lloyd was ninety and still had three
years to live. But she died in 1770, and Olive died in 1775; and once
again Sampson Lloyd had his domestic situation to repair, leaning
now upon an unmarried daughter of his brother Charles of corn
mill days. In 1769 he had been obliged to spend some time at
Bristol, taking Nehemiah with him, where the Warmley brassworks company had failed[4] and William Champion had become a
bankrupt, and in 1771, as we saw, he had been recalled to the ironmerchants business; but to Sampson junior he left the formation,
with Taylor, of the bank in London, and as the 1770s advanced he
became increasingly a spectator.

In 1770 he lost his daughter Mary Hanbury who died at Coggeshall aged thirty-four. 'The rudest girl in town', the first to marry, was the first to depart. Her virtues are clear to posterity from an epitaph which surprises by the candour of its avowal that 'as a memorial to as much excellence as any religion could bestow this faithful tribute is paid to a Quaker by a Clergyman of the Church of England'. Her husband carried on the home and brought up the children for another fourteen years until his death in 1784.

In 1772 Osgood Hanbury, who had just added banking to tobacco through the setting up of Hanbury, Taylor, Lloyd & Bowman, took John Lloyd, then aged twenty-one, into his tobacco business at Tower Street. Barclay's American proposal for John had not been adopted, but a spell in America now came his way, made desirable on account of the tobacco connection. This arrangement brought John Lloyd, between 1775 and 1777, something more than business experience for it landed him in the midst of the War of Independence (1775–83). The Lloyds being, as required by the Society, a wholly unmartial family, it is interesting to read the impressions of a war situation upon one of the younger members. Something of this, as well as of John's 'firmness and stability', is to be seen in a letter from West River, Maryland, written in September 1775 to his brother Nehemiah:

I was in hopes before now to have received a letter from thee and still please myself with the expectation that there is one upon its passage. But the ships are all going home and I apprehend it will be with great difficulty I shall convey intelligence to England. You must therefore not be uneasy if you should not hear from me. Many people are preparing to leave America and if matters are not settled in a twelvemonth Englishmen (I mean such whose connections are in Great Britain) will be rarities on this side of the Atlantic.

The provincial Convention met at Annapolis a few weeks ago and drew up a paper called an 'association' for everybody to sign. I'm in hopes they will not tender it to me; if they do I shall be obliged to return home sooner than what I intended. I wish as well as any man to Liberty and to America but at the same time cannot put my name to a paper which would make me obnoxious in England. The appellation Tory is immediately applied to those who make use of the least discordant expression; *in civitate libera linguam mentemque liberas esse debere* was the saying of a celebrated Roman, I wish it was verified in America.

The military exercise is now learned by everybody and a man makes a despicable appearance without a stick-frog by his side. Where matters will end no one knows. The storm is coming nearer to these southern provinces, as I see by the papers that the *Asia* man-of-war has cannonaded New York. You are happy in old England out of the way of these commotions. I wish my business was done that I might make one amongst you. The Scotch are by no means favourites with the people here. As an Englishman and a friend to America I think myself safe. If affairs should go to such extremities as to endanger my personal security I must then make a retreat, but this I hope and believe will not be the case. Excuse my writing so much about politics. It is a subject now in everybody's heart and consequently flows frequently from their pens.

I have been out a-shooting two or three times. Partridges and other kinds of game are here in great abundance. How soon I may be deprived of the means I don't know. Gunpowder is very scarce and I should not be surprised if one of the Committees was to send for my little stock; this article is not to be wasted at *birds* but used against *Britons*.[5]

John Lloyd was not obliged to retreat, he was still in America in 1777, but he returned to England some time that year for he begins to keep a memorandum book which opens with the entry '1 First Month 1778, at London'.

The last five years of Sampson Lloyd's life saw the marriages of all his younger sons except for Nehemiah who never married. Charles, on returning from his training in London, was married in 1774 to Mary Farmer, the only daughter of a Birmingham family with distinguished Quaker connections. This was a match which would both interest and gratify his father and will concern us again on a later page. John's bride, whom he married in 1779 about a year after his return from America, was Elizabeth Corbyn, the daughter of Thomas Corbyn of Bartholomew Close near the Royal Exchange. Ambrose, the youngest, in 1777 married Elizabeth Talwin, a niece of the master to whom he had been apprenticed, and settled at Bromley, between Clapton and the Isle of Dogs. Ambrose was considered 'a promising young man', but unfortunately both he and his young wife died in the 1780s, leaving an only daughter, and they disappear from this history. His only surviving letter contains little but a note of their being 'entertained at Blackwall a few days ago to eat White Bait which is now in season and dressed there to

perfection'. All these were Quaker marriages. Their father would
be present at Charles's in Birmingham but not at the others. He
was nearing eighty and did not make the journey to London any
more.

Thus he ended his days, in the house which had been his home
for sixty years, observing the events of his circle. The disgrace of
his nephew Pemberton in 1770 must have distressed him, for it
brought discredit on the family and upon Friends in Birmingham
as well. He would feel in a particular way the death of Taylor
senior, 'my friend John Taylor', in 1775. Taylor would be a loss
to the partnership, and Sampson Lloyd, the senior partner now,
would watch to see how their standing would be affected. But, with
ten years to its credit, the bank was providing a needed service
and was securely established; and had not the profits in that time
represented a yearly average of 45 per cent on the capital?[6] Sampson
Lloyd's last will was made in 1777. He would not be like his brother
Charles, who died intestate, to make work for the representatives
of his estate; Sampson Lloyd was of the opposite make-up. He was
'regular and methodical in his business and extremely accurate in
his accounts'.[7] He declares in his will that he has 'laboured ardu-
ously' in the disposal of his property, for 'every branch of my dear
family', and hopes that they will respect his endeavours. He had
been 'a man of good figure', we are told, 'full six feet in height and
stout made', but now he was troubled with shortness of breath.
He continued to spend time at Farm to the end and had a bedroom
in either house. 'I shall be glad to hear,' Rachel writes in her last
letter before his death, 'that the proposed change of thy chamber at
Farm is effected and that thou art quite comfortable in thy new
apartment.' Two weeks later, as John Lloyd tells us, on 30 November 1779, 'he quietly departed this life at his house in Birmingham in
the eighty-first year of his age' and was buried in the old burying-
ground at Bull Lane.[8] He had suffered hard blows in his life, but he
had built continuously and most things that he touched had come
right. 'A plain Friend both in dress and language', his reputation is
summed up by the local newspaper: 'Mr Sampson Lloyd senior, an
eminent iron merchant and late one of the proprietors of the bank
in this town, a gentleman of the strictest probity and most unsullied
character.'[9] Sampson Lloyd was more. He was the maker of the
Lloyds.

The will of Sampson Lloyd II was at once a family directory, a blueprint for the continuation of his affairs and a more human document than most wills of the present day.[10] The legacies, ranging in importance from £100 for an unmarried niece to a guinea for an unsatisfactory nephew 'if he ever calls to receive it', bring vividly to mind the marriage structure of the family group, detailing in turn, besides Lloyds, representatives of the Good, Crowley, Parkes and Champion connections. The recital concludes with employees in house and business, several sums for poor neighbours and – charming tailpiece – 'unto Richard Simes my barber forty shillings'. Had we an authentic portrait of Sampson Lloyd we might know what fashion of wig it had been Simes's privilege to dress.

Through the disposal of his properties, his businesses and his funds can be seen the pattern that Sampson Lloyd planned for his successors. To his son Sampson, holding the Parkes interest and two banking partnerships in addition to his share in the older business, he simply gives the property at Farm. The girls being provided for, his residuary estate is left among the sons of the younger family, the Edgbaston Street house going to the eldest, Nehemiah, who was unmarried and without a home of his own. At the same time a tribute is paid to the two senior sons by specific additional gifts, to Sampson £400 for 'his services to me in the bank', and to Nehemiah £300 for having acted over several years to settle his affairs in Bristol, 'as a token of acknowledgment that I do affectionately resent it'.

But most significant is the succession that he creates at the Digbeth mill and at the bank. The ironmerchants business of Sampson Lloyd and Son with its offshoot mills and forges had for several years past been committed to a new partnership under the style of S., N. & C. Lloyd,[11] which already controlled Powick, Burton and the Trent navigation interests; but the lease of the slitting mill Sampson Lloyd had retained and this he now gives to the same three Birmingham sons equally. Finally, to Nehemiah and Charles he gives his quarter share in Taylor & Lloyds,* making them partners in this business too. In this way the year 1780 saw the whole of the family's Birmingham interests pass into the hands

* The adjustment of the style of a firm on the death of a partner was a normal practice. Several examples occur in this history.

of the three elder sons, the younger ones being separately established in London, with Sampson, a partner in both banks, as the
bridge between the two.

At this date the Birmingham brothers all lived in the town close
to their business premises. Sampson was in the Square, Nehemiah
took over his father's establishment in Edgbaston Street, and
Charles was living next door to him. Sampson now made preparations to occupy Farm. These consisted of enlarging the dining-room,
making a new entrance at the side instead of facing down the
avenue, and substantial additions at the rear (Plate 30). His large
family, which had nearly reached its total of seventeen, was not
to be the last Lloyd household which in generations to come
would be glad of the extra capacity.

Charles and Mary Lloyd had had five children during the six
years of their marriage. To have a child a year was not at that
period uncommon, indeed a state of almost perpetual pregnancy
may seem to have been considered normal if we are to regard a
remark of his brother John. A few months after the birth of No. 1,
John writes in a letter from America 'the press I suppose is set
again at Charles's and before I return I expect a third will be upon
the stocks'. Mary Farmer is said to have brought her husband a
fortune of £30,000. Through Plumsteds and Freames she was already a cousin of David Barclay, and through her marriage to
Charles many fresh interlinkings were formed in the Quaker net.

In Birmingham, while Charles Lloyd's father was still alive, the
Farmers and the Lloyds had been friends as well as neighbours,
the Lloyds in the town and the Farmers at their dignified, newly
finished residence of Bingley, standing in what today is Broad
Street but was then still 'in the country'. Charles had privately
declared that he would not marry till he could see further into his
settlement in the world. But already, two years before the marriage,
Priscilla Farmer had written to Mary that 'it is desirable to retain
the esteem of a young man that everybody speaks well of'.[12] And
so, in 1774, it had come off, though there is a story that on receiving
his offer Mary had replied, with tongue in cheek, 'Yes, if thy brother
Nehemiah don't want me.'

But Nehemiah Lloyd was not a man of decision. He did not marry
anyone. A partner in both Birmingham businesses, comfortably off,
in his younger days he was evidently acceptable and well-meaning.

That he was trusted can be seen from his endeavours on his father's behalf at Bristol, but his health proved no more robust than his resolution. It was to S., N. & C. Lloyd that he mainly gave his time. The counting house and warehouse at Edgbaston Street, behind his house, continued as the headquarters of this business, where the records were kept and the buying and selling went on, Nehemiah taking charge of Powick and Charles of Burton. Down to about 1775 the older partner, Sampson was active here as well as at the Bank, overseeing both the business and his brothers, corresponding with the Sykes firm at Hull and reporting to his partners upon prices and deals when they were away. But soon the younger men, now approaching thirty, take over a good deal of the load, and if Nehemiah was away in Bristol it was Charles who would now write him the bulletins: that so much brass was sold last week, but the discount from the Bristol Brass Wireworks was not satisfactory; they were nearly out of tin and 'the sooner thou orderest ten more blocks from John Champion the better'; and, some weeks later, not ten but forty blocks are being dispatched from the Cornish suppliers at Falmouth 'per the Truro sloop for Bristol', with thirty more offered by another boat a little later on.

On the slitting mill at Digbeth the record is almost silent in these years, But, though we may not hear much about it, the surrounding district was unceasing in its demand for rod to convert into nails. Matthew Boulton was advised in 1775 that there was annually rolled and slit into rods for nails about 12,000 tons of iron and that 'there is near 10,000 people employed in the trade in this neighbourhood'.[13] A paper in Charles Lloyd's writing reflects the sharp watch that was kept on comparative slitting costs at Digbeth and at Powick;[14] and subject to the swings of peace and war the Birmingham mill was to continue steadily at work for another quarter of a century.

At Burton, Charles writes of the need to 'put the double rolls down soon'; this was to improve the equipment in the rolling department, where iron was rolled into plate to make hoops for beer barrels and copper into sheets for the processers in the toy industry at Birmingham. The same paper shows that cottages for employees are being built beside the forge, the vestiges of which may still be seen. At Burton, in 1774, they are out of 'coke pigs', i.e. pig iron made by the new coke-fired method, but they are

18. The Birmingham of the Lloyds in 1750; from Samuel Bradford's *Plan of Birmingham*.

19. View of Dale End, Birmingham (Taylors & Lloyds' premises through right-hand arch); a reconstruction by Paul Braddon (1864–1937) 'from an original painting on copper of 1780'.

20. John Taylor I, 1711–75, a founding partner of Taylors & Lloyds.

21. No. 60 Lombard Street, London (on left of church), premises of Hanbury, Taylor, Lloyd & Bowman; from a drawing by G. Shepherd about 1811.

22. Quakers at worship: Gracechurch Street meeting in the 1770s. Artist unknown.

23. A view of the Hotwells near Bristol, by T. Morris, 1802.

24. Charles Lloyd the banker, 1748–1828; from a bust by Peter Hollins.

25. David Barclay II, 1728–1809, brother-in-law of Charles Lloyd the banker, by John Zoffany.

26. Bingley in the 1820s, home of Charles Lloyd the banker. Artist unknown.

receiving 150 tons of 'Seaton pigs', of the best charcoal-made quality, all the way from Seaton in Cumberland.[15] From Burton the manager, James Lynam, mindful of his output, reports that he had put off some other business 'as the water was good and I thought to get as much forward with the work as possible'. S., N. & C. Lloyd all this time were still as dependent as ever upon water as their source of power, and as exposed to its vagaries. It is recorded that on one occasion when the Trent was in flood hundreds of pounds worth of precious charcoal was swept from the forge yard and they were obliged 'to employ men to recover it from the river and surrounding meadows at the rate of 4d. per bushel'.[16]

At Powick quite a compound had developed since Sampson Lloyd senior first took on the forge. There were the two works side by side, the one a forge, the other a rolling and slitting mill. A survey plan (Plate 17) shows that these were flanked by a pig wharf, coal yards, charcoal yard and barn, carpenters' yard and shop, blacksmiths' shop, and of course the stables. Besides this there were cottages for ten or fifteen employees, and a manager's house and garden where Nehemiah Lloyd often lodged, all on the same site.[17] Letters of 1780, when Charles Lloyd had been only a few years married and his eldest child was five years old, offer some glimpses of the scene. The first brings out the risks that were run from the flooding of the Teme. Charles Lloyd writes to his wife at Hotwells where she is staying with her mother and little Charles. It is the month of June:

About three weeks ago, as Joseph Shaw was putting up a very large piece of timber at the forge here, one of the forgemen slipped and tumbled into the water where the current was very strong, and it being a flood he was carried some distance and was unable to help himself. Another of our men, seeing him in this situation, leapt into the water and laid hold on him but without effect for he seemed lost also. A third man leapt in after these two poor creatures and entangled himself so with them that he also would have been drowned had not a fourth man leapt in and providentially brought them all out. One man did not recover for a fortnight being dead to all appearance, the other two were speechless. The wives and children of some of the men being on the spot made it a most affecting spectacle; however they are now all well and at work.

A week later, writing from Birmingham, he proposes that the Hotwells party should make a stop at Powick on their way home.

'I think you will like to spend an hour or two on our own premises; and Charles will see the wheels and the hammers, and if the sun shines Papa will show him a rainbow in the wheel'.[18] Two water-colour drawings have been preserved, done within three years of their visit, showing us more vividly than any letters what the ladies were to see and the house where they would be received. These convey the impression of a purposeful, orderly layout, with its clustered buildings, domestic detail, and the two neat mills, con-fronted on the opposite bank by the corn mill.* Of all this Nehemiah Lloyd was in charge, and it is Nehemiah's name as the proprietor that appears in survey plans; but he often needed help and it comes out from fragments such as those quoted that his brother's activities were not confined to Burton.

During more than thirty years following his marriage Charles Lloyd made at least one visit to London every year and sometimes more. This we know because his wife saved his letters.[19] He wrote inde-fatigably to Mary during these and other absences while she for her part was occupied with the children, of whom she had fifteen in nineteen years. He would be in London for a fortnight or three weeks at a time. He would lodge with family or friends, attend Yearly Meeting over many days in May, and keep in contact with affairs and causes and with the bank in Lombard Street. Through a change from Birmingham and the children he also achieved refresh-ment. His visits were much more than business trips.

To walk into 60 Lombard Street (Plate 21), where Hanbury & Co. had removed from No. 14 in 1779, and there to exchange banking intelligence as between country banker and London agent, was a proper part of his duty as an executive partner in Birmingham, and indeed – as his brother Sampson grew older – as principal executive partner, for John Taylor grew old too; and it was a convenience to have a desk at their premises. For Charles Lloyd well understood the value of responsible men getting to London and the contribution that this could make to his own usefulness.

The proceedings of Yearly Meeting, with its general and special-

* The drawings, in the Worcestershire County Record Office, were done in 1783 by E. F. Burney, the brother of Fanny Burney, during a visit to his relations at Worcester. (Plate 16.)

purpose forums, would be attended by Quakers from all parts and of all degrees, men and women, able and ordinary, contributors and hearers. In this atmosphere Charles Lloyd's abilities were soon noted and his services were in demand for this and that committee, and, in due course, for the central committee of all, known (and still known) by its evocative, seventeenth-century name of the 'meeting for sufferings'. During the time of Yearly Meeting, opening on *the first 3rd day after the third 1st day in fifth month* (i.e. the Tuesday following the third Sunday in May), a 'well concerned' Friend might be engaged many hours a day, perhaps for three meetings in succession, beginning before breakfast as Charles Lloyd tells us, and not ending until eight or nine at night. But it was also a great time of gathering, a stimulus and a treat, when Friends came to London in numbers and Quaker houses were thrown open; and the event was noticed in the town. 'Every Quakeress is a lily,' wrote Charles Lamb, 'and when they come up in bands to their Whitsun conferences, whitening the easterly streets of the metropolis, from all parts of the United Kingdom, they show like troops of the Shining Ones.' In addition, Yearly Meeting was an opportunity for the furthering of other kinds of concern, not excluding either the business or the matrimonial sort, as every Quaker tacitly understood.

During ordinary visits Charles Lloyd would attend one or other of the meeting houses of the metropolis, such as 'the Peel', Devonshire House or Gracechurch Street (Plate 22). He lodged chiefly with his London brothers and brother-in-law, with John at Tower Street, with Ambrose at Bromley, and with 'brother and sister Barclay' whose town house was now in Red Lion Square. From such addresses Charles Lloyd could call upon friends in the City at will. He dined here, breakfasted there, and 'drank tea', with great regularity, always at a fresh house, throughout his stay. And as he nearly always reported these encounters to Mary his letters give us a gallery of Quaker London of exceptional continuity and interest. Cousins, both on his own side and his wife's, apothecaries, bankers, widows, brewers, and the cousins of cousins, all Quakers, made up a good deal of the circle; and if the inner ring of names such as Lloyd, Plumsted, Freame or Barclay figure the most often, those of Hanbury, Gurney, Hoare and Bevan come close behind, with a host of others, continuing over the years. The households of Samuel

Hoare at Hampstead and Robert Barclay (David Barclay's nephew) at Clapham frequently provided a bed. Two at least of the leading Quaker doctors and their families, John Fothergill and Thomas Knowles, were intimate friends. It was like a club, for in a private world of this quality the visiting Quaker had little need of the world around.

Not that the better sort of Quakers were oblivious of the world around or closed their eyes to it. That they were concerned, many of them, about neglect or misfortune among their fellow beings, where they met with it, may be seen from their activities in the causes of education and hospitals, in the putting down of the traffic in human beings for slaves and, later, in conditions in the prisons. A social conscience was among the characteristics of Quakers such as Barclay and the Lloyds. Barclay was a promoter of the new Quaker school at Ackworth, Charles Lloyd for years kept the accounts of the General Hospital at Birmingham, and both of these men, and John Lloyd in particular, 'full of truth and simplicity of character', were stalwarts in the slave-trade campaign. War they observed but rejected. Misery they were prepared to make their business. A letter of 1778 shows this in Charles Lloyd as quite a young man. In it he writes of an excursion to Greenwich with Ambrose and two cousins, and of going on to Woolwich 'to see the convicts', and offers some reflections on their condition. The convicts they expected to see were part of the country's prison population, hundreds of whom were confined at this date in floating prisons in the Thames, known as the hulks, and employed on work for the improvement of the river banks and upon docks, quays and yards for the Royal Arsenal at Woolwich. This arrangement had been devised when the ordinary overflow from the prisons, that of transportation to the colonies, had been closed by the American War, popular interest had been caught, and viewing the convicts had become one of the sights. To the Quaker it was not simply sightseeing. After giving an account of the row down the river and their visit to the Naval Hospital, Charles Lloyd goes on:

We then walked up to the Observatory and to One Tree Hill, from whence is a charming prospect, and so across the country three miles to Woolwich. The first thing we had in view was to see the convicts and accordingly we walked through the town to the place where they are employed. We found they were at dinner on board the two ships (or more properly hulks of ship, for the rigging and masts are taken away) where they eat and lodge. We had not been long before a boatload of perhaps 150 came on shore and walked close to us, and a more affecting scene I never saw. Some looked ashamed and confounded, but more, bold and impudent; the majority seemed neither one or the other. They had all chains about one or both of their legs. When they reached the place of working, which is two hundred yards from the river, they began their employment as usual which is raising a great bank of earth for cannon to fire against, and the sand they use is raised by other convicts from the bottom of the Thames. I apprehend the whole number of convicts cannot be less than 500. Their keepers are armed with sword and pistol and are about one-seventh the number of the prisoners. They dont suffer any person to go near them when they are at work, which is a good regulation. The depravity of human nature is most affecting. A bad education and bad company often render those miserable who, had they had a good education and good company, might have been orna-ments in society. How then can we, who have been favoured in these respects, pass harsh censures on these poor creatures?[20]

John Lloyd's fortunes became solid and comfortable quite early in his married life – conveniently for raising a family of ten. He had married Betsy the year after his return from America. Upon Osgood Hanbury's death in 1784, they moved from Bartholomew Close to the Tower Street house, the seat of the tobacco business, and this became their home (and a hotel for Charles) for the next twenty-five years. About the same time, through the influence of his brother Sampson, John Lloyd began to work at Hanbury, Taylor & Co. in Lombard Street, where he was friends with his cousin Osgood Hanbury junior, and where, in 1790, having finally closed the tobacco business, he became a partner. For the rest of his life he continued as a banker, playing an essential part in the business and graduating to senior managing partner. The firmness and stability which Barclay had noted in him in his teens contributed to making John Lloyd a better banker than his brother Nehemiah. These characteristics can almost be deduced from his orderly, consistent memorandum book, in which he makes brief objective notes of events and facts, mainly of a family aspect, quite different from the warm, copious reporting of Charles Lloyd's letters.

But John Lloyd's chief claim upon our interest is his part in the movement for putting an end to the slave trade,[21] a movement begun in the 1780s mainly by members of the Society of Friends. The trade, as understood in the seafaring countries of Western Europe, in Portugal for instance, in Spain and France and Holland, just as much as in England, had been carried on for a hundred years and more and was simple, profitable and increasing. Basically its plan was, in return for cheap articles of ornament or use such as beads, cooking-pots or low-grade muskets, to acquire Negroes on the African coast, transport them for sale in the plantation ports of the West Indies and America and upon the proceeds to bring home the products of those regions, such as cotton and sugar, the round trip clearing principally from Liverpool, Bristol or London. This was the pattern which gave rise to the expression 'the triangular trade'. It also explains that of 'the Middle Passage', in which the cargo, in a lying-down position and chained, were kept stowed like merchandise upon the racks with which every deck and corner was fitted. Slave-raiding and a trade in black Africans was also carried on in other parts of Africa, for example by the Arabs in the east; but what Europe condoned and the Quakers condemned, besides the Middle Passage, was the 'acquiring' on the coast and the conditions in the plantations. For the first amounted to the forcible carrying away of men and women for gain, to say nothing of 'the wars and hostilities among the Negro princes and chiefs for the sake of making captives of each other for sale',[22] stifling other trade and development, while the life of the Africans in the plantations was one of unremitting exploitation. But the temper of the times was beginning to reject the whitewash and the arguments of self-interest, that the Negro was by nature debased and did not feel as white men do, that he was better off away from his primitive village, or that the slave on a plantation did not starve like the man out of work at home, and consciences were beginning to prick.

In Quaker teaching, slavery had been formally condemned for sixty years past as an offence against humanity as well as against Christian principles and was regarded as an evil second only to war. And the fact is that the Quakers, besides being thus conditioned and brought up, were in a position to know more about the trade than most other religious bodies, owing to their two-way relations with members of the Society in America who on their part condemned the cruelties that they saw in their own country. John Lloyd, at twenty-seven, had come back from that country stirred by the iniquities of the system, and when in 1783 six Friends were commissioned to organise propaganda for abolition his name was among them. The names are given in Clarkson's *Abolition*: William Dillwyn, George Harrison, Samuel Hoare, Thomas Knowles, MD, John Lloyd and Joseph Woods. The timing of this move in relation to public sentiment was good and the group made headway. The Society in that year petitioned Parliament against the trade and in the year after began putting out printed publications about it. Besides the six, others would be invited to take part in their deliberations, among whom in 1785 David Barclay's name is recorded. But it was not long before a fresh stage was reached, when a wider committee took shape, twelve in number, not exclusively Quaker but still predominantly so. The drive behind this second group was that of Thomas Clarkson, a young cleric with a talent for relentless enquiry who became the principal collector of data for the campaign. Clarkson travelled tirelessly, cultivating support, raising subscriptions, researching everywhere to assemble authentic particulars for propaganda, spending at one time five weeks in the waterside taverns of Bristol, meeting what Negroes he could, and all but drowned in a Liverpool dock through the hostility of the slave-traders there.

Clarkson, when he visited Birmingham, carried letters to Sampson and Charles Lloyd – prompted by John of course – and from that time they and some others in leading positions in the town – Garbett, Priestley, Russell, men of all persuasions – began to hold meetings and stir up interest there. As in other towns, support grew, and Taylor & Lloyds were employed to transmit the funds collected for the expenses of the London committee. Wedgwood we now likewise meet with again, for it was he who, joining the committee in 1787, was responsible for creating their publicity emblem of a Negro in chains with the legend 'Am I not a man and a brother?' Charles Lloyd, on his visits to London, was constant in meeting members of the committee. In his letters between 1787 and 1791 their names occur frequently; 'drank tea with Wm. Dillwyn', 'called at T. Knowles', 'breakfasted with George Harrison', 'took a bed at Samuel Hoare's'. Charles Lloyd had his shoulder to the wheel. In February 1790 we read, 'I drank tea at J. Phillips and afterwards went to the Committee of the Slave Trade, where I met several of my friends, indeed all the company were Friends. This great cause of humanity rests very much upon the members of our

Society.' And early in 1791 there was another name in the situation: 'the day after tomorrow Robert Barclay and I intend to dine at William Wilberforce's.'

That Charles Lloyd was taking a solid part in all this and not just playing the spectator can be felt from a letter of March 1792 in which among other guests dining at Osgood Hanbury's house he encounters the Attorney General of Barbados and wife: 'I had to defend the cause of the poor African against a very able opponent in the Attorney General who, however, candidly acknowledged that the slave trade was a horrid one and wanted great regulations, and that the whip *was* used in most plantations.' Nor were the Barclays inactive. There was an episode in their affairs which illuminates David Barclay's character as well as his attitude to slavery. In 1795 he and his brother John become possessed, through a debt, of a farm in Jamaica with thirty-two slaves upon it. Disapproving of this, Barclay, already in his later sixties, laid out £10,000 in removing these slaves to Philadelphia, freeing them, training them and establishing them in new employment, 'and lived to receive testimonials of their gratitude'. David Barclay was ahead of events. It was the trading in slaves that the 1807 Act was to make illegal. It was not until 1833, nearly forty years after Barclay's action, that possession of them in British territory was finally to be put down.

Through the advocacy of Wilberforce and his friends an advance was achieved in 1792 when a bill was passed approving *gradual* abolition, the date to be left open. This at any rate was an important stage. We cannot tell here the long story of the twenty years that passed between the formation of Clarkson's committee and the date of Abolition itself. Enough to say that no fewer than four times – in 1795, 1797, 1798 and 1799 – was a date for abolition brought up in Parliament only to be deferred, that in 1804 a bill was at last approved in the Commons but the Lords threw it out, and not until 25 March 1807 was it enacted (and correspondingly in the United States) that from 1 May that year 'no vessel should clear for slaves from any port within the British dominions' and after 1 March 1808 no slave should be landed in the Colonies. At his death in 1811 John Lloyd had lived to see the aim of his committee achieved.

The opening years of the slave-trade campaign coincided with the French Revolution and the events resulting in the war with France. Whatever their principles, Quakers were obliged to live with the violence of men and nations and, like other people, to suffer from its effects, and it is of interest to see this happening to some of the Lloyds. Despite their peaceable attitudes, or perhaps because of them, some Quakers were not impervious to the glamour of military scenes, when they saw any.

Charles Lloyd's visit to Woolwich in 1778 had ended with an artillery practice. 'We afterwards took a view,' he writes, 'of amazing quantities of cannon, bombs and instruments of death, saw the soldiers firing cannon at a mark, and were bold enough to stand within a few yards of where we knew the balls would come.' In the same year John Lloyd, on a journey from Margate to London, goes out of his way to see a camp of 13,000 militia and regulars near Maidstone, 'the appearance whereof pleased me much', and he describes its arrangements and extent. 'The tents, each containing five men, were pitched in regular rows and the spaces between them called streets. There were thirteen or fourteen tents in each row and the officers' marquees in the rear, with places for the soldiers to dress victuals and their wives to wash in.' In 1780, while visiting Weymouth with two of his young family, Charles Lloyd reports seeing 'some large fleets at sea which appeared very agreeable'.

Ten years later, when the Revolution has begun, John Lloyd, out for an afternoon on the Thames with his wife and four children, is a witness of warlike preparation which touches him rather more nearly. 'We proceeded down the river to Woolwich and had a fine view of the *Windsor Castle* of 98 guns. Upon our return we met with a press gang, who took away our two watermen and put one of their men on board our boat who landed us safely at the Tower about 9 o'clock.'[23] The laconic record plays down a disagreeable experience.

At Birmingham in 1791 reaction against the friends of France touched off the Priestley riots which, during five days, terrorised the town, alarmed the bankers and cost one of them the loss of most of his property. Unfortunately no Lloyd pen mentions these events, John Lloyd excluding from his memorandum book what does not touch him personally and Charles writing letters only when either he or Mary are away. So far as the Birmingham brothers are concerned there is therefore no reason to doubt that they personally experienced those days of menace and destruction.

The pretext for the riots was a dinner to celebrate the Fourteenth of July. Joseph Priestley had been a target of controversy for several years and this now burst into hostility against him and his friends. Priestley was a Dissenter and a Whig. He was a scholar, a pioneer in physics, an ornament of the Lunar Society,* a political pamphleteer, and the minister of a Unitarian congregation in Birmingham.† He was also a 'friend of Liberty'. His advanced, polemical writings, his support of the American colonists in the War of Independence and his open approval of the new government in France had brought him considerable notoriety. Now, in the sensitive state of political sentiment, London cartoonists attacked him, Birmingham was in a turmoil, 'damn Priestley' appeared on the walls, and a spirit of faction developed between Church and Tory opinion on one side and Dissenters, especially of Priestley's kind, on the other. It needed little provocation to fire the train, and the announcement of a dinner to mark the second anniversary of the taking of the Bastille, coinciding with the circulation of a seditious handbill reputedly from a Unitarian pen, was enough. Priestley absented himself from the dinner but it was too late, a mob gathered and, under the slogan of 'Church and King', violence broke loose.

Such was the focus of opinion against Priestley that the ringleaders easily directed the crowd against the houses of the principal Unitarians, the property of other Dissenters going unharmed. Some of the latter were threatened by groups of the rioters but were reprieved; and there is a tradition that a detachment of them appeared at Farm where Sampson Lloyd placated them with calm words and bread but there is no evidence for this story. If Sampson Lloyd did so he must have relied upon declaring for the King, he could hardly have done so for the Church. In the town, the two Unitarian meeting houses were destroyed and the best Unitarian houses pulled down, while those outside the town were burnt, and as each

* Birmingham's celebrated society for amateur scientific enquiry, the Lunar Society, flourished during the fourth quarter of the century.

† Dr Priestley was minister of the New Meeting, in what is still called New Meeting Street. The fact that this and the Old Meeting have by some writers been called 'Presbyterian' is not due to a mistake, as this was the name by which, down to about that period, Unitarian congregations in England had been known.

mansion fell in and the cellars were drained so the crowd swept on to fresh pillage and destruction. This was a week in which Birmingham paid the price of its primitive town government, feeble if not partisan magistrates and the want of any proper police. The riot was only arrested on the fifth day by the appearance of some cavalry from Nottingham. Priestley escaped with his life, but his house, library and scientific equipment were destroyed and so were many handsome properties round about. Two of these belonged to Sampson Lloyd's partner, John Taylor II, part of his inheritance from his father, one at Bordesley, the 'elegant, costly residence' in which he lived, the other at Moseley, which, though let, still suffered destruction. After the riot, when the time came for public compensation, John Taylor's claim of £12,670 was the largest made, though his real loss was believed to be approaching double that amount. The sum that he received was £9902. He had had other anxieties as well, for we read that quite early in the riot the bankers in the town took steps to remove their convertible property such as cash and notes from their places of business and lodge it in safety 'before the moment of seizure and plunder came upon them'.[24] John Taylor would not have neglected this. At this date he owned nearly half the business.

That year, opinion in England had been shocked when Louis XVI, seeking to cross the frontier, had been stopped and brought back a prisoner to Paris. Upon his execution in January 1793 opinion in England was dumbfounded. War against the Republic would soon be declared. Charles Lloyd writes from London, in February, of 'the present awful appearance of affairs'. Everywhere confidence was shaken. In Birmingham at a public meeting a resolution was passed, in leading names, to continue accepting the notes of the bankers in the town. Sentiment focused upon the throne. Heads would not roll here. An address to the King from the Society of Friends, praying him not to approve a war, was presented by three senior members, one of them John Lloyd. 'John Eliot, Joseph Bevan and brother John,' writes Charles Lloyd,

presented Friends' address to the King. They were received very graciously, to use the court talk; but it was evident from the King's answer that he did not like some of the sentiments, which were, however, Christian and proper, and happy would it have been had such sentiments prevailed in the Cabinet.[25]

The King's reply, which the deputation brought away in writing and which is preserved by the Society of Friends, was as follows:

Whatever steps I may feel myself bound to take for the security of my people I am not the less inclined to judge favourably of the motives which have led you to present this Address, and you may depend upon the continuance of my protection.

But all this time life, and especially Quaker life in the provinces, went on its normal way. Charles Lloyd went to London only once or twice a year. In Birmingham he brought up his children, attended to business, became a valued townsman and served the Society at Bull Street; from Birmingham he set out on his many concerns and to Birmingham, to 'dear Edgbaston Street', he came home. Mary's mother Priscilla Farmer, with her ample house and gardens, was a personality in their lives. Twenty years a widow, she often helped by having the children to stay or to spend the day, until Friday came to be known in the family as Bingley day; and as fifteen children were born and only four died in infancy it is easy to see why they are referred to as the 'little flock'. There were five boys first and then a daughter, in fact six daughters who grew up. Charles Lloyd no doubt had his favourites. These were the two eldest boys, Charles and James, and the first of the girls, Priscilla; and how often in his letters does he send messages to these three, remembering almost as an afterthought to reel off some of the other names.

In 1787 he acquired a farm, at Olton, near the road to Warwick, four or five miles from Birmingham, where for the rest of his life he farmed the land himself, spending the day there on Wednesdays; and members of the family, visitors and, later, grandchildren constantly went there too. A favoured watering-place was Bristol, or more precisely Hotwells, where the rest, the medicinal waters and the air of Clifton Downs were among the attractions. Bristol itself was much more, it was a hive of Quaker relations, connected in part through Charles's mother, Rachel Champion, with their ramifying world, a little London; it was also a centre for business for, canals or no, was not Bristol still the seaport of Birmingham? Charles Lloyd's letters from Bristol are a guide to the local Quaker world. The Champion relatives, mainly his first cousins, include two or three rolling stones, and some of them are inclined to be eccentric. The Goldneys on the other hand are welcoming and rich and Charles Lloyd often stays in their households at Clifton; while names such as Tuckett and Fry, Collinson and Dimsdale, as well as his cousins the Harfords, people his correspondence. Charles Lloyd was also, in the fashion of the time, a believer in another kind of water, sea-water. To Weymouth he sends his wife for recuperation ('recruiting', this was called) with one or two of their children, and thither he takes Charles and James when they are little boys, his letters telling of the bathing, and the machines, and the details. He is on less sure ground over sea-water taken internally, as the children tend to be sick. Scarborough, Exmouth and Caernarvon are among places which he visits with one or another of the family.

In the midst of the upheaval of the Revolution, in 1792, between the riots at Birmingham and the death of the French King, Charles Lloyd's sister Rachel died at Youngsbury. Rachel Barclay was only forty-nine. The brothers were summoned. 'My dear sister,' John Lloyd notes, 'having laboured for about a week under a pleuritic fever, departed this life at Youngsbury this evening. Brothers Sampson and Nehemiah arrived about an hour before her decease.' Charles Lloyd got there for the funeral. The couple had had twenty-five years of married life. Childless, they had devoted part of their time to the landscaping and improvement of Youngsbury as an estate. In the carriage on the way to the funeral some of this was in Barclay's mind. 'When we left Youngsbury this morning at 6 o'clock,' writes Charles Lloyd,

in very mournful procession, he remarked how mutable and unstable are all human enjoyments; he and his wife had been labouring to make Youngsbury a perfect place ever since he had bought it and this spring all was perfection, when alas the partner of his pleasures was snatched from him. I never saw a place in such exquisite order.

The next year, in the first summer of the War, the two men took a considerable tour into Wales, accompanied by two of the younger generation and a groom. This tour Charles Lloyd presents as being for Barclay's good, 'I really think a journey was quite necessary for my worthy brother whose spirits are much sunk', but it made an excellent holiday for the others. David Barclay lived for another seventeen years, and withdrew from Youngsbury to live chiefly at

Walthamstow where his friends could reach him better. He was 'one of the finest characters of his time and a true humanitarian'.[26] He had been immensely rich, but it does not seem to have corrupted him. He constantly employed his money for worthy objects. 'To be preserved humble and retired in the midst of so much affluence is a favour,' Priscilla Farmer had written in the 1760s, an opinion reflected by one of Barclay's executors when he wrote in 1809, 'my grandfather was much too good a man to be an *amasser* of riches, his assets do not amount to £40,000.'[27] David Barclay is said to have distributed his ample fortune among his near relatives during his lifetime.

The word 'affluent', like 'opulent', today is on the whole either a little guilty or not applicable. In those days it was neither; it conveyed a satisfactory condition, if you could achieve it. 'Pray dont over-fatigue thyself,' Charles writes to Mary in 1786, 'for considering how we are blessed with a good deal of affluence we ought to get over anxious care.' In the same vein, for his old brother Sampson, in a letter to his eldest son in 1799, the blessings of tranquillity of mind were above 'the mere ability afforded me to impart wealth'. The Lloyds were not Croesuses like Taylor or Barclay, but all the four brothers were very comfortably off; and so the world was aware, if we may judge from the statement in Shaw's *History of Staffordshire*, that for some years the forge at Burton has been occupied by 'the opulent family of Lloyds, Quakers, of Birmingham'.[28]

Meanwhile Charles Lloyd was working as a partner in the Bank at Birmingham, and we can now consider its fortunes during the last quarter of the century in relation to those of the iron business.

Since the loss of Sampson Lloyd II in 1779 there had been no alteration in the number of the partners and it was the end of the century before any were removed by death. The four men who signed the accounts and divided the profits during these twenty years were the younger Sampson Lloyd and the younger John Taylor, founding partners, and Sampson Lloyd's brothers Nehemiah and Charles, ranging in age, at the outset, from fifty-one down to thirty-one. The capital in the firm was held equally by the two families, as it had been from the beginning, so that Taylor, after his

father's death in 1775, was holding half and his three partners the
rest. Each of the two seniors also held a quarter share in Hanbury,
Taylor, Lloyd & Bowman. Taylor therefore received a handsome
proportion of the results of the two enterprises and, with his vast
private income and imposing mansions, was known to be a rich man
and contributed in this way to the estimation in which the stability
of the Bank was held. Both banks were prospering. As early as
1773 Taylor & Lloyds were issuing their own notes. Hanbury &
Co. had yielded the proprietors an average of 11 per cent per annum
over the first five years, lower than at Birmingham where there
was then no competition, but not unsatisfactory. The fortunes of
Taylor & Lloyds can be traced in their partnership ledgers, now in
the possession of Lloyds Bank, although only to a limited degree
because the method of book-keeping is unlike that of the present
day. For how long after its formation the firm remained Birmingham's only bank does not appear to be known but probably for
fifteen to twenty years. The final quarter of the century, however,
was on the whole a period of expansion and credit activity, the
number of country bankers growing rapidly, and Birmingham in
1791 had four banks, Taylor & Lloyds, Coales's, Goodall's and
Spooner's, afterwards Attwood & Spooner. But in that busy time
there was business for all and the position of Taylor & Lloyds did
not suffer. The sums which the partners allowed themselves to
divide advanced progressively. In the twenty years from 1780 to
1800 the ledgers suggest that the rate of return on the capital,
which was now £30,000, was moving from about 16 to about 25
per cent. After 1800 larger amounts were divided. There was no
audit. Each year, in the private ledger, the partners certified that
'the above account as stated to 31 Twelfth mo. December 1782 is
agreed to by us', the formula used for the date satisfying both the
Lloyds, who were Quakers, and Taylor who was not.

Nehemiah and Charles Lloyd had been working at Dale End, as
well as in the iron business, for several years before their admission
as bank partners. Charles, as already mentioned, had trained at the
Barclay business in Cheapside; Nehemiah's training is not known.
Charles Lloyd, whose handwriting first appears in the books in
1775, had begun to work at the Bank about the time of his marriage;
Nehemiah's hand appears two years later, after his return from Bristol, but it does not continue for long. Certainly his talents did not

lie in book-keeping, for while there are columns of names and figures in Nehemiah Lloyd's handwriting the totals at the foot are in his brother's. Charles Lloyd on the other hand, who was a man of good order and precision, personally wrote up the private ledger of the firm for fifty years.

Before long it became evident that Nehemiah was unsuited to be a working banker and that it was enough for him to be employed in the iron. He had inherited from his mother's family a kind of nervous insecurity which tended to deprive him of confidence and sometimes even of appetite. Charles Lloyd's letters offer quite a commentary on this. Charles was sorry for Nehemiah and ready to see the good in him but sometimes is plain-spoken, as in London in 1799 when they are both at Tower Street: 'Brother Nehemiah is here and poorly. He is just the same irresolute character as at home.' Just occasionally Charles's patience gives out. Writing at Bristol in 1785, 'I really am sick to hear brother Nehemiah's complaints. . . but I have been his friend and intend still to be so, considering him as *a forlorn, broken down man who has by nature much to struggle with.*' No doubt Nehemiah could not help these things, but they are not the characteristics of a manager. Seedy though he became, he was still a partner in both businesses, still supposed to be responsible for the management at S., N. & C. Lloyd at Birmingham and certainly at Powick, and continued to sign the private ledger at Dale End with the other partners every year. He left his mark on these businesses by what he did not do rather than by what he did and, on the iron side, gave the signal by his death for the closing down of most of it.

Nehemiah Lloyd died on 22 February 1801 at the age of fifty-five. His partners at once set about breaking up the iron business, and some particulars of how in the next few years Powick, the mill at Digbeth, and the metal-merchants business itself were all disposed of are given on another page. Burton they did not close for another ten years.

The case of Burton throws light on the others, for several things single out the Burton unit from the rest of the organisation. It was the special preserve of Charles Lloyd who in 1801 was only fifty-three while his brother Sampson was seventy-three; it was the only works in which steam had replaced water-power, perhaps on Charles Lloyd's initiative; its situation connected it closely with the interests of the Boat Company in which Sampson Lloyd was still a partner; and more is known about it through Charles's letters than about the other works. Enough is recorded to give Burton its own interest. Some of its plate or sheet iron went as far as to Manchester customers, and even to the brewery at Southwark for Barclay & Perkins to make into hoops.[29] A product not previously mentioned was 'wire iron for screws to drive into wood' supplied to a firm which cut the screws by water-power 'with great velocity, eight or nine screws a minute'.[30] The rolling equipment was used not just for rolling iron but often for copper, a user of which was Matthew Boulton at Birmingham, and the sales language of a Quaker business man can be seen from a letter of Charles Lloyd to that important customer in 1800:

S., N. & C. Lloyd respectfully inform their friend Mr Boulton that they would undertake to roll from 6 to 8 tons copper weekly at the prices they mentioned to his clerk T. Kellett, vizt. 3/- per ton provided they are not liable to losses by robbery, or 3/6 if they take this risque on themselves. They are obliged to M.B. for his attention to them.[31]

The date when S., N. & C. Lloyd installed steam in the Burton works to power processes hitherto worked by Trent water is not recorded. Such a departure must have seemed a momentous step to take. It was taken in the 1780s or early 1790s, probably the latter, during which time the firm's overdraft was rising; for these years were the period when contemporary improvements to the Newcomen 'fire-engines' were being adopted in the ironworking districts and the much more advanced innovations of Boulton's new partner, James Watt, were beginning to be known and available.* The Burton installation does not figure in Watt's engine book; it was of the improved Newcomen type known as the *common* engine, and was fired by coke, which was cheaper than charcoal and more easily obtained. Just as Charles Lloyd had applied himself in the 1770s to the refinements of slitting costs, so he now concerned himself with the technicalities of steam engines. In 1798, when

* For steam and the iron industry in the eighteenth century see W. K. V. Gale, *The Black Country Iron Industry*, Iron and Steel Institute, 1966, pp. 23–36. The Burton engine (cf.p.26) was modified in 1798 by the addition of crank and flywheel (pp. 29, 30), probably by the Derby firm of James Fox to whom references occur in the correspondence.

T.Q.L.—H

money had been spent on some major modifications, he writes from London to the manager at Burton:

It has not been in my power to be much at Burton of late but I often think a great deal about you, being very anxious for the prosperity of the work and for its being carried on with spirit. I was sorry to find that the new cylinders would blow only one fire. I hope however they will be made to do for both. James [the ex-manager] seemed to think the new flywheel would be too heavy for the gudgeons. Let me know thy opinion and write me a letter with an account of what you are doing and how the work goes on in all respects.[32]

This letter was written, not by a technical director, but by a senior banker, probably in Lombard Street, for it carries as a postscript, 'Direct for me at Taylor, Lloyd, Bowman & Co's, Bankers, London'.

In comparison to Burton the other works were uncompetitive. Just as water-power was giving way to steam, which was more efficient, so the refining of iron with charcoal was giving place to the new coal process, which was cheaper.* But Burton did not have this process. Their bar was still made with charcoal, and was expensive, though with technical refinements it sold on quality. A letter of Charles Lloyd's in 1804, soliciting orders for bar, includes both the case for the price they were charging and a reference to the disposal of their interests at Birmingham:

Esteemed Friend Matthew Boulton,

We had the satisfaction of supplying B & W with iron for several years when we were concerned in the iron trade in Birmingham and this iron was made at our forge at Burton on Trent, which we continue to work, and we should be glad to be favoured with part of your orders. Your smith repeatedly informed us that our iron gave satisfaction and it was not till some time after we had sold our stock in Birmingham to Gibson & Co. that we heard any complaint of its quality. It's possible the iron complained of might not be of our making as we believe you bought considerable quantities from G. & Co. after we had declined the trade, and as we have the opportunity of manufacturing iron in the best manner and are much disposed to do so we should be obliged to you for another order.

---

* Henry Cort's method of refining iron with coal, the 'puddling' process, introduced in the 1780s, together with the progressive shortage of charcoal, was putting an end to charcoal iron.

Our last process in refining our iron is by charcoal. It is all stamped under the hammer, then broken and piled on cakes for the air furnace, and afterwards drawn under the hammer so that our iron must have a *much stronger body* than when it is rolled into cakes and bars, and as we often use a quantity of nut and scrap iron to mix with the stamped iron this adds to its toughness.

We are respectfully thy friends

S. & C. Lloyd.

We would deliver you from 10 to 50 tons at £21 per ton in Birmingham, quarter-day payment, of prime quality, or good best bars at £20 per ton.[33]

But despite money spent on steam, intelligent direction and a renewal of the lease, the forge at Burton was not very long in following its sister mills and by 1812 the Lloyds had ceased iron-working there. In that year they obtained the consent of Lord Uxbridge, upon payment of £800, to remove the equipment and convert the premises to corn-milling, though the latter they did not do themselves, and the forge soon afterwards passed into other hands. None of the young Lloyds went into charcoal iron. Only Charles was now left, Sampson Lloyd had died in 1807, and Charles Lloyd at sixty-four had other calls upon his energies and attention.

The dissolution of the iron connection brings out the fact that, for several years before the death of Nehemiah in 1801, S., N. & C. Lloyd owed the Bank about £20,000, and draws attention to their special position as borrowers. The record of the ledgers, which start in 1777, shows some striking swings in the level of the account. In about twenty-five years there are two periods of high borrowing, the first in 1777 and 1778 just as the record opens, and the second from 1793 to 1800. Each reaches about £22,000. In between, during the 1780s, there are eleven years of low overdraft, averaging £5,300 a year. Eighteenth-century book-keeping apart, these peaks raise several questions not easy to answer. Each corresponds in date to a war period, the American war and the war with France, but in each period the demand for iron was high and prices of both pig and bar iron rose. Were capital outlays a cause? Was the second peak, which concluded a fairly steady rise from 1792 onwards, related to the installation of steam at Burton and the 'heavy expense for buildings' undertaken by the Boat Company in combating the menace of the Trent and Mersey? How far was the overdraft an incentive for the sale of the business? On the other side of the account, how were these borrowings paid off? On each occasion the process was rapid. The time of the first reduction corresponds closely to that of the division of their father's estate, the second must have been facilitated by the proceeds of selling the assets; but to dispose of your business and not enjoy the proceeds may seem a little inglorious.

Finally there is the attitude of the Bank as lender and extender of these advances. S., N. & C. Lloyd were themselves the proprietors of half the Bank, so that, in regard to half of what was advanced, the family had been lending to itself. The other half was Taylor's, and what was Taylor's line? The lending, at its height, had amounted to more than the Lloyd family's total stake in the Bank. Did the Lloyds give the Bank security? Taylor could hardly be so rich as to disregard business hazards in a business bearing his own name. This lending to one's parent business was a trap into which many country bankers fell, only to find the parent business unable to put them in funds when the bank ran into stringency. The Lloyds belonged, after all, to a Society that came down hard on irregularity in business and there is evidence that they were conscious of it. Within a month of their brother's death they were writing in a letter to Taylor,

> It is the wish of S., N. & C. Lloyd to reduce their accounts, and they hope to dispose of a considerable part of their concerns in the iron trade before the end of the year, and they will then be ready to lodge security with Taylor and Lloyds for any sum due from them which shall exceed half the amount of their capital, which is the most agreeable to the original plan of the house.*

How uncomfortable were they feeling? And how uncomfortable had they been, and for how long, while their brother was still alive?

Disposal took longer than they had indicated to Taylor, but they were out of Powick by the end of 1801, they declined the trade at Edgbaston Street in 1802 or the year after, and the slitting mill at Digbeth was given up by 1804. The Powick property passed to Thomas Elwell, a Birmingham ironmaster, and afterwards to the Willis-Bund family;[34] the ironmerchants' stock was sold to Gibson

---

* Typescript at Lloyds Bank containing extracts from a paper dated 18 March 1801, formerly in the Lloyd family. It is so soon after Nehemiah's death that they are still writing 'S., N. & C. Lloyd'.

& Co. as we saw; and the transfer of the slitting mill from the name of Lloyd into that of Tomlinson emerges from the town's levy books. In the 1820s the sites of the slitting mill and millpool were being developed by under-tenants of the Lloyds, who continued as the leaseholders until the second half of the century. Nehemiah Lloyd died intestate and his brother Charles was appointed his administrator. Whether from the capital of Nehemiah's estate, which presumably passed to the brothers, or from the product of these disposals, the indebtedness of S., N. & C. Lloyd soon fell to modest levels at which it remained until the firm's account was finally closed in 1815. So ended, after a hundred years, the charcoal iron history of the Lloyds, leaving the field to the Bank and to the nineteenth century.

8

THE NEW CENTURY

Despite the influences of the French Revolution, the nineteenth century, as we think of it, did not really begin on 1 January 1800. Centuries seldom do this. In 1800, George III was still on the throne, Napoleon still the enemy, railways were unheard of, Queen Victoria had not been born, and for some time the eighteenth century went on. The industrial revolution meanwhile was continuing in full spate. Since 1765 the population of Birmingham had doubled and had now reached 70,000. For country banking the years around 1790 had been a prosperous time and many new banks had appeared. All the four Birmingham banks had weathered the anxieties caused by the war against France, including those of its onset in 1793, when many banks failed, and those caused under threat of invasion in 1797 when the Bank of England, ceasing to give gold for its own notes, shook confidence in those of other banks, and a Birmingham commentator could declare:

> The Credit of our BANKERS firmly stood,
> As sterling GOLD their NOTES were full as good,
> Nor e'er were question'd – all throughout the land.
> The Reason's plain – They pay 'upon demand.'[1]

Among the Lloyds with whom we are concerned the opening of the century was a time when, from all being Friends, some became more so, some less, and some left the Society altogether. It was also marked by the association of some of the family with an exceptional circle of literary figures including Charles Lamb, Coleridge and the Wordsworths.

In order to conclude the story of S., N. and C. Lloyd we have run ahead a few years and must pick up the threads at Dale End.

The turn of the century was a time of new partners at the Bank, two young Lloyds from one family, one from another, and presently a young Taylor all being admitted to partnership within less than ten years. The regulations for country banks limited the number of partners to six, so that for Taylor & Lloyds, with only four principals, there had for some time past been the option of appointing two more, but while the partners were growing older the sons had been too young. But at the end of 1795 it had been agreed that Sampson Lloyd, who would soon be seventy, should formally divide his share of the profits with his two eldest sons although 'without withdrawing his name and responsibility', upon which in part the goodwill and reputation of the undertaking rested. The sons whom he introduced were Sampson, the fourth of this name, and his brother Samuel. Samuel had already been working in the Bank since the beginning of 1794. His brother, Sampson IV as we have to call him, had been gaining experience in London and was a newcomer.

But after only four years, in the winter of 1800–1801, the partnership was distracted by two deaths within two months, those of Nehemiah Lloyd and, unexpectedly, of the new Sampson. These losses the firm repaired in two stages, first by the introduction, in 1802, of Charles Lloyd's son James and secondly by admitting in 1805 a son of John Taylor, another James, aged only twenty-two. But although this appointment brought the number of the Taylors up to two they continued at that time to accept only eight twentieths of the profits instead of ten twentieths, the load being still predominantly upon the other family. Indeed, in the matter of Nehemiah Lloyd's share, the Lloyds had made a case to John Taylor for these proportions to continue:

We know the value of thy capital, character and attendance, but feeling our independence and knowing that the weight of the business has rested and is likely to rest on us for some years to come, we cannot but think it would be hard for us to be deprived of our N. Lloyd's share till such time as thy sons might be in a situation to take their reasonable part in the attendance and attention which the business requires.[2]

It was not until 1815, after further changes in the partnership had taken place, that the fifty–fifty relationship between the two families was restored. But the new admissions bring out an aspect which has not appeared before. Not only were there the respective interests of the Taylors and of the Lloyds to be kept in balance, but there were now two branches of the Lloyds at Birmingham, the Sampson Lloyd and Charles Lloyd branches, and this feature was to continue right down to 1865 when private partnership gave place to another form of organisation.

At the turn of the century we have to think of the Sampson Lloyds at Farm with thirteen of their seventeen children living and the Charles Lloyds at Bingley with eleven out of fifteen.* For the biographer, many of Sampson Lloyd's sons and daughters fade from view like those of his grandfather, Sampson Lloyd I, so that once again the main interest of so copious a family comes down to just a few. Of the daughters, tall, handsome girls as tradition has it, Rachel, Charlotte and Catherine did not survive the birth of their first infants, Mary, unmarried, became a Quaker preacher, while Anne was wed over the anvil at Gretna Green, a somewhat less Quakerly proceeding. Sarah, the eldest, married Joseph Foster of Bromley, Middlesex, who comes into the next chapter. Five of the sons became bankers, Sampson and Samuel in Taylor & Lloyds at Birmingham, Henry in Hanbury, Taylor & Co. in London, David with the Gurneys of Norwich and Alfred in a bank at Leamington. Richard, the sixth son, was a brewer at Coventry. The seventh, George, not tempted by banking, yet found the means to make use of it. George Lloyd did not care for these sober occupations; he became a captain in the 3rd Light Dragoons, was disowned by the Society, and died in his thirties owing large sums all round the circle of his banker brothers.

One notices, in a number of these families, how there were usually some members uneasy under the Quaker upbringing although born 'with a birthright in the Society'; one thinks of great-uncle Jack, 'gone abroad, as is supposed, beyond sea', and there is one in John Lloyd's family whose story must strike the imagination. Llewelyn Lloyd, 'an insolent coxcomb' when he was twenty-two, became a man of independent spirit. It is recorded that, being much addicted to sport, 'he would engage a poacher to assist him, and walk down from London to Darlington, shooting all the

---

* If John Lloyd's family of ten children is brought into account we get forty-two children from three mothers. The ages of these three mothers at date of death averaged seventy-five years.

way, without regard to the rights of proprietors of the preserves en route'.[3] On one of these occasions Llewelyn Lloyd had the misfortune to shoot a gamekeeper. In consequence of this he was obliged to fly abroad, taking refuge in Sweden where in the course of a bear hunt he shot a peasant who was acting as a beater. He lived these things down, however, and became the author of *Field Sports of the North of Europe*, a work which was for many years regarded as a classic.

The names of the two Lloyds who became partners in 1796, Sampson IV and Samuel, it must be admitted, are too alike to be convenient. They had been named on the respected pattern by which the first six children were named after their parents and grandparents, only admitting a wider fancy when that had been achieved. So accepted was this in some Quaker circles that if a family had the misfortune to lose one of those bearing a parental name the next child was given the name again, a custom quite commonly reflected in family records where a child is entered as 'the second of that name'. Sampson and Samuel, therefore, the eldest sons had to be, the one after the Lloyds, the other after their grandfather Barnes. In 1796 both men had been recently married, the one to a Harman from London, the other to a Braithwaite from Kendal, and were settled in Birmingham, Sampson at Camp Hill and Samuel near Bingley at the Crescent. Of Sampson Lloyd IV one could wish that more were known. He died in 1800 at thirty-five and his only son, Sampson V, died when not yet of age, and thus the succession passed to Samuel, the second in the family:

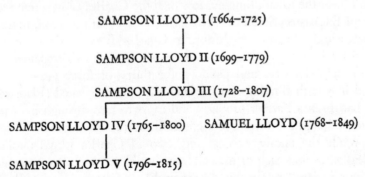

SAMPSON LLOYD I (1664–1725)

SAMPSON LLOYD II (1699–1779)

SAMPSON LLOYD III (1728–1807)

SAMPSON LLOYD IV (1765–1800)   SAMUEL LLOYD (1768–1849)

SAMPSON LLOYD V (1796–1815)

To Sampson Lloyd at Farm the death of his eldest son was a personal blow. It is known that they had worked closely together and that the father had leaned on the younger man and valued his judgement, both in banking matters and in matters to do with Wednesbury. That the son was a serious Quaker we also know, a better Quaker than his father had been in the days of the Bull's Head at Meriden, but little else is known. Of his father's career we have seen something in other chapters. Sampson Lloyd was old now. He had learned business under his own father. He had played a leading part in building up two banks. He had worked to form slave-trade opinion in the town. He had continued to uphold the Bull Street meeting and to support improvements there. He died on 27 December 1807, aged seventy-nine. 'His long life had been lived with integrity and honour,' so the Birmingham paper wrote, echoed by the *Gentleman's Magazine*. Sampson Lloyd III stands out to posterity as a Quaker, as a banker and as a good man of business.

Thin though the record may run at Farm just at this time, the same cannot be said of Charles Lloyd's family at Bingley. Like their father, most of Charles Lloyd's sons and daughters were writers of letters and several hundreds have survived, so that a good deal is known about them as a group, and as a group, in the 1790s, it is convenient to introduce them.[4]

A feature of this family was that, losing four children in infancy, the parents found themselves with five sons followed by six daughters, and each near in age to the next. 'When we walked out, we were often taken for a school,' one of the daughters noted. At Easy Hill 'near the town', Bingley, to which the Charles Lloyds removed from Edgbaston Street on Priscilla Farmer's death in 1796, though increasingly incommoded during Charles Lloyd's time by the 'smoky buildings which have rose up around us', remained an oasis with its trees and paddock for thirty or forty years more, and it is with Bingley that his later days are associated (Plate 26). It had been a Farmer property and came to him through his wife, and he himself did not live there until he was about fifty.

While the family were young, two of Charles Lloyd's ruling ideas were that each of his children should grow up 'an ornament to our Society' and that his eldest son should follow him at the Bank. Neither of these objects met entirely with the success that he desired, for two sons and a daughter married out of the Society, including Charles the eldest, and the successor at the Bank was not Charles, but the second son, James.

James Lloyd grew up to succeed to Bingley and become the senior partner in the Bank, but not without causing his parents plenty of headaches as a young man. It was in the autumn of 1794 that a bombshell burst upon Edgbaston Street. James had joined the Army. James was eighteen. Charles Lloyd hastened to London to do what he could, for it seemed that James was having second thoughts. 'I found our poor son in Tower Street,' his father writes to Mary, 'he was very much affected at seeing me.' Nothing has survived to fill out the background of this event, or to tell us through what influences or companions it came about, though doubtless from wartime motives, but 'I almost wonder at his escape from the military, considering the tempting offers he has had from one quarter or another'. Charles Lloyd did his best to be calm; 'I endeavour to act as the way opens and that every word may be fitly spoken, for on such occasions as these great caution is necessary.' He could not but note the expense which James had incurred but his recovery was cheap at the price: 'James had ordered regimentals and was obliged to pay 4 guineas on their being returned; his hat, &c, cost nearly 2 guineas, expenses at the hotel 6 guineas and other charges amount together to about 20 guineas, so that money has gone pretty rapidly. However, I don't regard this.' But the young man was not dressing like a Quaker and his father was embarrassed: 'My aunt and cousin Mary received us most kindly; I was apprehensive James's dress (for he is now quite in the mode, having a blue lappelled coat and powdered hair with a tail) would have caused a shyness, but it was quite the reverse.' Charles Lloyd, however, was mortified. 'My feelings have been deeply wounded. Oh, that this poor deluded youth had been his own friend, what a comfort would he have been to us!' At length a plan for James emerged. He was to learn to be a farmer, 'to throw off all fopperies of dress and to make himself perfectly acquainted with the use of everything that relates to husbandry.' He would be placed for two years with a Friend near Norwich and could then proceed to America if he wished. But James was not a countryman, and he was back at Birmingham in a year. He was, indeed, rather a townsman. He was also, as a young man, 'a great flirt and admirer of the ladies'. In Norfolk he had become engaged to Betsy Gurney, 'in her young and gay days', later well known as Elizabeth Fry, daughter of John Gurney of Earlham. This was a connection which, had it not been broken off, Charles Lloyd was disposed to have encouraged. In 1798 James again preoccupied the parents, this time by an alarming illness which was some form of paralysis; 'poor James is carried downstairs every day and with the assistance of a crutch and a stick he can hobble about the parlour now and then.' From this affliction James recovered at the end of about two years, but only after long absences for convalescence. But by 1801 he was working again at Dale End ('we value his assistance at the Bank'), and in 1802 he is married and made a partner. James Lloyd enjoyed a long and established marriage. The bride's father was Francis Hart, of Hart & Fellows, the Quaker bankers at Nottingham. The couple settled in the substantial house in Edgbaston Street which had been his uncle Nehemiah's and resided there until they succeeded to Bingley in 1828.

Why Charles, the eldest, was not meanwhile becoming a banker, and why his friends were often concerned about him, the picture of these years may suggest. By 1801, when still only twenty-six, Charles had worked in the Bank, had a breakdown, become a medical student in Scotland, published a book of verse, been domiciled with Coleridge in Somerset, made friends with Lamb, published more verse, had a second breakdown, broken off his engagement, lodged with Southey in Hampshire, brought out a two-volume novel, gone to Cambridge, married, rusticated in Cumberland, returned to Cambridge with his wife, become a father and taken a house in Westmorland. These are just the headlines. Charles junior was not banker material. To distinguish him from his father he has come to be referred to as 'Charles the poet'. He was a writer of sonnets and much other verse, also of plays and novels, and because of his sensitive, analytical mind, his poetical turn, and the literary figures with whom he was associated, the label of poet was ready to hand. But the performance, and perhaps the glamour, which the label suggests were overclouded by the emotional and mental imbalance which undermined him. For Charles was never a whole man, he was a misfit and unequal to the world. And because of this, because he was so different from the others of his name, because of his friends, and also because he was the eldest son, his story, often told, must claim attention.[5]

That he had been designed for a future in the Bank his father's letters abundantly show. Charles Lloyd had coached him, educated him, planned his holidays, introduced him in the London circle, and in 1793, about the time he was eighteen, had started him working in the business. Charles junior could not bear business. Within a year he suffered a collapse of health. Too sensitive to battle or persevere, he was of that temperament which under pressure becomes ill. Escape was essential. Business he must decline. 'Charles has excellent abilities,' his father now wrote, 'but his feelings are so opposite to the common maxims of life and so irreconcilable with his situation that he must suffer many mortifications I am afraid.'

Not without reservations and perplexity, as plan succeeded to plan, Charles Lloyd now did everything in his power to sustain the young man. In 1795 Charles is to study medicine at Edinburgh, but he is back at Birmingham in six months. In 1796, it is to be philosophy and poetry, as student and practitioner with Coleridge, two years his senior and lately married, at his cottage at Nether Stowey near Bridgwater. But it came to an end with another severe disturbance of mind and spirits. There is no doubt, however, that this time spent with Coleridge, through a chance encounter, opened the door for Charles to a glowing world of writing and of refinement, and not for Charles alone. His father, also, with his exceptional mind, gained richly from the minds of the gifted men it brought his way. For Coleridge's wife was sister to Southey's wife, and both were friends of Lamb, to whom the young Charles soon became attached, and so, through many more, the circle of letters widened.

In 1797, at twenty-two, Charles is in Birmingham recovered and about to marry. His bride is to be Sophia Pemberton, aged nineteen, the daughter of a Birmingham jeweller. A house has been found in Bromsgrove Street for £35 a year (his father pays, Charles does not earn a penny), 'eight small rooms', 'snug and comfortable', 'a nice little garden well stocked with fruit and a neat grape house and hot house'. But within three months everything is shelved and the house is being surrendered. It seems that the idea of working in the Bank had been revived but that the couple would not hear of it, and Sophia's father may have decreed delay until she should be twenty-one. Charles now stays with Southey near Christchurch in Hampshire and talks of resuming his medical studies, but he spends the winter in London with a friend of Lamb's. The next year, 1798, it is Cambridge.

Two other members who led the family a dance must now be mentioned, Robert the third in age, and Priscilla, the sixth. Both were allies of Charles's in the family, and both were trials to their parents in these closing days of the century. It was to Robert, aged sixteen, that the following illuminating, if backhanded, advice was addressed by Charles, who was three years more: 'be a good man, retain a pure heart, but oh! avoid alike the Methodist and the atheist, the Quaker and the libertine.' Robert, like some of his brothers, an intelligent, rather sensitive, gentle soul, never felt he could come up to the excellences of his father, much as he came to admire them; 'he is, really, a wonderful man.' One of Robert's closest satisfactions was found in the friendship of Lamb (whom he had met through Charles), in the exchange of private letters and, sometimes, in visits to Lamb in London.*

Priscilla, the first of the daughters, was the apple of her father's eye. She was a comely girl approaching seventeen, of average abilities, highly strung and unwilling to be managed. Charles, who now decided that he wished to continue his education, had become an undergraduate at Caius College. Making friends with his Greek tutor, Charles invited him to Bingley in the Christmas vacation, when the visitor on ten days' acquaintance became engaged to Priscilla. The tutor was Christopher Wordsworth, a brother of William Wordsworth and a clergyman of the Church of England. Charles and Robert abetted the affair. The parents were dismayed. A clergyman of the Church of England! Charles and Robert thought the parents unreasonable. Priscilla fled to the Clarksons, who were at this time living in Cumberland, and did not return to Birmingham for more than six months. 'Wordsworth writes to me respectfully and manly,' wrote her father, 'so that I think he is more to be depended on than Priscilla. At least he has his senses about him but *Priscilla is mad with passion.*'

Next it was Robert's turn. Ardently distressed on Priscilla's account, Robert, as Lamb wrote in London to Southey, 'hath eloped

* A sentiment of Lamb's in a letter to Robert, written on 17 December 1799, brings to mind the title of this chapter: 'Rob must contrive to pass some of his Christmas with us *or at least drink in the century with a welcome.*'

from the persecutions of his father and taken shelter with me'; and Robert likewise stayed many weeks away. All this time James was ill in the home. And the same year, in April, to fill the parents' cup, Charles, while still a student at Cambridge, attended only by Robert, was married to Sophia Pemberton at Edgbaston parish church. Charles Lloyd nevertheless was still able to write to his wife, 'don't be unduly affected, I have still hopes, indeed I believe my hope will never entirely fail'.

After all these rumpuses matters became rather more normal over the next two years. Priscilla settled down to what was to be a long engagement in the interests of Wordsworth's career, though she continued to have her independent ways. Like Robert, Priscilla was now acquainted with Lamb. 'Robert Lloyd is come to town,' writes Lamb in 1800; 'Priscilla meditates going to see *Pizarro* at Drury Lane tonight, from her uncle's, under cover of coming to dine with me.' Robert, sensitive and unsure of himself ('Robert's extreme feeling becomes really alarming'; and again, 'he cannot bear application to such business as ours at the counting house'), nevertheless advanced more steadily into his twenties. Charles junior settled into married life with the red-haired Sophia of the 'thoughtful cultivated mind'. Her father, who lived beyond the tollgate at Hagley Row near what is now the Five Ways, was only distantly linked with the Pembertons we have met in other chapters. The two fathers, it is clear, soon came to accept the marriage. After an extended honeymoon in the summer of 1799 at a cottage near Ullswater, Charles inclined to resume his studies at Cambridge and even talked of ordination; but 1800 saw the couple residing at Olton, expecting their first child. Within a short time after this, with his father's allowance and Sophia's income to live on, they removed to Ambleside and presently settled themselves at a respectable small country house at the head of Windermere, known as Old Brathay (Plate 27); and here among the fells, with Sophia's support and good management, Charles lived largely free from vicissitudes, raising a family, sociable at times, writing when his spirits allowed, and for a few years in fairly good health. 'Charles is become steady as a church,' Robert wrote to Lamb during this period, 'and as straight-forward as a Roman road. It would distract him to mention anything that was not as plain as sense. He seems to have run the whole scenery of life, *and now rests as the formal precisian of non-existence*';[6] but Robert, in his letters, was not above writing for effect and his brother's mind was yet to be much distracted.

If an excess of nervous sensibility was the inheritance of these elder members of the family, where are we to conclude that it came from? Charles was the acutest case, but Robert and Priscilla both displayed, in their degree, his alternations of spirits and readiness to go down under pressure. De Quincey declares that it was said of Charles, 'indeed by himself as well as others', that the malady which haunted him had been derived from an ancestress in the maternal line.[7] There we have no clue; but certainly some of the Champion family were unreliable or eccentric, and Charles's quality of in-decision brings to mind the inability of his uncle Nehemiah, who was half a Champion, to take decisions or stand up to events. Probably the tendencies of both Champion and some of the other stocks had come together in Charles with exceptional effect.

Upon both Robert and Priscilla, as upon Charles, marriage was to bestow an increased degree of stability and fulfilment. When Robert 'eloped' to London he had been escaping from what he regarded as the dull work of the counting house in Edgbaston Street as well as from the upheavals in the home. He had been unsettled during his apprenticeship too, and as it advanced he had veered away from the Quaker address and apparel. Quakers wore breeches, and to Robert's mother his fashionable trousers were *fantastical*; 'neither thy person or thy mind,' she wrote, 'are formed for eccentricities of dress or conduct.' But before long Robert is set up by his father as a partner in a business more suited to his in-clinations than the ironmerchant's. This was the High Street business of Thomas Aris Pearson, booksellers, the printers and publishers of many books and of the old-established weekly newspaper, *Aris's Birmingham Gazette*. On the death of the proprietor in 1800 the bookseller's side, and in 1804 the paper itself, passed into the hands of Knott & Lloyd. One assumes that it was Knott, not Lloyd, who was to supply the executive qualities. Their trade as booksellers was of the more select and expensive sort. The Wordsworths found themselves unable to patronise Robert, though from Charles who had no bookshops in his Lakeland valley he received many orders. 'Sophia seems rather inclined,' Charles writes in 1806, 'to have

Scott's *Lay of the Last Minstrel* and Scott's *Ballads,* with some other work, suppose I was to say Coleridge's poems, in a single volume by way of present to the Miss Watsons,' adding, 'all bound in green morocco and gold leaves'. Bishop Watson's family belonged to the cultivated circle in the Windermere district. 'The paper', however, is popular with all. Charles declares that it enables him to make a show of knowing what is going forward if he is obliged to go into company. For Priscilla in 1805, newly married and living in London, it keeps the talk of her home town before her, but she is not above twitting its new proprietor about it. 'Let me thank Robert for sending us the Birmingham paper. I hope he will continue to give us a sight of this *illustrious* and *unrivalled* Gazette,' which was an allusion to the announcement about the new management, and some months later, upon Nelson's return to England after chasing Villeneuve out of the West Indies, 'we are exceedingly obliged by Robert's papers; I could not help smiling at their eloquent harangue on Lord Nelson, which outshone anything I saw in other papers.'

But Robert was now in love, so much so that he did not correspond even with Lamb. Hannah Hart, who was the other daughter of the Hart family, he had met at James's marriage in 1802. It was Robert's fortune that a second Nottingham union was acceptable to his parents at Birmingham. Even in so small a family as the Harts, however, where there was but one brother besides the two girls, a loosening of the Quaker ties was to be found. Francis Hart junior was another of those who inclined towards military companions in time of war, ignoring the Society. How conscious of their pecularity the Quakers were is plain from the way in which Charles Lloyd retails the incident of Francis Hart on a visit to Birmingham. 'Lieutenant Hart,' he writes,

called on Daniel Woodhead in his regimentals. The old crusty Friend desired him at once to walk out of his house. Francis is cool and would not take this notice. At length the old man said, what would thy worthy grandfather have said hadst thou called upon *him*? Why, said Francis, he would have told me, as you have done, to get out of my house. Well, says the old man, if thou wilt not go, sit down. So I believe they parted friends.

Influenced, it may be, by his future brother-in-law, Robert had at this time one foot outside the Society himself and he was in a mood of some independence. In the autumn of 1803 he is a Captain in the third battalion of the Earl of Dartmouth's Loyal Birmingham Volunteers, and tells Hannah of the headaches he gets at the drills.* But he is embarrassed. He is to be married. The regular thing for the Hart family will be a Quaker marriage with the proper Quaker preliminaries, and this means being 'cleared' by the appropriate meetings. How will a military connection be viewed? Robert rather naïvely informs Hannah that he will leave to the Society what they are going to do about this. 'I have felt awkward,' he writes in February, 'on account of the suspense which the military business has caused. It is in my power to resign whenever I chuse.' But he extricates himself; 'I must inform you with uncommon pleasure that having had an interview with Lord D. he has accepted of my resignation. He behaved to me in a very gentlemanlike manner and expressed his concern to part with me as a member of the corps.' One wonders whether Hannah smiled. Friends, it appears, duly acquitted Robert, and the same year, in July 1804, after a season of alternating between ecstasy and self-abasement, he was married to Hannah at the Friends' meeting at Castle Donington near Nottingham.

The same autumn, after an engagement of nearly six years, Priscilla was at last married to 'Wordsworth' as he was called by everybody including herself. Her father had been right when he declared to Mary in 1799, 'I think it can be little short of a miracle that will prevent her having W.' He had written this not long after one of his own nieces at Farm had figured in a runaway marriage, and his letter goes on,

however...I never heard of a clergyman going to Scotland to be married. W. by such a step, would lose his Fellowship, his pupils probably, and I should think all future Church preferment, for marriage in the Church of England is considered a kind of sacrament, and for a clergyman to be married by a Scottish blacksmith at Gretna Green must be a degradation of clerical consequence.

Priscilla had seized the initiative, and she had kept it. 'Diffidence is not a quality,' she wrote to a sympathiser, 'that answers any good

---

* This was one of the Volunteer Corps sponsored by the War Office on the resumption of the war against Napoleon, when along the channel coast were assembled an invasion force of 200,000 soldiers and several thousand landing craft. (See C. J. Hart, *First Volunteer Battalion, the Royal Warwickshire Regiment*, 1906.)

end in this family.' We cannot doubt either that Priscilla's marriage took place in a church or that her parents were elsewhere on the occasion.

Wordsworth had been obliged to keep her waiting because his Fellowship disqualified him from marrying, but after the completion of five years he was presented to the living of Oby near Norwich, and it was here that they began their married life. However, within less than a year, at great inconvenience, they were removing to London where Wordsworth was unexpectedly appointed to be vicar of St Mary's, Lambeth, and private chaplain to the Archbishop of Canterbury; and their house at Essex Place, Princes Road, with its 'airy situation' and its 'kitchen garden in nice order' was where their children were to be born. As in the case of Charles and Sophia, so in that of Wordsworth and Priscilla relations with the parents at Bingley improved once marrying was accomplished, and soon became cordial. Clergyman or no, many letters testify to the regard in which Wordsworth came to be held, for his steadiness, his intellectual abilities and what appealed to his father-in-law, the good order of his domestic life; 'I feel the advantage of Wordsworth's example myself.' With Robert's choice, on the other hand, there had been no fault to find, and Robert's marriage brought a new asset into the circle for Hannah was the favourite of all.

Two other brothers, Thomas and Plumsted, who take their places before Priscilla in the family sequence, cannot be entirely left out.* Thomas Lloyd, the fourth son, was apprenticed to a merchant in Birmingham. Like his uncle John he was then sent for about eighteen months to America, where he rubbed some corners off, though there is no information as to his assignment; 'I soon found,' he wrote to his mother in 1801,

that a hundred cares which I thought were all nothing when other people undertook them for me were matters of great weight when obliged to look after them myself; for here servants will not do anything for you, they consider themselves your equals and are their own masters and mistresses.

As a partner in Wallis & Lloyd the only clues to his trade are a little puzzling, for at one moment he is supplying Charles at Brathay with

* The sequence of the elder children was: Charles born 1775, James 1776, Robert 1778, Thomas 1779, Plumsted 1780, Priscilla 1781. Five other sisters followed.

forks and hearth-brushes, 'black and gold, Indian pattern', and the next he is receiving remittances from America 'of £3,000 or £4,000'. In 1805 Thomas married Susannah Whitehead, the daughter of another Quaker banker, and set up house at Birmingham in Edmund Street.

The evidences of Plumsted Lloyd have much more colour. He was a colourful person. The fifth son, he was apprenticed to a brewer at Ipswich and lived his life in brewing and related avocations, and from Ipswich in 1804 came his wife, Fanny Bettenson, not from a Quaker family. Cheerful, talkative and impetuous, Plumsted, for a Lloyd, had bred quite different from the rest of his generation. Like most of his brothers, he too had made friends with Lamb. 'How,' Lamb enquires of Robert in 1801, 'is the benevolent, loud-talking, Shakespeare-loving brewer?' Ipswich, when Plumsted knew it in 1798, with a garrison of 12,000 soldiers, was an advanced anti-invasion base, as it was in 1940:

We have nothing stirring here but the talk of the long talked of invasion. This part of the coast is very strongly armed. The soldiers are ordered twice every week to have mock fights in the places where there is the most probability of the French landing. The soldiers wish the French would come and have it over for they had rather have one fair engagement man to man than to live in the nasty barracks. Temporary barracks are building in almost every part of the town. Things bear a very serious aspect here, where we are as it were upon the spot.

Plumsted always talked. He talked to the soldiers as well as attending to business or perhaps in the course of it. The Woodbridge monthly meeting wrote in his certificate that 'his conduct was in a good degree orderly although his conversation was not equally so'. His father put him into a brewing business near Birmingham.

This sketch of the first six members must serve for introduction to the Bingley family as the new century was beginning. It may be drawn together and, as it were, focused through the circumstance that, in 1806, portraits by a young artist named John Constable were commissioned by no less than five of these six *ménages*. During September that year, in a period when the Continent was closed to artists by the War, Constable had arranged a painting tour in the Lakes. At a musical evening given by the neighbours nearest to Old Brathay Charles and Sophia made the artist's acquaintance, and within a short time each had sat to him for their portrait. On the strength of his work at Brathay Constable was invited to stay at Birmingham where he painted first James and Sarah, then Hannah, and after that Susannah, known as Susan. This made six. 'Is Mr Constable gone yet?,' Charles enquires in a letter to Robert in November, 'I do hope he will not become troublesome.' Not only did Constable not become troublesome but soon afterwards he painted a seventh portrait, of Priscilla at Lambeth. Five of these pictures can be seen today, two in England, two in Wales and one in North America, a sixth is known in reproduction, and only Sarah is entirely lost to her descendants. Two of them are shown in Plates 28 and 29.

For posterity, it is a pity that while Constable was in Birmingham their father was not painted too. Charles Lloyd belonged to that eighteenth-century period of Quakerism when plain Friends, from principles of simplicity, would have few if any pictures in their houses, while to be painted themselves was avoided as an 'exaltation of the creature'. Some Quakers did not adhere to this strict line; his own wife's people in previous generations had had portraits on their walls which had come to Priscilla Farmer with Bingley. But she herself, after a somewhat fashionable youth, had become a Friend of the stricter sort, as her daughter and son-in-law were, and a grandchild of Charles Lloyd could remember in after years being called into his sanctum 'where were *hid* the old family portraits'. It is to this attitude, call it sectarian, call it conscience, that we owe the want of portraits, until the new generation breaks away, of the leading eighteenth-century figures in this history, whether of Charles of Bingley, his brother Sampson at Farm, their father Sampson Lloyd II, or their grandfather Sampson Lloyd I.*

While his elder sons and daughters were passing from youth to marriage and from Bingley to homes of their own Charles Lloyd was moving on past fifty towards the sixties, and for him, as for his family, the scene was by no means without change. By the time of the portrait-painting in 1806 he was no longer an ironmerchant, and

* The bust of Charles Lloyd, a photograph of which is reproduced in this book, was made only after his death. (Plate 24.)

only just a forgemaster, but in addition to being a banker he had become a person whose services were in demand in the commercial community. 'My father was a very active, clever man of business,' one of his daughters wrote, 'so that he was often called upon to take the lead in public measures.' In the 1790s, when the iron interest still continued, he had already been holding a leading place among the merchants in the town, as can be seen when he writes from London, 'W. Villiers, Geo. Simcox and myself are appointed to attend on the Minister respecting the high price of copper. &c.' In the next letter the name of the Minister is given, in the Quaker fashion: 'W. Pitt is indisposed, so it is uncertain when we shall see him. This Birmingham business deranges my engagements. If however I can render any service to my neighbours and the country in general I shall rejoice.' But a week later all he writes is that 'our interview with W. Pitt was last sixth day, and a very agreeable one it was'. This reflects the hazard of letters written when the writer is from home. Charles Lloyd was starting for Birmingham the next day and Mary would hear about the deputation by word of mouth, but posterity does not. However, the concerns that Charles Lloyd was to pursue in London in the succeeding years would be less those of the metal world and more upon the interests of country banking.

Through the late 1790s and early 1800s the London correspondence is punctuated by letters from new places. Some of the most frequent of the new journeys were to Westmorland and Cumberland. Near Penrith were the homes of two people who had befriended errant members of the family, of Thomas Wilkinson where Charles junior lodged and wrote in 1795, and of Thomas Clarkson of slave-trade fame with whom Priscilla took refuge in 1799. Both places were reached by way of Kendal, and so was Brathay where Charles and Sophia settled in 1801. Kendal soon became a port of call for other reasons, too, which are important for this narrative. The young Samuel Lloyd from Farm had been newly married, as we saw, in the 1790s. He had taken for wife Rachel Braithwaite, a daughter of one of the respected old families at Kendal, and this match proved the starting-point of a growing connection between Birmingham and that distant place. He and his brother, Sampson IV, had been boarders at the Quaker school in the town. Within a few years other Kendal marriages followed, two of them in the Bingley family, so that an increasing traffic and affection grew up between the two circles and Charles Lloyd was often in the north. In 1806 and 1808 his daughters Mary and Anna were married to Rachel's brothers George and Isaac Braithwaite, thus making Lloyd alliances for three members of a single Braithwaite family.* With these near connections, and as the grandchildren began to appear, Charles Lloyd thought little of the 156 coach-miles between the two towns, and besides he could visit, on the way, Burton for business and Matlock or Buxton for relaxation. It was by way of Kendal that he had travelled, with Charles and a nephew, when the business of the moment was to set the young man up as a medical student at Edinburgh, a city which impressed Charles Lloyd's imagination if the inns of the region did not. His letter the day after their arrival is worth quoting:

This is really a fine place, some of the streets and the Square strike more than most things in London, but the number of women walking barefooted gives me a very odd sensation. The old town seems in many places nasty enough, indeed grandeur and elegance and poverty and dirt are here most strikingly contrasted. The young men were exceedingly entertained by the novelty of our entertainment at Dinwoodie last night, thirty-five miles from Edinburgh. It was late when we got in and the first appearance was very disgusting for the kitchen was paved with stones in a very uneven manner like a street and covered with filth and dirt, though not over shoe tops. We were however shown into a carpeted room upstairs and the landlord would not let us be without a hot supper, for a *duke* should be roasted and some peas got directly. These we had in nice order soon after 10. We then tasted some whiskey and after a laughing evening went to bed *in clean sheets* which I had particularly attended to.[8]

Charles Lloyd was an inveterate housekeeper.

The scenes of some of his travels, Scotland, Wales, the Lakes, draw some well-observed descriptions from Charles Lloyd's pen. His mind had adopted the fashion for seeing the romantic in the spectacles of nature, of which he would build up word-pictures in his letters. From Kendal, the way to Scotland lay 'through a country increasing every mile in bold romantic scenery', upon which the mind might dwell, from a coach, with more of a spirit of contemplation

---

* This is the Anna Braithwaite who afterwards became known as a Quaker leader both here and in America, inheriting more of her father's qualities than some of her brothers and sisters did.

than when travelling upon the M6; in the Vale of Llangollen 'for ten miles our eyes were enchanted by the most romantic prospects'; while the Ambleside scene, about Brathay, he saw as 'a charming retired spot in a mountainous country, where cascades, shady lanes, majestical hills and craggy rocks irresistably strike the imagination with a pleasing rapture'. 'Romantic' is a concept that would have been foreign to his father's generation. In the whole of the letters of Sampson Lloyd II there is nowhere the least suggestion of his noticing any feature of scenery or natural beauty; he is more given to comment on the condition of the road. But Charles Lloyd and most of his children's generation were part of the romantic age. When a new 'W. Scott' was expected, a *Lord of the Isles* or a *Lay of the Last Minstrel*, they reported to one another in their letters. They were in tune with the attitudes of the group of poets resident in the Lakeland villages, the neighbours of Charles and Sophia, with Coleridge and with Southey, who had settled near Keswick, and with Wordsworth's brother at Grasmere—two of the three to be Laureate in their time. These Lakeland figures Charles Lloyd personally knew, and he called on them during his visits to Brathay, once upon all three in a day, recording how 'on 3rd day we went to Keswick, calling on W. Wordsworth before dinner, rode round the lake, and drank tea at Coleridge's with Southey, etc.'

After 1805 Charles Lloyd's visits to London began to include Lambeth, where he sometimes lodged. But soon Priscilla's mother was travelling too. After a few years free from bearing children herself, she was in demand for the births in her daughters' families, three of her own at a distance and Sophia's as well. Well connected among Quakers as she was, Mary Lloyd deserved some relief from the home, and to renew more freely, after so many years, her contacts of former days: 'My mother,' wrote one of the daughters, 'possessed great conversational talent, so that, until she became deaf, intellectual and refined society was her delight'. More of Charles Lloyd's letters than usual are now directed to Mary at the daughters' homes, at Lambeth and at Kendal, and the pattern goes on for a number of years in succession.

By the time of the death of Sampson Lloyd III, 'my late very dear brother', the eighteenth century was really left behind. This event was a break which made for changes both in the family and at the banks. At Farm, his eldest son took over. Samuel Lloyd, who had been a partner in Taylor & Lloyds for fourteen years, was in his forties and he and Rachel, with a dozen children, could easily fill the large Sparkbrook house. In the inner politics of the two Banks Sampson Lloyd's death had some interesting consequences, for his brother Charles now saw himself losing the share of Sampson's profits which he had for many years been receiving from the Lombard Street concern.[9] This income had been worth a tenth of the profits and had been showing him around £500 a year. But by 1807 Charles Lloyd had become so accustomed both to the situation, 'I have been a virtual partner at No. 60 for nearly thirty years', and to the income, 'my virtual share', that he was loth to surrender either and tried to avoid doing so.

His method was to lobby John Taylor who, himself a partner in both banks, was now involved in the revision of the London arrangements. From the time of Sampson Lloyd's death the correspondence between them extended over eighteen months. In his efforts to safeguard his valuable tenth Charles Lloyd tried everything he could think of. At one point he even pressed John Taylor to join him in starting a separate Bank, 'to strike a bold stroke and cooperate with us in forming a new house equally or more advantageous', stressing that under the proposed London arrangements there appeared no provision for a son of Taylor's to follow him there. Taylor thought that by such a plan the interests of the Birmingham house would suffer, and he pointed out that if Sampson Lloyd had shared out part of the income 'the other partners nor myself had nothing to do with that, it was an act entirely of his own'. Finally Taylor settled something. 'I am disposed to allow you £250 out of my profits of the London house, which is one fourth out of my profits of last year according to the annual statement, without you being in any way responsible for the transactions of the house.' Thus the matter was settled, and this allowance was continued by Taylor until he died in 1814, after which his son James Taylor agreed to continue it in his turn. After 1807 Sampson Lloyd's double interest separates into two streams. His participation in the Birmingham bank was continued through his eldest son Samuel and his line. In London, his name was carried on for years to come by his youngest son Henry and also by some of Henry's nephews. At the same time the name continued to be represented in Hanbury & Co. (as they were called for short) by John Lloyd of Tower Street until he died in 1811, and then by his son Corbyn, until that branch fell out upon the death of the latter without male issue in 1828.

As he moved on from his fifties to his sixties Charles Lloyd began turning his surplus energies to the classics, translating, between the years of Trafalgar and Waterloo, much of Homer into English verse and parts of Horace as well. His exceptional memory is noted in all the obituaries, and his liking for languages too. It was said of him, probably with some truth, that he carried accurately in his mind and could repeat almost all of the New Testament 'so that when his children were reading aloud he immediately detected the least false reading', and likewise the *Eclogues* and *Georgics* of Virgil in their entirety. One of his daughters, writing after his death, adds the information that 'he could read French, Italian, Spanish and Portuguese, he had an accurate knowledge of grammar, geography, history and astronomy, and a good general knowledge of the sciences, and in *belles lettres* he had read almost all the best authors of any standing'. Charles Lloyd was a natural scholar. At school at Worcester he had soon learned all that his master could teach him, who 'very much wished he should be put under a more able tutor or go to college'. Universities were closed to Quakers, but, possessing great application, what he did not learn at school Charles Lloyd taught himself. After translating a great part of the *Iliad*, and wishing to have something in print, he selected the Twenty-Fourth Book, upon the funeral of Hector, and arranged in 1807 for Knott & Lloyd 'to strike off a few copies' as Lucas writes.[10] There followed the interest for the author of obtaining the opinions, in that educated age, of the Southeys, the Coleridges, the Lambs and other competent critics on the merits of his work. Christopher Wordsworth introduced him to the best scholar he knew. 'Lamb,' Robert wrote to his father, 'is quite delighted and pleased with the idea of thy becoming a poet and would be highly gratified with a sight of the book of Homer which we printed for thee.' There followed a sequence of shrewd and engaging correspondence with Lamb in which the rhyming couplets of Bingley were compared with Pope's and Cowper's established translations, not altogether to Charles Lloyd's disadvantage. The correspondence extended also to his second and third publications. These were, in 1810, the first seven books of the *Odyssey*, of which he later translated the whole but only printed part, and the *Epistles* of Horace, some of which appeared in the *Gentleman's Magazine* in 1812.*

In the autumn of 1811 the Charles Lloyds experienced a change in their family and affairs more personal than any when they lost three of their children in six weeks. Two were married sons, not much past thirty, and the third a daughter aged twenty-one. The cause was typhus fever, sometimes known as putrid fever or gaol fever, which was still common in England at the time. Thomas, falling sick at the end of August, was dead by the middle of September. The second was his sister Caroline, the youngest but one in the family, and the third was Robert, both of whom succumbed in October. To add to the family's anxieties, two out of Thomas's three little girls went down with the same contagion as their father but survived it, while the infant Thomas, born at Christmas, lived for only three days. 'It was a furnace indeed for those left behind,' wrote one of the daughters, and the whole family was prostrated, except for Charles Lloyd, whose faith and fortitude could declare to Mary, 'I still endeavour in all states to be content.' Susan was left with three small children, Hannah with four. Both widows, escaping the infection, lived to bring up their families and to continue in affectionate relations with the numerous Bingley circle whose letters to Hannah over thirty years form part of the background for this chapter.

These afflictions were followed four years later by the untimely death of Priscilla. This was a particular blow to the parents, whose links with the Wordsworths had become closer every year. The three Wordsworth sons were to prove as able as, for those times, they were few in number. All were pre-eminent at school, all at their universities, and all were ordained. Two of them became bishops, of St Andrews and of Lincoln, and had not the other son died in his thirties he might have been a bishop too. Their father continued his career. Marrying again in due course, he was invited in 1820 to return to Trinity where he ruled as Master for more than twenty years. This was a turn of events not uncongenial to Charles Lloyd who, excluded as a Quaker from academic worlds, now ex-

* The published works both of Charles Lloyd and of Charles Lloyd junior are given in Appendix III.

changed Latin verses with his grandsons at the centre of one of them. The disqualification of Quakers from admission to the universities is reflected in Charles Lloyd's reaction to an invitation to visit Wordsworth at Trinity; 'I told him,' he records, 'that I did not know how Friends would sort with University society,' adding, 'but he answered, very well.'

When the distinction of their father is considered, the performance of Charles Lloyd's sons was a poor one. Plumsted, the youngest of them, unsuccessful as a brewer at Birmingham, presently became a grain merchant at Ipswich, but he seems to have overreached himself and to have required assistance from home. In 1816, to cap so many other losses in the family, his wife, Fanny, died, leaving Plumsted with four young children. After five years he married again and lived in London. Thomas, as his widow records, had been 'uneasy for some time about his worldly concerns,' but no more is heard after his death about the business he had been in. Robert had been in a still greater state of anxiety about Knott & Lloyd, exclaiming to his wife, 'Hannah, I am a ruined man.' His father had been concerned about the wellbeing of this business. The firm indeed seemed ill-fated, Knott himself emerging as a person 'of indolent habits, with no knowledge of accounts' and dying less than three years after Robert, after which *Aris's Gazette* had a new proprietor. James alone can be said to have led an established existence, but it was a sheltered one. That he was comfortably off, had a position in the Bank and would succeed to Bingley is true, but James was put there, he made nothing for himself that posterity can see, he was often unwell, inherited his mother's deafness, and in 1820 was rebuked by the Society for 'the payment of ecclesiastical demands', which was a Quaker expression for tithes. His only distinction in later life appears to have been that he was made a J.P. for Warwickshire. But, living to seventy-seven, he was unable in his later years to pursue an ordinary way of life, 'from the effects of a brain fever'. Through mental infirmity, as a sister records, he was unable to live at home,[11] and the annual accounts in the partners' ledger of Taylor & Lloyds were not signed by him personally during ten years before his death.

The most uncomfortable reading is the story of Charles junior. With intervals of relief, his instability advanced progressively and at times was alarmingly worse until he had to be accepted as a mental invalid. At Brathay in 1807 he writes to Robert of 'the suffering state of my mind', and the year after, 'it is a trial to me that I cannot come with Sophia to Birmingham, but really, without the greatest care, my spirits are in such a state that I must become a trial to those who love me and a subject of reproach to those who cannot feel for me.' As time went on, between about 1809 and 1815, he had a number of distressing seizures as his friends called them, through each of which the devoted Sophia had the care of him in addition to that of their eight children. The deaths in 1811 of two brothers and a sister only advanced his disorder. Robert had been one of his real friends. De Quincey, his neighbour at Grasmere, declares that his anguish was to know and dread the advancing intensification of his malady', and relates how he would pass times of intense exaggerated activity, sometimes physical, sometimes literary, as though to stave it off. To William Wordsworth he was 'his near and distressing neighbour'. The death of Priscilla in 1815, with whom Charles had felt so close a unity, again accelerated his derangement and that winter saw him for some months in confinement. In the spring of 1816 he was placed in The Retreat, a Quaker establishment at York, which today would be known as a mental hospital,* but in the summer he was transferred to the private asylum of Dr Willis, at Gretford in Lincolnshire, who had the principal share, with his father, in treating the recurrent illness of George III. The year after, though far from well, Charles was back at Birmingham where Sophia had removed with the children, having given up the home at Brathay, but Charles himself was taken in at Bingley. The reader interested in his case may turn to De Quincey, who tells of his friend in flight from restraint arriving in a distraught condition at Grasmere and 'retaken I knew he would be'; but he goes on to write nostalgically of Charles and Sophia as he first remembered them, 'young, rich, happy, full of hope, belted with young children, and standing apparently upon the verge of a labyrinth of golden hours'.

To set against these afflictions was the alliance of Olivia Lloyd with Paul Moon James, a son-in-law whose society and ability

---

* The Retreat had been started by the Quakers in the 1790s. It was one of the first hospitals where mental disorders were regarded as illness requiring sympathy and scientific treatment. It is well known as an establishment for psychiatric illness today and still operates under a Quaker governing body.

Charles Lloyd probably came to value even more than Wordsworth's. Olivia was the daughter next after Priscilla in the family.
There was no occasion for a family upheaval about a match with an
able young Birmingham Quaker. 'This young man's sense and
modesty interest everybody,' Charles Lloyd had written to Olivia's
mother in 1805, 'and if he had a fortune he would be much thought
of.' Olivia was married in 1808. Her husband, from the outset,
made common ground with his father-in-law. Not only did he write
verse but, obtaining a position in Galtons Bank in Steelhouse Lane,
later Galton, Galton & James, where he and Olivia soon resided,
he was beginning to be a banker; and the Galtons were Quakers
and cousins of Olivia's mother. During the next ten to fifteen years,
as Charles Lloyd grew older, spending more time at Bath and at
Malvern, he came to rely on this son-in-law for intelligence from
Birmingham, and the correspondence is a good deal garnished with
the news of the day, of the fluctuations of trade in the town, of
banking and banking reform, and of local politics, as well as of the
family and the cousins all around.[12] Although a competitor, Paul
Moon James was friendly with his brother-in-law James Lloyd down
the hill at Dale End, and his letters reflect the extent to which the
bankers in the town had their finger on the pulse of its business and
were serving its trade and expansion. Repeatedly also he writes
from London, where his contacts, including his appearances at
Yearly Meeting, recall Charles Lloyd's active days. Early in 1815,
as an observer of affairs, he is writing, from Birmingham, of defeat
abroad, commotions at home, trade bad and taxes increasing. 'A
long peace, a wiser administration and a reformed Prince' he con-
siders to be among 'the materials necessary to save the country';
and in June, 'the victory of Wellington affords, I think, little or no
cause for *rejoicing*. The slaughter has been dreadful, and where was
the necessity of the war? There has been no illumination here. Haymaking is becoming general.' How the juxtaposition bespeaks the
Friend.

In 1819, in a climate of reformers and 'ultra reformers'
Birmingham eyes were on the 'midnight drillings, inflammatory
placards, Caps of Liberty and other terrifying preparations for the
district meeting in Manchester', while in Birmingham itself 'the
leaders appear more active than ever'. Charles Lloyd is informed of
the state of local opinion, of popular unrest, of 'town's meetings',

and of measures taken, or not taken, by the Streets Commissioners. Birmingham at the time of Waterloo still had twenty years more of medieval town government before it, and, active and public-spirited, Paul Moon James served in turn as Chairman of the Board of Guardians, Chairman of the Streets Commissioners and, in 1835, as High Bailiff. In such circumstances, and perhaps a little because he and Olivia were childless, his activities were many and his reporting interesting.

The comments that Charles Lloyd received would often be on matters to interest a country banker. The years following the War were a time of economic unease and, as part of the money system, the country banks were among the objects of criticism. Since the 1790s too many new ones had sprung up, too many had failed and regulation was in the air. When trouble was in sight the country bankers came together. More than once, deputed by his partners, Paul Moon James found himself in London at meetings of country bankers expressing objections to interference or regulation, and he twice took part in deputations to Ministers. But firms such as the Galtons or Taylors & Lloyds, not themselves fearful of failure, did not mind seeing weaker banks go under, and P. M. James could remark in 1815 that 'a general mistrust of country bankers seems to pervade but after some more weeding the old stocks will flourish better'. In 1818 the country bankers were threatened with a restriction of their note-issues, a proposal which 'instantly brought to town a cloud of nearly two hundred country bankers with an equal number of proxies in their pockets', bent upon lobbying the Government.[13] This time it was not the Chancellor, Vansittart, but the Prime Minister, Lord Liverpool, who met the deputation of nine bankers and six M.P.s at an interview of which Charles Lloyd received a point-by-point account.

After Charles Lloyd's death the banking career of P. M. James was continued with distinction, partly at Birmingham and partly at Manchester. When the Galtons closed their banking business in 1829 their connection was taken over by the Birmingham Banking Co., the first Birmingham joint-stock bank, of which James became the manager; and in 1836, when in his fifties, he removed with Olivia to Manchester to be managing director of the new Manchester and Salford Joint Stock Bank, a position which he occupied until his death in 1854.

By good fortune the account has been preserved of a visit to Birmingham by two real-life visitors in the spring of 1819, taking the form of a day-to-day record of their four-weeks' stay at Bingley and some of the other Lloyd homes. The visitors were two young women from Falmouth, Catherine Payton Fox and Jean Melville, the one connected with the Birmingham circle at several points through marriage, the other, her friend, not a Quaker but a member of the Church of England. Their doings and impressions are those of a first visit to a rising industrial town as well as to its network of Quaker connections. Their reporting, for the consumption of themselves and probably their friends in Falmouth, the entries being sometimes by one and sometimes by the other, is intelligent and unbiased by hero-worship or intimate ties. What they saw was a Bingley, a Farm, a Quaker Birmingham at a time when the upheavals of 1799 and the bank deaths of 1800 were twenty years behind, and Birmingham itself had moved twenty years on in its thrusting, multiplying way.[14]

In a four weeks' visit the girls saw everyone and did everything. They stayed at four homes, first at Bingley, then at Steelhouse Lane with Paul and Olivia James, next at the Crescent at George Lloyd's, the eldest of the new generation from Farm, newly married, and later at Allesley in Warwickshire where some more of the Farm connection were centred;* and lodging with four they made the acquaintance of two or three times that number, being received and entertained at fully a dozen Lloyd establishments. With the brothers and sisters of Mary Dearman, George Lloyd's wife, the girls were old friends already which was another attraction of their stay (at her house they were 'a wild merry party' as the journal tells us), while her husband, they decided, 'quite shines a nonpareil among Birmingham beaux'; and it was George's brother, Samuel junior, installed as a bachelor at Wednesbury, who showed them the sights when they spent a day in the Black Country. To Charles and Mary Lloyd, in their seventies, the visitors quickly grew attached. On the day they left, 'we prepared to quit these dear kind Bingley friends'; and a year or so later, encountering Jean in London, 'no daughter,' Charles Lloyd wrote, 'could have welcomed a

* At Allesley they stayed at the house of William Payton Summerfield, a cousin of Catherine Payton Fox, whose wife was Ann Lloyd from Farm.

parent long absent with more warm affection than Jean welcomed me.'

Accompanied by one escort or another, the visitors' programme calls to mind that of 'R.P.' and his friend who visited Birmingham in 1755. But this was a Birmingham sixty years on; 'R.P.' did not write of it as 'the region of smoke and dust', he was not taken for a walk across 'the Navigation as the canal is termed in Birmingham', and it was water-wheels that he and his companion inspected, they could not write of seeing 'the largest steam engine in Birmingham, of 120 horse power'. The girls were taken to see 'the manufactories of the place', glass-cutting and the making of glass drops, plating on steel, the making of corkscrews, a papier mâché manufactory, the drawing of brass rods, machines for the making of shanks for buttons and the stamping of coins and medals. By their experiences in the Black Country, 'black by day and red by night', they were amazed and exhausted after seeing at Wednesbury the mining of coal and ironstone, at Gospel Oak near Bilston 'an immense iron foundry', and at Wren's Nest the tunnelled, subterranean limestone quarries of Viscount Dudley. At Birmingham they spent a morning at the Deaf and Dumb Asylum. In Warwickshire their tour, like 'R.P.'s', included Coventry, Kenilworth and Warwick, and in addition the 'newly arisen watering place' of Leamington.

Birmingham in 1819 thus gave an impression of urgency and growth, and likewise of growing rich. The price of this condition had been noticed, a few years before, by Southey in his imaginary *Letters from England*, translated from the Spanish:[15]

I am still giddy, dizzied with the hammering of presses, the clatter of engines, the whirling of wheels; my head aches with the multiplicity of infernal fires, – I may add, my heart also, at the sight of so many human beings employed in infernal occupations and looking as if they were never destined for anything better. Every man I meet stinks of train-oil and emery. Some I have seen with red eyes and green hair; the eyes affected by the fires to which they are exposed and the hair turned green by the brass works. The filth is sickening. Filthy as some of *our* old towns may be, their dirt is inoffensive; it lies in idle heaps, which annoy none but those who walk within the little reach of their effluvia. But here it is action, a moving, a living principle of mischief, which fills the whole atmosphere and penetrates everywhere, spotting and staining everything and getting into the pores and nostrils. I feel as if my throat wanted sweeping like an English chimney.

These were precisely the reactions of Catherine and Jean in 1819. A different aspect of the picture, for those who know Birmingham today, was the contemporary character of Edgbaston Street and the Aston Road, the girls recording in their journal an afternoon at the James Lloyds' at Edgbaston Street where they 'enjoyed a walk in the shady garden after dinner' and, still more, an excursion in the Bingley carriage when 'dear Mrs Lloyd took us a very nice ride to a pretty village called Aston through a country rich and cultivated. We could not have imagined trees growing so luxuriously, or grass looking so deliciously green, near so much smoke and dust.'

At the same time the two girls had an eye for a side of Birmingham's society which did not suit their conservative Falmouth ideas. This was something as essential to Birmingham as it had been when the Lloyds first settled there, the spirit of Dissent in the town.

Here, we feel ourselves alone in many things. There seems to reign in this place a latitudinarianism in religion and politics which quite startles our more aristocratic and less liberal views; not English liberty and law, but liberty and no law seems the ruling principle here. It is a perfectly dissenting republican place, – Presbyterians, Quakers, Independents, Unitarians, all seem placed here on the same level; the last we fancy have rather the preference. The poor Church alone seems the object of prejudice and animosity; and that excellent man, Mr Byrn,* seems not a little opposed. These sentiments are far from extending to our truly liberal friends at Bingley or their own children; but we are told that it would be quite dangerous here for persons to express themselves strongly, or what is here called harshly, on Socinianism,† and we have heard enough to make us rejoice that our lot was not cast in Birmingham, much as we enjoy our visit.

During their stay the girls had been thrown in touch with some members of the Bingley household who have not so far been mentioned. These were Grosvenor Lloyd, aged eighteen, the son of Charles and Sophia, and Grosvenor's unfortunate father himself.

---

* Mr Byrn was the minister of the church where Jean Melville went in Birmingham. The observations of the visitors are anticipated in Bisset's poetical guide to Birmingham when he declares, writing in 1800, 'Of Churches there are two, of Chapels four, And of dissenting Meetings near a score.'

† Socinianism: a term sometimes used at that time instead of Unitarianism.

The eldest son of the eldest son, Grosvenor was a favourite with his grandfather and had been accepted as a junior clerk at the Bank where he was making a more satisfactory start than his father had done. His mother, Sophia Lloyd, with the rest of her family, had taken a house in Birmingham where Grosvenor often went but 'Bingley he called his home'. His father, not now under care, was also living at Bingley. Up and down in health, Charles junior, grey-haired now though only in his forties, was an object of interest to the visitors and, from the first day, of comment in their journal. It happened that they had been late in arriving and they relate how, their host and hostess excusing themselves, Charles and Grosvenor bore them company that afternoon while they had their dinner:

We were rather awed at first by the presence of young Charles Lloyd who often imagines that all are spirits around him, that he alone, a never-dying frame, is embodied and bearing the sins of the whole world, hated by all. This fear, aided by Grosvenor's looks and light boyish spirits, was soon dispelled; and his poor unhappy father greatly interested our feelings and fascinated our attention by the animation and energy of his sensible conversation, although the wildness of his manner never suffers his state to be forgotten, whilst the gentle pensiveness of his tone claims strong sympathy and compassion.

Some further entries show the kind of impression made by his case upon a stranger at this time. At Hannah Lloyd's house, where 'poor Mr C. Lloyd' had accompanied them, 'he appeared very low and quietly went on with his drawing, but afterwards he seemed better and played a very good game of chess with Catherine'. A few days afterwards, 'poor C. Lloyd has been worse, and we have not seen him since the second day after our arrival. He often keeps his bed for days and sits up by night'; and three weeks later, 'Lydia told us of poor Mr C. Lloyd's having set off to walk to London; his friends had been most anxious, not knowing what was become of him, but at last they found he had walked as far as Olton.' Charles at this stage was declaring that only the sound of London traffic could ease his mind of its afflictions and he must seek lodgings in Cheapside to ensure it. They were indeed an afflicted family, Sophia declaring that 'she thought she must have an uncommon share of dross in her composition to require such deep probations'.

The respite in Charles's condition, however partial, lasted for three to four years. In 1821 he and Sophia did go to London for a while though before long they were back again in Birmingham. They took a house at Kensington Gravel Pits looking out at the back onto Kensington Gardens. Here, with revived hopes on their account, Charles's father lodged in 1821 during Yearly Meeting. He was seventy-three, and felt that this attendance would have to be his last. He could not know that Mary for her part, was already within six months of her death. This was the year when he saw again the Betsy Gurney of James's young days, now the Quaker matron, Elizabeth Fry. Her remarkable labours among the female prisoners at Newgate, destined only for the gibbet or for Botany Bay, were by this time established and accepted. In June, accompanied by his son, Charles Lloyd gained admission to that shocking place in order to attend one of her readings. What he wrote in his letter to Birmingham might serve as a caption to Barrett's well-known painting of the scene:

On 6th day Charles accompanied me to town and to Newgate, where we met Sophia. Elizabeth Fry had just begun to read (I think the 53rd chapter of Isaiah) and she also read the following chapter. A profound silence prevailed. Afterwards she expounded what she had read in a sweet low voice but being under an appointment I was obliged to leave this most impressive scene.

This was during the period of his son's last main literary and publishing activity. Taking advantage of what he feared must prove no more than an interval, Charles junior sought again the society of writing men and poets then in town, Hazlitt, Godwin, Leigh Hunt, the Lambs. The Lambs, not free themselves from mental infirmity, were uncertain in their welcome after the years. To his friend Thomas Manning at Cambridge, who was Charles's former mathematics tutor, Lamb had written in 1819,

C. Lloyd is in town with Mrs Lloyd...She is come for a few days, and projects leaving him here in the care of a man. I fear he will launch out, and heartily wish the scene of his possible exploits were at a remoter distance. But she does not know what to do with him. He run away tother day to come to London alone, but was intercepted, and now she has brought him. I wish people wouldn't be mad.

Charles, on his part, wrote with intensity until about 1823. But melancholy delusions thickened about him and at length, in 1825, the afflicted Sophia with her husband and the younger children left England to settle at Versailles. What determined this total change or particular destination has not been discerned. There in 1830 Sophia died, her husband surviving her for nearly ten years more as the inmate of an establishment at Chaillot. The list of his works in Appendix III shows the extent of his output in that last creative period. There is no doubt that his powers of analysis and thought had been highly estimated by his intimates, as were his translations from Italian authors, but his verse was often obscure. 'Your lines,' Lamb wrote to him once, 'are not to be understood reading on one leg.'

At the bank in Birmingham, since John Taylor's death in 1814, two partners had been brought in. The first was William Taylor, another of John Taylor's sons, whose signature to the accounts begins to appear in 1815. The second, admitted in 1821 was George Lloyd, the eldest of the new generation at Farm. By these additions the number of the partners had risen again to six. For the last fourteen years of his life Charles Lloyd was the senior partner. It has been stated that when in the panic of December 1825 there was a general run on the banks, which Taylors & Lloyds countered by galloping cash from London, 'that coup was Charles Lloyd's';[16] but Charles Lloyd was then seventy-seven and becoming infirm and his nephew Samuel was managing the Bank. The collapse of several banks in London and of their correspondents in various parts had sounded the alarm, and it was Samuel, 'having never before witnessed anything of a run', who reached the City before the panic became general and made the emergency arrangements. His recourse was to the firm's London agents, the operational reserve of the country banker, and through Hanbury & Co. action was arranged. The money arrived at Dale End in a post-chaise and four during business hours on Saturday, 17 December, the day of the main run in the town. In Lombard Street on the Monday, 'the storm does not yet seem much to abate,' Samuel Lloyd wrote; 'there is no increased bustle in H. & Co.'s office, but the anxiety and distress in too many is dreadful and the country bankers are pouring in.'[17]

Far from abating, the storm spread everywhere and more than sixty banks went out of business. The cash had reached Taylors & Lloyds just in time.

Since Nehemiah's death in 1801, Charles Lloyd had been entitled to a quarter of the Bank. It was the policy of the partners that this proportion, which was half the Lloyd interest, should continue to be held in his branch of the family, and it had already been divided with James. For many years Charles Lloyd had given thought to the question how, within the six-partners limit, his branch ought to be represented after his death. Events had made James his successor, but what was to happen after James? Anxious to do justice and perhaps a little more to his eldest son's family, Charles Lloyd's wish was that two grandsons should become partners, the eldest son of Charles and the eldest son of James. These were Grosvenor, born 1800, and Francis, born 1803. The training of Francis could be looked after by his father; but Grosvenor, effectually fatherless, Charles Lloyd had had trained at Dale End. The arrangement was without stipulation of future partnership but Charles Lloyd still hoped that at his death one would be offered. As the end of his life approached it became clear that there was only one vacancy to be expected. Which of the young men was to have it? Charles Lloyd wished that it should be Grosvenor. In his last days he made two codicils to his will, one to underline his wish that Grosvenor should be brought in, and one to regulate his inheritance if he were not. In the event Grosvenor Lloyd was not chosen and the Charles Lloyd quarter share with its important income was continued in the family of James Lloyd only, three of whose sons at various dates were brought in as partners in the Bank.

Charles Lloyd died on 16 January 1828 at the age of seventy-nine. He had been for seven years a widower and his surviving letters become fewer, Mary Lloyd having died in 1821. Bingley and the Bank were his anchors. Bingley was rather empty but was still visited by many of his sixty-two grandchildren. He continued to go a good deal to Bath, and also to Malvern and Cheltenham sometimes taking with him one or two of his grand-daughters, who could be of service to him as his years advanced; and he was apt to compose rhyming letters for this or that part of the family, to give an account of present doings or bestow affectionate Christian advice. Bath he particularly liked, for despite the saying of P. M. James that it was a place where 'Gout and Gaiety walk arm-in-arm down Pulteney Street, Dissipation and Disease go to the play together' there as an agreeable Quaker circle there, *mundulus mundus in mundo immundo*, and Charles Lloyd at his lodgings could work on his Homer and see his friends as well.

In causes of good will his interest was unabated. Trading in slaves having been stopped, to forbid the owning of them was now an object of propaganda. The decision of the Society of Friends 'to petition the legislature for the abolition of slavery itself' is reported by his son-in-law while in London for Yearly Meeting in 1822, and it was his own nephew Thomas Fowell Buxton, the grandson of his sister Mary Hanbury, under whose lead the campaign was to bear fruit in 1833. In his will Charles Lloyd left legacies both to the Birmingham General Hospital and to the young British and Foreign Bible Society in aid of which an association had been formed in Birmingham supported by many in the Society of Friends. The value of Charles Lloyd's estate is not known. In addition to about £25,000 in pecuniary legacies he disposes of seven or eight properties in houses or land, mainly on the Warwickshire side of the town.[18] Charles Lloyd was an exceptional personality, and his funeral was an exceptional occasion. The meeting house in Bull Street was too small for the large number of mourners who formed 'a solemn silent assemblage' outside. Elizabeth Fry travelled from London to be present. An eyewitness counted twenty-eight carriages.

9

THE SENIOR BRANCH

The theme of this book is the history of the Lloyds in the eighteenth century, of the trade on which their fortunes were built and of its superstructure, a private banking partnership. The event of the century that followed was the conversion of this partnership, in 1865, into a public joint-stock company. And since the whole story is in some sense the pre-history of a later and greater bank, so the 1860s are the time to which this final chapter must extend, to give perspective to the earlier century and bridge it to more modern days.

Before the end of Charles Lloyd's time the fortunes of the family were at a plateau, but the years to the 1860s were still a time of reaching out, both into new business activities and in matters of conscience as well. They were, of course, years of social and political change, but they were on the whole settled years, the times of William IV and of Victoria and Albert. The full history of the Lloyds in the nineteenth century is yet to be written. It will be a fascinating task and a weighty one but not something to be contained in a single chapter, and what the present chapter offers must be selective. From Bingley, the focus shifts to the senior branch, to Samuel Lloyd of Farm and the time of his sons and daughters,* and the selection is composed of four separate stories, of Samuel Lloyd's flint mill in Leicestershire, of the coal and iron inheritance in the Black Country, of the family after 150 years as Quakers, and of how Taylor & Lloyds became Lloyds Banking Co. Ltd; and as all of these belong to the same period of years we shall make a jump back in time as each fresh story is reached.

* For some of these see Appendix V.

The story of Samuel Lloyd and the flint mill is a surprising one. Until the time of his death in 1849, during at least forty years, this responsible townsman, a banker at Birmingham and a promoter of industry in the Black Country, at a period when steam-driven machinery was advancing on every side, ran a pair of water mills forty miles away on the Derbyshire–Leicestershire border. These were the Kings Mills on the Trent near Castle Donington, half way between Burton and Nottingham and about fifteen miles from each.[1] They were used for grinding various forms of flint and alabaster, also dyewoods, into products required by the building, pottery and paint-making industries, such as plaster, glaze, Paris white and other colouring materials. The mills were located, as we have already seen, on the part of the river once used by the Burton Boat Co., and it was through this connection that Samuel Lloyd had had the opportunity of acquiring them.

The long battle of the Boat Co. against the competition of the canals can be studied in excellent sources[2] but may not be enlarged upon here except as Lloyd interests or the Kings Mills are concerned. During thirty years the syndicate had tried hard. It had acquired new wharves, improved its facilities, constructed a lateral canal on the west of the town, the Bond End canal, at a cost of £3600, to join the Trent and Mersey, and had procured, in 1784, a new lease; it had extended its range far below its own stretch of the Trent, co-operated with other interests over the provision of towpaths, and opened depots on the canal network as far away as Birmingham, running its own canal boats to serve them. But by the turn of the century the battle had been lost, and in 1805 the Company had agreed with its principal competitors, in return for the rights and facilities of the local canal, that all through traffic between Burton and Wilden should cease.[3]

All this the family had been party to through Samuel Lloyd's father who had been a partner in the Boat Co. since the syndicate was formed in 1763. But, if he started with a one-fifth share, by the time of the Agreement he was almost the only partner, probably the only one, his Burton colleagues gradually withdrawing, whom presumably he had been willing to buy out. For on succeeding his father in 1807 Samuel Lloyd found himself the Boat Co.'s sole proprietor. A note by one of his grandsons records that a rent or annuity arising out of the lease continued to be paid by the Trent and Mersey Canal Co. up to the death of Samuel Lloyd in 1849, his being the last of the three lives during which the lease was to continue in force, and he having also become the owner of all the shares in the Boat Company and thereby the owner of sundry properties in Burton and of the Kings Mills near Castle Donington.*

It may perhaps be supposed that his father's incentive for persisting with the Boat Co., apart from its relationship with the Burton ironworks, had been partly the income and partly some predilection for these mills. Samuel Lloyd evidently shared in these sentiments, and in 1810 his name appears in an estate valuation as the Kings Mills lessee.[4]

It was like starting the eighteenth century over again, for the Kings Mills were a period piece. 'Delightfully situated on the Trent' as a directory described them, their history may be traced back to Domesday.[5] Backed by a high wooded escarpment, with water meadows all about, the mills made an arcadian scene. But nature had been aided by art. In the 1790s the Hastings family, the land-lords, having rebuilt their nearby mansion, Donington Hall, in the Gothic manner, had decided that the estate would be embellished if it displayed some gothic mills; and, as Plate 33 shows, the whole range of the mill buildings, house and all, had been encased in gothic trappings, so that the house became known as 'the priest's house', the flint mill as 'the chapel', and an air of fancy dress beguiled the eye.

This enterprise for forty years the solemn banker ran by remote control. Apart from the paper quoted only one contemporary family reference has been found to the whole operation, in a letter of 1823 to Charles Lloyd, written at Birmingham, in which Paul Moon James remarks that 'Cousin Samuel is gone to see his flint mills'. After Samuel Lloyd's time the mills were carried on for some years by one of his sons, William Lloyd, of whom some particulars are given in Appendix V; and in 1860 they were sold. Today only some cottages remain and the house with its gothic shell, but the foundations and orientation of the mills can still be traced from the

---

* From a paper by George B. Lloyd the younger (1824–1903) in private possession. The Boat Co. could not afford to let others hold mills which straddled the waterway and dominated the lock.

stark skeletons of their wheels, standing axle-deep, half in, half out of the ground, which indeed are very nostalgic.

The flint mill, however, was a side-show by comparison with the exploitation of the mineral inheritance which Samuel Lloyd initiated at Wednesbury. For this is the saga of the Heirs of Parkes, whose opportunity after ninety years had now arrived. Let us recall the plot and see what families were holding the inheritance, who the actors were, and how the omens were looking at the death of Samuel Lloyd's father in 1807.[6]

The land and rights were held by this time among three of the four original families, the one-fourth share of the eldest daughter, Mary Wilkinson, having been disposed of by her sons among the descendants of the other three, Scandrett, Lloyd and Pemberton. The Scandrett share had passed by marriage in the previous century to the Harford family of Bristol, being held by the head of that family, John Scandrett Harford; and the Pemberton share was held by Sarah Pemberton, now of Wakefield, the widow of Thomas Pemberton the younger who had left it to her by his will. The Lloyd share had for fifty years been held by Sampson Lloyd III who had the advantage of living quite near to Wednesbury when his cousins did not.

Since the partition of 1778 there had been little alteration in the aspect of the properties, the freehold parts held as separate estates and the leasehold parts in common. As in the time of Parkes and Fidoe, water was still the enemy, the primitive character of contemporary pumping still the limitation. The old Newcomen engine, if somewhat modified, was still basically the type in use for pumping as it had been throughout the eighteenth century, and the proprietors could quite normally record in a report upon a particular site that they had 'sunk a pit and raised a little ironstone about the year 1812 or 1813 but were overpowered by the water and could not go on'.

But the continuous increase in the population and in manufacture called for coal; Wednesbury was full of coal, and coal must be got. The innovations of James Watt were slowly becoming available, mining men had their eye upon them and Samuel Lloyd's father had had all this well in mind when making his will. In a clause which strikes the keynote of what was afterwards done by his successors he authorises his trustees, 'if they shall think it advisable and for the benefit of my estate', to join with the Harfords or others jointly interested in the minerals

in granting a lease or leases thereof for such term or terms of years as they may think proper or in letting the same upon a royalty rent or in boring for coal ironstone or other minerals or in erecting steam engines and other erections and doing any other act that shall be necessary for proving working and selling the said mines and minerals.*

The will directed that the Wednesbury rights and estate should be divided among his children equally. This meant that a single Heir, the testator, would be replaced by ten, which was the number of his children then living, but he had been able to foresee that even a one-tenth portion would be a valuable asset.

In the years 1818 and 1819 several important steps were taken. The interim since his father's death had been employed by Samuel Lloyd, who was the son on the spot as well as being the eldest, partly in opening up fresh workings at Wednesbury and partly in laying plans for larger operations. For these purposes he took into consultation his brother-in-law Joseph Foster. Joseph Foster of London, calico-printer, was the husband of Sarah, Samuel Lloyd's eldest sister, and as we saw in another chapter had been established since the 1780s at Bromley-by-Bow. He was also a co-executor of the will. Disposed to work together and spurred by the logic of the prospect, the two men had encouraged the formation of the Old Park Colliery Co., to conduct matters at Wednesbury, with representatives of the families as partners. The new firm had already, by 1818, 'erected a fire engine, opened old workings, and made levels, rail roads and other works', and had 'laid out and expended large sums of money in and about the said works and premises'. The Harfords were now approached by Lloyd and Foster with a view to a deal, and, willing now to shed the obligations of a distant estate, they consented to dispose of the whole of their share to Lloyd and Foster equally.† From this date the Parkes inheritance

* Will of Sampson Lloyd III, 1808, folio 123 Ely, Prerogative Court of Canterbury. At this period the words *mine* and *mines* were used of the ore, coal or other material to be extracted, and not normally of the place or pit where it was got.

† The price agreed was £10,000, made up of £3500 for their freehold estate as created at the partition and £6500 for their rights in the leasehold mines and minerals. Parkes Papers 12/19; indentures dated 21 January 1818 (counterparts at Bristol City Record Office, ref. 19835).

was held between two families only, those of Lloyd and Pemberton, and as their shares in the estate (considered as divided into forty-eight parts) were now Lloyd, thirty-four, and Pemberton, fourteen, it was the Lloyds who had the control.

The partners in the Old Park Colliery Co. were Samuel Lloyd's eldest sons, George and Samuel, Joseph Foster's sons, Joseph Talwin Foster and Sampson Foster, and a great-nephew of the widow Pemberton named John Rooth. The first four were all young men in their twenties. At a meeting of the Heirs of Parkes held at Birmingham on the day after the Harford business had been formally completed these young men made proposals which resulted in their obtaining a fresh lease for forty-two years. They also re-named their partnership 'Lloyds Fosters and Company', under which style the mines and lands were thereafter operated.* Of the partners, George Lloyd was located at Birmingham, one Foster was a merchant in London and the other a banker at Norwich, while Rooth resided in Wednesbury but does not appear to emerge as an executive. The partner designated for the management of the concern was Samuel Lloyd junior.

In the cat's-cradle of landholders and mine-owners at Wednesbury these developments produced their reactions, and the early days of the new company were not easy, 'a concern', as George wrote to his brother in 1821, 'which has so ill repaid thee hitherto'. The Heirs of Parkes had been accustomed to look after their assets locally, in ejecting bad tenants, issuing writs and, as a matter of business, 'in asserting their rights and in suits at law and in equity concerning the same'. But the new activities provoked a dispute with a bigger opponent than usual. This was Sir Horace St Paul, married to a member of Lord Dudley's family, who was a considerable owner of surface land under which the Heirs of Parkes claimed the minerals. In 1820 a long-drawn-out Chancery case began between the two sides, which continued in progress for nearly three years. St Paul was disputing some of their most valuable mining claims. The Lord Chancellor was to hear the case. Counsel

---

* The date of the new lease was 23 November 1819, the principal rents and royalties being £300 a year for rent of premises and plant and the following royalties on output: for coal, 12½ per cent of the selling price: for coke, 2d. per sack: and for ironstone, 12½ per cent on the selling price or if less than 12s. per ton then 10 per cent. Lease, 23 November 1818; Patent Shaft Deeds, Box 6, Parcel 13. See also Parkes Papers 12/22.

must be briefed. The Lord Chancellor, Lord Eldon, had a dilatory reputation. Would he sit to hear causes, would he not? The Fosters nursed the solicitors in London, the Lloyds travelled up and down. Deeds and evidences must be produced to prove every contention, acts of ownership must be established and old field names reconciled with new. Gradually proofs of title were produced, some of them going back to the time of William and Mary. Still the Lord Chancellor prolonged the matter until, in 1823, the property was finally freed from Chancery by a compromise under which St Paul secured forty acres and the Heirs of Parkes 500.[7] Had the case gone the other way the history of Lloyds Fosters and the royalties of the Heirs of Parkes would have been very different.

The firm was now free to press ahead and in the coming years the business grew until it was one of the largest in Wednesbury. In the same year that the settlement was reached their first blast furnaces were completed. The minerals were progressively exploited. As colliery-owners and coal merchants they maintained a depot at Baskerville Wharf in Birmingham;[8] as ironmasters they profited, for smelting, from the presence under their land of ironstone and limestone side by side and from their enterprise as pioneers in technical innovation. In 1833 in a report to the Heirs of Parkes, the partners record pioneering the 'hot blast' principle, through installing 'an apparatus for heating the blast before it is admitted into the furnaces, by which improvement the cost of our iron has been so much reduced that we do not doubt our being able in future to meet the utmost competition in the sale'. In 1849 they were the first in the West Midlands to make use of their own blast-furnace gas to raise steam for driving the blast-furnace, an innovation which saved them 10,000 tons of small coal annually and in due course became universal. In 1862, simultaneously with John Brown of Sheffield, they were the first licensees of the new Bessemer steel-making process.[9] As engineers and manufacturers they developed markets in structural ironwork and, with the spread of the railways, in wheels and parts for rolling stock both at home and abroad. They were an example of vertical integration. In addition they farmed a large estate of unmined land in Wednesbury including nearly a hundred acres of mowing grass.

In 1837, when the firm had been established for about twenty years, George Lloyd retired from the partnership in order to confine his attentions to the Bank, and was replaced by his youngest brother Sampson who became an executive partner and resided in Wednesbury. Their brother, Samuel Lloyd, after the early spadework was past, took the lead in developing the business and became a figure in the town. A Quaker both in ways and dress, well known in the district as 'Quaker Lloyd', he used a Quaker approach in his labour relations which made for loyalty among the workmen and contributed to the prosperity of the firm. An example was their policy as regards the payment of employees by the truck system.* 'This system,' says a local writer,

an employer was obliged to adopt for self-protection, but not all firms made an undue profit out of their workmen. Lloyds Fosters & Co. kept a truck shop in Wednesbury which was conducted on high moral principles. All the articles were of the best value and the prices were low and sometimes lower than in the shops. Samuel Lloyd, the founder, took pride in buying the chief articles himself, especially the tea, the bullocks and the sheep, and the shop was noted for the best butcher's meat in Wednesbury.[10]

At Wednesbury Quaker Lloyd resided during the whole of his married life and brought up his family. (It is convenient to use this form of his name to keep him distinguished from his father.) His wife, Mary Honychurch, was a Quaker from Falmouth. Twice every week, from 1823 when he married to 1862 when he died, he and Mary Lloyd drove the eight miles to Birmingham with their family to attend Bull Street meeting for worship. Mary Lloyd herself became an acknowledged minister in the Society; she was also the founder of the Ladies' Negro Friend Society, a body which, concerning itself with the lot of slave women wherever slavery remained lawful, continued active for more than ninety years.

In about 1850 Quaker Lloyd's eldest son Samuel (1827–1918), who had been learning the business, was admitted as a partner in Lloyds Fosters, the first of the next generation. The names of the partners may sometimes have caused confusion, comprising as they did at this time Samuel Lloyd, Joseph Foster, Sampson Foster, Sampson Lloyd and Samuel Lloyd the younger, and more so again

---

* It was common at this period to pay workmen partly in kind through vouchers on a provision shop run by the employer. This was known as the truck shop or 'tommy shop'. Though open to abuse by profiteering, many wives preferred a system which saved wages from being spent in other ways.

when the elder Foster was followed by Sampson Foster's son, Sampson Lloyd Foster. They were, it is true, all cousins, in descent from the Sampson Lloyds, but it was through chance that so many bearers of the same names should have come together from the two families. For a sequence of Sampsons, however, to be capped by a series of Samuels must have made it more confusing still. Lloyds Fosters were saddled with both, and how the partners addressed one another it might be curious to know. But the business continued to prosper; Quaker Lloyd, growing older, could feel satisfied at what it had become, and with trade advancing and the minerals unexhausted look with confidence to its future. He died at sixty-seven in 1862.

Within five years of his death Lloyds Fosters were on the rocks. The story has been told before,[11] of the ironwork for a bridge over the Thames, of the calculated risk, of the unknowns that upset those calculations and of the consequent crippling loss. In 1862, when the old Blackfriars Bridge was to be replaced by a new wrought-iron bridge, Lloyds Fosters were appointed sub-contractors for the ironwork. Quite early in the course of the work the main contractors, whose tender had been unrealistically low, found themselves unable to make the monthly cash payments for deliveries of material. Lloyds Fosters, on consideration, resolved to retain the business by financing the contractors until completion and engaged themselves accordingly. Difficulties not foreseen beset the project. One was in the sinking of the iron caissons into the clay below the bed of the river, 'with the tide rushing to and fro night and day', so as to be watertight for constructing the foundations of the stone piers. Another arose at the City end of the bridge from the want of a good bottom, for here it was found that the old river Fleet, pouring its waters for thousands of years into the main river, 'had burrowed down and made the ground so soft that there seemed no bottom to it'. Costs mounted continually, and by the time that the ironwork was completed Lloyds Fosters had incurred a loss of a quarter of a million pounds. A going concern, profitable and respected, they could find no more working capital, and on 1 January 1867, when the bridge was still unfinished, the business was sold to their principal competitors in Wednesbury, the Patent Shaft and Axletree Company. The bridge, which is still in use, was opened by Queen Victoria in 1869 (Plate 34).

27. Old Brathay near Ambleside, home of Charles Lloyd the poet; by John Harden, about 1810.

29. Priscilla Wordsworth, 1781–1815, daughter of Charles Lloyd the banker and sister-in-law of William Wordsworth; by John Constable.

28. James Lloyd I, 1776–1853, a partner in Taylors & Lloyds; by John Constable.

30. 'Farm' near Birmingham, residence of the Lloyds; by A. E. Everitt, 1855.

31. The Quaker meeting house at Bull Street, Birmingham, as it was from the 1770s to the 1850s.

32. Samuel and Rachel Lloyd of 'Farm'; by Samuel Metford, about 1840.

33. The Kings Mills at Castle Donington; engraving by H. L. Pratt, 1852.

34. Opening of the new Blackfriars
Bridge by Queen Victoria,
November 1869, showing
ironwork made at Wednesbury by
Lloyds, Fosters. (*Illustrated
London News.*)

35. Sampson Samuel Lloyd,
1820–99, a partner in Taylors &
Lloyds, afterwards chairman of
Lloyds Bank; by Terry Burnett,
1849.

All but one of the partners had voted for financing the contractors. The only contemporary account of the matter is that of the
minority voice, Samuel Lloyd the younger, who resisted the proposal on commercial grounds and declared that his father, had he
been alive, would have done likewise, but the managing partner, his
uncle Sampson Lloyd, was backed in the decision by the other
partners. In ordinary circumstances they could probably have stood
the expense; but, it may be asked, ought not someone to have
foreseen some of the hazards encountered, 'which were greater,'
Samuel Lloyd writes, 'than my partners, or the contractors, or even
the engineer, Mr Cubitt, had contemplated'? At this distance of
time it is difficult to judge. What seems likely is that an undertaking
once given by these men was something that they would not go
back on.* Lloyds Fosters had been the largest firm in Wednesbury,
employing 3000 workpeople. Upon the amalgamation, the Patent
Shaft became the largest in Staffordshire, Samuel Lloyd noting that
within the next eight years the profits were enough to have paid
the whole of the purchase money in dividends.

So ended, 'in needless calamity', the fifty years' history of Lloyds
Fosters. The royalties of the Heirs of Parkes, who still owned the
land and minerals, now came from the Patent Shaft to whom the
lease had been assigned. The sequel may be touched in. Lucrative
for a few years longer, the deposits then began to be worked out in
common with the district at large. The remaining land was disposed
of by degrees. This process continued slowly until well into the
next century, a small company, the Heirs of Parkes Ltd, being
formed in 1896 to carry it on, but by the end of the 1880s, a century
and a half after Parkes's death, the long saga of the inheritance was
to all intents and purposes at an end.

After the smash the partnership of the Lloyds and Fosters was
dissolved, each of them going their several ways. The young
Samuel, removing to Birmingham, started the tube-making partner-

---

* The price received for the business was £410,000 made up of £300,000 in cash
and shares and £110,000 to Lloyds Banking Co. Ltd to pay off a mortgage which
the firm had been obliged to raise while in difficulties. Patent Shaft records. Agreement for Sale 21 November 1866, in the Company's Minute Book, 12 December
1866, and solicitors' notice to pay, 11 May 1870, Box 8 (unnumbered). The latter is
among documents in possession of the Patent Shaft Steel Works Ltd taken over from
Lloyds Fosters after the sale. The author is indebted to the Secretary for access to
these documents which are in many respects complementary to the Parkes Papers.

ship of Lloyd & Lloyd, a firm which later developed into Stewarts & Lloyds. Sampson Lloyd became the vice-chairman of the Patent Shaft, a position he continued to occupy until his death in 1874. Apart from a few years of training with Taylors & Lloyds, Sampson Lloyd had served Wednesbury nearly all his life. His bride, whom he brought there in 1842, had been Sarah Zachary of Areley Kings in Worcestershire, and at Wednesbury their family was brought up. In later life he resided at Wassell Grove near Stourbridge, from which place there was now access to Wednesbury by rail; and he lived for a few years, in his old age, at Areley Hall itself, just across the Severn from Stourport. A Wednesbury obituary declared that he was 'truly one of nature's noblemen'. Though outside the scope of this book it must be added that one of his sons, Francis Henry Lloyd, became likewise a noted figure in the Black Country as the creator of F. H. Lloyd & Co., the steelfounders, and some other well-known companies.

In 1839 an exceptional occurrence took place in the senior branch of this large family when, at the age of seventy-one, Samuel Lloyd of Farm ceased to be a Friend. He had been a pillar of the Quakers in Birmingham most of his life, an acknowledged minister for twenty years, and, counting from Charles Lloyd of Welshpool gaol, he was the fifth Quaker head of the family. His case offers no parallel to those of forty years before in the Bingley family, of young people leaving Friends in their twenties, from intolerance, indifference or in order to marry. Samuel Lloyd resigned for conscience's sake, at a time of ferment in the Society, and so did some of his children. At the same time his wife did not, and the background to such a situation needs to be suggested, even if a brief account risks appearing over-simplified.[12]

The end of the eighteenth century and the beginning of the nineteenth were a period when revolutions of thought were taking place and when Quaker teaching itself, little modified for more than a hundred years, was beginning to be reviewed and debated. After toleration had eased the path in the time of William and Mary, the Quaker ministry had shed its campaigning character and taken its stand upon the more mystical aspects of Fox's teaching. At the core of his message, rejecting the forms and rituals of the churches which he saw as corrupt and plunged in error, stood reliance upon a direct relationship between God and the individual through the Spirit. This was made possible, Fox said, because of the seed of grace or 'inward light' that is present in every man, by which light he may learn God's will and be guided in his thought and actions. Such had likewise been the theme of Barclay in the *Apology*, making the scriptures secondary to the inward light as a guide to religious truth. The impact of the teaching of these men lived fresh in Quaker minds through the first half of the eighteenth century and its influence was still dominant in the second. To depend upon the promptings of the Spirit, to preach only if so inspired, to be receptive, and by turning inward to achieve calmness in all situations were the attitudes of the Quaker tradition, a tradition which came to be known by the term used of other mystical religions, that of 'quietist'. It was a teaching which in men of the right spiritual quality bore notable fruit; but Quakers, like other men, are of divers sorts and temperaments, and spiritual needs may be met in divers ways. The influences of the day were stirring new thought among them, the afterglow of John Wesley's ministry and the new evangelical climate among Anglicans were having their effect, and some Friends were questioning whether the doctrine of the perceptible guidance of the Spirit, 'the inward light', was satisfactory, and whether they were placing enough reliance upon New Testament teaching concerning matters such as salvation and the sacraments. Thus, by Samuel Lloyd's time, there were the makings of more than one outlook within the Society. There were many who held to the quietist position, others much affected by the evangelicalism about them, and a variety of opinions in between.

At home, in an established community, there might have been room for diversities of this extent, but in America, in its radical, unformed state, controversy took a form which resulted, in 1828, in several thousand Friends breaking with their Yearly Meetings (of which there were several in that country) to set up new ones of their own. These events became known as the Great Separation. The Friends who seceded were, in general, of the quietist tradition, which, however, they carried to extremes. They were spurred on by the preaching of a farmer named Elias Hicks which exalted the guidance of the Spirit but was sceptical of the divinity of Christ, so that they were mistrusted as 'unitarian' in their views while regarding the opposite party, who were largely evangelical in thought, as the slaves of Holy Writ. Each side doubtless overplayed its hand, but the outcome was a sign of the times and its echoes disturbed Friends in England. In a climate of growing unease the differences at home came more into the open. In 1835, the concern which was felt by the more advanced evangelical Quakers over the strength of the secession in America and their fears as to its effects in this country were brought to the fore in a small book, *A Beacon to the Society of Friends*, by Isaac Crewdson, a Kendal Friend who had been many years a minister at Manchester. Designed as an indictment of the seceders, this publication caused a turmoil, implying, as to some it did, that the gospel of the inner light, rereceived of Fox, had been all this time more Fox than gospel. This and the disunity of the Manchester meeting the leaders of the Society felt bound to notice and Crewdson was deprived of his position as a minister. He resigned from membership, followed soon after by three hundred more who, like him, placed the gospel before the inner light.

Among the three hundred was Samuel Lloyd. Through their Kendal connection the Lloyds were kept close to the situation, and the fact that Isaac Crewdson was from Kendal and his brother married to Rachel Lloyd's sister* did not make the crisis less trying. Samuel Lloyd left Friends himself at the end of 1838 about three years after the *Beacon* was published, but already its repercussions had drawn one of his daughters out of the Society. This was an occurrence which had its influence on his own course of action and needs to be filled in. Rachel Lloyd junior in 1825 had married Robert Howard of Tottenham, one of two Quaker brothers, the sons of Luke Howard, the pioneer meteorologist. The wife of the other brother, John Eliot Howard,† was a daughter of W. D. Crewdson of Kendal and thus niece both to the Lloyds and to Crewdson of the *Beacon*. And it was Robert and John Eliot Howard and their wives, Samuel Lloyd's daughter and niece, who first in the Lloyd circle, in 1836, had felt it right to leave Friends, to be baptised, and to partake of the Lord's supper; for these matters,

---

* Isaac Crewdson's brother, W. D. Crewdson of Kendal, was the husband of Rachel Lloyd's sister, Deborah Braithwaite.

† John Eliot Howard, FRS, FLS, is usually known by his three names in full to distinguish him from John Howard, the prison reformer.

baptism and the breaking of bread, rejected by Fox long before as 'empty external rites', were among the issues on which the controversy turned and which, for Crewdson and his friends, the new focus on gospel teaching made all-important.

But if you left Friends where did you go? With what body did you worship? Most turned in one of three directions, some to the Baptists and some direct to the Anglicans, while others were attracted to the simpler worship and the broader, very evangelical thinking of Brethrenism.* This was the solution adopted by the Howards, who built up at Tottenham a Brethren meeting which prospered both in their time and after. It was also the solution adopted by the Crewdsons in the North-West and, in turn, by Samuel Lloyd at Birmingham.

Disagreement with old friends and fellow worshippers can be of the harshest kind, and this time of separation in the family was attended by every degree of heart-searching. Conflict, reluctance and conviction succeeded each other from stage to stage. In Fox's time new truths brought persecution, in Samuel Lloyd's they brought emotion and distress. 'Agitation seems the order of the day,' writes one of his daughters in her journal, 'schism and separation are at work amongst us.' His wife, Samuel Lloyd is persuaded, 'continues happier than she was previously although she talks of never being happy again'. To W. D. Crewdson at Kendal, who had taken the step when Lloyd had not, Samuel Lloyd writes of facing the large meeting for worship at Bull Street from his minister's place, his convictions known, his ministry silenced, his resignation or disownment awaited. A few weeks later, 'there was quite a scene,' wrote a grandson, 'at monthly meeting when Samuel Lloyd offered his resignation and walked out, Uncle Theodore weeping like a child and others much affected'. But, as in the wars of religion, so in great schisms, action comes from forces within, and 'I cannot be sufficiently thankful,' Samuel Lloyd wrote to a sympathiser, 'that in my old age I have been so *marvellously extricated.*'

Like the Howards at Tottenham, he soon found himself the leader of a small Brethren group in Birmingham, in Waterloo Street, 'our little room', and one of his sons with him, for so the

---

* The Brethren were a fairly new body. After the 1840s several forms of Brethrenism developed, the best known being the Plymouth Brethren, but at the time of the *Beacon* controversy they were simply 'the Brethren'.

loosening advanced. This was Sampson, the youngest, who by this time was in Lloyds Fosters and living at Wednesbury. 'I wish,' Sampson writes to his sister Rachel, 'that more of the family would see with us.' The new group did what they could to push out the frontiers of Brethrenism a little further. Support grew and they took a better room, this time at the Athenaeum rooms in Temple Row. 'Our numbers are increased, and with enquirers our large room is often nearly half full,' writes Samuel Lloyd in 1841; 'I am going to take a journey tomorrow, with dear C. Hargrave, to visit some of the little churches and scattered Brethren in and about Stafford, and from thence to Stanton and Salop.'

To leave the Society meant leaving behind the externals of membership, the plain speech and the Quaker apparel. The 'thou', 'thy' and 'thee' were not easily shed, even by the young. Their letters at first use 'thee' and 'you' alike, sometimes with the one struck out and the other written over, and some of them, when addressed to seniors who were Friends, still employ the accustomed 'thee'; for this was a custom already two centuries old. Its use had been modified, with time, till it no longer matched the strict biblical turn of Fox's day. 'Thou seest' had become, first, 'thou sees', and later, when, 'thou' dropped out, 'thee sees'. This last was ungrammatical but easy, and, where it survives, is the form in use today. But the plain speech was a testimony of membership and if you left Friends you must learn to give it up. To give up the Quaker dress was a still more public act. Apart from members of ecclesiastical orders the Friends were the only sect or Church to have a uniform, and a uniform it was. Sampson Lloyd III, when his Quaker suit came, 'felt as though they had brought him his coffin'; but when he was old he always wore grey, 'because that was the natural colour of the wool and dyes were vain things'. George Fox had not prescribed what Quakers should wear, he had only said let it be plain, let it be your testimony. Insistence on detail had developed thereafter, at first from a desire to preserve the style of Fox's day, and afterwards, in a time of foppery and parade, to depart from it as little as might be practicable, and it had come to be valued by many Quakers for its peculiarity. By Samuel Lloyd's time the principal features, for a man, were coats of low collar instead of the high ones then in vogue, keeping your hat on when others took them off, and, although trousers had come in, to continue the wearing of breeches. For a woman they included the neutral greys, discretion in style, and not least the Quaker cap, of clear-starched muslin for the home* and of a more bonnet-like substance for the street. In either case it was obvious that the wearer was a Quaker; and if, to them, the apparel was a thing they got used to, to the world it was still apt to seem comic.†

In the crisis of exit from the Society, to give up the dress was also a testimony, if in the opposite sense to Sampson Lloyd's experience, and the widow of John Eliot Howard could still recall the embarrassment of it fifty years later; 'On the 6th October 1836 we resigned our connection with the Society of Friends,' she writes, 'and a few days afterwards we renounced the Quaker garb, a step far more painful and formidable than can at this distance of time be understood.' Samuel Lloyd, it seems, took his time in adopting the change, which he made in 1841. At Farm when he made it there were more hard feelings, on which his son Sampson reports to Rachel at Tottenham:

Poor mother worked herself up into quite a pet about Father's alteration in dress and I understand poured out her troubles to you. She gave me a dose on reaching Farm last Saturday, as if I had been the cause. I spoke my mind clearly to her and I hope in a Christian spirit. I told her that if she was determined to make trouble on such a little matter she would drink a bitter cup when she might and ought to have a sweet one. She knew that Father's object was to serve the Lord, and why should he wear the garb of a sect he believed to be greatly in error, telling a lie to the world. She cooled down after a short time.[13]

Sampson Lloyd's mother was seventy-three.

It was a tangled time of change both inside the Society and out of it. At Farm, husband and wife chose separate ways, the husband following that of his daughter Howard. Their son Sampson, united with the Brethren at heart, was married in a church. His brother Theodore, marrying as a Friend, turned presently to Anglican ways. But six others of the family make Quaker marriages and

---

* See R. J. Lowe, op. cit., p. 61: 'Clear-starching was an acquired art which the daughters of the family practised on starching days.'

† When Friends, maintaining their testimony against bearing arms, sent a deputation to the Tsar on the eve of the Crimean War, it was noted that 'three gentlemen of unwonted humility and diffidence have volunteered ... to try the effect of the undoffable broadbrim upon Tsar Nicholas', *John Bull*, 28 January 1854.

ended their days as Quakers. Samuel Lloyd himself did not have many years to minister among his new-found brethren. He lived to eighty but in declining health and died in 1849. The Society of Friends, having suffered, in quality, more than might be thought from the loss of Crewdson's three hundred, drew itself together to move on again through the nineteenth century. As Methodism had stimulated the Church, so Beaconism had stimulated the Society, its bias for a time becoming more evangelical than not though it swung back in after times to the Light Within; but its advance to the twentieth century is not to be followed here.

By the close of Samuel Lloyd's life, alterations were coming both in the disabilities and the attitudes of members of the Society, some of which he lived to see. The admission of dissenters to the universities, that is, to Oxford and Cambridge, did not come until 1871, but the situation in regard to tithes was relaxing. Passive resistance through the non-payment of these and similar levies had been the classic Quaker testimony against 'hireling priests'. It had meant, since Fox's time, a conflict between their religious profession and the requirements of the law, but they had suffered indefensible extortions for non-payment. Charles Lloyd had been no exception at Bingley, and as lately as 1830 goods of Samuel Lloyd had been seized at Farm comprising hay, straw, sheep, cows and a horse, to an estimated value of £180,[14] but through an act of 1836 legislation towards the commuting of tithe had begun. On 'plainness of speech' and 'plainness of apparel', it was not until the middle of the century that opinion among Friends modified. Conservatism died hard, but in 1860 both these requirements were at length declared optional.* In the same year, more important still, the rule was dropped against marrying out, the restriction which in earlier days had favoured the rise of a Quaker élite but which, the more it came to be disregarded, had drawn off through disownment so much good material for so long. There was thus a loosening at work, a mixing and a reorienting which continued in progress until, two generations later, a majority of the Lloyds were no longer Quakers. But these things took place after Samuel Lloyd's lifetime. Banker, mill-owner, an Heir of Parkes and, until he was seventy, a Quaker, he had

---

* Returning from Yearly Meeting at about this date, a Quaker of the old school is said to have reported that 'many Friends had gone down into longs but there was a precious remnant in shorts'.

reigned at Farm in sober state, the last of the Lloyd Quaker patriarchs.

While these enterprises were being carried on, these lives lived,
and these spiritual crossroads faced, the firm of Taylor & Lloyds
had been carrying on their daily business in a thrusting, fast-growing
Birmingham, the population during this same time advancing from
100,000 to 300,000. During the span of about forty years from
Charles Lloyd's death to the Bank's great change in 1865 the
proprietors, all Taylors or Lloyds, lived through many profitable
years, saw important changes both in Birmingham and in banking,
and several times replenished their number as death removed this
one or that. One of the banking changes which was brought in after
the failures of the 1820s had been the right for a bank to have
more than six partners provided it was located over sixty-five miles
from London (and the Bank of England) and that it was organised
on the joint-stock method. But, liability being still unlimited, share-
holders were not protected from ruin, and not all the banks so
formed were either successful or well run. Confronted with this
new option, Taylor & Lloyds preferred the personal touch of a
partnership and the risks that they understood and they successfully
continued as a private bank for more than a generation to come.
But they had their critical years, their shocks and their anxieties,
and some of these moments of upheaval are of interest to record.

The understanding still was that the Bank should be owned half
by Taylors and half by Lloyds. The situation in the 1830s shows
this plan in operation, when James Taylor and his brother William
held a quarter each and the two branches of the Lloyds a quarter
each, Samuel Lloyd and his son George from the Farm family, and
James Lloyd and his son Francis from the Bingley family. But, tidy
though the example may appear, it recalls one of the handicaps of
private banking under the six-partners system. For what if a partner
became an invalid? It was undesirable either to alter the partnership,
so losing a name which was probably an asset, or to deprive one's
partner of his livelihood. He had to be carried. Taylor & Lloyds
were more than once faced with this problem, in two cases from
reasons of mental health. For from 1820 until his death in 1839
William Taylor was incapacitated in this way and, though remaining

a partner, did not sign the annual accounts,[15] while, as we have seen, from 1843 until 1853 James Lloyd was in similar case, so that during thirty years there could be only five effective partners in the Bank.

Francis Lloyd had been admitted on Charles Lloyd's death in 1828. Popular and able, a bachelor all his life, he served in 1833, under Birmingham's system of town government, in the office of High Bailiff, which may be likened in some ways to that of a mayor without a corporation. But when still in his thirties his services to Taylor & Lloyds were cut short through one of those episodes which lead Ministers of the Crown to resign and will not do in banks. In 1839, to the dismay of his partners, the Bank was sued for £1281 by a dishonest and eccentric woman in her seventies who accused Francis Lloyd of malpractice; the case was brought to court and so improbable did his counsel consider the charges to be that Francis Lloyd's witnesses, ten in number, were never called and he was declared guilty. It was revealed later that the case was a put-up job relying on perjured witnesses.[16] Francis Lloyd, however, had no choice but to offer his resignation which, considering the competition in the town and the adverse publicity caused by the case, the Bank felt obliged to accept. Francis Lloyd had been a partner for eleven years and must have been a loss to the Bank. Research has not disclosed what he subsequently did in life beyond the fact that he held a commission in the Warwickshire Yeomanry and became a J.P.

The other young partner, George B. Lloyd (1794–1857), spent nearly fifty years in the Bank's service and was a partner for thirty-seven. As the eldest son, his line in due course became the senior branch of the family and both his sons became Bank partners. George Lloyd was a back-room figure, the back room that he knew best being the partners' room at Taylor & Lloyds, where his contribution was that of continuity and of the cordial regard which he inspired in the Bank's customers. That he held himself apart from public work and the activities of the town was due mainly to two handicaps: the spasmodic asthma of the Crowley strain in the family and the loss of his young wife after only seven years of married life. George Lloyd had married Mary Dearman in 1819, the year of Caroline Fox's journal, and had settled at a house in Broad Street, near the tollgate at Five Ways. Mary Lloyd was everybody's favourite. Not long after her death, believing it to be best for his young boys, George Lloyd accepted his parents' invitation to return to Farm where he took up residence as a widower, a decision which he afterwards spoke of as 'the great blunder of his life'. About fifteen years later, when his father and mother were rising eighty and he was in his fifties, he married again. A consistent Quaker himself, he may have become uncomfortable in the home climate with one parent a Quaker and the other not. Little is known of his second wife, a Birmingham Friend named Mary Shipton. They resided not far from Farm, returning to live there again for a brief spell between his mother's death in 1854 and his own in 1857.

During George Lloyd's banking life innovations were taking place in Birmingham such as can barely be mentioned here but which included the grant of borough status in 1838 to a town newly endowed with Town Hall, Market Hall and a railway station. By the 1840s the new revolution in transport was in full career. Not much more than two generations had passed since the canal frenzy had begun sweeping the country and Birmingham's first canal had been opened. During this time, with the improvement in the principal roads, coach transport too had reached new levels of reliability in many parts, but first the coach and later the barge were destined to be superseded. The new railways, operating from Liverpool and from London, came into Birmingham at Curzon Street station, on the east side of the town, which was opened in 1837. In 1842 Samuel Lloyd could reach Farm from Kendal in a day, and so could Edward Pease from Darlington, 'the father of railways', who travelled to Birmingham to stay with Samuel Lloyd the same year, and by 1846 New Street station was beginning to be used.[17]

Five years later the creation of another new station, at Snow Hill, caused a problem for Birmingham's Quakers and an unexpected task for George Lloyd, when it became necessary to cut right through the old burying-ground at Monmouth Street, formerly Bull Lane, and to transfer the remains to the newer burying-ground at Bull Street. It was George Lloyd, now the head of the family, who during the first five days of September 1851 personally supervised the gruesome process of transfer and reinterment and the recording of those remains that could be identified. One of his sons recalls the scene:

My father undertook the task of watching the disinterment and removal of the remains to a large vault in the burial ground adjoining the Friends meeting house in Bull Street. My grandfather had left a plan which shewed the position of the graves of members of our family from the year 1698, when Charles Lloyd of Dolobran who had been imprisoned in Welshpool was buried there. The lead coffins were still perfect, but many ghastly sights were presented of those who had not been so buried and whose remains were only partially decayed. Charles Lloyd's skeleton was found in an almost perfect state, having been protected from rain by a projecting corner of building and I had the melancholy interest of holding his skull in my hand.[18]

So numerous were the Lloyd buryings that a bronze plate was provided by the family to record the names, nearly fifty in number, going down to about 1820 when Bull Lane ceased to be used (*see endpaper*). Besides Lloyds, these include Pembertons, Fidoes, Richard Parkes, Olive Kirton and indeed very many of those in this book. When redevelopment disturbed the site a century afterwards the en-graved plate was still in its place and can be seen at Bull Street today.

From this digression we come back to Taylor & Lloyds. During the 1840s the firm had had a further reorganisation of partners and had also moved into new premises. In a single month in 1839 they had lost both William Taylor and Francis Lloyd. No junior Taylor being available, it was thought proper for James Taylor to assume his brother's holding and the Taylor half of the Bank thus passed into his sole name. On the Lloyd side, Samuel Lloyd being now old and James Lloyd ill, there were two newcomers, first James Lloyd junior, thirty-six, 'of Gloucester, merchant', replacing his brother Francis, and two or three years later Sampson Samuel Lloyd, twenty-three, son of George Lloyd, to continue the senior branch (Plate 35). The opportunity of securing better premises had come when James Taylor had offered the firm his family's former town house in High Street. The lease at Dale End was running short and the offer was accepted. Having acquired likewise a next-door shop, the combined premises were opened, in 1845, as No. 65 High Street, and continued to be the headquarters of the Bank until the establishment of the Colmore Row office in the 1870s. The cost of the operation was £6,000.

But in 1852 the firm had to face an upheaval of a much more disturbing kind, which was to prove a turning-point in its long

history. This was the sudden breakdown and death of James Taylor
himself who, under a delusion that he had no money and that his
affairs were in disorder, unexpectedly took his own life. Holding
half the business, his name and known wealth had been a main
foundation of the firm's credit. The Taylors indeed used to say
that they 'always kept £100,000 outside the bank business in the
Funds'. The partners were thrown into disarray. Taylor's eldest
son was a landed gentleman at Strensham in Worcestershire with
pursuits of his own. The partners had known that the son who
should succeed, Francis Taylor, was already of age and likely soon
to be one of their number, but on his father's death this plan did
not come into effect. The young Taylor was offered a quarter of the
Bank but declined it, and the Lloyds were left as the proprietors of
the business. 'We were thus left,' one of them wrote, 'to bear the
responsibility of the Bank alone, and anxiety could not but be felt
lest our credit should not suffice to keep the business together.'
The name of Taylor had been part of it since 1765 and what would
Birmingham say if it dropped out? It was a critical issue for the
family. But the decision was taken, they would stand their chance,
and in April 1853 the firm was changed to the new name of Lloyds
& Co. The partners were four: James Lloyd senior, George Lloyd,
and their respective sons James junior and Sampson Samuel. James
Lloyd senior was 'hopelessly ill and inacapacitated' but, to the relief
of the others, lived until the new firm had been established a year,
and 'his name and property as a partner materially aided its credit'.[19]
The surviving partners, who were now in receipt of the Taylor
income, while prudently limiting the distribution of profits for two
or three years, were better off themselves and were able, by saving,
to increase the paid-up capital of the firm.

In London, Taylor's death was likewise a disturbance at Hanbury
& Co. Bad publicity apart, he proved to be the last of that firm's
Birmingham partners, his son declining an offer there as he had at
Birmingham. In this way, after eighty-seven years, the name of
Taylor disappears from Lombard Street, that of Lloyd continuing
from Sampson Lloyd's death in 1807 through younger sons, nephews
and grandsons,* down to the takeover by Lloyds in 1884.

* These included his brother John's son, Corbyn Lloyd (d.1828), his own son
Henry Lloyd (d.1864), and a grandson and great-grandson, Richard Harman
Lloyd (d.1867) and Richard Borrodaile Lloyd (d.1907).

At Birmingham Lloyds & Co. prospered. It was not long, however, before the loss of another senior, George Lloyd, who died
in 1857, had to be made good. Suitable candidates were not wanting,
and two new Lloyds were admitted within a year of each other,
George B. Lloyd junior and Thomas Lloyd, one each from the
Farm and Bingley branches, brothers of those were were running
the business. Neither was a young man. Both had been in other
businesses. Both were town councillors. Both became mayors of
Birmingham. George Lloyd, an engineer, had been head of his
own business of G. B. Lloyd & Co., boiler-tube manufacturers in
Gas Street;* Thomas Lloyd had been a partner in the merchants
business of Rabone Brothers in Broad Street, travelling widely for
the firm in overseas markets; and both men served the Bank for
thirty or forty years into the future. A fragment of family tree will
show the connection of the four Lloyds at this time, the same
who were to face and carry through the great conversion of the
1860s, though as James Lloyd was then a sick man it was carried
through in fact by three of them:

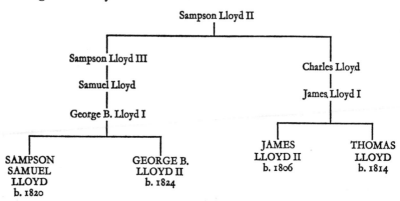

Why did the Lloyds convert the partnership into a public company? They did so because of increasing competition from the
joint-stock banks.[20] It was forty years since joint-stock banking
had been introduced, but only recently, through the Companies
Act of 1862, had Parliament approved the limitation of liability by
shares. This much enhanced the attractions of shares in joint-stock
banking companies, which, raising new money and improving their

* G. B. Lloyd & Co. was the first of the Lloyd tube businesses. Others included
the Albion Tube Co., the Weldless Steel Tube Co., and Lloyd & Lloyd, the last-
named later forming part of Stewarts & Lloyds Ltd.

facilities to the customer, besides rapidly increasing in numbers, were taking away accounts from private banks. Again, business and trade, in their expanding state, were calling constantly for more accommodation from banks of all types; more than once at recent dates, as minutes in the ledgers show, Lloyds & Co. had taken what steps they could to increase the firm's paid-up capital, but only within the limitations of their own resources. Thirdly, the very magnitude of contemporary business was pressing on private bankers as individuals. For if confidence in a private bank depended largely on the supposed substance of its partners their ultimate reserve in time of trouble was their actual substance, and both the pace and the risks were increasing; but in the new type of joint-stock concern liability would be limited by shares. The private banker, as an individual, had long been under certain constrictions; it was desirable that at least some of the partners should be seen to own property or estates, 'gentlemen,' in Paul Moon James's phrase, 'who had landed estates near their banks as well as money capital.'* And therefore, in the interest of the business, a partner in a private bank needed to provide handsomely for his own bank successors, probably at the expense of his other children; but after 1862, if his liability were limited, his firm's credit would depend no longer on individual fortunes and he could distribute his shares as he pleased.

Private banking in fact was out of date, and these were some of the considerations which induced the Lloyds in 1865 to change the business into a limited liability company. A particular spur had been the startling failure of Attwoods Bank on account of the check that it gave to confidence in private banking in the district. Attwoods & Co. of New Street, old-established and respected, were one of the three remaining private banking houses in the town. Early in 1865, this bank was found to be insolvent by many shillings in the pound and 'the thunderclap reverberated through Birmingham that Attwoods had stopped payment'. Such a failure was a shock for private banking and the Lloyd partners began to consider conversion more seriously.

In March, to counter local distrust, they took the unheard-of step

* Braithwaite MSS, packet 18. The Taylor establishment at Moseley is an example; so are Farm and Bingley; and The Priory at Warwick, the great house which Thomas Lloyd took in 1858; and it is relevant that in March 1865, when Lloyds & Co. published their balance-sheet, one of the entries reads: 'Partners' capital and accumulated profits *exclusive of their private property.*'

for a private bank of publishing in the press an audited and certified balance-sheet, an event which stirred and reassured public opinion and improved the climate for the step that they were contemplating. The ground being thus prepared, the decision was taken and the private partnership of the Lloyds was brought to an end, the business of the new Company opening on 1 May 1865, one hundred years from the foundation of Taylors & Lloyds. Just as the firm had been the first private banking house in the town so it was the last, the one other private bank, Moilliet & Co., being joined with Lloyds at its own request in the offer which was made to the public. The account of the operation can be sketched in, of the prospectus and its terms, the partners receiving £100,000 for the goodwill, half cash, half premium value, of the impressive committee of townsmen and customers, of the new name, Lloyds Banking Co. Ltd, chairman Timothy Kenrick, managing director Sampson Samuel Lloyd, of the issue eagerly over-subscribed, the shares at once reaching a high premium, of how 'new accounts flowed in'.[21] Lloyds Fosters might be in trouble at Blackfriars and the Kings Mills lately sold, but this operation was conspicuously successful and the decision to convert had been right. Nevertheless the key decision had been that of twelve years before when the Lloyds carried on on their own.

The story ends here. The Bank in the second part of the century is not our business, neither are the Lloyds. Yet a further glance may be spared for one character in the cast, Sampson Samuel Lloyd, on account of two particular occurrences in his long and bustling life. In 1869 Sampson Samuel Lloyd succeeded Kenrick as chairman of the new company, a position which he occupied during eighteen years of its greatest expansion. This was not because he was the head of the family, it was because of the estimation of the directors who retained him as chairman of the board. But his position in the family may have had something to do with his purchase, a few years later, of the Dolobran estate, which had been out of Lloyd hands since 1780. The history of the first Quaker Lloyd and the traditions of ancestral persecution had never ceased to stir family sentiment, as they stir it today, and more than one of those in a position to do so had dreamed of recovering the property. As early as 1735, when it was encumbered but not sold, Sampson Lloyd II had gone into the question and discussed what price it ought to fetch. Seventy years later Charles Lloyd had been tempted, and 'prudence alone,' as Olivia James wrote in her memoirs, 'prevented my dear father from purchasing it.' In the year 1878 Sampson Samuel Lloyd did purchase it, 'the dream of my younger days,' as he wrote, however contrary to the advice of his father, '*never thou buy Dolobran!*' The purchase is understood to have cost him £20,000. Returning to a Lloyd after ninety-eight years, Dolobran has remained with his descendants for nearly as long again, one of them taking the name of the property for his title. The estate, in extent, is much as it was at the time of the opening chapters of this book, and the house not much altered externally, the features which the visitor might notice being the up-to-date farm buildings and yards and the peacocks that embellish the scene.

But Sampson Samuel Lloyd wore Dundreary whiskers and a top hat, he did not wear the breeches of the Quaker. Only one partner was a Quaker at the time of the conversion, for the Quaker Lloyds were of the past, of the time that this book is about, 'the tall forms and noble presences to be seen in those days', 'the ways and style of a previous age'. The mind turns back to the quality and talents of Charles the banker, to John in London, as consistent and useful as Nehemiah in Birmingham was useless, to their brother, Sampson the Third, established, right-minded, able, but not talented like Charles; to the father of these men, Sampson the Second, for whom everything came right, who built for the future; to Sampson the First, who took the risk, the stage-setter; to his well-meaning brother at Dolobran; to their father in Welshpool gaol. These men exchanged country for town; they made themselves merchants in iron, and manufacturers too, using forges to refine it and corn mills to slit it; spoke the speech of the Quaker, declined to pay tithes and were willing to go it alone. They dealt plainly and fairly in business and they met with success; gave a bank to a region that had no bank, made another in London and a name in a Black Country town. They were part of the Quaker élite. They lent weight to the improvement of Birmingham and leadership to causes of the day. For them, no degrees and no honours. What the world accorded them was esteem. These are the men that this book is about. These were the Quaker Lloyds.

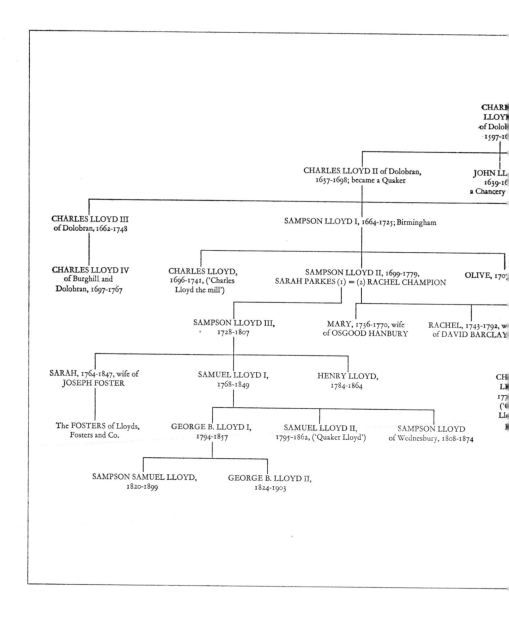

CHARLES
LLOYD
of Dolobran
1597-16

CHARLES LLOYD II of Dolobran,
1637-1698; became a Quaker

JOHN LL
1639-16
a Chancery

CHARLES LLOYD III
of Dolobran, 1662-1748

SAMPSON LLOYD I, 1664-1725; Birmingham

CHARLES LLOYD IV
of Burghill and
Dolobran, 1697-1767

CHARLES LLOYD,
1696-1741, ('Charles
Lloyd the mill')

SAMPSON LLOYD II, 1699-1779,
SARAH PARKES (1) = (2) RACHEL CHAMPION

OLIVE, 170

SAMPSON LLOYD III,
1728-1807

MARY, 1736-1770, wife
of OSGOOD HANBURY

RACHEL, 1743-1792, w
of DAVID BARCLAY

SARAH, 1764-1847, wife of
JOSEPH FOSTER

SAMUEL LLOYD I,
1768-1849

HENRY LLOYD,
1784-1864

CH
LL
177
('
Ll

The FOSTERS of Lloyds,
Fosters and Co.

GEORGE B. LLOYD I,
1794-1857

SAMUEL LLOYD II,
1795-1862, ('Quaker Lloyd')

SAMPSON LLOYD
of Wednesbury, 1808-1874

SAMPSON SAMUEL LLOYD,
1820-1899

GEORGE B. LLOYD II,
1824-1903

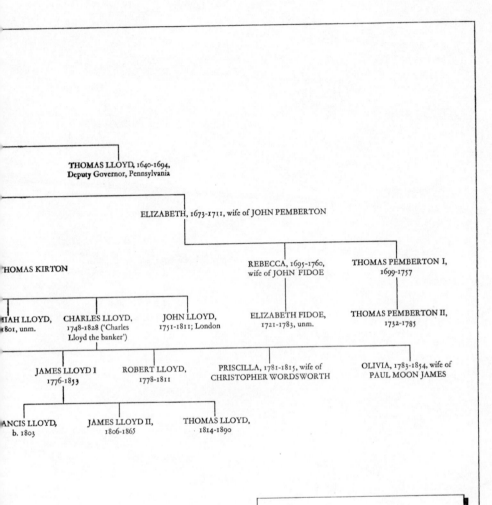

THOMAS LLOYD, 1640-1694,
Deputy Governor, Pennsylvania

ELIZABETH, 1673-1711, wife of JOHN PEMBERTON

THOMAS KIRTON

REBECCA, 1695-1760,
wife of JOHN FIDOE

THOMAS PEMBERTON I,
1699-1757

IAH LLOYD,
801, unm.

CHARLES LLOYD,
1748-1828 ('Charles
Lloyd the banker')

JOHN LLOYD,
1751-1811; London

ELIZABETH FIDOE,
1721-1783, unm.

THOMAS PEMBERTON II,
1732-1785

JAMES LLOYD I
1776-1853

ROBERT LLOYD,
1778-1811

PRISCILLA, 1781-1815, wife of
CHRISTOPHER WORDSWORTH

OLIVIA, 1783-1854, wife of
PAUL MOON JAMES

ANCIS LLOYD,
b. 1803

JAMES LLOYD II,
1806-1865

THOMAS LLOYD,
1814-1890

GENEALOGICAL TABLE
SHOWING DESCENT OF THE PRINCIPAL QUAKER
LLOYDS DURING THE PERIOD OF THIS BOOK.

THE ARMS OF LLOYD AND STANLEY

The heraldic panel (see frontispiece) was made by Charles Lloyd I (1613–57), probably in the 1650s. It displays Charles Lloyd's shield of fifteen quarterings impaled with Stanley of Knockin, of six, for his wife Elizabeth Stanley.

An accurate knowledge of ancestry was a characteristic of Welsh society, such studies being in the seventeenth century the pride of the gentry classes, and there is some interest in considering what coats this shield presents. So far as the Lloyd side is concerned, Charles Lloyd's method was, in accordance with Welsh genealogical practice, to include the coats of the most distinguished or interesting of his ancestors through whatever marriage they might be claimed. In English heraldry, only the coat of an 'heiress' might be quartered with the parental coat, that is, only that of a woman representing her line because male representatives were wanting; but in Charles Lloyd's shield 'ancestress' coats are included whether claimed through heiresses or not. The Stanley traditions, on the other hand, were English, and on the Stanley side the shield respects the English rules, admitting no coats of wives who were not heiresses also.

Specialists in Welsh genealogy agree that the fifteen quarterings in the Lloyd part of the shield stand for the ancestors named below, and are able to indicate from Welsh sources those wives in the pedigree through whom each ancestress coat came down. The lines of descent represented by the six coats in the Stanley part of the shield (or seven, since one of the quarterings contains two coats) are similarly established on the authority of English records.

LLOYD SIDE OF SHIELD

Quartering

1. Aleth, reputed king of Dyfed
2. Brochwel Ysgythrog, prince of Powys
3. Einion Efell, a son of Madog ap Maredudd prince of Powys
4. Einion ap Seisyll of Meirionydd
5. Maredudd ap Cynan, lord of Eifionydd
6. Bleddyn ap Cynfyn, king of Powys
7. Cynwrig ap Rhiwallon of Maelor
8. Aleth, as quartering No. 1

9. Strange of Knockin
10. Tudur Trefor, king of the border territories
11. Alo ap Rhiwallon of Trefnant in Castle Caereinion
12. Elystan Glodrydd, king between Wye and Severn
13. Broughton of Owlbury in Salop
14. Howell ap Ieuaf ap Owen, lord of Arwystli
15. Cadwaladr Fendigaid, king of Gwynedd

STANLEY SIDE OF SHIELD

Quartering

1. Stanley of Knockin
2. (*above*) Strange of Knockin; (*below*) de Bamville of Chester
3. Silvester of Storeton
4. Hooton of Hooton
5. Heleigh of Flint
6. Stanley of Knockin, as quartering No. 1

An exchange of correspondence on this shield with Dr Michael Siddons, to whom the author is indebted for much genealogical and heraldic assistance, is deposited at the Birmingham Reference Library. See also the article, 'An approach to Welsh genealogy' by Major Francis Jones, now Wales Herald Extraordinary, in *Transactions of Honourable Society of Cymmrodorion* for 1948.

APPENDIX II

THE EXCAVATION OF MELBOURNE FURNACE

The account of the excavating of the Melbourne iron furnace in Chapter 5 is supplemented by the following report of Mr W. H. Bailey which appeared in *Bulletin No. 3 of the Historical Metallurgy Group* (June 1964):

The remains yielded the plan of a typical 17th–18th century blast furnace with a hearth or crucible. All the furnace structure above this level had disappeared, but the arrangements for driving the wheel, and the ponds, were well preserved.

There appeared to have been two ponds of different dates. The first pond was on the same side of the stream as the furnace itself, and may have been used for an earlier bloomery. At some later stage the water storage facilities were improved by building a dam 160 ft upstream of the old dam and right across the valley. This water was led to a pitch-back or breast wheel, a system that makes the most economic use of water. The wheel was 2 ft wide and 17 ft diameter and operated bellows (about 17 ft long) on the downstream side of the furnace, the water passing under the charging bridge.

The bellows terminated in a conical tuyere consisting of two semi-circular stones. The tap-hole consisted of a circular hole about 18 ins. diameter and the base of the hearth was a large piece of sandstone. On the bottom of the hearth was a 'bear' consisting of a saucer-shaped piece of cast iron which is being examined. All traces of the fore-hearth had gone.

The hearth itself was originally square in plan, about 4 ft by 4 ft, and about 5 ft high, but was now 'D' shaped due to slag accretion. The remains showed the beginning of the well-flared bosh and it would seem that this furnace belongs to the normally accepted type, like that of Lamberhurst, Kent, shown in Swedenborg's '*De Ferro*' of 1724.

One feature that was well preserved in the remains was the ventilation system. This comprised a series of brick-built passages running horizontally round the structure, set inside the rubble core of the masonry and connected by vertical passages at intervals.

An analysis of the slag has been carried out. Both roasted and unroasted remains of the local coal measure nodules were found on the site. The low lime-content of the coal measure nodules suggests that limestone or dolomite additions were made to the burden, but no limestone was found on the site.

APPENDIX III

PUBLICATIONS OF CHARLES LLOYD THE BANKER AND CHARLES LLOYD THE POET

CHARLES LLOYD THE BANKER (1748–1828)

1807   *A Translation of the 24th Book of the Iliad*
1810   *A Translation of the First Seven Books of the Odyssey*
1812   *The Epistles of Horace, translated into English Verse*

CHARLES LLOYD THE POET (1775–1839)

1795   *Poems on Various Subjects*
1796   *Poems on the Death of Priscilla Farmer*
1797   *Poems, Second Edition*: poems by Coleridge, Lamb and Lloyd; Lloyd's poems, pp. 153–213, 267–72

1798 *Blank Verse*: contains also poems by Charles Lamb; Lloyd's poems, pp. 7–72

1798 *Edmund Oliver*, 2 vols; a novel

1799 *Lines Suggested by the Fast*

1799 *A Letter to the Anti-Jacobin Reviewers*

1815 *The Tragedies of Vittorio Alfieri*, 3 vols.; a translation

1819 *Nugae Canorae*

1820 *Isabel, a Tale*, 2 vols.

1821 *Desultory Thoughts in London, Titus and Gisippus, with Other Poems*

1821 *Poetical Essays on the Character of Pope*

1821 *Memoirs of the Life and Writings of Vittorio Alfieri*; a translation

1822 *The Duke d'Ormond, A Tragedy; and Beritola, A Tale*

1823 *Poems*

APPENDIX IV

LLOYDS FOSTERS AND ELIZABETH FIDOE'S INHERITANCE

In 1839 the Lloyds, and through them Lloyds Fosters, became possessed of further land and minerals at Wednesbury in addition to those which they were already working under the Heirs of Parkes. The new properties, 108 acres in extent, were the inheritance of Elizabeth Fidoe, who had died more than fifty years before. The line of succession was devious but the value was considerable, approaching that of the Lloyd or Harford portions of the Parkes inheritance.*

The history of the Fidoe inheritance goes back to the brothers of Sarah Parkes, Henry Fidoe's successors, among whom his Wednesbury property had been divided. In the next generation, through agreement and purchase, the lion's share was in the hands of one grandson, John Fidoe of Birmingham, whose daughter Elizabeth inherited in 1737.† Elizabeth Fidoe was rich and unfortunate. Carefree in youth, never married, eccentric in middle age, she had inherited from the Fidoes, besides property, the family's mental infirmity. One of her uncles stands in the record as 'lunatic', which was the term then in use for those who

---

* In 1818 the total Parkes inheritance had been valued at £28,235; the Fidoe estate was valued in 1855 at £13,500.

† John Fidoe acquired the portion of his cousin Henry Fidoe junior by purchase in 1722. (Family paper in private possession.)

had to be certified. Elizabeth's end was the same. By the 1770s, resident in London at or near Red Lion Square, Holborn, she had become 'poor cousin Fidoe', the object of charitable visits by members of the family circle. For David Barclay, in 1777, she was 'much calmer than she before had been but rambled widely in her discourse on some points'. In 1779, after a formal enquiry into her condition, the custody of her person was committed to David Barclay who was her neighbour in London, and the care of her estate to Sampson Lloyd at Birmingham.[1] She died intestate in 1783.

For the succession it was necessary to go back to a grand-daughter of Henry Fidoe, whose descendant, John Burr, was declared the heir-at-law. John Burr was a surgeon at Ware. He was already a holder of property in Wednesbury, presumably through his Fidoe grandmother, and this, with Elizabeth's, made up a valuable estate.* He inherited likewise Elizabeth's Birmingham property including the house at No. 13 the Square† where she herself was born and where Johnson had been the guest of the Lloyds. After her death the Lloyds for the next forty years acted as agents for John Burr's estate, reporting to him on his tenants and remitting his rents annually. As a result of these associations and the regard between the parties, Burr, dying unmarried in 1821, left all his Wednesbury property to the Lloyds. It was left for life to David Lloyd, a banker in Suffolk, who was a brother of Samuel Lloyd, and after him

* The course of the inheritance from Fidoe to Burr may be followed by a simplified Table:

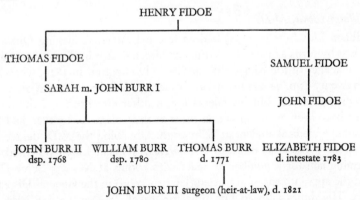

HENRY FIDOE

THOMAS FIDOE SAMUEL FIDOE

SARAH m. JOHN BURR I JOHN FIDOE

JOHN BURR II WILLIAM BURR THOMAS BURR ELIZABETH FIDOE
dsp. 1768 dsp. 1780 d. 1771 d. intestate 1783

JOHN BURR III surgeon (heir-at-law), d. 1821

John Burr's own Wednesbury property, of which a 1767 survey plan survives (Parkes Papers 14), had come down through his uncle, John Burr II.

† The tradition given in J. Hill and R. K. Dent, *Memorials of the Old Square*, Achilles Taylor, Birmingham, 1897, p. 104, that Burr acquired this property for services rendered is not borne out by his will. He acquired it as heir-at-law. Folio 314 Mansfield (1821), Prerogative Court of Canterbury.

to Samuel Lloyd and any living brothers or sisters equally. David Lloyd died childless in 1839. By this intricate, crab-like route did the inheritance of the Fidoes come into the hands of Lloyds Fosters; for, besides Samuel Lloyd, the brothers and sisters then living were two only, his sister Sarah Foster whose sons were in the firm already, and his brother Henry, a partner in Hanbury & Co. and a bachelor. Under these three, by appropriate arrangements,* the firm obtained substantial additional resources on their very doorstep.

APPENDIX V

THE CHILDREN OF SAMUEL AND RACHEL LLOYD

Samuel and Rachel Lloyd of Farm had nine sons and daughters who grew up and married. Three were in one or other of the family businesses described in Chapter 9, namely George Lloyd, the eldest, who was a partner in both Lloyds Fosters and Taylor & Lloyds, Samuel Lloyd junior, otherwise 'Quaker Lloyd', the head of Lloyds Fosters, and Sampson Lloyd, the youngest, a partner in the same firm. Some particulars of the six other sons and daughters are given below.

William Lloyd, M.D.

William Lloyd (1798–1875) had an unusual career. A lifelong Quaker, he was by turns a farmer in Worcestershire, a doctor in Birmingham and the manager of the Kings Mills at Castle Donington. In 1820, when he was twenty-two, he was set up as a farmer by his father at Strensham near Upton-on-Severn. But his talents lay in other directions and the farm must have been given up within three or four years, for by then he had become a medical student at Edinburgh. Obtaining the M.D. degree in 1832 for a thesis *de Mucosis Membranis*, William Lloyd practised at Birmingham for a number of years with rooms at No. 135 Snow Hill and the appointment of physician (later surgeon) to the General Dispensary. His duties allowed him time for travel. In 1830 he had been at Versailles on the occasion of the death of Sophia Lloyd, the wife of

---

* Samuel Lloyd's one-third portion was purchased from the trustees of his estate by his sons Samuel and Sampson in 1855, who also purchased Henry Lloyd's portion in 1857, while that of Sarah Foster passed to her sons Joseph and Sampson under her will in 1846. (Parkes Papers; Patent Shaft Deeds.)

Charles the poet; in 1836 he travelled with Joseph Sturge and another Friend to the West Indies to enquire into the conditions of the slaves still employed there, publishing upon his return *Letters from the West Indies, 1836 and 1837*, with illustrations from his own drawings; and in 1845 he accompanied the young Arthur Albright, afterwards co-founder of Albright & Wilson, on a journey to the Danube region to buy bones for the making of phosphorus.

About 1846, when in his upper forties, there occurred a crisis in William Lloyd's affairs which obliged him to throw up his medical career. It seems that he had taken to the treatment of patients by the homoeopathic method then attracting attention, and, as enquiry shows no sign of disciplinary measures against him, it is probable that hostile medical opinion undermined his practice.* The move to Castle Donington followed. Here the local manager had grown old, Samuel Lloyd, rising eighty, was glad to find a successor whatever his experience, and from 1847 until 1860 the mills were in William Lloyd's hands. Within a year of taking over, at the age of fifty, he announced his engagement to be married. 'Thou art likely, my dear, to be blessed with another aunt – guess who,' wrote one grown-up niece to another. His Leicestershire bride, twenty years younger than himself, was Caroline Ellis, a relative of the old Quaker whom he succeeded. Little is known of William Lloyd's period as mill manager. In 1860, at the age of sixty-two, he gave up, the business was sold to a competitor in Derby, and the sale of the mills thus brought to an end, after more than a hundred years, the Lloyd connection on the Trent.

Isaac Lloyd

Isaac Lloyd (1801–83) was apprenticed to his maternal uncle George Benson, a wholesale grocer at Kendal. In 1824 he started in life as a private banker, in partnership with William Miller Christy and two others, J. Worsley and J. K. Winterbottom, in the newly formed Stockport and East Cheshire Bank, usually known as Christy, Lloyd & Co.† Christy was a Quaker hat-manufacturer, based on Gracechurch Street in London, who had interests in the Stockport felt hat industry. He probably required Isaac Lloyd's services to relieve the others of manning the

* Neither the University of Edinburgh Medical School, the Royal College of Physicians, nor the Wellcome Institute of the History of Medicine are able to trace any record of action against William Lloyd. For the attitudes of some of the medical profession, see essay 'Homoeopathy and its Kindred Delusions' in Oliver Wendell Holmes, *Medical Essays*, 1861.

† The tradition that this bank was wound up with heavy losses (R. S. Sayers, *Lloyds Bank in the History of English Banking*, 1957, p. 65) seems, on later information, to be unfounded.

bank and is believed to have advanced part of his partnership capital. The new firm successfully weathered the banking panic of 1825, sustained by the reputation of Christy and of the local partners and fortified by the receipt of emergency cash supplies, 'sufficient to cover its outstanding paper', from Hanbury & Co., the bank's London agents.[2] In 1829, upon being approached to become part of a new joint-stock co-partnership, the Manchester and Liverpool District Banking Company (afterwards the District Bank), the firm ceased to be a private partnership and Isaac Lloyd retired in 1830 with a handsome honorarium. He had married in 1828 a Kendal Quaker, Mary Rigge, and, leaving the North, he reappears, at a time of active banking expansion, in another joint-stock, the Wilts and Dorset Bank, about 1835. This company he served for ten years in various branches, as a manager, resigning about 1845 when he was in his forties.

From then on Isaac Lloyd resided variously at Bath, Weston-super-Mare, Bristol and, in his old age, at Birmingham. He was a faithful, orthodox Friend, but he was an unfortunate man and something of a ne'er-do-well. It is said that he never found himself able to repay what Christy had advanced, and he was probably an expense to his father who by his will created trusts for Isaac and Isaac's family which he did not consider necessary for his other sons. One of Isaac Lloyd's most unfortunate experiences was the loss of his young child Henry while travelling from Bristol to Poole, the shock of which left his wife an invalid for the rest of her life. The event is reported by one of his sisters, herself in the course of a journey, who records how 'about thirty miles from Bristol, near Shaftesbury or Gillingham, the coach door flew open and one of the children, we suppose Henry, fell out and was crushed under the wheel, which passed over his head and killed him almost instantly'.[3] Isaac Lloyd's claim to fame is as the father of Howard Lloyd, a distinguished servant of Lloyds Bank during a time of great growth, who was born the year after the accident.

Theodore Lloyd

Theodore Lloyd (1806–80), 'with his sensitive interesting face',[4] made his career as a stockbroker in London, but stockbroking was not his first employment. Theodore Lloyd began life as a carpet-manufacturer. He was married as a Friend at Worcester in 1833, to Anna Ash, a spirited young widow, formerly Newman, lived for seven years at Bewdley, and occupied a position, unspecified, in carpets, presumably at Kidderminster. He removed to London about 1840 and established himself as a stock-broker, with the help of his father who mentions in 1842 'the large advance made to Theo the beginning of this year'. Theodore Lloyd was a Stock Exchange member for between thirty and forty years and his firm of Lloyd & Ward continued in business well into the twentieth century. He made his home in the Croydon area but, though far from Birmingham, he remained in touch with his brothers and his name appears as a trustee in a number of deeds relating to the family and its West Midlands interests. In the 1840s he and his wife left Friends and turned to the Church of England.

Deborah Stacey, Rachel Howard and Sarah Fox

The three daughters, Deborah, Rachel and Sarah Lloyd all made Quaker marriages. Between them, they had twenty-six children who grew to man's estate, the ancestors of countless Lloyd descendants not of the name of Lloyd.

The marriage of Deborah (1796–1841), the eldest, to George Stacey of Tottenham in 1818 was of comparatively short duration, for while each of her sisters lived to an advanced age Deborah died in 1841 aged only forty-four. Her husband was by origin from Kendal and a cousin to Deborah on her mother's side. 'An able, energetic little man', he was a partner in Corbyn, Beaumont, Stacey & Messer, chemists, at No. 100 Holborn, and the fact that in the 1830s and 1840s he was chosen twelve consecutive times as clerk of the London Yearly Meeting was a matter of close interest to Friends at Birmingham.

Rachel (1803–92), the middle sister, figures in Chapter 9 in connection with the *Beacon* controversy. Her husband, Robert Howard of Tottenham, was a partner with his father and brother in Luke Howard & Co. at Plaistow, the manufacturing chemists, a firm which became well known for its work in the development of quinine.

Sarah (1804–90), the youngest sister, made her home much further away than Tottenham, being married in 1828 to Alfred Fox of Falmouth; Alfred Fox was a partner in G. C. Fox & Co., ship agents, and in other Cornish businesses, and a cousin of Catherine Payton Fox whose journal is mentioned in Chapter 8.

NOTES

Preface

1. Letter of Robert Southey to Charles Lloyd the banker, 25 November 1820, quoted in E. V. Lucas, *Charles Lamb and the Lloyds*, Smith, Elder & Co., London, 1898. (Southey did not, unfortunately, write the projected history.)

Part I: DOLOBRAN

1. CALLED IN SCORN QUAKERS

1. See Meyrick's edition of Lewys Dwnn's *Heraldic Visitations of Wales 1586 to 1613*, ed. S. R. Meyrick, Llandovery, 1846, vol. I, p. 332.

2. A source used generally for parts of Chapters 1 and 2, not referenced in detail, is the personal memorandum book of Charles Lloyd III (1662–1748), Lloyd MSS 1/166.

3. This communion plate bears marks signifying *Goldsmiths Hall, London, 1679*.

4. For a glimpse of some of the local families, see 'The Dolobran Family in Religion and Industry in Montgomeryshire', *Montgomeryshire Collections*, 56, II, 1961, pp. 124–7, by E. R. Morris of Llanfyllin, to whom the author is indebted for information and guidance on aspects of Chapters 1 and 2.

5. For particulars about Lort the author is indebted to Major Francis Jones, the county archivist of Carmarthenshire, and also to those of Staffordshire and Salop; and see, among other sources, Lewys Dwnn, op. cit.; the article under Lort in *Dictionary of Welsh Biography*, 1959; and the will of Sampson Lort, proved 1667, Prerogative Court of Canterbury.

6. G. M. Trevelyan, *History of England*, Longman, 1926.

7. *Victoria County History, Oxfordshire*, Constable and Oxford University Press, 1907– , vol. III.

8. Richard Davies, *The Convincement*, p. 78.

9. Joseph Besse, *A Collection of the Sufferings of the People called Quakers from 1650 to 1689, from original records and other authentic accounts*, 2 vols, London, 1753.

10. Besse, op. cit., vol. I, p. 755.

11. See *The Christian Progress of that ancient Servant and Minister of Jesus Christ, George Whitehead, historically relating his experience, ministry, sufferings, trials and service in defence of the Truth and God's persecuted people commonly called Quakers*, 1725.

12. Besse, op. cit., in his concluding chapter.

13. Davies, op. cit., p. 172.

14. These letters of Charles Lloyd II are in the Lloyd MSS, Collections 1 and 2. The present extracts are mainly from letters 1/165/15, 17 and 18, and from letter 2/6.

2. FORGES IN WALES

1. E. Wyndham Hulme, 'Statistical History of the Iron Trade of England and Wales 1717 to 1750', *Transactions of the Newcomen Society*, vol. IX, 1928–9.

2. See also Humphrey Lloyd, 'The Iron Forges of the Vyrnwy Valley, *Montgomeryshire Collections*, vol. LX, 1968, p. 104.

3. Rent rolls of the Manor of Caereinion Iscoed. National Library of Wales, Aberystwyth.

4. House of Lords Calendar, 1660; see *Historical MSS Commission, Seventh Report*, 1879, appendix, p. 86.

5. Minute-book of Dolobran meeting; County Record Office, Glamorgan.

6. Survey of Manor of Caereinion by parishes, 1774; at Agent's Office, Powis Castle.

7. Ref. 898.2; 1204/21, County Record Office, Worcestershire.

8. Records of Society of Friends, item 2, County Record Office, Glamorgan.

9. Notes in handwriting of Charles Lloyd's son. Lloyd MSS, 1/143.

10. Kelsall, op. cit., 10 February 1722 and 16 August 1725.

11. ibid, 20 July 1722.

12. Hulme, op. cit.

13. Lloyd MSS, 1/41; letter of 28 August 1734.

14. Dolobran Deeds, National Library of Wales, Aberystwyth.

Part II: CHARCOAL IRON

3. THE IRONMONGER

1. Lloyd MSS, 1/167.

2. Map reference: OS 1 in., sheet 129, SO 538622.

3. Proved 20 October 1686, Prerogative Court of Canterbury.

4. Lloyd Deeds, ref. 440842, Bond of Sampson Lloyd I, 1713, Birmingham Reference Library, to restore the capital value to the trustees of the settlement.

5. William Hutton, Birmingham's first historian; author of *The History of Birmingham*, published in 1781.

6. R. K. Dent, *The Making of Birmingham*, J. L. Allday, Birmingham, 1894, p. 131.

7. Camden, *Britannia*, 1586.

8. John Leland, *Itinerary of Britain*, 1538.

9. Rev. T. R. Nash, *Collections for the History of Worcestershire*, vol. I, p. 279.

10. Lloyd Deeds, ref. 440578, Birmingham Reference Library.

11. Articles of Agreement, 29 April 1697; in *Glamorgan Miscellaneous Deeds*, Cardiff Central Library. In 1727 Ambrose Crowley's Estate received £275 on account of the Crowley share in this South Wales undertaking; Lloyd MSS, 2/18b.

12. Crowley's ultimatum, Lloyd MSS, 1/53.

13. 1699, Prerogative Court of Canterbury.

14. See M. W. Flinn's article 'The Marriage of Judith Crowley' in the *Journal of the Friends Historical Society*, vol. XLVII, 1955.

15. Proved 3 July 1725; folio 157, Prerogative Court of Canterbury.

4. THE TOWN MILL

1. For Wednesbury, the indispensable work is J. F. Ede's *History of Wednesbury*, Wednesbury Corporation, 1962.

2. B. L. C. Johnson, 'The Foley Partnerships: the Iron Industry at the end of the Charcoal Era', *The Economic History Review*, 2nd series, IV, Longman, Green, 1952.

3. Notebook of Sampson Lloyd II (extracts); Friends House Library.

4. Local History Pamphlet No. 1, *An Early Steam Engine*, Central Library, Wednesbury, 1966.

5. Parkes Papers 5/6.

6. Lloyd MSS, 2/31.

7. Fidoe letter No. 24. About two dozen letters of John Fidoe are deposited at Birmingham Reference Library.

8. Sparry's *Plan of the Manor of Edgbaston*, surveyed 1718 for Sir Richard Gough of Edgbaston Hall, with thumbnail sketch of a mill; reprint, 1884, Birmingham Reference Library.

9. Kelsall, Diary, 10 February 1729.

10. Some particulars of Nehemiah Champion's trade are given in A. Raistrick, *Quakers in Science and Industry*, Bannisdale Press, London, 1950.

11. Lloyd MSS 1/85; a paper in the writing of George B. Lloyd I. Written down probably in the 1820s, it is likely to have been prompted by his father (Sampson Lloyd's grandson), with whom he then lived, if not copied from an earlier paper.

12. Lloyd MSS, 1/154.

13. John Sanders, pamphlet, *An iron rod for the Naylors and Tradesmen near Birmingham*, B.M., Thomason Tracts, 669.19.72; quoted in W. H. B. Court, *The Rise of the Midland Industries, 1600–1838*, Oxford University Press, London, 1938, p. 62.

14. M. W. Flinn, *Men of Iron*, 1962, Edinburgh University Press, p. 253.

15. Lloyd MSS, 2/150.

16. Lloyd MSS, 2/15.

17. H. R. Schubert, *History of the British Iron and Steel Industry to 1775*, Routledge & Kegan Paul, 1957, p. 311.

18. Lloyd MSS, 2/18a.

19. *Four Topographical Letters Written in July 1755, from a Gentleman of London to his Brother and Sister in Town*, 1757, p. 56.

20. Westley, *Plan of Birmingham*, 1731.

21. Bradford, *Plan of Birmingham*, 1750.

22. J. Bisset, *A Poetic Survey round Birmingham, with a brief description of the different curiosities and manufactories of the place, intended as a guide to strangers*, Swinney & Hawkins, Birmingham, 1800.

23. These letters, upon which the remainder of Chapter 4 is largely based, are contained in the Lloyd MSS at Friends House Library, Collection 2, especially letters 28 to 73 and 146 to 148. Only the longer extracts are referenced in notes.

24. See article by R. A. Pelham, 'The West Midland Iron Industry and the American Market in the Eighteenth Century', *University of Birmingham Historical Journal*, vol. II, no. 2, 1950, p. 156; and cf. T. S. Ashton, *Iron and Steel in the Industrial Revolution*, Manchester University Press, 1924, p. 117.

25. Lloyd MSS, 2/42, 11 February 1738.

26. Lloyd MSS 2/60, 22 September 1739.

27. Lloyd MSS 2/146, 12 December 1737.

28. Gooch papers, No. 206558, 1731, Birmingham Reference Library; and some other dates.

29. Lloyd MSS, 2/70.

30. The levy books are preserved at Birmingham Reference Library.

5. IRON AND WATER

1. The letters of Sampson Lloyd II, from some of which unreferenced quotations

are given in the opening section of this chapter, are numbered 28 to 90 in the Lloyd MSS, Collection 2.

2. Lloyd MSS 166; memorandum book of her husband, Charles Lloyd III of Dolobran.

3. Notebook of Sampson Lloyd II (extracts); Friends House Library.

4. Lloyd MSS, 2/82.

5. See *The British Seaman*, Collins, 1968, pp. 248 and 252, by Christopher Lloyd, to whom the author is indebted for the nautical particulars in this paragraph.

6. Lloyd MSS, 2/149.

7. Lloyd MSS, 1/41, 1/42, 1/43.

8. Lloyd Deeds, 440032, Birmingham Reference Library.

9. Bathurst Estate Papers, D421/B1, County Record Office, Gloucestershire; paper endorsed 'Mr Champion's first proposals, 1761'.

10. See 'The Water-Power Crisis in Birmingham in the Eighteenth Century', *University of Birmingham Historical Journal*, vol. IX, no. 1, 1963, by Dr R. A. Pelham, to whom the author is indebted for help and information in this context.

11. Lloyd MSS, 2/84.

12. Map Reference: O.S. 1 in., Sheet 120, SK 262239.

13. S. Shaw, writing of conditions in 1745, in his *History of Staffordshire*, 1798.

14. Lloyd MSS, 2/46.

15. The source is the printed account of a tour into the midland counties in the form of four journal letters. The short title is: *Four Topographical Letters Written in July 1755, from a Gentleman of London to his Brother and Sister in Town* (1757). The extracts quoted are from Letter IV. It has been stated by the British Museum that the initials of the writer, 'R.P.' stand for Rista Patching.

16. Alice Harford, *Annals of the Harford Family*, Westminster Press, London, 1909, pp. 39, 40.

17. S. Lloyd, *The Lloyds of Birmingham*, Cornish Bros., Birmingham, 1905, p. 103.

18. Lowe, op. cit., pp. 38, 66.

19. Lloyds Bank; letter of Sampson Lloyd III to his father, dated in 1755.

20. Bond of Arbitration, 18 November 1757, preserved at Lloyds Bank.

21. Records at offices of North Warwickshire monthly meeting, Bull Street, Birmingham, and at Woodbrooke College, Selly Oak.

22. T. S. Ashton, *Iron and Steel in the Industrial Revolution*, Manchester University Press, 1924, ch. 6.

23. Schedule of Hastings Deeds, ref. DE362/1, County Record Office, Leicester.

24. 'A survey of the estates in Land of the Right Honourable Lord Theophilus Hastings Earl of Huntingdon, 1735,' ref. DE4210/2/8, County Record Office, Leicester. The map reference of the furnace site is: O.S. 1 in., Sheet 121, SK 378239.

25. Map reference: O.S. 1 in., Sheet 143, SO 835525.

26. *Victoria County History, Worcestershire*, St Catherine Press, vol. III, p. 408. The author is indebted for this and much other information and help to A. J. Clinch, whose thesis 'The Mill at Powick in the Eighteenth Century', 1969, is deposited at County Record Office, Worcestershire, Class 989.9:484, BA5361.

27. Deed of Covenant, Hadley to Elwell, 24 December 1801; at Central Electricity Generating Board, Midland Region, Moseley, Birmingham.

28. E. Wyndham Hulme, 'Statistical History of the Iron Trade of England and Wales 1717 to 1750', *Transactions of the Newcomen Society*, vol. IX, 1928–9.

29. Undated plan of about the end of the eighteenth century, 438/14, County Record Office, Worcestershire.

30. So specified in a survey plan, ref. 705:349, BA 3835/6 (iii), County Record Office, Worcestershire. See Plate 17.)

31. Ministers' Certificates and Testimonies at Bevan-Naish Quaker Library, Woodbrooke College; BN5.K30.

32. William White, *Friends in Warwickshire*, 1873.

33. Lloyd MSS, 2/83.

34. Lloyd MSS, 2/91.

35. MS No. 218, Friends House Library.

36. Birmingham levy books, Birmingham Reference Library.

37. Paget Deeds, D603 unlisted, E472 and 17/3. County Record Office, Staffordshire.

38. Paget Deeds, D603 unlisted, Burton 18. Lease dated 10 February 1763. County Record Office, Staffordshire.

39. Leases dated 10 February 1763 and 29 December 1766: Paget Deeds, Burton 18 and 20.

Part III: 'THIS TRADE OF BANKERING'

6. INTO BANKING

1. Kelsall, Diary, 12 August 1727; and see A. Stanley Davies, 'The Charcoal Iron Industry of Powys Land', *Montgomeryshire Collections*, 1939, vol. XLVI, Part I, p. 34.

2. William Hutton, *The History of Birmingham*, 6th edn, 1835, p. 201.

3. R. S. Sayers, *Lloyds Bank in the History of English Banking*, Clarendon Press, Oxford University Press, 1957, p. 111.

4. Lloyd MSS, 2/36, 4 September 1736. For the Sykes family as merchants at Hull, afterwards bankers themselves, see Gordon Jackson, *Hull in the Eighteenth Century*, Oxford University Press, 1972.

5. W. Hawkes Smith, *Birmingham and its Vicinity as a Manufacturing and Commercial District*, 1836, Part III, p. 19.

6. Hutton, op. cit., p. 488.

7. See A. Raistrick, *Quakers in Science and Industry*, Bannisdale Press, London, 1950, p. 120, and Sketchley, *Birmingham Directory* for 1767.

8. Lloyd MSS 1/92, draft letter, 24 November 1764, Sampson Lloyd III to Osgood Hanbury.

9. Extract from letter of Samual Garbett, 10 December 1764, addressee not stated, in private possession.

10. Quoted by permission of the Curator, the Wedgwood Museum, Barlaston, Stoke-on-Trent.

11. Ernest Allison, *Fruitful Heritage*, n.d, p. 54.

12. British Transport Historical Records; Birmingham Canal minute-book.

13. J. T. Bunce, *The Birmingham General Hospital and Triennial Musical Festivals*, 1858, p. 3.

14. Letter, 20 April 1771, William Wyatt to R. Brown: Paget MSS, County Record Office, Staffordshire.

15. Lloyd MSS, 2/175, David Barclay to Sampson Lloyd II, 5 July 1771.

16. Rentals-book of Francis, Earl of Huntingdon, for period 1771 to 1779, in County Record Office, Leicestershire.

17. Parkes Papers 1/10.

18. Minute-books of the Commissioners, Birmingham Reference Library; and

see the account in C. Gill and A. Briggs, *History of Birmingham*, Oxford University Press, 1952, vol. I.

19. See Bunce, op. cit., ch. 2.

20. Letter, 12 August 1777, Sampson Lloyd junior to Matthew Boulton, at Birmingham Assay Office.

21. Bevan-Naish Quaker Library, Woodbrooke College, Birmingham, 7.K9, p. 70, quoting a Bull Street minute-book.

22. James Boswell, *The Life of Dr Johnson*, first appeared in 1791. See Birkbeck Hill edn, 1934, vol. II, p. 458.

23. C. C. Lloyd, *Fanny Burney*, Longmans, Green, 1936, p. 52.

24. *An Apology for the True Christian Divinity, being an Explanation and Vindication of the Principles and Doctrines of the People called Quakers*, by Robert Barclay. First published 1675.

25. R. J. Lowe, *Farm and its Inhabitants* (privately printed), 1883, p. 41; S. Lloyd, *The Lloyds of Birmingham*, Birmingham, Cornish Bros., 1905, p. 108.

26. Lloyd, op. cit., p. 56.

27. *The Gentleman's Magazine*, 27 December 1807.

7. THE BANKERS

1. See the chapter on David Barclay II in R. H. Fox, *Dr John Fothergill and his Friends*, 1919.

2. For smallpox research by Quaker doctors see A. Raistrick, *Quakers in Science and Industry*, Bannisdale Press, London, 1950, p. 308.

3. E. V. Lucas, *Charles Lamb and the Lloyds*, Smith, Elder & Co., London, 1898, p. 107.

4. See R. A. Buchanan and N. Cossons, *The Industrial Archaeology of the Bristol Region*, David & Charles, Newton Abbot, 1969, pp. 118–19.

5. Lloyd MSS, 1/107.

6. Private Ledger of Taylors & Lloyds in the possession of Lloyds Bank.

7. This and some of the other personal particulars about Sampson Lloyd are from the biographical notice about him, Lloyd MSS 1/85.

8. John Lloyd's diary, in possession of Lloyds Bank, entries for 30 November and 6 December 1779.

9. *Aris's Birmingham Gazette*, 6 December 1779.

10. 1780, folio 91, Prerogative Court of Canterbury.

11. Lloyd MSS, 1/104, 22 October 1774.

12. For Priscilla Farmer's letters see Braithwaite MSS, packet 2.

13. Birmingham Assay Office. Thomas Green's survey of the nail trade, commissioned by Matthew Boulton, 1775.

14. Lloyd MSS 1/100, dated '1777'.

15. Lloyd MSS 1/99a.

16. W. Molyneux, *Burton on Trent, its History, its Waters, and its Breweries*, Trubner, 1869, p. 286.

17. Survey Plan, BA3835/6 (iii), ref. 705:349, County Record Office, Worcestershire.

18. For these episodes see Braithwaite MSS, 6/27 and 6/30.

19. Braithwaite MSS, packets 6 and 7.

20. Braithwaite MSS, 6/16; and see W. Branch-Johnson, *The English Prison Hulks*, Phillimore, Chichester, 1957.

21. For the slave trade see Thomas Clarkson, *History of the Rise, Progress and*

Accomplishment of the Abolition of the Slave Trade by the British Parliament, 2 vols., 1808, and J. Pope-Hennessy, *Sins of the Fathers*, Weidenfeld & Nicolson, 1967.

22. Malachy Postlethwayt, *Universal Directory of Trade and Commerce*, 2 vols., 1751 and 1754.

23. John Lloyd's diary at Lloyds Bank, 8 July 1790.

24. H. D. Symonds, *An Authentic Account of the Dreadful Riots in Birmingham occasioned by the celebration of the French Revolution on the 14th July, 1791, when the property of the Inhabitants was destroyed to the amount of Four Hundred Thousand Pounds*, London, 1791, p. 8.

25. Braithwaite MSS, 6/95.

26. Karl Pearson, *The Life, Letters and Labours of Francis Galton*, 1914, vol. I, p. 32.

27. Letter of Hudson Gurney quoted by Charles Lloyd; Braithwaite MSS, packet 7, 10 June 1809.

28. S. Shaw, *History of Staffordshire*, 1798, p. 14.

29. Gurney MSS, 1/16, Friends House Library; Robert Barclay to Charles Lloyd, 23 January 1789.

30. Shaw, op. cit., p. 13.

31. Birmingham Assay Office. Boulton collection. S., N. & C. Lloyd to Matthew Boulton, '8.11 mo. 1800'.

32. Lloyd MSS 1/101, Charles Lloyd to Samuel Bamford.

33. Birmingham Assay Office. S. and C. Lloyd to M. Boulton, '20, 11 mo, 1804'.

34. See deeds of Powick Mill in possession of Central Electricity Generating Board, Midland Region, Birmingham.

8. THE NEW CENTURY

1. J. Bisset, *A Poetic Survey round Birmingham*, Swinney & Hawkins, Birmingham, 1800.

2. Typescript at Lloyds Bank containing extracts from a paper formerly in the Lloyd family.

3. Memorandum book of C. D. Sturge, at Society of Friends, Bull Street, Birmingham.

4. The letters of Charles Lloyd and his family upon which much of this chapter is based are comprised partly in the Lloyd MSS at Friends House Library, Collection 3, but mainly in the Braithwaite MSS, which are in private possession, especially packets 6, 7, 8, 18, 19 and 20.

5. See the *Dictionary of National Biography*, Oxford University Press, and, among other works, Thomas De Quincey, *Reminiscences of the English Lakes and the Lake Poets*, 1834; E. V. Lucas, *Charles Lamb and the Lloyds*, Smith, Elder & Co., London, 1898; Samuel Lloyd, *The Lloyds of Birmingham*, Cornish Bros., Birmingham, 1905; Malcolm Elwin, *The First Romantics*, 1947; Frederick L. Beaty, *The Lloyd–Manning Letters* (Indiana University Press, Bloomington, Ind.), 1957; also R. I. Aldrich, unpublished doctoral thesis, 'The Life, Works and Literary Relationships of Charles Lloyd', University of Wisconsin, 1961. The Author is indebted to Dr Aldrich for much information and help over a number of years.

6. Quoted by Lamb in a letter to Coleridge, 20 May 1803.

7. De Quincey, op. cit.

8. Braithwaite MSS 6/125, 25 August 1795.

9. See copies of contemporary letters of C. Lloyd at Lloyds Bank Head Office.

10. Lucas's book, *Charles Lamb and the Lloyds*, offers much the best account of

this and Charles Lloyd's two subsequent translations, as well as affording material for other parts of the present chapter.

11. J. Bevan Braithwaite, *Memoirs of Anna Braithwaite*, Headley, London, 1905.

12. Braithwaite MSS, packet 18.

13. L. S. Pressnell, *Country Banking in the Industrial Revolution*, Oxford University Press, 1956, p. 134.

14. The Journal of Catherine Payton Fox and Jean Melville, 1819, is preserved in private possession.

15. Written in the name of an imaginary foreigner, Don Manuel Alvarez Espriella, Southey's *Letters from England; translated from the Spanish*, in three volumes, had appeared in 1807.

16. S. Lloyd, op. cit., p. 67.

17. Letter of Samuel Lloyd, '19th of 12 mo. 1825', in private possession.

18. Probate 25 February 1828, Prerogative Court of Canterbury.

9. THE SENIOR BRANCH

1. Map reference: OS 1 in. Sheet 121, SK 417275.

2. See Dr C. C. Owen's thesis, 'The Development of Industry in Burton-upon-Trent prior to 1900', 1968, in Sheffield University Library.

3. John Farey, *General View of the Agriculture and Minerals of Derbyshire*, 1815, vol. III, p. 470.

4. This document is reported among the Hastings MSS at the Huntington Library, San Marino, California; see MS notes by George H. Green in Loughborough Public Library.

5. See W. E. A. local history pamphlet, *Historical Account of the Ancient Kings Mills*, 1960, edited by George H. Green; also J. M. Lee, 'Castle Donington in the Nineteenth Century: the Rise and Fall of a Market Town', *Leicestershire Archaeological and Historical Society Journal*, vol. XXXII, 1956. The author is indebted also for many local particulars to Mrs E. Fryer of Castle Donington.

6. Apart from the writings of F. W. Hackwood and J. F. Ede's *History of Wednesbury*, Wednesbury Corporation, 1962, the principal sources for this section are the Parkes Papers at Staffordshire County Record Office, some letters at Lloyds Bank Head Office (the Sydney Raine deposit), and records in possession of the Patent Shaft Steel Works Ltd, Wednesbury.

7. Parkes Papers; and see *Ryders Annual*, 1898.

8. Birmingham levy books, 1829.

9. Lloyds Bank Head Office, Sydney Raine deposit, envelope 'J'; Samuel Lloyd, *Reminiscences*, 1914; Ede, op. cit., p. 242.

10. *Ryders Annual*.

11. S. Lloyd, *The Lloyds of Birmingham*, pp. 199–201.

12. Sources for this section, in addition to R. J. Lowe, *Farm and its Inhabitants*, and S. Lloyd, *The Lloyds of Birmingham*, include E. Isichei, *Victorian Quakers*, Oxford University Press, 1970, and F. Roy Coad, *A History of the Brethren Movement*, Paternoster Press, 1968, also letters of Samuel Lloyd to W. D. Crewdson in the Westmorland County Record Office, the journal of Sarah Fox in private possession, and discussions with Mrs M. E. Grubb.

13. Letter of Sampson Lloyd, Wednesbury, 15 June 1841, to Rachel Howard, in the possession of the author.

14. Records of Sufferings, Warwickshire Monthly Meeting, Bull Street, Birmingham.

15. Particulars from the firm's ledgers at Lloyds Bank Head Office; also MS book (in private possession) of George B. Lloyd II, a partner in the Bank.

16. *Statement of facts and exposure of the perjuries of the witnesses which, uncontradicted at the trial, obtained a verdict at the late Summer Assizes at Liverpool against the bank of Taylor and Lloyds*, 15 December 1839, Birmingham Reference Library 68505.

17. For the town's early railway history see C. Gill and A. Briggs, *History of Birmingham*, Oxford University Press, 1952, vol. II.

18. Sampson Samuel Lloyd 'Memoranda of the events of my life', written in the 1890s, typescript in private possession. See also Lloyd, op. cit., pp. 14–15.

19. Several of these quotations are from Sampson Samuel Lloyd's 'Memoranda of the events of my life'.

20. See, among works on banking, P. W. Matthews and A. W. Tuke, *History of Barclays Bank Ltd*, 1926; W. F. Crick and J. E. Wadsworth, *A Hundred Years of Joint Stock Banking*, Hodder & Stoughton, 1936; L. S. Pressnell, *Country Banking in the Industrial Revolution*, Oxford University Press, 1956; and J. A. S. L. Leighton-Boyce, *Smiths the Bankers, 1658–1958*, National Provincial Bank, London, 1958.

21. S. Lloyd, *The Lloyds of Birmingham*, Cornish Bros., Birmingham, 1905, and sources in private possession, e.g. Sampson Samuel Lloyd, 'Some Memoranda of the Events of my Life', and Howard Lloyd, 'Notes and Reminiscences of Lloyds Bank', 1917. For the history of the new company see R. S. Sayers, *Lloyds Bank in the History of English Banking*, Clarendon Press, Oxford University Press, 1957.

Appendices

1. Lloyd, MSS, 2/185; Parkes Papers 38; C.211/9, Public Record Office, London.

2. Letter of Samuel Lloyd, 19 December 1825, in possession of the author.

3. Letter dated '12, 4 mo. 1836' in possession of the author, from Sarah Fox to her sister Rachel Howard.

4. Anon., *Memorials of the Families of Shorthouse and Robinson*, 1902.

BIBLIOGRAPHY

The principal sources drawn upon for this book are summarised under three sections: Manuscript Material; Printed Sources; Theses. The Printed Sources are arranged according to areas of interest as follows: The Welsh Chapters; Charcoal Iron; The Birmingham Scene; Banks and Banking Matters; The Quakers; Lloyd Family and Connections; History and General Background. A number of works not given in the bibliography are referred to in the footnotes and notes.

I. MANUSCRIPT MATERIAL

IN PRIVATE POSSESSION

Many Lloyds and other individuals
Braithwaite MSS: collection of family letters and papers in the possession of the Braithwaite family
Journal of Catherine Payton Fox
Letters, journals and memoranda bearing on the Lloyd family
Sampson Samuel Lloyd, 'Memoranda of the events of my life'

CORPORATE BODIES AND ESTABLISHMENTS

Birmingham Assay Office
Correspondence of the Lloyds with Matthew Boulton

City of Birmingham Reference Library
Letters, leases and many other documents relating to Birmingham and the Lloyds
Levy Books
Lloyds Deeds

City of Bristol Archives Office
Correspondence and documents
Harford MSS
Local Quaker records

County Record Office, Stafford
Heirs of Parkes Deeds
Leases and other papers in the Paget Deeds relating to Burton-upon-Trent

County Record Office, Worcester
Local Quaker and family records
Deeds and documents concerning Powick

House of Lords Record Office
Documents bearing upon the Lloyd Act, 1731

Lloyds Bank Ltd, Lombard Street, London
Diary of John Lloyd (1751–1811)
Family correspondence
Ledgers and other records of Taylors & Lloyds

National Library of Wales, Aberystwyth
Dolobran Deeds
Papers in the Chirk Castle MSS relating to the Dolobran Lloyds

Patent Shaft Steel Works Ltd, Wednesbury
Deeds of Lloyds, Fosters & Co.
Minute-books of the Patent Shaft and Axletree Co. Ltd

Public Record Office, London
Discharge of John Lloyd (1704–51) from the Navy
Lunacy of Elizabeth Fidoe

Society of Friends

   Bevan-Naish Library, Woodbrooke College, Birmingham
   C. D. Sturge's draft history of Bull Street meeting
   Documents bearing on Quakers and Quakerism at Birmingham

   Friends House Library, London
   John Kelsall's Diary
   Many written evidences on Quaker history
   Stacey letters and other papers on the Lloyd family
   Three collections of Lloyd MSS

   Warwickshire Monthly Meeting, Bull Street, Birmingham
   Documents referring to the Lloyd family
   MS book of C. D. Sturge
   Records of the Quakers at Birmingham

Somerset House, London
About twenty-five Lloyd wills and Letters of Administration, from 1664 to 1849

II. PRINTED SOURCES

THE WELSH CHAPTERS

Cymmrodorion Society, *Dictionary of Welsh Biography to 1940*, 1959
Davies, A. Stanley, 'The Charcoal Iron Industry of Powys Land', *Montgomeryshire Collections*, vol. XLVI, Part I, 1939
Davies, Richard, *An Account of the Convincement, Exercises, Services and Travels of that Ancient Servant of the Lord, Richard Davies: with some Relation of Ancient Friends and the Spreading of Truth in North Wales*, 3rd edn, 1771
Dineley, Thomas, *The Beaufort Progress through Wales*, 1684
Dodd, A. H., *The Industrial Revolution in North Wales*, University of Wales Press, 1933
Dwnn, Lewys, *Heraldic Visitations of Wales 1586 to 1613*, ed. S. R. Meyrick, Llandovery, 1846
Edwards, Ifor, 'The Charcoal Iron Industry of Denbighshire 1690–1770', *Transactions of Denbighshire Historical Society*, vol. x, 1961
Fenton, R., *Historical Tour through Pembrokeshire*, 1811
Jones, Major Francis, 'An Approach to Welsh Genealogy', *Transactions of Honourable Society of Cymmrodorion*, 1948
Jones, Richard, *Crynwyr Bore Cymru 1653–1699*, Abermaw, 1931

Jones, T. G. Cyffin, 'Parish of Meifod, Sketch of the history of Nonconformity therein', *Montgomeryshire Collections*, vol. XI, Part I, 1878

Lloyd, Humphrey, 'The Iron Forges of the Vyrnwy Valley', *Montgomery Collections*, vol. LX, 1967–8

Lloyd, John Edward, *A History of Wales from Earliest Times to the Edwardian Conquest*, London, 1911

Lloyd, Rev. W. V., 'The Armorial Insignia of the Vaughans of Llwydiarth with memorials of the Lloyds of Dolobran', *Montgomeryshire Collections*, vol. XIV, Part I, 1881

Morris, E. Ronald, 'The Dolobran Family in Religion and Industry in Montgomeryshire', *Montgomeryshire Collections*, vol. LVI, Part II, 1960–61

Nuttall, G. F., *The Welsh Saints, 1640–1660*, Wales University Press, Cardiff, 1957

Owen, Henry, *Old Pembrokeshire Families*, London, 1902

Owen, Robert, *In the Heart of Powysland*, 1930

Palmer, A. N., 'John Wilkinson and The Old Bersham Iron Works', *Transactions of Honourable Society of Cymmrodorion*, reprinted with Appendix, 1899

Reynolds, John, *Herauldrie of North Wales*, 1639

Wynne-Edwards, Rev. Canon, 'History of the Parish of Meifod' (second part), *Montgomeryshire Collections*, vol. IX, Part II, 1876

CHARCOAL IRON

Agricola, Georgius, *De Re Metallica*, (1556), trans. H. and L. H. Hoover, Dover Publications, 1950

Ashton, T. S., *Iron and Steel in the Industrial Revolution*, Manchester University Press, 1924

Bulletin of the Historical Metallurgy Group. Reports on the excavation of Melbourne Furnace; Bulletins No. 2, 1963, No. 3, 1964

Clinch, A. J., Dissertation, 'The Mill at Powick in the Eighteenth Century', 1969 (typescript at Worcestershire Record Office)

Court, W. H. B., *The Rise of the Midland Industries, 1660–1838*, Oxford University Press, London, 1938

Diderot, M., 'Les Fenderies', *Encyclopédie des Sciences, des Arts, et des Métiers*, vol. VII, 1773

Emerson, William *Principles of Mechanics*, 1757

Fairbairn, W., *Mills and Mill Work*, Longman, 1864

Farey, John, 'Iron', *Pantalogia, a Dictionary*, vol. VI, 1812–15

Flinn, M. W., 'The Lloyds in the Early English Iron Industry', *Business History*, vol. II, no. I, November 1959

—— *Men of Iron*, Edinburgh University Press, 1962

Flinn, M. W., and Birch, A., 'The English Steel Industry before 1856', *Yorkshire Bulletin of Economic and Social Research*, vol. VI, 1954

Gale, W. K. V., *The Black Country Iron Industry*, Iron and Steel Institute, 1966

Hulme, E. Wyndham, 'Statistical History of the Iron Trade of England and Wales 1717 to 1750', *Transactions of the Newcomen Society*, vol. IX, 1928–9

Johnson, B. L. C., 'The Stour Valley Iron Industry in the late Seventeenth Century', *Transactions of Worcestershire Archaeological Society*, XXVII, 1950

—— 'The Charcoal Iron Industry in the Early Eighteenth Century', *The Geographical Journal*, vol. CXVII, 1951

—— 'The Foley Partnerships: the Iron Industry at the end of the Charcoal Era', *The Economic History Review*, 2nd series, IV, 1952

Lloyd, G. I. H., *The Cutlery Trades*, Longmans, Green, 1913

Minchinton, W. E., *The British Tinplate Industry*, 1957

Molyneux, William, *Burton on Trent, its History, its Waters, and its Breweries*, Trubner, 1869

Pelham, R. A., 'The West Midland Iron Industry and the American Market in the Eighteenth Century', *University of Birmingham Historical Journal*, vol. II, no. 2, 1950

—— 'The Water Mills of Edgbaston, Birmingham', *Transactions of the Birmingham Archaeological Society*, vol. LXXXVIII, 1962

—— 'The Water Power Crisis in Birmingham in the Eighteenth Century', *University of Birmingham Historical Journal*, vol. IX, no. 1, 1963

Raistrick, A., *Dynasty of Ironfounders*, Longmans, Green, 1953

Rolt, L. T. C., *Thomas Newcomen: the prehistory of the Steam Engine*, David & Charles, Newton Abbot, 1963

Schubert, H. R., *History of the British Iron and Steel Industry to 1775*, Routledge & Kegan Paul, 1957

Scrivenor, Harry, *History of the Iron Trade*, 1854

Swedenborg, Emanuel, *Regnum Subterraneum*, 1734

THE BIRMINGHAM SCENE

Allen, Bernard M., 'Priestley and the Birmingham Riots', *Transactions of Unitarian Historical Society*, vol. V, no. 2, 1932

Bickley, W. B., and Hill, J., eds., *Survey of the Manor of Birmingham, 1553*, 1890

Bisset, J., *A Poetic Survey round Birmingham with a brief description of the different curiosities and manufactories of the place, intended as a guide to Strangers*, Swinney & Hawkins, Birmingham, 1800

British Association, *Birmingham and its Regional Setting*, 1950

Bunce, J. T., *The Birmingham General Hospital and Triennial Musical Festivals*, 1858

Dent, R. K., *The Making of Birmingham*, J. L. Allday, Birmingham, 1894

—— *Old and New Birmingham*, Houghton & Hammond, Birmingham, 1880

Edwards, Eliezer, *Personal Recollections of Birmingham and Birmingham men*, 1877

Gill, Conrad, and Briggs, Asa, *History of Birmingham*, Oxford University Press, 2 vols., 1952

Hill, J., and Dent, R. K., *Memorials of the Old Square*, Achilles Taylor, Birmingham, 1897

Hutton, William, *The History of Birmingham*, 1781

Langford, J. A., *A Century of Birmingham Life, 1741–1841*, 2 vols., Osborne, 1868

Lines, S., *A few incidents in the life of Samuel Lines senior*, 1862

Matthews, A. B., ed., *An Authentic Account of the Dreadful Riots at Birmingham, July 1791*, reprint, 1863

Smith, W. Hawkes, *Birmingham and its Vicinity as a Manufacturing and Commercial District*, 1836

Timmins, Samuel, *Birmingham and the Midland Hardware District*, 1866

Wilkinson, K. Douglas, ed., *History of the Birmingham Medical School 1825–1925*, 1925

BANKS AND BANKING MATTERS

Ashton, T. S., paper, 'The Bill of Exchange and Private Banks in Lancashire, 1790 to 1830', *Papers in English Monetary History*, ed. Ashton and Sayers, Oxford University Press, 1953

Cave, C. H., *A History of Banking in Bristol.* 1899
Child, J., *A New Discourse of Trade,* 1693, 4th edn., n.d. (eighteenth century).
Crick, W. F., and Wadsworth, J. E., *A Hundred Years of Joint Stock Banking,* Hodder & Stoughton, 1936
Defoe, Daniel, *The Complete English Tradesman,* 1725
Gilbart, J. W., *The History, Principles and Practice of Banking,* 1827
Gillett Brothers Discount Co. Ltd, *The Bill on London,* Chapman & Hall, 1952
Hilton-Price, F. G., *A Handbook of London Bankers,* 1876
Holden, J. M., *The History of Negotiable Instruments in English Law,* Athlone Press, 1955
Joslin, D. M., 'London Private Bankers', *Economic History Review,* vol. VII, no. 2, December 1954
Leighton-Boyce, J. A. S. L., *Smiths the Bankers, 1658–1958,* National Provincial Bank, London, 1958
Matthews, P. W., and Tuke, A. W., *History of Barclays Bank Ltd,* 1926
Postlethwayt, Malachy, *Universal Dictionary of Trade and Commerce,* 2 vols, 1751 and 1754
Pressnell, L. S., *Country Banking in the Industrial Revolution,* Oxford University Press, 1956
Rae, George, *The Country Banker,* 4th edn, 1885
Richards, R. D., *The Early History of Banking in England,* F. Cass, 1965
Sayers, R. S., *Lloyds Bank in the History of English Banking,* Clarendon Press, Oxford University Press, 1957

THE QUAKERS

Barrow, Walter, pamphlet, *Centenary Address to Birmingham Friends Reading Society,* 1930
Besse, Joseph, *A Collection of the Sufferings of the people called Quakers from 1650 to 1689, from original records and other authentic accounts,* 2 vols., London, 1753
Clarkson, Thomas, *A Portraiture of Quakerism,* Longman, Hurst, Rees & Orme, London, 1807
Coad, F. Roy, *A History of the Brethren Movement,* Paternoster Press, 1968
Crewdson, Isaac, *A Beacon to the Society of Friends,* 1835
Doncaster, Hugh, *Quaker Organisation and Business Meetings,* Friends Home Service Committee, 1958
Fox, R. Hingston, *Dr John Fothergill and his Friends,* 1919
Grubb, Isobel, *Quakerism and Industry before 1800,* Williams & Norgate, 1930
Isichei, Elizabeth, *Victorian Quakers,* Oxford University Press, 1970
Lidbetter, Hubert, *The Friends Meeting House,* Sessions, York, 1961
Lloyd, Arnold, *Quaker Social History 1669–1738,* Longmans, 1950
London Yearly Meeting of the Religious Society of Friends, *Church Government,* 1968
——*Extracts from the Minutes and Advices of the Yearly Meeting of Friends held in London from its first institution,* 2nd edn. (1802), with Supplement, 1822
Newton, B. W., *A Remonstrance to the Society of Friends,* 1835
Raistrick, A., *Quakers in Science and Industry,* Bannisdale Press, London, 1950
Stunt, Timothy C. F., pamphlet, *Early Brethren and the Society of Friends,* C.B.R.F. Publications, Pinner, 1970
Vipont, Elfrida, *The Story of Quakerism,* Bannisdale Press, London, 1954
White, William, *Friends in Warwickshire,* 1873
Whitney, Janet, *Elizabeth Fry,* Harrap, 1937

LLOYD FAMILY, AND CONNECTIONS

Beaty, Frederick L., *The Lloyd-Manning Letters*, Indiana University Press, Bloomington, Ind., 1957

Benson, M. E. and J. S., *Descendants of Isaac and Rachel Wilson*, W. Appleyard & Sons, Middlesbrough, 1949

Braithwaite, J. Bevan, *Memoirs of Anna Braithwaite*, Headley, London, 1905

Carr, Mary, *Thomas Wilkinson, A Friend of Wordsworth*, Headley, London, 1905

Flinn, M. W., 'The Marriage of Judith Crowley', *Journal of the Friends Historical Society*, vol. XLVII, 1955

Foster, S. B., *The Pedigree of Wilson of High Wray and Kendal* (private circulation), 1890

Hankin, Christiana C., *Life of Mary Anne Schimmelpenninck*, Longman, Brown, Green, Longmans & Roberts, London, 1858

Harford, Alice, *Annals of the Harford Family*, Westminster Press, London, 1909

Lloyd, Edyth, *Anna Lloyd 1837–1925*, Cayme Press, London, 1928

Lloyd, Mrs Richard Harman, *The Pedigree of the Lloyds of Dolobran* (private circulation), 1877

Lloyd, Samuel, *Reminiscences* (private circulation), 1914

—— *The Lloyds of Birmingham*, Cornish Bros., Birmingham 1905

Lowe, Rachel Jane, *Farm and its Inhabitants* (privately printed), 1883

Lucas, E. V., *Charles Lamb and the Lloyds*, Smith, Elder & Co., 1898

Owen, Hugh, *Two Centuries of Ceramic Art in Bristol*, 1873

Pearson, Karl, *The Life, Letters and Labours of Francis Galton*, Cambridge University Press, 1914, vol. I

Pemberton, R. C. B., *Pemberton Pedigrees*, 1923

Smith, Charles Perrin, *Lineage of the Lloyd and Carpenter Family* (U.S.A.), 1870

Somervell, John, *Isaac and Rachel Wilson, Quakers of Kendal, 1714–1785*, Swarthmore Press, London, 1924

Sturge, Sara W., *Memoir of Mary Lloyd of Wednesbury, 1795–1865* (private circulation), 1921

GENERAL HISTORY AND BACKGROUND

Ashton, T. S., *Economic History of England*, Methuen, 1955

—— *The Industrial Revolution, 1760–1830*, Oxford University Press, 1948

Boswell, James, *The Life of Dr Johnson* (1791), ed. Birkbeck Hill, 1934

Branch-Johnson, W., *The English Prison Hulks*, Phillimore, Chichester, 1957

Buchanan, R. A., and Cossons, N., *The Industrial Archaeology of the Bristol Region*, David & Charles, Newton Abbot, 1969

Burton, John R., *A History of Bewdley*, 1883

Clarkson, Thomas, *History of the Rise, Progress and Accomplishment of the Abolition of the African Slave Trade by British Parliament*, 1808

Defoe, Daniel, *A Tour through the Whole Island of Great Britain*, 3 vols, 1724–6

De Quincey, Thomas, *Reminiscences of the English Lakes and the Lake Poets*, 1834

The Dictionary of National Biography, Oxford University Press

Ede, J. F., *History of Wednesbury*, Wednesbury Corporation, 1962

Elwyn, Malcolm, *The First Romantics*, 1947

Farey, John, *General View of the Agriculture and Minerals of Derbyshire*, 1815

Green, G. H., ed., pamphlet, *Historical Account of the Ancient Kings Mills*, W. E. A. Group, Castle Donington, 1960

Hackwood, F. W., *Odd Chapters in the History of Wednesbury*, 1920, *Olden Wednesbury*, 1899, and *Religious Wednesbury*, 1900, Borough News Press, Wednesbury

Hadfield, Charles, *The Canals of the East Midlands*, 1966, and *The Canals of the West Midlands*, 1966, David & Charles, Newton Abbot

Harral, T., *Picturesque Views of the Severn*, 1824

Jackson, Gordon, *Hull in the Eighteenth Century*, Oxford University Press, 1972

Lloyd, Christopher, *The British Seaman*, Collins, 1968

—— *Fanny Burney*, Longmans, Green, 1936

Mantoux, Paul, *The Industrial Revolution in the Eighteenth Century*, Jonathan Cape, 1961

Mathias, Peter, *The First Industrial Nation*, Methuen, 1969

Minchinton, W. E., 'Bristol the Metropolis of the West in the Eighteenth Century', *Transactions of Royal Historical Society*, 5th series, vol. IV, 1954

Nash, Rev. T. R., *Collections for the History of Worcestershire*, vol. I, 1781, vol. II, 1782

Nixon, Frank, *The Industrial Archaeology of Derbyshire*, David & Charles, Newton Abbot, 1969

Owen, C. C., 'The Early History of the Upper Trent Navigation', *Transport History*, vol. I, no. 3, November 1968

Phillips, J., *A General History of Inland Navigation*, 4th edn, 1803

Plot, R., *The Natural History of Staffordshire*, 1686

Pope-Hennessy, J., *Sins of the Fathers*, Weidenfeld & Nicolson, 1967

Shaw, Rev. S., *History of Staffordshire*, 1798

Snell, L. S., *Essays towards a History of Bewdley*, Birmingham, Snell, 1972

Tawney, R. H., *Religion and the Rise of Capitalism*, Murray, 1926

Trevelyan, G. M., *English Social History*, Longmans, Green, 1942

Warner, G. T., Marten, C. H. K., and Muir, D. E., *The New Groundwork of British History*, London and Glasgow, Blackie & Son, 1943

Willan, T. S., 'The River Navigation and Trade of the Severn Valley, 1600–1750', *Economic History Review*, vol. VIII, no. 1, November 1937

Yarranton, Andrew, *England's Improvement by Sea and Land*, 2 vols., 1677 and 1681

III. THESES

Aldrich, Ruth I., 'The Life Works and Literary Relationships of Charles Lloyd', Ph.D., University of Wisconsin, 1961

Blundell, D. W., 'Transport in the West Midlands, 1660–1840', M. Com., University of Birmingham, 1933

Davies, E. I., 'The Hand-made Nail Trade of Birmingham and District', M. Com., University of Birmingham, 1933

Jones, Harri Gwynn, 'John Kelsall, a Study in Religious and Economic History', M.A., University College of North Wales, 1938

Lewis, R. A., 'Two Partnerships of the Knights', M.A., University of Birmingham, 1949

Owen, C. C., 'The Development of Industry in Burton-upon-Trent prior to 1900', Ph.D., University of Sheffield, 1968

INDEX

A figure printed in italics indicates an illustration. Personal names and places occurring only once in the text are not all given in this Index. Certain recurring place-names such as Birmingham and London are only lightly indexed.

314   *Index*

CHARLES LLOYD OF DOLOBRAN IN THE COUNTY OF
  MONTGOMERY   DIED 26. OF 11.MO. 1698 AGED 60 YEAR

ANN LLOYD	,,	6.MO.1708	,, 70	,,
CHARLES LLOYD	,,	21. OF 1.MO.1747	,, 84	,,
SARAH LLOYD	,,	1736	AB⊤61	,,
SAMPSON LLOYD	,,	3. OF 1. MO.1724	AB⊤60	,,
MARY LLOYD	,,	1. OF 9.MO.1770	,, 95	,,
SAMPSON LLOYD	,,	30. OF 11.MO.1779	,, 79	,,
SARAH LLOYD	,,	16. OF 3.MO.1729	,, 29	,,
RACHEL LLOYD	,,	16. OF 9.MO.1756	,, 43	,,
OLIVE KIRTON	,,	27. OF 11.MO.1775	,, 68	,,
SAMPSON LLOYD	,,	27. OF 12.MO. 1807	,, 79	,,
RACHEL LLOYD	,,	20. OF 3. MO.1814	,, 69	,,
NEHEMIAH LLOYD	,,	22. OF 2.MO.1801	,, 55	,,
RACHEL SUMMERFIELD		3. OF 6.MO.1793	,, 26	,,
LUCY LLOYD	,,	12. OF 12.MO.1793	,, 12	,,
ELIZABETH BIDDLE	,,	15. OF 8.MO.1797	,, 26	,,
ELIZABETH MORRIS	,,	18. OF 10.MO.1726	,, 24	,,
MARY GILL	,,	20. OF 7. MO.1736	,, 25	,,
SUSANNAH LLOYD	,,	15. OF 7.MO.1766	,, 27	,,
SARAH GULSON	,,	12. OF 11.MO.1753	,, 59	,,
SARAH LLOYD	,,	1780	,,	,,
CHARLES LLOYD	,,	12. OF 2.MO.1741	,, 11	,,
CHARLES LLOYD	,,	1. OF 11.MO.1760	,, 36	,,
AMBROSE LLOYD	,,	11. OF 2.MO.1742	,, 11	,,

ALSO THE REMAINS OF MANY O⊤